America and Iraq

This edited volume provides an overview on US involvement in Iraq from the 1958 Iraqi coup to the present day, offering a deeper context to the current conflict.

Using a range of innovative methods to interrogate US foreign policy, ideology and culture, the book provides a broad set of reflections on past, present and future implications of US–Iraqi relations, and especially the strategic implications for US policy-making. In doing so, it examines several key aspects of the relationship such as: the 1958 Iraqi Revolution; the impact of the 1967 Arab–Israeli War; the impact of the Nixon Doctrine on the regional balance of power; US attempts at rapprochement during the 1980s; the 1990–1991 Gulf War; and, finally, sanctions and inspections. Analysis of the contemporary Iraq crisis sets US plans against the 'reality' they faced in the country, and explores both attempts to bring security to Iraq, and the implications of failure.

This book will be of great interest to all students of US foreign policy, Middle Eastern politics, Strategic Studies and IR in general.

David Ryan is a member of the Department of History, and Associate Dean, Graduate Studies in the College of Arts, Celtic Studies and Social Sciences, University College Cork. **Patrick Kiely** is a Research Fellow in the Department of History, University College Cork.

Contemporary security studies
Series editors: James Gow and Rachel Kerr,
King's College London

This series focuses on new research across the spectrum of international peace and security, in an era where each year throws up multiple examples of conflicts that present new security challenges in the world around them.

America and Iraq

Policy-making, intervention and
regional politics

Edited by David Ryan and Patrick Kiely

LONDON AND NEW YORK

First published 2009
by Routledge
2 Park Square, Milton Park, Abingdon, Oxon OX14 4RN

Simultaneously published in the USA and Canada
by Routledge
270 Madison Ave, New York, NY 10016

Routledge is an imprint of the Taylor & Francis Group, an informa business

Typeset in Garamond by Wearset Ltd, Boldon, Tyne and Wear
Printed and bound in Great Britain by TJI Digital, Padstow, Cornwall

British Library Cataloguing in Publication Data
A catalogue record for this book is available from the British Library

Library of Congress Cataloging in Publication Data
America and Iraq : policy-making, intervention and regional politics /
edited by David Ryan and Patrick Kiely.
p. cm. – (Contemporary security studies)
Includes bibliographical references.
1. United States–Foreign relations–Iraq. 2. Iraq–Foreign relations–
United States. 3. Iraq War, 2003– I. Ryan, David, 1965–
II. Kiely, Patrick.
E183.8.I57A54 2009
327.730567–dc22   2008024866

ISBN10: 0-415-46621-0 (hbk)
ISBN10: 0-203-88634-8 (ebk)

ISBN13: 978-0-415-46621-9 (hbk)
ISBN13: 978-0-203-88634-2 (ebk)

For Heidi, Daniel, Hannah and Luca
and
For the Kiely family and Claire
for their support over the years

Contents

Contributors

James Denselow is a doctoral candidate in geopolitics at Kings College London. He is researching the political geography of the Syrian-Iraqi borderlands, which he has visited extensively. He worked as a researcher at Chatham House from 2003–2005. Since 2007 Mr. Denselow had been a board member of the 'Council for Arab-British Understanding' (CAABU). His articles have appeared in *The World Today*, the *Daily Telegraph* and the *Yorkshire Post*. He is a frequent guest on the BBC World Service, Sky News, ITN and CNN. He is currently working on a book entitled *New Iraq, Old Neighbours* with Richard Schofield.

Toby Dodge is Reader in International Politics at Queen Mary, University of London and Consulting Senior Fellow for the Middle East at the International Institute for Strategic Studies. He is a frequent visitor to Iraq both before and after the 2003 US invasion. He is the author of several books and articles including *Inventing Iraq: the Failure of Nation Building and a History Denied* (2003), *Iraq's Future: the Aftermath of Regime Change* (2005), and co-editor of *Iraq at the Crossroads: State and Society in the Shadow of Regime Change* (2003) with Steven Simon and *Globalisation and the Middle East, Islam, Economics, Culture and Politics* (2002) with Richard Higgott.

Cary Fraser is the author of *Ambivalent Anti-Colonialism* (1994) and teaches American foreign policy, Caribbean history, and the politics of race in twentieth century America at the Pennsylvania State University. His research and writing focuses upon the history of international relations over the course of the twentieth century.

Patrick Kiely is a doctoral candidate in the Department of History, University College Cork. He has conducted extensive research in the Ford Presidential Library and the Nixon Project as well as the recently declassified material in the National Archives and Records Administration, Washington, DC on US policy in the Persian Gulf and the Middle East 1969–1976.

Scott Lucas is Professor of American Studies at the University of Birmingham and the Founding Director of Libertas: The Centre for US Foreign Policy. He is the author of numerous books and articles on British and American foreign policy, amongst which are *Divided We Stand: Britain, the US, and the Suez Crisis* (1991), *Freedom's War: the US Crusade against the Soviet Union, 1945–1956* (1999), and *Betrayal of Dissent: Beyond Orwell, Hitchens, and the New American Century* (2004). He is currently working on a two-volume study of the foreign policy of the George W. Bush Administration.

Melani McAlister is Associate Professor of American Studies and International Affairs at George Washington University in Washington, DC. She is the author of *Epic Encounters: Culture, Media, and U.S. Interests in the Middle East since 1945* (2005, orig. 2001). Her current project examines Christian evangelicals, popular culture, and global issues; it is tentatively titled: *Our God in the World: The Global Visions of American Evangelicals.*

Trevor B. McCrisken is Associate Professor in US Politics and International Studies at the University of Warwick and Chair of the British American Security Information Council (BASIC). He is author of *American Exceptionalism and the Legacy of Vietnam: US Foreign Policy since 1974* (2003) and co-author with Andrew Pepper of *American History and Contemporary Hollywood Film* (2005).

Lara Marlowe is the Paris correspondent for the *Irish Times*. Throughout her career as a journalist with CBS, *Time* and the *Irish Times* she has covered the conflicts in Nicaragua, Lebanon, Algeria, Somalia, Rwanda, the former Yugoslavia and the two Gulf Wars. She has won numerous awards including the Amnesty International Press Award and was made Chevalier of the Légion d'Honneur in 2006. She has written extensively on the 2003 US invasion of Iraq and its aftermath.

John Morrissey is Lecturer in Political and Cultural Geography at National University of Ireland, Galway. His research focuses on the study of identity and conflict, especially in the contexts of colonialism and geopolitics. He is the author of *Negotiating Colonialism*, an examination of resistance in early colonial Ireland, and his forthcoming book is *Key Concepts in Historical Geography*. He is currently a Fellow at the Center for Place, Culture and Politics at CUNY Graduate Center in New York, where he is writing a geopolitical history of United States Central Command.

Kenneth Osgood is Associate Professor of History at Florida Atlantic University. He is the author of *Total Cold War: Eisenhower's Secret Propaganda Battle at Home and Abroad* (2006), which won the Herbert Hoover Book Award for best book on any aspect of American history during 1914–1964, and co-editor (with Klaus Larres) of: *The Cold War after Stalin's Death: A Missed Opportunity for Peace?* (2006). He has been the Visiting Mary Ball Washington Chair in American History at University College Dublin, a postdoctoral fellow at the Mershon Center for International Security Studies at The Ohio State University and a pre-doctoral fellow of the Institute on Global Conflict and Cooperation at the University of California.

Jon Roper is Professor of American Studies at Swansea University. His research interests encompass American political ideas, the American Presidency and the impact of war on American politics, culture and society. He is the author of *Democracy and Its Critics* (1989), *The American Presidents: Heroic Leadership from Kennedy to Clinton* (2000), and *The Contours of American Politics* (2002). Other edited books include (with John Baylis), *The United States and Europe: Beyond the Neoconservative Divide* (2006) and *Over Thirty Years: The United States and the Legacy of the Vietnam War* (2007).

David Ryan is in the Department of History, University College, Cork, Ireland. He is author of several books and articles including *US-Sandinista Diplomatic Relations* (1995), *US Foreign Policy in World History* (2000), *The United States and Europe* (2003), and *Frustrated Empire* (2007), and co-editor of *The United States and Decolonization* (2000), *Vietnam in Iraq* (2007). He is currently working on a history of the Vietnam Syndrome and US intervention.

Maria Ryan is a Lecturer in American History at the University of Nottingham. She has published scholarly articles on various contemporary and historical aspects of neoconservatism, intelligence and the CIA and their impact upon foreign policy making. She is currently writing a book about the development of neoconservative foreign policy from 1989–2001.

Marilyn B. Young is Professor in the Department of History at New York University. She has written and researched extensively on US foreign policy and US-Asian relations and is the author of *The Vietnam Wars, 1945–1990* and *Vietnam and America* (with Marvin Gettleman, Jane Franklin and Bruce Franklin), and *Reporting Vietnam: American Journalism, 1959–1975*, two volumes. *The Vietnam Wars* was recipient of the Berkshire Women's History Prize. Most recently she has co-edited two books with Lloyd Gardner, *The New American Empire* (2005) and *Iraq and the Lessons of Vietnam* (2007).

Preface

Lara Marlowe

In late 2002 and early 2003, it was obvious that George W. Bush was determined to invade Iraq and topple Saddam Hussein, with or without a UN mandate. It was equally obvious that the invasion would plunge the region into ever greater chaos and violence. There are times when a journalist would rather not be vindicated.

Although we wrote about Saddam Hussein's murderous dictatorship, journalists who criticized the invasion were accused of supporting Saddam. The Pentagon and British Ministry of Defence went to great lengths to prevent us covering the March and April 2003 bombardment from Baghdad.

The results of the war were writ large in its initial conduct. As the US Air Force pounded away at Iraq's infrastructure, we were constantly reassured that telephone exchanges, government ministries and other infrastructure would be rebuilt; they never were.

On 8 April 2003, a tank from the 4th Infantry Division fired a shell at the Palestine Hotel – where the whole world knew the press were staying – killing two of my colleagues. Washington never accepted responsibility for the deaths of Taras Protsyuk and Jose Couso, no more than it acknowledged the deaths of hundreds of thousands of Iraqi civilians.

If a US soldier felt threatened, Gen. Ricardo Sanchez said, he had orders to shoot. On the Dora highway south of Baghdad, I saw the blackened, bloated bodies of dozens of civilians who were picked off by US gunners as they entered the capital.

I asked US Ambassador Ryan Crocker in May 2008 whether, as the representative of the United States, he felt responsible for the destruction of the country. 'I got here in March 2007 and history starts for me then,' he replied. It was up to the historians of the future to determine what had happened. 'The scholars of the future will be spending generations on what happened in 2003 and after,' he predicted.

Present-day scholars writing in this book give keys for understanding what has happened in Iraq. Kenneth Osgood's chapter on 'Eisenhower and regime change in Iraq: the United States and the Iraqi Revolution of 1958' notes the perennial US oscillation 'between conflict and cooperation, between working with the regime in Baghdad and conspiring against it.' The Eisenhower administration considered going to war in Iraq in 1958 but feared it would have a disastrous effect on world public opinion. It's a pity the Bush administration did not have the same foresight in 2003.

Jon Roper's chapter on 'The imperial presidency redux: presidential power and the war in Iraq' chronicles the assumption of US conservatives over the past half century that authority and power should be concentrated in the executive branch. George W. Bush, he concludes, 'is the latest American "Caesar" to become a casualty of a failed war that lost him the public confidence necessary to the exercise of effective Presidential power.'

John Morrissey's chapter on 'US central command and the war in Iraq' lends credence to suspicions that whatever presidential candidates may promise, the US will never leave Iraq, because Iraq's oil and location are vital to US interests.

A West Point graduate serving in Iraq recently spoke to me of John Nagl's book *Counterinsurgency Lessons from Malaya and Vietnam: Learning to Eat Soup with a Knife*, whose title was inspired by a quote from T.E. Lawrence. Marilyn B. Young shrewdly picked up on the US military's romantic, comical and alarming fascination with Lawrence. Americans may see themselves as Lawrence-like would-be liberators, but Iraqis see them as invaders and occupiers.

Cheerleaders for the Bush invasion persisted through the failed mandates of Gen. Jay Garner and Paul Bremer, through the corruption and discredit of two Iraqi governments and the disgrace of the torture at Abu Ghraib prison. As Iraq descended into the world capital of suicide bombings and beheadings, the Americans blamed savage Iraqis. A US mercenary in Baghdad told me in May 2008: 'The Iraqis are like the Watts rioters: hell-bent on destroying their country.'

The neo-con cheerleaders fell silent around 2006; Iraqis called it 'the year of disaster.' Hostilities between Sunni and Shia started as soon as Saddam fell, but burgeoned into civil war proportions when al-Qaeda in Iraq blew up the Shia golden mosque in Samarra in February 2006.

It took Bush's 'surge,' the defection of 90 000 Sunnis from the insurgency to the US-backed Sahwa or Sons of Iraq militia and relative restraint by Moqtada al-Sadr's Jaish al-Mehdi militia to bring the bloodshed of 2006 and 2007 down to manageable proportions. In May 2008, the US announced that violence had reached its lowest level in four years.

Yet the words 'fragile and reversible' accompany every US announcement of improvement. The retired four-star General Barry McCaffrey summed up the situation before the Senate Foreign Relations Committee in April 2008:

> It's a hell of a mess. I mean, you know, there's just no way about it. It's a USD 600 billion war, 34,000 (US servicemen) killed and wounded. We've alienated most of the global population. The American people don't support the war. And the Iraqi government's dysfunctional.

There is no guarantee that the security gains of late 2007 and 2008 will survive substantial US troop withdrawals. At least seven conflicts are still brewing in Iraq: Arabs vs. Kurds over possession of oil-rich Kirkuk; the upper-class Shia of the Supreme Islamic Council in Iraq vs. the poor Shia who follow Moqtada al-Sadr; al-Qaeda in Iraq vs. the Shia; al-Qaeda vs. Sunni 'traitors'; US forces vs. al-Qaeda and US forces vs. al-Sadr's Jaish al-Mehdi. Last and certainly not least is the rivalry between Iran and the US for influence in Iraq, a veritable new Cold War.

If Iraq is to overcome these wars within wars, it must reach consensus on how to share oil revenues and how to govern itself. Pressures by some US lawmakers and the Kurds for 'soft partition' could set a dangerous precedent for the dismemberment of an Arab state. Yet the Sunni and Shia who 'ethnically cleansed' most of Baghdad over the past two years seemed to arrange themselves by design, to achieve contiguity between the Sunni neighbourhoods of west Baghdad and the Sunni heartland of Abu Ghraib, Ramadi and Falluja.

More than five years after the invasion, there are only questions, no answers. Will the US stay? In what form, and for how long? Will the US attack Iran? And will the war between Sunni and Shia reignite? History has taught us to fear the worst.

Lara Marlowe, May 2008
(Lara Marlowe covered the 2003 invasion of Iraq and its aftermath for
The Irish Times.)

Acknowledgements

A selection of the papers were drawn from a conference held at the Clinton Institute for American Studies, University College Dublin, Ireland. The editors would like to thank Professor Liam Kennedy and Catherine Carey for their encouragement, enthusiasm and above all organization. They would also like to thank the Institute for its support.

David Ryan would like to acknowledge the generous support of the College of Arts, Celtic Studies and Social Sciences, University College Cork and the Department of History at UCC.

Together the editors would like to thank Andrew Humphrys and Emily Kindleysides at Routledge for adopting the project and for patience throughout.

Introduction

David Ryan

The US intervention in Iraq has had a profound impact on that country, the region and for the future of US foreign policy and power. The impact is made all the more significant because, after all, this was a 'war of choice.' The intervention has not only largely defined the foreign policy of the Bush administration but also partly characterized the identity of the United States at the beginning of the twenty-first century. It is an irony of significant proportions that in 1990 and early 1991, the administration of George Bush Sr. made the case for repelling the Iraqi invasion of Kuwait on the basis of protecting notions of sovereignty in the then 'new world order.' Despite the many shortcomings of the normative element of international relations during the Cold War, as both superpowers fuelled local conflicts, there was a pervasive sense of balance that characterized the period and compromised various readings of sovereignty. Obviously the issue of sovereignty was extensively debated and compromised across the 1990s too, but the war started in 2003 in Iraq, again based on choice, violated the strict interpretations of sovereignty. The consequences are obviously significant and profound. Following the fraught transatlantic diplomacy and reflecting on the repercussions of the Iraq war, Jürgen Habermas concluded that 'the normative authority of the United States of America lies in ruins.'[1] More recently examining the fallout, Richard Falk too has highlighted the 'normative costs' and the war's implications for world order and the 'evaluation of the neoconservative blueprint for U.S. foreign policy from the perspectives of world order.' Though the Baker-Hamilton Report (2006) provided an opportunity for disengagement, negotiation and 'Iraqification', Bush chose otherwise, to initiate the 'surge' and 'stay [...] the course.' The implications are profound in terms of the erosion of the 'legitimacy of American global leadership.'[2] The costs and implications for Iraq are unfathomable as one considers the extent and depth of suffering, since 2003, but also for decades under the brutal regime of Saddam Hussein. The implications for Iraq's viability are still to be played out with regional and global repercussions. The costs are far more widespread than the limited focus here. There is already a revival in the literature on US Decline[3] and on the 'post-American' world and the prospects of an era of 'nonpolarity.'[4] In 1977 when Jimmy Carter assumed the presidency he explicitly sought to restore the moral authority of the nation. As he indicated in his inaugural, 'I have no new dream to set forth today, but rather urge a fresh faith in the old dream.' The United States could be better and stronger than before, 'let our recent mistakes bring a resurgent commitment to the basic principles of our Nation...' were themes that he tried to develop alongside concepts of 'shared leadership,' which is a theme he has revisited in recent months.[5]

This volume aims to provide a broad set of reflections on the US intervention in Iraq placing it within a broad temporal approach provided by perspectives informed by a range of leading US historians as well as contributions from some younger scholars using innovative methods to interrogate US foreign policy, ideology and culture. The current period is prefaced with a set of essays that examine the US–Iraqi relationship since 1958 and earlier US justifications and strategies used to legitimate their involvement. Kenneth Osgood examines the bilateral and regional relationship surrounding the 1958 Iraqi Revolution and its aftermath. The impact of the 1967 War and the Nixon Doctrine on the regional balance of power and its implications for Iraq are developed by Patrick Kiely. I then trace the US attempts at rapprochement during the 1980s and its ultimate failure prior to the 1990–1991 Gulf War and crucially the decision to end that engagement short of Baghdad. Marilyn B. Young moves between the US romance of Lawrence of Arabia and the contemporary counterinsurgency debates and provides a study on how the romantic framework informed current tactics.

The chapters on the contemporary crisis investigate the causes and consequences of regime change and its failure. Iraq expert Toby Dodge sets US plans against the 'reality' they faced in the country. John Morrissey provides an analysis of CENTCOM within the context of US grand strategy and geopolitics. Three chapters then focus on domestic influences on the Bush administration. Trevor B. McCrisken examines the prevailing influence of US exceptionalism and the manner in which the administration was informed by these ideologies and framed their policies within that context. Melani McAlister provides an analysis of the influence of Evangelical Christians on US policy and the administration. Scott Lucas and Maria Ryan scrutinize the quest for unipolarity and the use of Iraq as a demonstration case for US foreign policy. Jon Roper then revisits the questions of presidential power and the 'imperial presidency,' while Cary Fraser reflects on the question of US empire and the potential decline of regional hegemony. Finally, James Deneslow, with extensive regional expertise, looks at the attempts to bring security to Iraq through rapidly changing norms and conventions on border control, with a particular focus on the Iraqi–Syrian border. Hence the collection aims to provide historical and contemporary analysis combined with reflections on US policy-making, culture and an analysis on the local, regional and global impact of war in Iraq.

The debate on the future direction and identity of US foreign policy begins to take sharp relief, as President Bush and Senator John McCain chastised Senator Barack Obama for offering to talk to US regional opponents, through the divisive invocation of the Munich analogy and tactics of appeasement.[6] In part the Iraq War of 2003 was brought on by the belief, held by some, that it offered an opportunity to transform US strategic interests and identity after Vietnam and after the inhibited closure of the 1991 Gulf War. These beliefs cut against other lessons of an earlier devastating war. In 1975 an NSC study on the 'lessons of Vietnam' informed Kissinger:

> Having been badly burned in Viet-Nam, the American people now appear to have quite different, and more limited, vision of our proper role in the world and our ability to influence events. In a sense, a control mechanism has evolved within our society which is likely to prevent for the foreseeable future any repetition of a Viet-Nam style involvement. The danger may therefore be not that we will ignore the lessons of Viet-Nam, but that we will be tempted to apply them too broadly, in East Asia and around the world.... It is tempting to say, as many do, that we should either use our power totally or not use it at all.[7]

Apart from all the local, regional and international repercussions and dynamics resulting from the Iraq War, how the United States reads, remembers and narrates its experience will be pivotal in years to come.

Notes

1 Jürgen Habermas, *The Divided West* (Cambridge: Polity, 2006).
2 Richard A. Falk, *The Costs of War: International Law, The UN, and World Order After Iraq* (New York: Routledge, 2008), 1.
3 See a good review by Michael Cox, 'Is the United States in decline – again?' *International Affairs*, vol. 83, no. 4 (2007), 643–653.
4 Fareed Zakaria, 'The Future of American Power: How America Can Survive the Rise of the Rest,' 18–43; and Richard Haass, 'The Age of Nonpolarity: What Will Follow U.S. Dominance,' 44–56, both in *Foreign Affairs* (May/June 2008).
5 President Jimmy Carter, The Capitol, 20 January 1977, Inaugural Address of President Carter, 1/20/// (44), Jimmy Carter Library; David Ryan, 'Dilemmas and Lessons of Carter's Constructions of Foreign Policy: We are now free of that inordinate fear' paper delivered at The Carter Presidency: Lessons for the 21st Century, University of Georgia, 19 January 2007; Jimmy Carter, 'Reclaiming the Values of the United States,' in Robert Harvey (ed.), *The World Crisis: The Way Forward after Iraq* (London: Constable, 2008).
6 Sheryl Gay Stolberg and Jim Rutenberg, 'Bush Assails "Appeasement," Touching Off Storm,' *New York Times*, 16 May 2008; Larry Rohter, 'Obama Says Bush and McCain are "Fear Mongering" in Attacks,' *New York Times*, 17 May 2008.
7 W. R. Smyser memorandum to Secretary Kissinger, Lessons of Vietnam, 12 May, 1975, NSA, Presidential Country Files for East Asia and the Pacific. Country File: Vietnam, Vietnam (23), box 20, Gerald R. Ford Library.

1 Eisenhower and regime change in Iraq

The United States and the Iraqi Revolution of 1958

Kenneth Osgood*

Shortly after the 1991 Gulf War, the Mexican-American comedian Paul Rodriguez joked that war was God's way of teaching geography. 'Before the war in the Middle East,' he confessed, 'I didn't know what the hell Kuwait was. I thought it was a fruit from New Zealand.'[1] Rodriquez's humorous observation captured the ethos of an American public that is often poorly informed about the wider world, but which, in moments of crisis, scrambles to make sense of its role in the global community. Rodriguez could also have pointed out that America's wars abroad have acted as catalysts for tutorials in US diplomatic history. This is especially true with respect to the Middle East, where the pace of historical inquiry has largely followed the emergence of crises in such places as Palestine, Egypt, and Iran. This volume is itself testimony to the power of contemporary problems – in this case, the ongoing war in Iraq – to provoke scholars and the wider public to reflect more deeply on the historical background of crises in the Middle East.

Prior to 1991, you could search in vain for books or articles that focused on the history of US foreign policy toward Iraq. To the extent that Iraq figured at all in historical writing on US foreign relations, it did so only indirectly – as but a small component of broader studies of such issues as the Arab–Israeli dispute, the British Empire, Arab nationalism, and the Cold War. The situation has improved slightly during the last 15 years, but Iraq effectively remains a black hole in US diplomatic history. We know more about the 1991 Gulf War than we do about US–Iraqi relations during the five decades of Cold War that led up to it. Indeed, we know more about the conduct of the *present* war in Iraq than we do about the historical events that preceded it. Thus, putting the current conflict in its proper historical perspective is as difficult as it is important. So too is it necessary to examine US–Iraqi relations on their own terms. As Nathan Citino has written, 'more research is sorely needed to prevent America's wars with Saddam Hussein from distorting historical interpretations of previous US–Iraqi relations.'[2]

A broadened historical perspective reveals that America's troubled relationship with Saddam Hussein was anything but an aberration in US–Iraqi relations. For over a half century, US policy toward Iraq oscillated between conflict and cooperation, between working with the regime in Baghdad to conspiring against it. At recurring intervals, American policymakers carefully considered various types of interventions in Iraq – from direct military intervention, to covert operations, to more subtle efforts to shape, manipulate, or influence Iraqi politics. Iraq was hardly unique in this regard, of course: the history of US foreign policy is to a great extent the history of American intervention abroad. As Stephen Kinzer has expertly chronicled, the most drastic form of intervention, 'regime change,' has been a recurring feature of US foreign policy since the nineteenth century. At least 14 times since 1893 the United States played a decisive role in overthrowing foreign governments. On many other occasions Americans played a supporting role in campaigns directed against leaders and regimes at odds with the United States. American leaders often considered regime change to be a legitimate objective of US foreign policy, even if they usually hid that sentiment from the public.[3]

Well-intentioned critics of George W. Bush's foreign policy were mistaken, then, in concluding that his policy of 'preemptive war' to spark 'regime change' in Iraq somehow represented a dramatic break from the normal course of American foreign relations. What was unique about George W. Bush was not that he used American power to topple a foreign government, but the *way* that he went about it: openly and brazenly declaring his determination to do so. President Bush also was not the first to seek regime change in Iraq. His immediate predecessors, George H. W. Bush and Bill Clinton, had made overthrowing Saddam Hussein a top priority, though they opted to use clandestine measures, rather than direct military force to do so.[4]

American leaders seriously considered regime change at earlier moments as well. The first instance was a half-century ago, near the end of the presidency of Dwight D. Eisenhower. The precipitating incident was the Iraqi Revolution of July 14, 1958. Early that morning, a group of army officers surrounded the royal palace in Baghdad and executed the king and his family. The Hashemite dynasty, which had ruled Iraq as a virtual proxy of the British Empire since the 1920s, was dead. When the coup plotters announced on the radio that the army had liberated Iraq from British imperialism, Iraqis poured into the streets to celebrate the downfall of the old regime. Shortly thereafter, army officers found and shot the former prime minister of Iraq, Nuri al-Sa'id. Nuri had been one of Britain's closest allies in the Middle East, and he was widely regarded by ordinary Iraqis as a tool of the British Empire. Cheering crowds celebrated Nuri's death by parading his mutilated remains through the streets of the capital.[5]

The events of that day triggered a wave of panic among other pro-Western regimes in the Middle East. Leaders in Saudi Arabia, Jordan, and Lebanon feared that they might be the next victims of nationalist revolution. Washington and London went into crisis mode. Concerned about their interests and their allies, the American and British governments promptly dispatched troops to shore-up the pro-Western governments of Lebanon and Jordan respectively.[6] These interventions have overshadowed the more complex and confused set of politics that the United States pursued with respect to post-revolutionary Iraq. Much of the historical writing on the Iraqi Revolution has focused on the impact of the Iraq crisis on other areas of the Middle East or on Anglo-American relations. Mirroring the neglect of Iraq in the broader historiography, diplomatic historians have devoted little attention to the impact of the 1958 crisis on US–Iraqi relations.[7]

In the aftermath of the July revolution, American officials debated quite seriously the possibility of invading Baghdad and toppling the new government of Iraq. Detailed operational plans were developed, but the invasion never happened. The Eisenhower administration chose restraint. It also labored to ensure that other governments followed suit. For differing reasons, the British, Iranian, Turkish, Egyptian, and Israeli governments also explored the possibility of invading Iraq, but were persuaded not to do so, in part because of US efforts. Why the Eisenhower administration rejected military intervention as an option for itself and its allies is the subject of this chapter. It argues that the Eisenhower administration refrained from military action to provoke regime change not for idealistic reasons stemming from the morality and legality of overthrowing a foreign government, but for pragmatic reasons stemming from the consequences of doing so. Remarkably, the Eisenhower administration expressed little concern that military intervention would precipitate war with the Soviet Union, despite the blustery threats made by Nikita Khrushchev during the Iraq crisis.[8] But it was deeply troubled by the probable impact an intervention would have on the broader battle for hearts and minds in the Cold War. The Eisenhower administration calculated that military intervention would damage the broader geopolitical position of the United States because it would have a catastrophic impact on world public opinion. It would damage the US reputation in the world and severely undermine American efforts to win friends and allies in the Middle East and the broader Third World. Moreover, American officials acknowledged, an invasion would be disastrous within Iraq itself. A hostile nationalist backlash would precipitate armed resistance against US forces, if not civil war. Any government imposed on Iraq would be overthrown in time. Civil war and chaos would probably result, and radical movements hostile to the United States would gain influence in Iraq and elsewhere in the region. In short, intangible 'psychological' factors – the impact on hearts and minds – restrained the Eisenhower administration from using military power in Iraq.

The chapter also examines the secret debate that took place within the Eisenhower administration about clandestine operations. Believing that direct military action would inflict irreparable harm on America's reputation and capacity for global leadership, the Eisenhower administration explored the possibility that it could achieve its goals in Iraq by working covertly with Iraqi opposition groups and various foreign intelligence services. Because many sources remain classified, it is impossible to determine what kinds of covert operations the United States implemented in response to the Iraqi revolution. This chapter does suggest, however, that the available records provide circumstantial evidence linking the Eisenhower administration to various assassination and coup attempts perpetrated at the end of the 1950s. If the Eisenhower administration was prudent and restrained in its application of military power, it appeared less so in the matter of covert action.

Dual containment in the Middle East

US policy toward Iraq in the aftermath of the revolution was primarily shaped by the larger strategic calculations that governed US foreign policy to the region as a whole. Generally speaking, the overarching objective of US national security strategy can be stated simply: preserve Western access to the region's oil resources. The imperative of protecting Western access to Middle Eastern oil is one of the most consistently argued themes running through US national security documents after 1946. A top State Department official articulated this theme clearly in the midst of the 1958 Iraq crisis, announcing succinctly: 'The principal Western interest in Iraq ... is oil.'[9]

Although today US prosperity virtually demands a continued flow of oil from the Middle East to the United States, in the early Cold War years the American interest in the region's oil resources was less directly linked to the American economy. To be sure, by 1958 American oil companies had developed an important stake in the petroleum reserves of Iraq, Iran, Saudi Arabia, Kuwait, and other overseas locations. Yet because the United States imported only a small percentage of its petroleum needs until the early 1970s, the flow of oil from the Middle East did not have as direct an influence on the American economy as it does today.[10] The same could not be said of Western Europe. By the early 1950s, key European economies appeared reliant on Middle Eastern petroleum for their economic and strategic health. The United Kingdom especially depended on Persian Gulf oil for both fuel and hard currency. As Eisenhower's Secretary of State, John Foster Dulles, noted: 'If the oil fields of Iraq and Kuwait fell under hostile control, the financial impact on the United Kingdom might be catastrophic.'[11] The turmoil in Iraq loomed especially large for American officials because the economic health of America's closest Cold War ally was at stake.

Because the military strength and economic prosperity of America's NATO allies were intertwined with Persian Gulf oil, US policy toward the Middle East was, in a sense, hostage to European fuel needs. The National Security Council (NSC) established, as a matter of policy, that the United States had to do everything in its power to ensure the uninterrupted flow of oil to Western Europe from the Middle East – an area known in the 1950s as the Near East. 'The critical importance of Near Eastern oil to our NATO allies requires that we make every effort to insure its continued availability to us and to our allies,' the NSC announced in its November 1958 statement of US policy toward the region. Accordingly, the United States should be

> prepared to use force, but only as a last resort, either alone or in support of the United Kingdom, to insure that the quantity of oil available from the Near East on reasonable terms is sufficient ... to meet Western Europe's requirements.[12]

Such a clear statement of US readiness to employ any measure to preserve Western access to Middle Eastern oil on favorable terms surfaced time and again in US policy papers during the postwar period.

Two interrelated concerns also dominated US thinking with respect to the Middle East. First there was the Cold War with the Soviet Union. Washington was determined to prevent the region from falling under communist control or Soviet influence. The United States was especially concerned to keep the Soviets from encroaching on the region's oil reserves, which would have a disastrous impact on strategic plans for the defense of Western Europe. The second concern was Arab nationalism. Led by the Egyptian president Gamal Abdel Nasser, Arab nationalists threatened to undermine Western hegemony in the Middle East. Nasser and his supporters opposed foreign military establishments on Arab territory, railed against the exploitive economic practices of European colonial powers, and conspired against the conservative autocratic regimes that dominated the region's politics and appeared to do the bidding of the West. Many also called for Arab unity and the building of a single pan-Arab state. This dream appeared possible at about the same time as the Iraqi coup. Egypt and Syria had merged to create the United Arab Republic (UAR) five months earlier, in February 1958, and Nasser signaled his interest in bringing more Arab states into the fold. This seemed to jeopardize the pro-Western regimes of the area which ruled with the thinnest base of popular support. Further exasperating the United States, many nationalists urged a neutralist path between the opposing power blocs of the Cold War. For much of the 1950s, American officials ranked nationalism as a greater concern than communism, for the simple reason that nationalism had much wider popular appeal than atheistic communism in the widely Islamic Middle East. In addition, Arab nationalism posed a direct threat to the conservative, pro-Western, and often authoritarian regimes that guaranteed Western access to Persian Gulf oil at reasonably low prices.

Accordingly, US strategy toward the Middle East evolved into a form of 'dual containment.' It was directed at preventing communist encroachment while simultaneously limiting the appeal of Arab nationalism. Since Nasser was often the chief spokesperson and most powerful promoter of Arab nationalism, this dual containment strategy in practical terms meant containing both Egypt and the USSR. The American response to the Iraqi revolution would be shaped by this dual containment strategy as well as by the related goal of protecting Western oil access.[13]

The Iraq Revolution

US policy would be complicated, however, by a murky understanding of the Iraqi political scene. The 1958 revolution was spearheaded by a group of army officers who loosely modeled themselves after the group that had brought Nasser to power in Egypt. The Iraqi conspirators were a less cohesive group, however. United only by a shared hatred of the Hashemite monarchy, they were bound by an alliance of convenience that masked deeply rooted ideological and political differences. The most contentious issue concerned Arab unity. Should Iraq follow Nasser's lead and join the UAR, or should it challenge Nasser's leadership and remain an independent force?[14]

The differences on this issue were exemplified by the two most prominent leaders of the Iraqi Revolution: 'Abd al-Karim Qasim and Abd al-Salam 'Arif. Qasim was the highest-ranking officer involved in the coup. He emerged as head of the new Iraqi regime almost immediately. 'Arif was Qasim's subordinate, but also his rival. The most divisive issue between them concerned Iraq's relationship to Nasser. 'Arif, generally speaking, had pan-Arabist sympathies. He supported a close relationship with Nasser and suggested that Iraq might join the UAR. He in turn was supported by pan Arabists in the officer corps and by members of the Ba'ath Party: a small, but well-organized, political force. Qasim, on the other hand, was deeply suspicious of Nasser. He believed that union with the UAR would undermine Iraqi sovereignty. It also would mean that Qasim would have to play second fiddle to Nasser and Qasim was not interested in playing second fiddle to anyone. He was supported by his allies in the army and others, including Iraqi communists, who shared Qasim's distrust of Nasser and the UAR.[15]

Further complicating the political picture was the status of the Iraqi Communist Party (ICP). Before 1958, it was a well-organized underground movement opposed to the Iraqi monarchy. After the revolution, the ICP came out into the open. Because it was the largest, best-organized, and most cohesive political group in Iraq, the Communist Party would play a pivotal role in shaping the balance of power in the months to come. Its capability to mobilize crowds in the streets of Iraq's cities proved to be a particular asset in the chaotic post-revolutionary atmosphere. In the course of Qasim's reign, he performed a delicate balancing act between the nationalists and the communists. He often vacillated between seeking support from the Iraqi Communist Party and seeking support from Iraqi nationalists, a dangerous game of playing one group against the other that rendered Qasim's regime highly vulnerable to opposition from both sides – and to meddling from abroad.[16]

In the early days of the Iraqi revolution, these subtleties in Iraqi politics were invisible to American officials, who displayed a murky understanding of both Arab nationalism and communism in the Middle East. It was widely assumed that Qasim was simultaneously a tool of both Nasser and the Kremlin. American officials assumed that Nasser was not only behind the July revolution, but that he was the puppeteer pulling the strings of the Qasim regime. Simultaneously, American officials assumed that Nasser's strings were in turn being pulled by the Kremlin. Eisenhower remarked that the events of July 14 were 'fomented by Nasser under Kremlin guidance.'[17] In his mind lurked a Middle Eastern version of the domino theory. Eisenhower feared that Iraq would spark a wave of defections to communism. If Iraq fell to communism, the rest of the region would sooner or later fall with it. Something needed to be done, he decided, because 'to lose this area by inaction would be far worse than the loss of China, because of the strategic position and resources of the Middle East.'[18]

To a great extent, British officials shared American fears about the implications of the Iraqi Revolution. If anything, they were more anxious than their American counterparts and more interested in exploring military solutions. The events in Iraq seemed to signal the 'virtual end of the British empire in the Middle East,' as William Rogers Louis observed. The British were especially concerned about the potential threat Qasim and his crew posed to their oil interests and to the sprawling British air base at Habbaniya. They were equally concerned about the threat to their client states in Jordan and Kuwait, both of which appeared highly vulnerable to nationalist upheaval. British Prime Minister Harold Macmillan argued for a forceful response. Regarding Nasser as the Hitler of the Middle East, he perceived Nasser's hand in the Iraqi Revolution. Macmillan initially argued for a broad Anglo-American intervention to restructure the Middle East region as a whole. This would involve not only joint military action in Lebanon, Jordan, and Syria, but also 'regime change' in Iraq. His plan would resuscitate the British position in the Middle East which had declined markedly since the disastrous Suez invasion two years before.[19]

Eisenhower quickly nipped these grandiose plans in the bud. After the debacle in Suez, the British knew they needed American support for any broad-based intervention in the Middle East, and this Eisenhower refused to give. He hesitated for three main reasons. First, there was the opposition of his military advisors. The Joint Chiefs of Staff did not want to become embroiled in an unpopular neocolonial war in the Persian Gulf. Second, Eisenhower worried that such an intervention would stretch the limits of his constitutional powers. Respectful of Congressional prerogatives, he believed Macmillan's plans were 'far beyond anything I have the power to do constitutionally,' and he doubted he could rally American opinion to support a seemingly colonial enterprise.[20] Most importantly, there was world public opinion. Eisenhower feared that overt military intervention to provoke regime change would isolate the United States morally and politically. He had pulled the plug on the Suez invasion two years earlier largely because its blatant neocolonialism threatened American efforts to win friends and allies in the Third World. He argued in 1956 that the resort to arms 'might well array the world from Dakar to the Philippine islands against us.'[21] The same concern inspired restraint in 1958. Viewing the Cold War as a global battle for hearts and minds, Eisenhower felt he needed a compelling moral reason to justify a major military intervention. Although Eisenhower worried about Western access to Persian Gulf oil, he was reluctant to make that the basis for war. He understood that unprovoked war to spark regime change in Iraq would inflict terrible damage to America's reputation and its global leadership.[22]

The new Iraqi leadership also acted in ways that encouraged American and British restraint. The day after the July 14 coup, Qasim met personally with the ambassadors from the United States and Britain and expressed his interest in pursuing friendly relations. Three days later, his government announced that Iraq would not disrupt the flow of oil to the West. Qasim had taken steps to protect oil wells, pumping stations, and other oil-related facilities in Iraq. He also denied having any plans to nationalize the oil industry. He seemed to understand that the oil nationalization project was what had led the US and UK to overthrow Mohammed Mossadeq in Iran five years earlier.[23] For nearly two years following the revolution, Qasim repeatedly vocalized concerns that Anglo-American agents were conspiring against him.[24] Undoubtedly Qasim realized he needed to assure the Western powers that their oil interests would not be disrupted. His announcement to that effect provoked sighs of relief in London and in Washington. Western officials were less pleased that Qasim signed a mutual defense agreement with the United Arab Republic and even more chagrined that the Soviet government extended recognition to his regime. Yet, taken together, these developments led the US and UK to suspend any plans for regime change. They did not want a regional conflict that would send the Arab world into Soviet arms. American and British forces would do little more than stage a brief show of force in Lebanon and Jordan. They would dramatize Western willingness to defend their conservative allies in the region, but they would not seek a wider war.

On August 3, the United States and Britain extended diplomatic recognition to Qasim's regime. For the next several months, the discussion in US foreign policy circles focused not on whether or how to get rid of Qasim, but rather how to use the new situation in Baghdad to further the American strategy of dual containment of Arab nationalism and communism. Officials would discover, however, that applying this strategy to the new Iraq was difficult indeed.

Working with Nasser

The problem came as Nasser's ambition to lead the Arab world collided with internal Iraqi politics. As Qasim sought to consolidate his power, he moved against 'Arif and his supporters in the army – the faction that represented Nasser's best chance for garnering influence in the new Iraqi state. In the aftermath of the July revolution, 'Arif had given numerous speeches praising Nasser and calling for union with the UAR. Qasim perceived this as a threat to both his own authority and the independence of the new Iraq. He pushed 'Arif into a marginal government post, then had him arrested. Others who supported union with the UAR or collaboration with Nasser were demoted or imprisoned. Nasser took this assault on his closest supporters in Iraq as a grave challenge. A bitter personal feud and a hostile propaganda war erupted between Qasim and Nasser.[25]

The fallout from the Qasim–Nasser split had two significant consequences. In the first place, Qasim became more closely tied to the Iraqi Communist Party. His moves against 'Arif and the pan-Arabist faction in the army may have eliminated rivals for power, but they also cut him off from a significant base of potential support. To compensate for this, Qasim swung left. He developed a working alliance with the Iraqi communists, who had their own reasons for opposing Nasser. Qasim's hold on power increasingly relied on the ability of his communist allies to mobilize popular demonstrations of support. Qasim also turned to the USSR for help, and signed trade and arms deals with the Soviets in October 1958. These developments increased the sense of alarm in Washington. Some officials in the State Department and CIA concluded that Iraq was on the way to becoming a Soviet satellite.[26]

The other major consequence of the Nasser–Qasim feud produced happier results for American foreign policy. Nasser, who had previously been cultivating ties to Moscow, now moved in the other direction. He began launching a heated propaganda assault on both Qasim and communism. He also nurtured ties with his sympathizers in the Iraqi army and lent his support to various schemes for ousting Qasim. Nasser's anti-communist campaign threw the 'dual containment' strategy into sharp relief. The Eisenhower administration now confronted a difficult choice: support Nasser's campaign against Qasim and risk seeing Iraq engulfed into an enlarged UAR, or continue to maneuver against Nasser and risk seeing a communist takeover of Iraq. A clear consensus emerged in the administration. Far better to see Nasser in control of Iraq than the Soviet Union. Although the British, Israelis, Turks, and pro-Western Arab elite recoiled at the idea of encouraging Nasser's regional ambitions, the United States nevertheless reappraised its policy toward the Arab leader. Containment of Arab nationalism would give way to cooperation.[27] Relations between the UAR and the United States improved, and Nasser began seeking American help in waging his anti-communist assault on Qasim. The Eisenhower administration pursued ways to reward Nasser with enlarged US aid, including sales of wheat, urgently desired by Nasser, and a $100 million loan for improving the Suez Canal.[28]

US cooperation with Nasser highlighted the bizarre twist in Cold War logic taking root in Washington. American officials saw a silver lining in communist success in Iraq: it made other countries in the Middle East take the communist danger more seriously. American officials were especially elated that Nasser, the most influential spokesperson in the Arab world, was using his voice to attack communism. The State Department was enthralled: at last, Nasser had seen the light. His prestige lent the assault on communism much greater credibility than would be accorded to American pronouncements. 'To give [the] devil his due,' the American ambassador to the UAR noted, 'Nasser has dealt body blows to both Communists and Soviets recently which [the] West, with all its psychological warfare potential, could not equal.'[29]

Yet there was an unfortunate by-product of Nasser's newfound anti-communism. The more Nasser attacked Qasim for being a communist stooge, the more Qasim became alienated from Iraqi nationalists, and the more dependent he became on support from the Iraqi Communist Party. In a seeming paradox, Nasser's anti-communist broadsides had the effect of moving Qasim closer to the communists. American analysts predicted that as Qasim became more and more dependent upon his communist allies, he would feel compelled to begin staffing his government with communists, thus initiating a chain of events that would lead to a communist takeover in Iraq.

The crises came to a head in March 1959. In the northern city of Mosul, nationalist officers in the army, working with Nasser, plotted a revolt against Qasim's regime. Communist Party leaders heard of the plot and helped foil it by rallying hundreds of their supporters for demonstrations in Mosul on March 6. As events unfolded, Qasim crushed the coup with communist support, and hundreds of nationalist officers were killed. The Mosul uprising followed other coup plots, several of which appeared to have had Nasser's support. Qasim now appeared dependent upon the communists for his very survival, and communist party leaders asked to be rewarded with key posts in Qasim's government. That same month, Qasim signaled shifts in Iraqi foreign policy by accepting a large loan from the Soviet Union and by officially withdrawing Iraq from the Baghdad Pact, a Western security arrangement created in 1955.[30]

Falling dominoes

Qasim's changing fortunes exacerbated the Eisenhower administration's sense of alarm. Even before the Mosul revolt, the CIA was predicting that Iraqi communists were poised to take direct control of the government. The agency doubted Qasim's ability to stem the movement toward a communist takeover of his regime. Qasim had become so dependent on the communists to balance the nationalists, that it was only a matter of time before the communists held the upper hand. The agency warned in February:

> Iraq is the scene of a determined and so far effective Communist drive toward power. This drive threatens important US interests: the maintenance of assured Western access to Middle East oil, the denial of the area to Soviet control, and the security and stability of non-Communist governments in the area as a whole.[31]

After the Mosul revolt, reports from CIA director Allen Dulles and other sources painted an even gloomier picture; the trend seemed to be toward a communist government without any arresting factors in sight.[32] On March 26, the American ambassador to Iraq, John D. Jernegan, sent Washington his most pessimistic report to date. The 'Iron Curtain [was] descending' upon Iraq, he announced. Qasim, by aligning himself with the communists to defeat the Nasserists, was abandoning his balancing act and choosing sides. 'Overt signs point sharply left,' Jernegan grimly reported. The government of Iraq was now too far along the road to communism to turn back, he added, predicting that Iraq might become 'the first Soviet satellite in [the] Arab world.' Ominously, Jernegan concluded that 'control could be wrested from Qasim only by assassination.'[33]

Washington again went into crisis mode. Eisenhower's advisors foresaw falling dominoes in the Middle East. American officials used the same logic to describe the communist threat to Iraq that they had used to explain the strategic significance of Vietnam: it was the pivotal domino keeping the rest of the region from falling to communism. A Defense Department policy paper concluded:

> The situation in Iraq is cause for grave concern. If matters proceed along their present course it seems but a matter of time before Communist control of the country will be established ... If the Communists take over Iraq, they will be in a position to extend their influences into Syria and the Persian Gulf areas, particularly Kuwait, thus threatening the West's control of the Middle East oil reserves. The repercussions of a Communist takeover in Iraq could well include the downfall of the regime in Iran.[34]

The discussion again turned to military intervention. By the spring of 1959, the Pentagon had already developed plans to use two or three army divisions to gain control over Baghdad and other strategic locations. American planners believed they could easily topple the regime in Baghdad.[35] But the Eisenhower administration also recognized that unprovoked, preemptive warfare would stimulate fierce resistance from the Iraqi populace. Any new government set up by the United States would be discredited, the State Department warned: 'As soon as US forces left Iraq the revulsion against any government set up [by the US] ... would be so great that it would probably be swept away.' Its replacement assuredly would be hostile to the United States. Moreover, 'such military action would set the whole Middle East against us.' It would also destroy America's reputation throughout the broader Third World. According to the State Department, military intervention to provoke regime change would have a 'catastrophic psychological reaction throughout Africa and Asia which would inevitably portray us as being worse aggressors than the Communists.'[36] The often more hawkish Defense Department agreed, adding that the US reputation would be damaged and long-standing US principles would be violated by what would in effect be unprovoked aggression. 'The capacity of the United States to take decisive action,' a Defense policy paper concluded, 'is limited.'[37] Despite an urgent sense of crisis, the administration ruled out military intervention on grounds that the United States would lose more than it would gain by fostering regime change in Iraq with military force.

The State and Defense departments evinced a remarkable understanding of the limits of US power and the psychological consequences of an unprovoked assault on a sovereign state. Overthrowing the Iraqi government was one thing; dealing with its consequences was quite another. The State Department advocated a 'wait and see' policy. Believing that Qasim personally was no communist, the State Department believed he might be convinced to keep the communists at arm's length if the United States could win his trust. The job, then, would be cautious, patient, and friendly efforts to earn Qasim's confidence.

This 'wait and see' policy had the support of the UK. British military planners saw nothing but disaster in an invasion of Iraq without a clear moral rationale. The Chiefs of Staff argued that such an invasion would provoke a strong nationalist backlash in Iraq that would unite the country in opposition to the West. It would also 'arouse wide-spread hostility throughout the Middle East and cause world-wide damage to Western interests.' The Chiefs concluded that the psychological stakes were too high: 'Severe damage would be done to the standing of the United Kingdom and the United States throughout the world.'[38]

American officials discussed another possibility for dealing with Qasim: intervention by Turkey, Iran, Jordan, the UAR, or some combination. For different reasons and at different times, each of these governments considered sending forces into Iraq. Such a possibility portended serious psychological ramifications. The State Department's Assistant Secretary in charge of the Near East, William Rountree, noted that intervention by these countries would still be viewed as 'Western-instigated aggression.' It would provide little beyond a short-range fix, and would 'probably have the long-range effect of strengthening Communism in the Arab world and permanently alienating Arab nationalist sentiment from the West.'[39] Accordingly, staving off a precipitous invasion by other regional powers became a major objective of American foreign policy toward post-revolutionary Iraq.

The Mossadeq option

While most members of the Eisenhower administration agreed that military intervention would create more problems than it would solve, some doubted that the United States could risk sitting passively while Iraq slid into communism. Speaking before the National Security Council, Treasury Secretary Robert B. Anderson drew an unfavorable comparison with recent events in Indochina. When the French were losing to the communists in 1954, he recalled, there was a lot of talk about how the United States could not afford to lose Indochina. 'Much of Indo-China was lost to the

Communists while we were here talking and planning about saving it. We must not now repeat this error in the Middle East. ... We do not want another Dienbienphu.'[40] Eisenhower's National Security Advisor, Gordon Gray, expressed similar frustration:

> We sit and watch unfolding events which seem to point inevitably to Soviet domination of Iraq, acknowledging, I am afraid, an inability to do anything about it. It is almost like watching a movie whose end we do not like but which we are committed to see.[41]

Eisenhower shared such frustrations. Viewing Qasim as a 'prisoner of the Communists,' he opined that 'we are facing the complete loss of Iraq to the Communists.'[42]

Pressing his advisors to continue searching for options, Eisenhower ordered the National Security Council to look for ways to influence the course of events in Iraq.[43] At the beginning of April, he created a high-level committee to explore overt and covert means of preventing a communist takeover in Iraq. Chaired by the State Department's William Rountree and later by his successor G. Lewis Jones, the committee included representatives from the CIA, the Defense Department, the Joint Chiefs of Staff, and the US Information Agency – the propaganda agency created by Eisenhower in 1953. The Iraq Committee met regularly from April 1959 to March 1960, and evaluated a wide range of measures to influence the internal politics of Iraq, including covert operations to spark regime change.

It is difficult to discern what exactly came of these efforts. As Douglas Little notes, 'Nowhere has the story of American covert action in the Middle East ... been shrouded in greater mystery than in Iraq.'[44] Some evidence suggests that US intelligence may have cooperated with Nasser in supporting the March 1959 revolt in Mosul. A few journalists have alleged that the CIA was complicit in an assassination attempt on Qasim in October 1959 that involved the Ba'ath Party, including a young Saddam Hussein. Other observers have seen the agency's hand in the more successful plot that took place during the Kennedy administration: the 1963 coup that brought the Ba'ath Party to power for the first time and resulted in a murderous anti-communist bloodbath.[45] We do not know precisely what the US role was in these and the myriad other plots that were hatched against Qasim's regime during the Eisenhower and Kennedy administrations. The documentary record is filled with holes. A remarkable volume of material remains classified, and those records that are available are obscured by redactions – large blacked-out sections that allow for plausible deniability. While it is difficult to know exactly what actions were taken to destabilize or overthrow Qasim's regime, we can discern fairly clearly what was on the planning table. We also can see clues as to what was authorized.

Within days of the coup in Iraq, the US and British governments began contemplating covert action. When John Foster Dulles met with his British counterpart, Selwyn Lloyd, on July 18 the two concluded that 'the best way to handle the Iraqi situation was to wait and watch developments, building up assets within the country which might at some future time make it possible to bring about a change.' They cited 'the Mussadiq example' as an option for Qasim.[46] The Iraq Committee, formed a few months later, counseled military restraint while considering covert options. It shared the consensus view within the administration that dramatic military action by the United States was not desirable at that time. Although many of the committee members were hawkish about Iraq and hostile to Qasim, they acknowledged that a military invasion would produce civil war or an insurgency within Iraq that would lead to the collapse of any government installed by the West. They also understood that an invasion would weaken American power and influence in the region and in other parts of the world. Covert action, however, appeared more promising. By minimizing or obscuring US involvement, a successful covert action campaign might achieve US objectives without sparking the unwanted psychological and political ramifications that would accompany an invasion.

Eager to come up with a workable covert operations plan, the Iraq Committee set itself to work building up assets for possible future operations against Qasim.[47] Discussions within the NSC alluded to the committee's charge. It was working 'in very great secrecy' to explore 'all possible courses of action' to 'change the situation' in Iraq.[48] The tenor of the Iraq Committee's deliberations and discussions within the NSC revolved around a search for sources of opposition to Qasim that would not be viewed as imperialist agents. William Rountree told the council that he foresaw three possible outcomes from the political turmoil in Iraq. Tellingly, none of these alternatives involved Qasim remaining in power. The first, and most dreaded, possibility was a communist takeover in Iraq. The second possible outcome would involve Nasser's sympathizers assuming control of Iraq with the UAR's help. The third alternative was a 'nationalist' regime, not connected to Nasser, that would come to power and remove both the Communists and the pro-Nasser leaders from the Iraqi government. This latter possibility, while remote, shaped the US outlook toward Iraq. For the next several years, American officials would search for a 'third force' in Iraq that was neither communist nor aligned with Nasser.[49]

Hawkish calls for regime change came from the Joint Chiefs of Staff. A few days after the Iraq Committee was established, the JCS urged the committee to develop a covert action campaign to weaken communist influence and destabilize the Qasim regime. In addition to clandestine political and propaganda operations against Iraqi communists, the Chiefs recommended drawing up plans for the 'replacement of [the] Qasim government.' A top priority was identifying 'acceptable replacement leaders' to take over after Qasim's downfall. The United States should help pro-Western leaders to escape from Iraq so that they could 'provide a rallying point of elements opposing the Iraqi regime.' The United States should also find out the 'sources of support available to them, and determine manner in which they may achieve control of the government.' To facilitate a pro-Western takeover in Iraq, the Chiefs advocated measures to destabilize Qasim's regime and the development of 'assets in coordination with US Allies which could be used to promote revolts.' Other courses of action recommended by the JCS included economic sanctions to ratchet up the pressure on Qasim and weaken his government, as well as the preparation of plans for military intervention by Turkish, Jordanian, Iranian, and Egyptian forces. Military intervention was to be a last resort action to keep Iraq from communist hands. The Chiefs hoped covert operations would render this course of action unnecessary. Their template for clandestine regime change mirrored the range and type of operations the United States had employed to overthrow the governments of Iran and Guatemala a few years earlier.[50]

The Central Intelligence Agency fueled the sense of urgency. CIA Director Allen Dulles publicly called the Iraq situation 'the most dangerous in the world,' and consistently presented the National Security Council with the direst estimates about the future of Iraq.[51] Dulles and his intelligence analysts left little doubt that Iraq was fated to become the next communist satellite. The CIA pressed the Iraq Committee to pursue an aggressive covert action program, including possibly assassination, which intelligence analysts saw as the only sure way of removing Qasim from power. The CIA's representative on the Iraq Committee argued forcefully: 'We should move with all dispatch to throw the Communists out of Iraq, working with the UK, Egypt, Turkey, Iran and Jordan all in different degrees.'[52] A partially declassified document prepared for the Iraq Committee listed overt and covert measures being planned or implemented by the United States. The covert section of the document is almost entirely blacked out, but telling passages indicate the tenor of its recommendations. 'We should not embark upon a campaign of minor pin-pricks and harassments which will not individually or collectively strike the regime a mortal blow,' the document announced. 'We do not want merely to infuriate the enemy, but to eliminate him.' It called for greater risk-taking to pursue regime change in Iraq. 'We should also be prepared to accept some exposures, some losses, and hostile propaganda attacks. The Soviets regularly accept these risks and continue to do their dirty work.... We must become thick skinned.' These and other sources leave little doubt that the CIA's preferred course of action involved decisive measures to remove Qasim from power.[53]

Still, the Eisenhower administration was divided about the merits of covert operations. The State Department consistently opposed extreme measures to bring down Qasim's regime. Jernegan, the US ambassador to Iraq, briefed the Iraq Committee on the principle question facing the group: 'shouldn't we start gathering up our assets and seeing if we could get rid of [Qasim]?'[54] To the chagrin of the more hawkish intelligence and defense communities, Jernegan cautioned against drastic actions until the situation was truly beyond hope. Counseling restraint, he felt the only solution should come from within Iraq. Outside efforts by Nasser and others, including the US, Turkey, and Iran, would only exacerbate the situation.[55] 'The situation is not lost,' he argued in May 1959, 'Kassem is not a Communist, and ... the Iraqi Premier may find it possible to hold the line against the Communists.' Besides, Jernegan cautioned, 'there was no one now in sight who could replace Kassem if we succeeded in ousting him.' Overthrowing Qasim without a strong alternative would merely provoke chaos. Jernegan believed the best policy would be to try to reassure Qasim and entice him away from the communists.[56] He and other State Department officials met repeatedly with Qasim and members of his government to reassure them the United States was not plotting against Iraq.[57]

While publicly reassuring Qasim about US intentions, the Eisenhower administration secretly nurtured contacts with his opponents. It did not have to look hard to find them. The capitals of the UAR, Jordan, and Lebanon were littered with committees of Iraqi exiles, supported by one or other foreign government, plotting ways and means of returning to power. Jordan's King Hussein, working with Iran, pursued his dream of restoring Hashemite rule in Iraq. Nasser, meanwhile, actively supported several conspiracies against Qasim by nationalist factions in Iraq.[58] The American intelligence community was well-informed about anti-Qasim conspiracies and well-connected with the conspirators. Indeed, the intelligence community seemed to be aware of virtually every assassination and coup attempt before it happened.[59]

Of the many who were conspiring against Qasim, Nasser appeared to have the best chance for success. Officials recognized that Nasser had more assets, more credibility, and better capabilities to operate in Iraq than the United States.[60] This realization, combined with the American hope for regime change, led the Eisenhower administration to cast aside its policy of dual-containment. Arab nationalism, once regarded as the scourge of Western policy in the region, now appeared to be the only realistic bulwark against communist expansion in Iraq. The administration's rapprochement with Nasser, already in the works, was now accelerated. Nasser, the same man whom Eisenhower had once blamed for instigating the Iraqi Revolution, now looked like the only one who could reverse it.

Yet working with Nasser was risky business. The United States had spent the past three years trying to weaken and isolate him; the UK and America's regional allies were deeply suspicious of Nasser's ambitions; and any public effort to cooperate with Nasser was sure to provoke both consternation among US allies and domestic opposition from supporters of Israel. There was also the risk that Nasser would become both emboldened and empowered by his increased influence in Iraq, especially if that brought him access to Mesopotamian oil revenues. The Eisenhower administration recognized all these risks, and for that reason was careful to conceal its contacts with Nasser. CIA operatives believed that the United States could run the risk of encouraging Nasser's ambitions because the Iraqis would not permit UAR domination over their affairs for very long. 'In the long run,' an unnamed

CIA operative predicted, 'an independent, neutralist, Iraq would probably emerge.'[61]

It seems probable that the CIA provided covert assistance to Nasser's plotting against Qasim, as has been suggested by Said Aburish, a Palestinian-American journalist who worked for Saddam Hussein's regime in the 1970s.[62] The documentary record does not provide conclusive evidence, however, and the precise nature of US connivance with Nasser and Iraqi opposition elements cannot be determined from available records. Still, it is clear that the Eisenhower administration actively considered a range of measures to assist Nasser and oppositional elements working with him against Qasim. It is also clear that the US extended at least some level of support and encouragement to the Egyptian leader in this regard.[63]

Even before the Iraq Committee was tasked with finding ways to change the situation in Iraq, the Eisenhower administration was exploring its options for achieving this goal by working with Nasser. The possibility of a Nasserist coup, with US support, was discussed at several NSC meetings in late 1958 and early 1959. These discussions happened to take place just prior to the Mosul revolt against Qasim, which involved Nasser's agents and sympathizers. 'Nasser does not want to be dominated by the Kremlin,' Eisenhower observed in one of these meetings, adding that 'it might be good policy to help the UAR take over in Iraq.'[64] Eisenhower expressed a key interest in helping Nasser by providing money or other assistance to help him wage his anti-communist campaign.[65] On another occasion, Eisenhower noted that cooperating with Nasser had distinct advantages. His prestige in the region meant that 'Nasser could oppose Communists better than can the US in the three-cornered struggle of the Middle East.'[66] Though it may be merely a suggestive coincidence, the timing of these remarks provides circumstantial evidence supporting the possibility that the United States secretly assisted Nasser in his campaign against Qasim.

Reporting by the intelligence community also provides some supporting detail for this theory. Well in advance of the Mosul revolt, the Eisenhower administration knew about Nasser's plotting. In February 1959, US intelligence reported to Eisenhower that Nasser was conspiring to overthrow Qasim's government by working through nationalists in the Army. The CIA noted that an assassination attempt against Qasim on February 22 would be followed by another coup attempt a few weeks later. Nasser's Iraqi allies would move against Qasim between March 2 and 5, US intelligence predicted, accurately forecasting the Mosul revolt.[67]

It is not clear what role, if any, the United States had in the Mosul plot. At the very least, the United States gave its tacit approval to the scheme. Knowing of the plot well beforehand, the Eisenhower administration did nothing to thwart it and did not alert Qasim to the danger. Qasim himself concluded that Mosul resulted from a joint US–UAR conspiracy. He complained to US officials that he had documentary proof that 'five or six Americans had been engaged [in] improper activities.'[68] The Iraqi press amplified and reinforced his suspicions by publishing numerous accounts of US collusion with Nasser. As one Iraqi paper put it, 'Nasser became first agent of American imperialism in Arab world and executer of aggressive Eisenhower Doctrine under mask of combating Communism danger.'[69] The State Department regarded such statements as bogus and attributed them to Iraqi paranoia and communist propaganda. Yet circumstantial evidence in declassified records suggests that Iraqi suspicions cannot be dismissed out of hand. The United States was working with Nasser on some level, even if the precise nature of that collaboration is not known.[70]

Regardless, the Mosul uprising encouraged the administration to continue improving US relations with Nasser in the hopes of halting communist advances in the Middle East. Even though the Mosul plot's failure exposed the limits of Nasser's abilities to change the regime in Baghdad, it also pointed to new possibilities. In April, JCS chairman Nathan Twinning urged the National Security Council to explore 'on [an] urgent basis the feasibility and desirability of supporting action by Nasser against Iraq.'[71] By May 1959, the administration approached Nasser to discuss 'parallel measures' that could be taken by the two countries against Iraq.[72] US officials also consulted with Nasser regarding his propaganda offensive against Qasim. They were concerned that calling Qasim a communist stooge might become a self-fulfilling prophesy. It would further alienate Qasim from the nationalists and drive him straight into communist arms. So the Eisenhower administration urged Nasser to attack communism broadly and ease-up on Qasim himself. This would leave Qasim at least some freedom to change course; he could still ally himself with the nationalists against the communists. To the great satisfaction of the Eisenhower administration, Nasser took this advice and turned his considerable prestige and formidable propaganda assets to a broad ranging attack on communism in the Middle East. One State Department official remarked approvingly, 'Nasser's recent attacks on Communism had done more to stay the advance of Communism in the Middle East than anything that the Western Powers could have achieved in years of work.'[73]

A similar range of ambiguous evidence links Nasser and the Eisenhower administration to the October 1959 assassination attempt against Qasim. Perpetrated by the Iraqi Ba'ath Party, the plot has provoked recent controversy because of Saddam Hussein's participation. Then in his early twenties, Saddam was part of a seven-man assassination team that ambushed Qasim as he drove down a main Baghdad thoroughfare. Saddam was supposed to provide covering fire while the other assailants took aim at Qasim. The plan broke down, everyone fired uncontrollably, and one of the gunmen was killed. Saddam and the others escaped. A seriously wounded Qasim survived. Although at the time Hussein was an inconsequential thug playing a bit-part as a trigger man in the plot, years later the attempt on Qasim's life would become a central part of the folklore of his rule in Iraq.[74] It also would provoke unpleasant allegations of a US role in helping to bring to power the same tyrant it would later depose.[75]

As with the Mosul plot, there is little direct documentary proof of US involvement. But the circumstantial evidence is such that the possibility of US–UAR collaboration with Ba'ath Party activists cannot be ruled out. The details are murky. Most accounts indicate that the UAR was involved on some level. Some of the gunmen were probably trained in Damascus by Nasser's agents, though it is doubtful Saddam himself was among them. He was recruited to participate late in the planning.[76] US intelligence believed Nasser was working closely with the Iraqi Ba'ath party. 'Nasser is counseling conspirators involved in plan for coup in Iraq ... including assassination of Qasim,' the agency reported in September. Again American intelligence knew about the plot several weeks in advance.[77] Some administration officials perceived the impending plot as an opportunity for the United States to rid itself of Qasim. An urgent meeting of the Iraq Committee was called by the Defense Department representative, Assistant Secretary John Irwin, who drew attention to the interesting 'possibilities' raised by news of the impending plot. 'Increased partisan tensions [in Iraq] point to the possibility of an attempt to overthrow the Qasim government by violence,' he wrote. These reports 'do draw attention to possibilities that merit serious consideration.'[78]

The Iraq Committee meeting, held on September 24, involved a heated debate about US options. The two State Department representatives urged a cautious approach, while the 12 others in attendance argued for more active measures against Qasim. The Defense Department and CIA made a particularly 'strong pitch for a more active policy toward Iraq, or at least broadened contingency planning to cover situations in which Kassem might be removed from the scene through a coup or assassination.'[79] Two CIA representatives on the committee described Qasim as 'an unstable, psychotic personality' who had forfeited his chance to earn nationalist support. Another official linked to the intelligence community, William Lakeland, argued that the United States should abandon all hope of working with Qasim. The US should 'be looking for alternatives' to Qasim, Lakeland argued – an ominous assertion from a man some believe later masterminded Qasim's removal in 1963.[80]

The Iraq Committee approved 'contingency' planning, coordinated with the UK in deep secrecy, to assist a new anti-communist regime should one come to power in Iraq.[81] The committee members also agreed that the US would be better off working through local intermediaries – regional governments and Iraqi exiles – than by initiating direct action itself. Plots involving the UAR, Jordan, Saudi Arabia, Turkey, and an unidentified power (redacted in the minutes) were discussed. The CIA was prepared to act. 'We have done all we can operationally to get ready,' an agency representative noted. 'There is a small stockpile in the area. We could support elements in Jordan and the UAR to help Iraqis filter back to Iraq.'[82] UPI reporter Richard Sale and the British journalist Adel Darwish separately interviewed several anonymous US officials from the period, and concluded that the CIA and UAR were working with the coup plotters, including Saddam Hussein. An Iraqi dentist served as the CIA's handler for Saddam, who monitored Qasim's movements from an apartment directly opposite Qasim's office in Iraq's Ministry of Defense. The apartment was funded through payments from the assistant military attaché at the Egyptian embassy.[83] Some evidence also suggests that, following the failed assassination attempt, Saddam Hussein escaped to Cairo where he was in frequent contact with US officials and intelligence agents.[84] Whatever the validity of these charges, at the very least currently declassified documents reveal that US officials were actively considering various plots against Qasim and that the CIA was building up assets for covert operations in Iraq.

The October assassination attempt put Qasim in the hospital until December, but did not fundamentally weaken his regime. As some American intelligence analysts had feared, the failed assassination brought another shift in Qasim's policies. Maneuvering against his nationalist rivals, Qasim again provoked concerns about his relationship to the communists. Released from the hospital on December 10, Qasim denounced the nationalists in an emotional six-hour press conference. Briefing the NSC on the episode, the CIA's Richard Bissell predicted that 'if Qasim had to make a choice, he would rely heavily on the Communists which he has been seeking to maintain in the past.' The situation was bleak, Bissell reported, but there was a bright side: at least now Qasim was vulnerable. His popularity had greatly declined and many officers in the army were ready to move against him. Bissell hinted that assassination might be the only viable option. Recent intelligence estimates supported his argument. A special intelligence estimate stressed that 'the most likely way to remove Qasim would be by assassination' and that the 'chances of success would be best if [the] coup appeared to be wholly internal.'[85] Bissell warned if no further assassination attempts were made, communist power in Iraq would continue to grow.[86] Such intelligence reporting led to one conclusion, and it skirted across the murky boundaries between intelligence analysis and policy recommendation.

Classified discussions increasingly revolved around the pros and cons of assassination. Even Bissell and his agency's analysts acknowledged that the risks were high. Although covert operations to assassinate or depose Qasim might shield the United States from the world outrage that would accompany an invasion, it would do little to address the other major obstacles to regime change. In the first place, even if Qasim were deposed, there was no 'suitable' (strong and pro-Western) replacement in sight. In addition, Qasim's assassination would probably provoke civil unrest which would redound to the benefit of the communists. Moreover, if nationalist elements tried and failed to assassinate Qasim, he might move even further into the communist camp. Any of these developments could spark intervention by Iraq's neighbors and a big regional clash.[87]

For these and other reasons the State Department had doggedly opposed both overt and covert attempts at regime change since the July revolution. The department, an NSC staffer grumbled, was 'basically opposed to covert activities.'[88] The force with which State Department officials made their arguments was one indication of how the department was swimming against the tide. The rest of the national security bureaucracy clamored for action. Bureaucratic tensions were high. Some CIA officials suspected that the department was sabotaging their efforts by making it difficult for operatives to get visas.[89] At one point the Iraq Committee was so paralyzed over the issue that the State Department gave up 'any effort to coordinate a report as a result of frustration with the views of other action agencies.'[90]

By early 1960, there were some signs that the State Department's preferred approach of wooing Qasim was producing success. Relations between the US and Iraq improved somewhat. The two countries reached a cultural exchange agreement and resolved some of the minor issues that had troubled their relationship since the 1958 revolution.[91] Such hopeful signs were overshadowed in the minds of most American officials by Qasim's greatest liability: his weakness. Virtually everyone in Washington assumed that it was only a matter of time before Qasim succumbed to communist pressure or fell to an assassin's bullet. Concerned by the instability of Qasim's government and the strength of the Iraqi Communist Party, the Eisenhower administration continued searching for a possible successor regime. By January 1960 even the cautious Ambassador Jernegan was open to extreme measures. In a cable to the State Department, he indicated that 'the situation in Iraq is now such that, while there were risks involved, the possibilities of developments adverse to US interest are such as to justify a more active' policy in Iraq. Within the Iraq Committee, talk of covert operations peaked. Unfortunately the records of those discussions have not been declassified in full, and extensive passages have been blacked out. The context of the redacted portions is such that it is clear US officials were discussing whether or not to implement existing covert operations plans. One official, for example, confessed to being 'worried about pushing the button,' following a large and heavily censored discussion about assassination. Within the CIA, assassination was occasionally and euphemistically referred to as the 'magic button.' Another line of conversation, again heavily redacted, suggested that the administration was appraising the merits of working through various Iraqi groups opposed to Qasim.[92]

One important source suggests that the CIA proceeded to act against Qasim at about this time. A Senate investigation conducted in the 1970s revealed that, in the spring of 1960, the CIA's Near East Division had created a 'health alteration committee,' overseen by Richard Bissell. The committee proposed a 'disabling operation' whereby a poisoned handkerchief would be sent to Qasim from an unnamed Asian country. Ostensibly the objective was to incapacitate Qasim. 'We do not consciously seek subject's permanent removal from the scene; we also do not object should the complication develop.'[93] Not surprisingly, this plot failed. But it did indicate a growing sense of frustration within the government that something needed to be done about Qasim. The administration broadened its contacts with opposition elements, and was communicating with supporters of the old regime, nationalists, and military personnel.[94]

Taken together, the existing evidence supports, but by no means proves, the theory that the United States actively conspired against Qasim. Clearly a number of options were explored and undoubtedly some measures were implemented. Regrettably, the evidence is too inconclusive to reach firmer conclusions. If the CIA's handkerchief assassination attempt did happen, then it came at a peculiar time since the general attitude of the US government was improving. Qasim was making new, if limited, moves against the communists and taking measures to improve Iraqi relations with the United States. There had been 'a quiet but nonetheless significant improvement in US–Iraqi relations,' one administration report acknowledged in December 1960.[95] A few months earlier, the CIA declared that Qasim's tenuous hold on power had stabilized, though sooner or later he would be deposed 'most likely by nationalist-minded officers.' The agency even predicted that it was unlikely that the communists would be able to seize power.[96]

Such contradictions point to the state of confusion that existed within the Eisenhower administration. Its views on how to handle Qasim fluctuated wildly in the years following the 1958 revolution. The Eisenhower administration saw no easy solution to the state of affairs in Iraq. John Foster Dulles admitted, in a rare moment of humility, that the United States was 'simply not sufficiently sophisticated to mix into this complicated situation.'[97] Doing nothing raised the increasingly likely possibility that Iraq would slide into communism. Invading Iraq would create an anti-American backlash throughout the Middle East, if not the entire Third World. The closest thing to a middle option, supporting a coup by Nasser's allies, also was unattractive. The possibility of a Nasserist takeover in Iraq was preferable to communist takeover, but it was hardly a desirable scenario. If Iraq came under Egypt's control, Nasser would be able to exert extraordinary pressure on Kuwait and Saudi Arabia, thus presenting a grave peril to Western oil access. Moreover, the UK and all key US allies in the region were deeply suspicious of Nasser and appeared to regard the UAR with greater apprehension than the Soviet Union. The choice between Qasim and Nasser, Eisenhower remarked, was like choosing between two mobsters – John Dillinger and Al Capone.[98]

Hard and soft power

Throughout the Iraq crisis, American officials also exhibited a striking degree of realism in assessing US foreign policy toward Iraq, realism in two different meanings of the word. First, there was the realism of international relations theory, realpolitik. On this score, the United States was guided primarily by cold-hearted calculations of power and interest. The Eisenhower administration was shaped less by ideological or Orientalist perceptions of Qasim and revolutionary Iraq, than by assessments of how the Qasim regime would affect the strategic and economic interests of the West. Likewise, American officials did not make their policy choices on the basis of moralistic or legalistic principles; they had no moral qualms about regime change;

they did not feel constrained by international law. They were prepared to take any measures to ensure that Iraqi oil resources continued flowing to Western sources.

Yet, at the same time, the Eisenhower administration's decisions were tempered by a more conventional kind of realism: pragmatism, an assessment of what was achievable and desirable with the resources at their disposal. The Eisenhower administration decided against drastic action purely for the pragmatic reason that it could not see an immediate solution to the problem of Qasim that did not carry with it an excessively high price. American officials may have had few qualms about regime change per se, but they did have reservations about the broader geopolitical consequences of an invasion. They understood that the reckless use of American hard power – its military might – would jeopardize the efficacy of American soft power – its ability to lead through persuasion and diplomacy.[99] Even if US forces could topple the Qasim regime, as everyone in the Eisenhower administration expected, an invasion would unleash a nationalist backlash in Iraq and elsewhere that would ultimately undermine American security and weaken US influence. Moreover, without a compelling moral rationale, military intervention would damage American prestige and undermine US efforts to win friends and allies in the Third World. As Salim Yaqub observes, 'fear of offending Arab or world opinion was a major constraint on the United States, and US officials took pains to craft Middle East policies that were legally and morally defensible in the international arena.'[100] The battle for hearts and minds, and the related perception that world public opinion mattered, exerted a restraining influence on the Eisenhower administration's exercise of military power.

There was a flip-side to this line of thinking, however. If the fear of enraging world public opinion was the most significant reason for rejecting regime change by military force, that made clandestine intervention seem all the more promising. It is doubtful that the Eisenhower administration played a *decisive* role in fostering plots against Qasim, who seemed to have a special talent for creating enemies on his own accord. But the administration did encourage and support Qasim's opponents. In so doing, it contributed to the destabilization of Iraqi politics. It also helped prepare the way for the eventual downfall of the Qasim regime. Working with Nasser, the Ba'ath Party, and other opposition elements, including some in the Iraqi army, the CIA by 1963 was well positioned to help assemble the coalition that overthrew Qasim in February of that year. It is not clear whether Qasim's assassination, as Said Aburish has written, was 'one of the most elaborate CIA operations in the history of the Middle East.' That judgment remains to be proven. But the trail linking the CIA is suggestive. Aburish postulated that the operation was organized by William Lakeland, who had indeed advocated such a policy while serving on the Iraq Committee a few years earlier. According to Aburish, Lakeland 'put together a collection of anti-Kassem army officer elements of the Ba'th Party in Iraq, fellow Ba'thists in Syria, and an assortment of people who genuinely feared a Communist takeover of their country.' He also provided the conspirators with lists of suspected communists and Qasim supporters that they then used to perpetrate a bloody elimination campaign.[101] Whatever the nature of US involvement, the coup and subsequent developments did little to improve the long-term relationship between the US and Iraq. Ensuing events bore out a prediction made by the US embassy in Baghdad in the summer of 1959: 'Iraq [was] likely to be a turbulent trouble-spot for years to come.'[102]

Notes

* The author would like to thank the Division of Sponsored Research at Florida Atlantic University for funding this research, Michael Bocco for research assistance, and Eric Hanne for his helpful comments.

1 Paul Rodriquez, Comic Relief 1996, quoted at: www.comedyave.com/archive/ 102201.html (March 7, 2008).

2 For a thoughtful critique of the historiography of US–Iraqi relations and a superb analysis of the events discussed in this chapter, see Nathan J. Citino, 'Middle East Cold Wars: Oil and Arab Nationalism in US-Iraqi Relations, 1958–1961,' in Kathryn C. Statler and Andrew L. Johns, eds. *The Eisenhower Administration, the Third World, and the Globalization of the Cold War* (Lanham, MD.: Rowman and Littlefield, 2006), 245–270. The Iraq experts Marion Farouk Sluglett and Peter Sluglett point out that the neglect of Iraq by historians has not been limited to the subject of foreign relations. 'A bleak picture' is how they described the historiography of modern Iraqi history since 1958. See Marion Farouk-Sluglett and Peter Sluglett, 'The Historiography of Modern Iraq,' *The American Historical Review* (December 1991), 1408–1421. See also Edwin Moise's comprehensive bibliography of works on modern Iraq and US foreign policy: www.clemson.edu/caah/history/facultypages/EdMoise/iraqbib.html#iraniraq.

3 Stephen Kinzer, *Overthrow: America's Century of Regime Change from Hawaii to Iraq* (New York: Times Books, 2004). William Blum has written a broader, and somewhat polemical, chronicle of US interventions since 1945. See Blum, *Killing Hope: US Military and CIA Interventions Since World War II* (Monroe, Maine: Common Courage Press, 2004).

4 On attempts to overthrow Saddam Hussein in the 1990s, see Kenneth M. Pollack, *The Threatening Storm: The Case for Invading Iraq* (New York: Random House, 2002), 58–104, esp. 59, 94.

5 Although a military coup d'état brought down the old regime, most historians of modern Iraq describe the events of July 1958 as a revolution because of the broad popular support for the overthrow of the monarchy and the shift in power among Iraq's social classes. It was, William Rogers Louis has written, 'not just another Middle East coup but a major social and economic revolution.' See Louis, 'Harold Macmillan the Middle East Crisis of 1958,' *Proceedings of the British Academy* 94, 207–228, quote on 217. The most comprehensive accounts of Iraq during the revolutionary period are Hanna Batutu, *The Old Social Classes and the Revolutionary Movements of Iraq* (Princeton, NJ: Princeton University Press, 1982) and Uriel Dann, *Iraq Under Qassem: A Political History, 1958–1963* (New York: Praeger, 1969). For details regarding the July 14 revolution, see also Michael Eppel, *Iraq from Monarchy to Tyranny: From the Hashemites to the Rise of Saddam* (Gainesville: University Press of Florida, 2004), 147–148; Said K. Aburish, *Saddam Hussein: The Politics of Revenge* (New York and London: Bloomsbury Publishing, 2000), 38–39; Charles Tripp, *A History of Iraq* (Cambridge, UK: Cambridge University Press, 2000), 145–147; and

Marion Farouk-Sluglett and Peter Sluglett, *Iraq Since 1958: From Revolution to Dictatorship*, rev. edn. (London: I. B. Tauris, 2001), 48–70.

6 The Eisenhower administration, which sent US forces to Beirut, presented its intervention in Lebanon as a successful test of the Eisenhower Doctrine toward the Middle East – the president's January 1957 statement asserted that the United States would act to guarantee the security of friendly governments in the region that were threatened by communist encroachment. Once praised by revisionist historians of the Eisenhower presidency as a successful and measured use of American force, the Lebanon intervention has been criticized in more recent scholarship on the Eisenhower Doctrine. Most authors now see the intervention as a clumsy and misguided effort to contain Arab nationalism and to shore up American credibility. See especially Douglas Little, 'His Finest Hour? Eisenhower, Lebanon, and the 1958 Crisis in the Middle East,' *Diplomatic History* vol. 20, no. 1 (Winter 1996), 27–54; Ray Takeyh, *The Origins of the Eisenhower Doctrine: The US, Britain and Nasser's Egypt, 1953–57* (New York: St. Martin's Press, 2000); Salim Yaqub, *Containing Arab Nationalism: The Eisenhower Doctrine and the Middle East* (Chapel Hill: University of North Carolina Press, 2004); Robert J. McMahon, 'Credibility and World Power: Exploring the Psychological Dimension in Postwar American Diplomacy,' *Diplomatic History* vol. 15, no. 4 (Fall 1991), 455–471, esp. 464–465.

7 William Roger Louis, 'Harold Macmillan the Middle East Crisis of 1958,' Nigel J. Ashton, 'Harold Macmillan and the "Golden Days" of Anglo-American Relations Revisited, 1957–63,' *Diplomatic History* vol. 29, no. 4 (September 2005), 691–723; Ashton, '"A Great New Venture"? – Anglo-American Cooperation in the Middle East and the Response to the Iraqi Revolution July 1958,' *Diplomacy & Statecraft*, vol. 4, no. 1 (March 1993), 59–89; Avi Shlaim, 'Israel, the Great Powers, and the Middle East Crisis of 1958,' *Journal of Imperial and Commonwealth History* vol. 12, no. 2 (May 1999), 177–192; Irene L. Gender, *Notes from the Minefield: United States Intervention in Lebanon and the Middle East, 1945–1958* (New York: Columbia University Press, 1997); Ritchie Ovendale, 'Great Britain and the Anglo-American Invasion of Jordan and Lebanon in 1958,' *International History Review*, vol. 16, no. 2 (May 1994), 284–304; Orna Almog, 'An End of an Era – the Crisis of 1958 and the Anglo-Israeli Relationship,' *Contemporary Record*, vol. 8, no. 1 (Summer 1994), 49–76; Lawrence Tal, 'Britain and the Jordan Crisis of 1958,' *Middle East Studies*, vol. 31, no. 1 (January 1995), 39–57; Stephen Blackwell, 'Pursuing Nasser: The Macmillan Government and the Management of British Policy Towards the Middle East Cold War, 1957–63,' *Cold War History*, vol. 4, no. 3 (April 2004), 85–104; W. Taylor Fain, 'John F. Kennedy and Harold Macmillan: Managing the "Special Relationship" in the Persian Gulf Region, 1961–63,' *Middle Eastern Studies*, vol. 38, no. 4 (October 2002), 95–122; Elie Podeh, '"Suez in Reverse": The Arab Response to the Iraqi Bid for Kuwait, 1961–63,' *Diplomacy & Statecraft*, vol. 14, no. 1 (March 2003), 103–130. Two articles that focus specifically on US–Iraqi relations include Citino, 'Middle East Cold Wars,' and Daniel C. Williamson, 'Understandable Failure: The Eisenhower Administration's Strategic Goals in Iraq, 1953–1958,' *Diplomacy & Statecraft*, vol. 17, no. 3 (September 2006), 597–615.

8 Aleksandr Fursenko and Timothy Naftali, *Khrushchev's Cold War: The Inside Story of an American Adversary* (New York: W. W. Norton, 2006), 158–184, esp. 163–164.

9 Memorandum from the Assistant Secretary of State for Near Eastern and South Asian Affairs (Rountree) to Acting Secretary of State Dillon, December 22, 1958, *FRUS 1958–1960*, vol. XII, 368–371.

10 For a succinct overview of the role of oil in US foreign policy see Douglas Little, *American Orientalism: The United States and the Middle East since 1945* (Chapel Hill, NC: University of North Carolina Press, 2002), 43–76. For more detailed treatment, see Daniel Yergin, *The Prize: The Epic Quest for Oil, Money, and Power* (New York: Free Press, 1991).

11 Discussion at the 373rd Meeting of the National Security Council, July 24, 1958, *FRUS 1958–1960*, vol. XII, 100–109.

12 NSC 5820/1, 'US Policy Toward the Near East,' November 4, 1958, *FRUS 1958–1960*, vol. XII, 187–199.

13 Recent scholarship has stressed the importance of containing Arab nationalism to US policy toward the region. See Yaqub, *Containing Arab Nationalism*; and Takeyh, *Origins of the Eisenhower Doctrine*.

14 Farouk-Sluglett and Sluglett, *Iraq since 1958*, 52–53.

15 Tripp, *A History of Iraq*, 152–154; Farouk-Sluglett and Sluglett, *Iraq since 1958*, 55–61.

16 The division between nationalists and communists in Iraq was blurry, and the ICP itself blended socialist ideas with those of national independence. Iraqi communists issued appeals for Arab unity, but opposed joining with Nasser in the UAR. Iraqi nationalists were divided into disparate factions that espoused varying ideas for Iraq's future. The question of union with the UAR provided the most salient dividing line among the various nationalist factions. The Slugletts suggest that the split within Iraq over union with the UAR was more tactical and symbolic than substantive, union was not so much 'a genuine political aim' as it was a useful issue to hammer political rivals, especially the communists, who were outspoken in their opposition to joining the UAR. See Farouk-Sluglett and Sluglett, *Iraq since 1958*, 53–55, 62–66; Eppel, *Iraq from Monarchy to Tyranny*, 176–183; Tripp, *A History of Iraq*, 153–154.

17 Quoted in Fursenko and Naftali, *Khrushchev's Cold War*, 160.

18 Memorandum of Conversation with the President, July 14, 1958, *FRUS 1958–1960*, vol. XI, 211–215.

19 Louis, 'Harold Macmillan the Middle East Crisis of 1958,' 209; Memorandum of Telephone Conversation between Eisenhower and Macmillan, July 14, 1958, *FRUS 1958–1960*, vol. XI, 231–234; Message from Prime Minister Macmillan to Eisenhower, July 14, 1958, *FRUS 1958–1960*, vol. XI, 234–236.

20 Memorandum of Telephone Conversation between Eisenhower and Macmillan, July 14, 1958, *FRUS 1958–1960*, vol. XI, 231–234.

21 Memoranda of a Conference with the President, July 31, 1956, *FRUS 1955–1957*, vol. XVI, 62–68; Memorandum of Conversation, July 17, 1958, *FRUS 1958–1960*, vol. XII, 776–778.

22 Memorandum of Conversation with the President, July 14, 1958, *FRUS 1958–1960*, vol. XI, 211–215; Fursenko and Naftali, *Khrushchev's Cold War*, 164. On Eisenhower's view of the Cold War as a contest for hearts and minds, see Kenneth Osgood, *Total Cold War: Eisenhower's Secret Propaganda Battle at Home and Abroad* (Lawrence: University Press of Kansas, 2006), 46–55.

23 On the overthrow of Mossadeq, see Mark J. Gasiorowski, 'The 1953 Coup D'etat in Iran,' *International Journal of Middle East Studies*, vol. 19, no. 3 (August 1987), 261–286; Stephen Kinzer, *All the Shah's Men: An American Coup and the Roots of Middle East Terror* (Hoboken, NJ: John Wiley & Sons, 2003); Moyara de Moraes Ruehsen, 'Operation "Ajax" Revisited: Iran, 1953,' *Middle Eastern Studies*, vol. 29 (July 1993), 467–486.

24 According to US officials who met with Qasim, the Iraqi leader was convinced that the United States was conspiring against him, possibly by working through Iran, Egypt, or the Iraqi Kurds. See, for example, Memorandum from

the Assistant Secretary of State for Near Eastern and South Asian Affairs (Rountree) to Acting Secretary of State Dillon, December 22, 1958, *FRUS 1958–1960*, vol. XII, 368–371; Embassy in Baghdad to Department of State, December 11, 1958, US National Archives (College Park, Maryland), Record Group 56, Central Decimal File, 611.87/12–2258; Embassy in Baghdad to Department of State, December 23, 1958, US National Archives, Record Group 56, Central Decimal File, 611.87/12–2358; Embassy in Baghdad to Department of State, January 1, 1959, US National Archives, Record Group 56, Central Decimal File, 611.87/1–1959; Embassy in Baghdad to Department of State, January 20, 1959, US National Archives, Record Group 56, Central Decimal File, 611.87/1–2059; Stuart W. Rockwell to William Rountree, March 13, 1959, US National Archives, Record Group 56, Central Decimal File, 611.87/3–1359; Embassy in Baghdad to Department of State, April 9, 1959, US National Archives, Record Group 56, Central Decimal File, 611.87/4–959; Embassy in Baghdad to Department of State, April 27, 1959, US National Archives, Record Group 56, Central Decimal File, 611.87/4–959.

25 Said K. Aburish, *Nasser: The Last Arab* (New York: St. Martin's, 2004), 178–186; Farouk-Sluglett and Sluglett, *Iraq since 1958*, 58–60.

26 Memorandum from the Director of Intelligence and Research (Cumming) to Secretary of State Dulles, November 25, 1958, *FRUS 1958–1960*, vol. XII, 353–354. See also notes 1 and 2.

27 The policy change was approved by the National Security Council in November 1958. 'It has become increasingly apparent that the prevention of further Soviet penetration of the Near East ... depends on the degree to which the United States is able to work more closely with Arab nationalism,' the NSC concluded, prescribing a policy of establishing an effective working relationship with Arab nationalism while at the same time seeking constructively to 'contain its outward thrust.' See NSC 5820/1, 'US Policy Toward the Near East,' November 4, 1958, *FRUS 1958–1960*, vol. XII, 187–199. This shift in US policy made several American allies nervous. The United Kingdom, Turkey, Jordan, Israel, Kuwait, and Iran were mortified at the prospect of an enlarged UAR that put Iraq under Nasser's control, and urged greater caution in US dealings with Nasser. For a summary of their views, see: Chairman of JCS Nathan Twinning to Secretary of Defense, April 22, 1959, Dwight D. Eisenhower Presidential Library (Abilene, Kansas), Special Staff File, NSC Staff Papers, box 4, 'Philip J. Halla Files (4).'

28 John A. Calhoun to Gordon Gray, Department of Defense paper on Iraq, April 15, 1959, Eisenhower Library, Special Staff File, NSC Staff Papers, box 4, 'Philip J. Halla Files (4).' Yaqub, *Containing Arab Nationalism*, 261. For documentation regarding negotiations and discussions related to US aid to Egypt, see *FRUS 1958–1960*, vol. XIII, 401–611.

29 Telegram from Embassy in the United Arab Republic to the Department of State, April 1, 1959, *FRUS 1958–1960*, vol. XIII, 519–525; John A, Calhoun to Gordon Gray, Department of Defense paper on Iraq, April 15, 1959, Eisenhower Library, Special Staff File, NSC Staff Papers, box 4, 'Philip J. Halla Files (4)'; Discussion at the 402nd Meeting of the National Security Council, April 17, 1959, Eisenhower Library, Ann Whitman File, NSC Series, box 11.

30 Farouk-Sluglett and Sluglett, *Iraq since 1958*, 66–70; Eppel, *Iraq from Monarchy to Tyranny*, 155; Dann, *Iraq Under Qassem*, 164–194.

31 Special National Intelligence Estimate 36.2–59, 'The Communist Threat to Iraq,' February 17, 1959, *FRUS 1958–1960*, vol. XII, 381–388.

32 Paper by the President's Special Assistant for National Security Affairs, Gordon Gray, April 1, 1959, *FRUS 1958–1960*, vol. XII, 401–402.

33 Telegram from the Embassy in Iraq to the Department of State, March 26, 1959, *FRUS 1958–1960*, vol. XII, 395–398.

34 John A. Calhoun to Gordon Gray, Department of Defense paper on Iraq, April 15, 1959, Eisenhower Library, Special Staff File, NSC Staff Papers, box 4, 'Philip J. Halla Files (4).' See also discussion at the 402nd Meeting of the National Security Council, April 17, 1959, Eisenhower Library, Ann Whitman File, NSC Series, box 11.

35 Discussion at the 402nd Meeting of the National Security Council, April 17, 1959, Eisenhower Library, Ann Whitman File, NSC Series, box 11; JCSM-156–159, Suggested Courses of US Action, Iraq, April 22, 1959, Eisenhower Library, Special Staff File, NSC Staff Papers, box 4, 'Philip J. Halla Files (4).'

36 Paper prepared in the Department of State, 'The Situation in Iraq,' April 15, 1959, *FRUS 1958–1960*, vol. XII, 414–422.

37 John A. Calhoun to Gordon Gray, Department of Defense paper on Iraq, April 15, 1959, Eisenhower Library, Special Staff File, NSC Staff Papers, box 4, 'Philip J. Halla Files (4).'

38 February 1959, Chiefs of Staff Committee, Military Intervention on Iraq, Memorandum by the Chiefs of Staff, British National Archives (Kew, United Kingdom), AIR 8/1958.

39 Memorandum from the Assistant Secretary of State for Near Eastern and South Asian Affairs (Rountree) to Acting Secretary of State Dillon, December 22, 1958, *FRUS 1958–1960*, vol. XII, 368–371.

40 Discussion at the 402nd Meeting of the National Security Council, April 17, 1959, Eisenhower Library, Ann Whitman File, NSC Series, box 11. The Joint Chiefs of Staff also argued for continued planning for possible military or covert intervention. 'The US should decide now to initiate action,' the Chiefs advised. 'Prudence requires … that our planning be based on the assumption that Qasim will not reverse his British National Archives-USSR policies.' See JCSM-156–159, Suggested Courses of US Action, Iraq, April 22, 1959, Eisenhower Library, Special Staff File, NSC Staff Papers, box 4, 'Philip J. Halla Files (4).'

41 Paper by the President's Special Assistant for National Security Affairs, Gordon Gray, April 1, 1959, *FRUS 1958–1960*, vol. XII, 401–402.

42 Memorandum of Discussion at the 401st Meeting of the National Security Council, April 2, 1959, *FRUS 1958–1960*, vol. XII, 402–406.

43 Memorandum of Discussion at the 401st Meeting of the National Security Council, April 2, 1959, *FRUS 1958–1960*, vol. XII, 402–406.

44 Douglas Little, 'Mission Impossible: The CIA and the Cult of Covert Action in the Middle East,' *Diplomatic History*, vol. 28, no. 5 (November 2004), 663–701, quote on 694.

45 Adel Darwish, *Unholy Babylon: The Secret History of Saddam's War* (New York: St. Martin's Press, 1991); Said Aburish, *A Brutal Friendship: The West and the Arab Elite* (New York: St. Martin's Press, 1998); Richard Sale, 'Saddam Key in Early CIA Plot,' UPI, April 10, 2003; Hanna Batutu, *Old Social Classes*, 985–987. Roger Morris, 'A Tyrant 40 Years in the Making,' *New York Times*, March 14, 2003; Farouk-Sluglett and Sluglett, *Iraq since 1958*, 86.

46 Quoted in Little, 'Mission Impossible,' 694.

47 Memorandum from the Assistant Secretary of State for Near Eastern and South Asian Affairs (Jones) to Secretary of State (Herter), September 28, 1959, *FRUS 1958–1960*, vol. XII, 484–486.

48 Discussion at the 402nd Meeting of the National Security Council, April 17, 1959, Eisenhower Library, Ann Whitman File, NSC Series, box 11.

49 Discussion at the 402nd Meeting of the National Security Council, April 17, 1959, Eisenhower Library, Ann Whitman File, NSC Series, box 11; Memorandum of

Discussion at the 428th Meeting of the National Security Council, December 10, 1959, *FRUS 1958–1960*, vol. XII, 494–495; Memorandum from the Assistant Secretary of State for Near Eastern and South Asian Affairs (Rountree) to Acting Secretary of State (Dillon), December 22, 1958, *FRUS 1958–1960*, vol. XII, 368–371; Meeting of Special Committee on Iraq, October 22, 1959, Eisenhower Library, Special Staff File, NSC Staff Papers, box 4, 'Philip J. Halla Files (2)'; Telegram from the Embassy in Iraq to the Department of State, February 26, 1960, *FRUS 1958–1960*, vol. XII, 502–506.

50 Chairman of JCS Nathan Twinning to Secretary of Defense, April 22, 1959, Eisenhower Library, Special Staff File, NSC Staff Papers, box 4, 'Philip J. Halla Files (4)'; JCSM-156–159, Suggested Courses of US Action, Iraq, April 22, 1959, Eisenhower Library, Special Staff File, NSC Staff Papers, box 4, 'Philip J. Halla Files (4).'

51 Dana Adams Schmidt, 'C.I.A. Head Warns of Danger in Iraq,' *New York Times*, April 29, 1959.

52 Meeting of Special Committee on Iraq, May 20, 1959, Eisenhower Library, Special Staff File, NSC Staff Papers, box 4, 'Philip J. Halla Files (3).'

53 NSC memorandum re. measures by US Government, n.d. (May 1959), Eisenhower Library, Special Staff File, NSC Staff Papers, box 4, 'Philip J. Halla Files (3).'

54 John D. Jernegan Oral History Interview, John F. Kennedy Library.

55 Telegram from the Embassy in Iraq to the Department of State, March 26, 1959, *FRUS 1958–1960*, vol. XII, 395–398; Memorandum from the Assistant Secretary of State for Near Eastern and South Asian Affairs (Rountree) to Acting Secretary of State (Dillon), May 20, 1959, *FRUS 1958–1960*, vol. XII, 456–458; Discussion at the 405th Meeting of the National Security Council, May 7, 1959, Eisenhower Library, Ann Whitman File, NSC Series, box 11; Briefing Note for NSC Meeting, May 6, 1959, Eisenhower Library, Special Staff File, NSC Staff Papers, box 4, 'Philip J. Halla Files (3).'

56 Telegram from the Embassy in Iraq to the Department of State, August 9, 1959, *FRUS 1958–1960*, vol. XII, 474–477; Discussion at the 409th Meeting of the National Security Council, June 4, 1959, Eisenhower Library, Ann Whitman File, NSC Series, box 11; Rountree Briefing Note for NSC, June 17, 1959, Eisenhower Library, White House Office [WHO], Office of the Special Assistant for National Security Affairs [OSANSA], NSC Series, Briefing Notes Subseries, box 13, 'The Middle East (1) [1957–1959].'

57 See note 23 for US meetings with Qasim.

58 CIA Staff Memorandum No. 606–660, The Outlook for Iraq, September 22, 1960, Eisenhower Library, Special Staff File, NSC Staff Papers, box 4, 'Philip J. Halla Files (1)'; NIE 36.2–60, 'The Outlook for Iraq,' November 1, 1960, *FRUS 1958–1960*, vol. XII, 516–523.

59 See, for example: Memorandum of Discussion at the 393rd Meeting of the National Security Council, January 15, 1959, *FRUS 1958–1960*, vol. XII, 375–377; Memorandum of Discussion at the 420th Meeting of the National Security Council, October 1, 1959, Eisenhower Library, Ann Whitman File, NSC Series, box 11; SNIE 36.2–4-59, 'Possible Developments in Iraq,' September 24, 1959, *FRUS 1958–1960*, vol. XII, 481–483; Editorial Note regarding intelligence materials presented to the president, December 16, 1960, *FRUS 1958–1960*, vol. XII, 500; Telegram from the Embassy in Iraq to the Department of State, February 26, 1960, *FRUS 1958–1960*, vol. XII, 502–506; Assistant Secretary of Defense John N. Irwin, II to Assistant Secretary of State for Near Eastern and South Asian Affairs G. Lewis Jones, September 18, 1959, Eisenhower Library, Special Staff File, NSC

Staff Papers, box 4, 'Philip J. Halla Files (3)'; Philip J. Halla to Marion Boggs, September 21, 1959, Eisenhower Library, Special Staff File, NSC Staff Papers, box 4, 'Philip J. Halla Files (3)'; CIA Office of National Estimates Staff Memorandum 42–60, Current Prospects for Iraq, July 12, 1960, Eisenhower Library, Special Staff File, NSC Staff Papers, box 4, 'Philip J. Halla Files (1).'

60 Meeting of Special Committee on Iraq, January 4, 1960, Eisenhower Library, Special Staff File, NSC Staff Papers, box 4, 'Philip J. Halla Files (1).' The meeting was held on December 28, 1959.

61 Philip J. Halla to Marion Boggs, September 21, 1959, Eisenhower Library, Special Staff File, NSC Staff Papers, box 4, 'Philip J. Halla Files (3).'

62 Aburish, *Nasser*, 182, 201–202, 214.

63 John A. Calhoun to Gordon Gray, Department of Defense paper on Iraq, April 15, 1959, Eisenhower Library, Special Staff File, NSC Staff Papers, box 4, 'Philip J. Halla Files (4).'

64 Memorandum of Discussion at the 391st Meeting of the National Security Council, December 18, 1958, *FRUS 1958–1960*, vol. XII, 363–364.

65 Memorandum of Discussion at the 393rd Meeting of the National Security Council, January 15, 1959, *FRUS 1958–1960*, vol. XII, 375–377.

66 Memorandum of Conversation with the President, December 23, 1958, *FRUS 1958–1960*, vol. XIII, 509–511.

67 *FRUS 1958–1960*, vol. XII, 385, note 1.

68 Embassy in Baghdad to Department of State, April 27, 1959, US National Archives, Record Group 56, Central Decimal File, 611.87; Embassy in Baghdad to Department of State, August 27, 1959, US National Archives, Record Group 56, Central Decimal File, 611.87.

69 Embassy in Baghdad to Department of State, April 30, 1959, US National Archives, Record Group 56, Central Decimal File, 611.87/4–3059.

70 If the CIA had been involved in plotting against Qasim, it is quite possible that the State Department was unaware of the fact. The US ambassador to Iraq, Jernegan, for example, was not alerted to US discussions with Nasser about possible cooperation against Qasim. See P. J. Halla to Gleason, May 11, 1959, Eisenhower Library, Special Staff File, NSC Staff Papers, box 4, 'Philip J. Halla Files (3).' One diplomat later believed that he had been kept in the dark about US covert operations to stir up the Kurdish resistance movement in Iraq. The Foreign Affairs Oral History Interview with David A. Fritzlan, May 29, 1990, Library of Congress, http://hdl.loc.gov/loc.mss/mfdip.

71 Chairman of JCS Nathan Twinning to Secretary of Defense, April 22, 1959, Eisenhower Library, Special Staff File, NSC Staff Papers, box 4, 'Philip J. Halla Files (4)'; CSM-156–159, Suggested Courses of US Action, Iraq, April 22, 1959, Eisenhower Library, Special Staff File, NSC Staff Papers, box 4, 'Philip J. Halla Files (4).'

72 Scattered references to US overtures to Nasser can be found in several sources. For example: Discussion at the 404th Meeting of the National Security Council, April 30, 1959, Eisenhower Library, Ann Whitman File, NSC Series, box 11; Outline of Planning for Iraq Situation: Interagency Draft II 2, n.d. (May 6, 1959), Eisenhower Library, Special Staff File, NSC Staff Papers, box 4, 'Philip J. Halla Files (3)'; P. J. Halla to Gleason, May 11, 1959, Eisenhower Library, Special Staff File, NSC Staff Papers, box 4, 'Philip J. Halla Files (3)'; John A. Calhoun to Gordon Gray, Department of Defense paper on Iraq, April 15, 1959, Eisenhower Library, Special Staff File, NSC Staff Papers, box 4, 'Philip J. Halla Files (4).'

73 Telegram to Foreign Office, May 23, 1959, FO 371/140957, British National Archives; Telegram from the Embassy in Iraq to the Department of State,

April 3, 1959, *FRUS 1958–1960*, vol. XIII, 406–409; Memorandum of Conversation, April 30, 1959, *FRUS 1958–1960*, vol. XIII, 534–540.

74 Aburish, *Saddam Hussein*, 46–49; Murray J. Gart and Dean Brelis, 'An Interview with Saddam Hussein,' July 19, 1982, *Time*, www.time.com/time/magazine/article/0,9171,953554,00.html; 'Iraq Saddam Hussein Reminisces about Assassination Attempt on Qasim in October 1959,' BBC Summary of World Broadcasts, October 12, 1991; 'Iraq Saddam's Further Reminiscences on Assassination Attempt on Qasim in 1959,' BBC Summary of World Broadcasts, October 14, 1991.

75 Sale, 'Saddam Key in Early CIA Plot.'

76 Aburish, Saddam Hussein, 46–49.

77 'Synopsis of Intelligence Items Reported to the President,' September 30, 1959, in *FRUS 1958–1960*, vol. XII, 489, note 6. As early as September 21, CIA analysts knew of the plot, predicting that 'a move against the Kassem regime by nationalist elements might occur at any time.' See Philip J. Halla to Marion Boggs, September 21, 1959, Eisenhower Library, Special Staff File, NSC Staff Papers, box 4, 'Philip J. Halla Files (3)'; Memorandum of Discussion at the 428th Meeting of the National Security Council, December 10, 1959, *FRUS 1958–1960*, vol. XII, 494–495.

78 Assistant Secretary of Defense John N. Irwin, II to Assistant Secretary of State for Near Eastern and South Asian Affairs G. Lewis Jones, September 18, 1959, Eisenhower Library, Special Staff File, NSC Staff Papers, box 4, 'Philip J. Halla Files (3).'

79 Philip J. Halla to Marion Boggs, Meeting of the Special Committee on Iraq, September 24, 1959, Eisenhower Library, Special Staff File, NSC Staff Papers, box 4, 'Philip J. Halla Files (2).'

80 The discussion was recorded in convoluted minutes transcribed two months later. See Meeting of the Special Committee on Iraq, September 24, 1959 (notes transcribed November 12, 1959), Eisenhower Library, Special Staff File, NSC Staff Papers, box 4, 'Philip J. Halla Files (2).' Aburish, *Nasser*, 213.

81 Telegram from the Embassy in Iraq to the Department of State, February 26, 1960, *FRUS 1958–1960*, vol. XII, 502–506; Discussion at the 423rd Meeting of the National Security Council, November 5, 1959, Eisenhower Library, Ann Whitman File, NSC Series, box 11; Discussion at the 432nd Meeting of the National Security Council, January 14, 1960, Eisenhower Library, Ann Whitman File, NSC Series, box 12; Meeting of Special Committee on Iraq, June 8, 1959, WHO, OSANSA, NSC Series, Briefing Notes Subseries, box 13, 'The Middle East (1) [1957–59].'

82 Meeting of the Special Committee on Iraq, September 24, 1959 (notes transcribed November 12, 1959), Eisenhower Library, Special Staff File, NSC Staff Papers, box 4, 'Philip J. Halla Files (2).'

83 Sale, 'Saddam Key in Early CIA Plot'; and Darwish, *Unholy Babylon*.

84 PBS Frontline Interview with Said K. Aburish, www.pbs.org/wgbh/pages/frontline/shows/saddam/interviews/aburish.html; Aburish, *Saddam Hussein*, 54–55.

85 SNIE 36.2–5-59, 'Short-Term Prospects for Iraq,' December 15, 1959, *FRUS 1958–1960*, vol. XII, 496–499.

86 Memorandum of Discussion at the 428th Meeting of the National Security Council, December 10, 1959, *FRUS 1958–1960*, vol. XII, 494–495.

87 SNIE 36.2–4-59, 'Possible Developments in Iraq,' September 24, 1959, *FRUS 1958–1960*, vol. XII, 481–483; Memorandum of Discussion at the 428th Meeting of the National Security Council, December 10, 1959, *FRUS 1958–1960*, vol. XII, 494–495.

88 Philip J. Halla to Marion Boggs, November 23, 1959, Eisenhower Library, Special Staff File, NSC Staff Papers, box 4, 'Philip J. Halla Files (2).'

89 Philip J. Halla to Marion Boggs, November 23, 1959, Eisenhower Library, Special Staff File, NSC Staff Papers, box 4, 'Philip J. Halla Files (2).'

90 Philip Halla to Lay, October 26, 1959, Eisenhower Library, Special Staff File, NSC Staff Papers, box 4, 'Philip J. Halla Files (2).'

91 Memorandum from Evan M. Wilson of the Policy Planning Staff to the Director (Smith), March 18, 1960, *FRUS 1958–1960*, vol. XII, 507–508; Memorandum of Discussion at the 438th Meeting of the National Security Council, March 24, 1960, *FRUS 1958–1960*, vol. XII, 508–510; Memorandum of Discussion at a Meeting of the Operations Coordinating Board, August 10, 1960, *FRUS 1958–1960*, vol. XII, 511; NIE 36.2–60, 'The Outlook for Iraq,' November 1, 1960, *FRUS 1958–1960*, vol. XII, 516–523.

92 Meeting of Special Committee on Iraq, January 13, 1960, Eisenhower Library, Special Staff File, NSC Staff Papers, box 4, 'Philip J. Halla Files (1).' The meeting was held on January 12. On euphemisms for assassination, see US Senate Select Committee to Study Governmental Operations with Respect to Intelligence Activities, *Alleged Assassination Plots Involving Foreign Leaders*, 94th Cong., 1st Sess., 1975, 183.

93 *Alleged Assassination Plots Involving Foreign Leaders*, 181.

94 Phillip J. Halla to Lay, January 23, 1961, Eisenhower Library, Special Staff File, NSC Staff Papers, box 4, 'Philip J. Halla Files (1).'

95 Operations Coordinating Board Operations Plan for Iraq, December 14, 1960, *FRUS 1958–1960*, vol. XII, 524–530.

96 CIA Staff Memorandum No. 606–660, The Outlook for Iraq, September 22, 1960, Eisenhower Library, Special Staff File, NSC Staff Papers, box 4, 'Philip J. Halla Files (1).' See also NIE 36.2–60, 'The Outlook for Iraq,' November 1, 1960, *FRUS 1958–1960*, vol. XII, 516–523.

97 Memorandum of Discussion at the 393rd Meeting of the National Security Council, January 15, 1959, *FRUS 1958–1960*, vol. XII, 375–377.

98 Memorandum of Discussion at the 393rd Meeting of the National Security Council, January 15, 1959, *FRUS 1958–1960*, vol. XII, 375–377; Chairman of JCS Nathan Twinning to Secretary of Defense, April 22, 1959, Eisenhower Library, Special Staff File, NSC Staff Papers, box 4, 'Philip J. Halla Files (4)'; Memorandum from the Assistant Secretary of State for Near Eastern and South Asian Affairs (Rountree) to Acting Secretary of State Dillon, December 22, 1958, *FRUS 1958–1960*, vol. XII, 368–371.

99 On the concept of 'soft power,' see Joseph S. Nye Jr., *Soft Power: The Means To Success In World Politics* (New York: Public Affairs, 2004).

100 Yaqub, *Containing Arab Nationalism*, 279.

101 Aburish, *Nasser: The Last Arab*, 213–216; Aburish, *A Brutal Friendship*, 136–143.

102 Telegram from the Embassy in Iraq to the Department of State, August 9, 1959, *FRUS 1958–1960*, vol. XII, 474–477.

2 Through distorted lenses
Iraq and balance of power politics 1969–1979

Patrick Kiely

On 16 January 1979 the Shah fled Iran in his self-piloted Boeing 707.[1] Commentary from inside Iran in the wake of his ignominious exit reported the prevalence of US-made M16 rifles amongst the 'Islamic Guards'.[2] The 'Made in America' stamp was evident everywhere in Iran, from the US-supplied telecommunications equipment to the cutting edge jet fighters of the Iranian Air Force. From 1969 to 1979, Iran had been built up as an anti-Soviet bulwark in the Persian Gulf, an important pillar of the regional Nixon Doctrine tripod which included Saudi Arabia and Israel. A major component of the rationale forwarded for Iranian militarization was Iraq and the closeness of Iraqi–Soviet relations. The analytical lenses trained by US policymakers on the Persian Gulf provided a distorted view of the region which impacted on US policy towards Iraq and in turn contributed to the deposition of the Shah and the renegotiation of the balance of power in the Middle East. The two lenses which yielded these distortions were a realist-inspired reductive focus on the US–Soviet balance of power and an over reliance on the Shah of Iran to provide regional stability.

Nixon, Kissinger and balances of power

Viewing regions and regional conflicts through the Cold War lens was hardly an exclusive trait of the Nixon administration. As Richard Clarke, a career member of the Senior Executive Service from 1973–2003, maintained, 'Cold War America saw all foreign policy issues through the prism of the conflict between the two superpowers.'[3] Nixon and Kissinger were also not the first or last US statesmen to use balance of power calculus in their formulation of foreign policy, but they were the first to use the realist rationale so frequently in public discourse.[4] In January 1969 the Nixon administration was presented with the legacy of three conflicts: the Soviet achievement of strategic missile parity in the Cold War, the ongoing Vietnam War and in the Middle East, the far reaching repercussions of the 1967 Arab–Israeli War. Coming to office with the awareness of the limits of US power exposed in Vietnam and facing a Soviet Union with strategic nuclear parity, Kissinger argued that the balance of power politics was the only logical path for the US to follow; there was no place for the ambitious agendas of the 1960s. The moral superiority and rigid anti-communism that had accompanied the now obsolete US preponderance of power had to be abandoned, he maintained, as 'we are in the position that every other nation has been throughout history'.[5] Vietnam, described by Kissinger as a cancer,[6] had fractured the Cold War consensus and had a debilitating impact on the US capacity to project conventional military power abroad. Realism and the focus on national interests would facilitate a period of US retrenchment.[7]

Given Nixon and Kissinger's realism[8] their penchant was to view the world through the bi-polar prism and the shifts in the balance of power. Despite the development of détente[9] the US quest for unilateral advantage continued apace in the Middle East and particularly in the Persian Gulf.[10] Kissinger expressed caution on the prospects for détente. In 1971 he indicated,

> I'm not sure how the Soviets view détente with the United States. Whether détente should come through defeating the United States or through negotiating for world peace. Our part therefore is to try in Moscow to get a long enough period of détente to let momentum and pressure build up for maintaining the peace.[11]

Despite the improvement in relations with the Soviets Nixon and Kissinger remained very suspicious of their motives and, as this chapter will illuminate, tended to view regional developments through Cold War prisms. Despite détente, Nixon had no intention to 'reduce arms to spend on ghettos' and intended to remain vigilant until 'adversaries really changed'.[12]

Vietnam brought the limitations of US power into sharp focus. On 5 July 1969 Nixon announced what would become his eponymous doctrine in Guam. The United States, while honouring existing treaties, would provide the shield against threats to allies from nuclear powers but 'in cases involving other types of aggression we shall furnish military and economic assistance when requested and as appropriate' and 'we shall look to the nation directly threatened to assume the primary responsibility of providing the manpower for its defense'.[13] The Nixon Doctrine intended to continue the longstanding policy of containment although in a more acceptable guise as 'the costs of Vietnam were assumed by other regional powers'.[14] The application of the Nixon Doctrine in the Middle East and Persian Gulf augmented Iran's regional role and facilitated the Shah's regional ambitions.

Building pillars: US Persian Gulf policy 1969–1972

The United States had no formal diplomatic or consular relations with Iraq in 1969. Although US officials believed relations with Iraq to be steadily improving during the 1960s, the Iraqi government had severed ties in 1967 following President Gamal Abdul Nasser's claim that the US collaborated with Israel during the Arab–Israeli War.[15] Communications were maintained through the

US appointment of personnel to the Belgian embassy in Baghdad and the Iraqis reciprocated by placing staff in the Indian embassy in Washington. While in 1969 the Iraqis had three members of staff at the Indian embassy, no US staff had been assigned to Baghdad.[16] Transition reports revealed the US considered Iraq as a pro-Soviet, radical Arab state similar to Syria and Egypt. US officials reported that Moscow used the Arab–Israeli conflict to penetrate the Middle East through diplomatic support and by replacing military hardware lost in the war.[17] The United States also had a series of outstanding economic grievances with Iraq; the boycott of US goods and supplies harmed commercial interests, a long running dispute with the Iraq Petroleum Company (IPC) risked the investments of US companies Mobil and Esso and the ban on overflights by all US aircraft forced Pan American airlines to take a roundabout flight-path over Turkey on the Beirut–Tehran route.[18] Although there were no diplomatic relations and outstanding commercial issues with Baghdad, the US would eventually attempt to improve relations in the early 1970s.

The transition files reported little prospect of the resumption of diplomatic contact without progress towards a Middle Eastern settlement and considered that the presence of an unstable military regime in Baghdad made the prospect of an improvement in relations and a resolution of bilateral disputes unlikely for some time.[19] Nixon's National Security Adviser, Henry Kissinger, pursued the same line as the Johnson administration regarding the resumption of diplomatic relations with the Arab states that had severed ties in response to Nasser's claims in 1967. Kissinger outlined in strident terms how the Nixon administration was unwilling to countenance the preconditions placed by the radical Arabs for a reinstatement of diplomatic communication: that US pressure Israel to withdraw from occupied territories.[20] As the Arab states broke off diplomatic contact it was up to the same states to take the initiative to reinstate those relations.[21]

Furthermore, as the resolution of the Arab–Israeli conflict did not rank high among the priorities of the new administration the chances of a US–Iraqi rapprochement were slim. Secretary of State William Rogers and the Department of State were given nominal control of the US policy on the Arab–Israeli conflict. The Department of State had been systematically sidelined since January 1969 as Nixon and Kissinger asserted White House control over foreign policy and elevated the National Security Council to 'the principal forum for the consideration of policy issues requiring presidential determination'. This provided further indication of the urgency with which the White House viewed the Middle East.[22] The region was relegated to a linkage device in US–Soviet relations and as a pressure point to extract concessions on Vietnam.[23] The tension between the State Department and the White House's view of the Middle East was manifest; State favoured a regional interpretation of the difficulties and potential solutions, while Kissinger and Nixon maintained their global Cold War perspective. In a telephone conversation between Nixon and Kissinger in June 1970, the President criticized the State Department for viewing Middle East problems primarily resulting from the Arab–Israeli issue; as Nixon indicated in conversation, 'That's what matters Henry. Unless you bring the Russian thing in there is no stroke as you know.... We have to put the Russians in the game.'[24] They imposed a global view on the Persian Gulf as well.

In January 1968 the British government announced that it would withdraw all its military forces from the Persian Gulf by the end of 1971. The US encouraged the British to maintain political and commercial ties with the area. Although the Johnson administration had no ambition for the US to replace the British, the increased Soviet presence did provoke concern.[25] Delighted with the apparent progress made by Iran's 'White Revolution' in economic growth and social reform, the Johnson administration felt confident the Shah was well positioned to replace Great Britain as the 'chief pillar of pro-Western stability in the Persian Gulf'.[26] Transition papers prepared for Kissinger emphasized the close relations the US enjoyed with the Shah while also observing that arms sales were the key to that relationship. Noting the increasingly large Iranian arms requests following the British announcement, the policy inherited by the Nixon administration carefully weighed the consequences of these requests for regional stability and Iranian economic development with a concern that a US refusal might damage Washington's strategic interests.[27] In May 1968, Johnson approved a $600 million military sales credit package for Iran which would run for six years from fiscal year (FY) 1968 to 1973.[28]

In contrast to Iraq where the Nixon administration had a series of unresolved grievances, for Iran there were ambitions. The State Department briefed Kissinger for his 31 January 1969 meeting with the Iranian Ambassador Hushang Ansary. The objectives included: US support for Iran as a pro-Western, self-reliant nation vigilant against Soviet aims and amenable to US interests including commercial investment, oil exports, overflight rights, and intelligence gathering privileges.[29] The Shah proved more than willing to accept the role envisaged by Washington. In a series of meetings with Kissinger, Rogers and Secretary of Defense Melvin Laird on 1 April 1969 the Shah reiterated his concerns about reckless Iraqi behaviour, Soviet designs on warm water ports and aspirations to dominate the Persian Gulf.[30] The meeting with Kissinger concluded with the Shah's description of the US and Iran as 'natural allies' who needed to coordinate their policies 'for the next four hopefully eight years'.[31]

On 12 July 1969, two weeks prior to Nixon's announcement of his doctrine, he commissioned National Security Study Memorandum 66 to assess US options in the Gulf following British withdrawal. The general consensus in the State Department was that a joint Iran–Saudi Arabia guardianship of the region was the optimal arrangement. However, doubts were expressed about the Saudi capacity to fill the role given its weak military, especially relative to Iran, and King Faisal's preoccupation with the Arab–Israeli conflict.[32] Hence, the draft report credited Iran 'as the strongest and most effectively ruled state in area' and observed the mantra often used by the Shah about his fears of the 'serious radical Arab nationalist threat to the Gulf'. It was noted that the Shah was amenable to a joint Iranian–Saudi endeavour on the condition that King Faisal played the junior role. It was also noted that the Shah would act unilaterally to maintain regional stability should the Saudis prove unwilling to cooperate.[33]

Coordinating US policies with those of the Shah was a particularly problematic exercise for the Nixon administration from 1969–1972. The Shah persisted in his requests for increased income for Iranian oil and for more sophisticated military hardware. In April 1969 the NSC Interdepartmental Group endorsed the request by the Shah for an additional two squadrons of F4 Phantom fighter bomber jets to address the threat to Iran posed by land forces entering the region and the reported delivery of Soviet missile boats to Iraq.[34] The group also agreed that the annual review of Iran's economic situation and capacity to pay for military purchases was important. Kissinger summarized the position for Nixon in an 29 April memorandum commenting that the general issue on arms sales was its effect on the Iranian economy especially as 'Iran's future financial soundness is still fragile, depending as it still does on the continued flow of oil revenues at high levels.'[35] US policymakers were aware of the Iranian economy's precarious position but US strategic interests were paramount. The White House still nurtured the Shah's ambition for regional power and provided him with ever increasing quantities of US military hardware. By 1972, Iran was spending over $600 million on foreign military purchases and devoting 10 percent of the total budget to the military.[36]

US officials were aware of the Shah's concerns about 'the inherent Soviet threat' and the potential for Soviet-supported radical Arab inroads in the Gulf, particularly following British withdrawal.[37] Yet, the Iranian arms requests provoked considerable disagreement within the administration from 1969–1972. A key feature of these debates was the US perception of the threat posed by Iraq to Iran and the regional balance of power. From 1969–1972, Iraq was considered particularly weak. The series of secret trials, televised confessions and public executions launched by the Iraqi government which led to the 27 January 1969 hanging of 14 Iraqis, nine of whom were Jews, and the detention of US citizens as al-Bakr promised 'to arrest and execute all of the spies for the United States, Israel, imperialism and Zionism,'[38] was interpreted in Washington as a further indicator of Iraqi weakness. The executions prompted Walworth Barbour, the US Ambassador to Israel, to urge the Department of State to issue a strong condemnation to appease the outraged Israelis.[39] The lack of US capacity to exert direct influence in Iraq was exposed when US citizens were detained by the Iraqi authorities and the US had to rely on the efforts of the Belgian Ambassador to Baghdad, Marcel Dupret, to secure their release.[40] What US officials took from these Iraqi developments was that the Ba'athist regime was weak and was indulging in these enterprises to shore up fragile domestic support and attempt to solidify the loyalty of the army.[41] This perception was reinforced as several coup attempts were mounted against the al-Bakr regime. The US policy as stated by Rogers was that of non-involvement in any coup attempts but 'should new government prove to be moderate and friendly, we would be prepared to consider prompt resumption of diplomatic relations'.[42]

The Department of Defense was the most active in its opposition to increased Iranian military purchases as doubts persisted over the level of threat posed to Iran and the capacity of the Iranian military to meet the manpower requirements of the new purchases. Accentuating these difficulties was the Shah's continuing insistence that US Air Force technicians, 'blue suiters', provide training in the maintenance of his F4 aircraft and that Iran receive further slots for pilot training.[43] Bureaucratic infighting and disputes over the staffing, financing and provision of arms to Iran persisted until 1972. In September 1970, responding to the latest arms requests from Iran the Department of Defense requested a Special National Intelligence Estimate (SNIE) on the military threat to Iran. NSC Middle East expert Harold Saunders conceded in a memorandum to Kissinger that the military threat was not sufficiently great to warrant the hardware requested by the Shah. Generally, the NSC looked at Iran in broader terms seeing not just the visible threat but also the fact that the Shah sought to build a military establishment to serve as a deterrent.[44] Saunders reported that efforts were already underway to broaden the scope of the SNIE so that it would 'not turn out to be so limited as to make it more difficult for us to operate from a broader view of the situation'.[45] The broader view advanced by the NSC was primarily informed by the global balance of power and bilateral US–Soviet relations. As the Jordanian Civil War erupted in September 1970 this reductive lens was trained on the Middle East and on Iraq as it had troops stationed in King Hussein's Jordan.

Iraq and US Policy during the Jordanian Civil War

Kissinger viewed the events of September 1970 as a US–USSR proxy war.[46] The US could not afford to allow a moderate pro-Western regime in the Middle East be toppled by radical pro-Soviets. The capacity for Iraq to influence regional affairs was demonstrated during the crisis as Washington feared a pro-Soviet tilt in the Middle Eastern balance of power. Iraqi assertions of force served to underline the importance of the Shah of Iran to the White House as a counterweight to Baghdad's ambitions. On 1 September, the Jordanian army, responded to a failed Fedayeen assassination attempt on King Hussein by shelling Fedayeen positions. The Iraqis informed Jordan if the shelling did not cease 'it would not be able to stop individuals from the Iraqi forces from intervening in favour of the Fedayeen'.[47] On 2 September, the American Ambassador to Moscow Jacob Beam impressed on Soviet Deputy Foreign Minister Sergei Vinogradov the need for the Soviets 'to take whatever useful steps possible to prevent Iraqi intervention' since the US had no relations with Iraq.[48] Kissinger regarded the approach to the Soviets as proof of State Department weakness in crises and sought a tougher US approach to the perceived Soviet threat.[49] The Iraqis did not act on their ultimatum prompting Kissinger to believe the worst of the crisis had passed.[50] When the Popular Front for the Liberation of Palestine (PFLP) highjacked four commercial passenger jets and landed three at Dawson Field in the Jordanian desert the tension ratcheted up again. The PFLP sought to upstage other Palestinian groups, in particular the Yasser Arafat-led Fatah, to secure the release of Fedayeen prisoners in exchange for hostages and to provoke a confrontation between the Fedayeen and King Hussein with a view to toppling the Hashemite dynasty.[51] The internal struggle within the Fedayeen which precipitated a civil war in Jordan was viewed by the White House as a confrontation with the Soviets.

On 9 September, Kissinger, at Nixon's request, activated the Washington Special Action Group ensuring White House control over the management of the crisis. The potential of Iraqi action dominated White House thinking prior to the announcement on 19 September that Syrian armour had invaded northern Jordan. Nixon authorized the deployment of the US Sixth Fleet to the coast off Lebanon on 11 September as a signal of intent. On 16 September, King Hussein announced the formation of a military government and launched an offensive against the Fedayeen.[52] The NSC staff had prepared contingency plans in the event of an outbreak in fighting. The three principal contingencies prepared for at that point were Jordanian army versus Fedayeen alone, Jordanian army versus Fedayeen and Iraq, and a US armed intervention for evacuation of American citizens. On 18 September NSC Soviet expert Helmut Sonnenfeldt compiled a memorandum for Kissinger entitled 'Soviet Reaction to US Involvement in Jordan'.[53] He argued that the potential for regional chaos and a potentially Maoist leaning radical guerrilla regime in Jordan would not be entirely welcomed by Moscow but argued that 'the disappearance of regime influenced by, and sympathetic towards the US would also represent a gain of sorts for the USSR'.[54] Viewing the Soviet threat to beleaguered US ally King Hussein, Nixon was adamant that US force should be employed rather than the use of Israeli military forces that Kissinger favoured.[55] The White House received intelligence that the Iraqi troops had not intervened when nearby Fedayeen positions were being attacked by Jordanian forces.[56] Iraqi passivity has since been attributed to the pro-King Hussein disposition of the Iraqi Vice President Hardan al-Takriti who had taken personal control of forces in Jordan at the onset of the civil war.[57] On 17 September, Nixon deviated from the planned 'bull session' and delivered a backgrounder in Chicago which warned that it was better for the US to intervene in Jordan than for King Hussein to fall.[58] Later that evening, Nixon called Kissinger in ebullient humour after his backgrounder commenting that, 'The Russians are really stewing right now.' Speaking of the Soviet reaction to his deployment of an additional aircraft carrier, the USS *Kennedy* to the Eastern Mediterranean, Nixon commented 'They will know we are ready to do something … Makes them think we might do something.'[59] The Iraqi decision to refrain from intervention and the Jordanian repulsion of the Syrian intervention between 19–23 September was seen as vindication of the US balance of power policies in the region and a victory over the Soviets. The Israeli willingness to intervene in accordance with King Hussein's request reinforced the White House view that Israel was a strategic asset to be firmly installed as a pillar of the Nixon Doctrine.[60] Nixon and Kissinger dramatically increased military aid to Israel almost tenfold in the wake of the Jordanian Civil War; for fiscal years 1968–1970 Israel received $140 million in military credits but for fiscal years 1971–1973 they received $1152.5 million.[61] The White House commitment to supply Israel prompted Golda Meir to comment in March 1973 that 'we never had it so good'.[62] Kissinger regarded the Jordanian Civil War as the nearest the administration had, at that point, come to a superpower confrontation and credited the US policy for its favourable resolution.[63]

Studies of US policy during the Jordanian Civil War have exposed the regional nuances that were sidelined by the bipolar focus of Nixon and Kissinger. Iraqi–Syrian Ba'ath rivalry could have influenced Iraqi decisions; a victory for the Fedayeen would have bolstered Syrian power in the region.[64] Furthermore, an internal power struggle between Syrian air force commander Hafez al-Assad and his principal rival Salah Jadid, who commanded the invading force, was partly responsible for Syria's refusal to commit air-support for its ground forces.[65] In a 1974 meeting with Kissinger in Damascus al-Assad, then Syrian President, claimed that Syria had very limited objectives in September 1970 and did not intend to conquer Jordan nor destroy its army: 'the decision was to occupy northern Jordan, and hand it over to the Fedayeen. Then leave.'[66] These regional dynamics were wholly ignored by the White House. The Iraqis, having taken a passive stance during the war, did not emerge unscathed. Hardan al-Takriti was removed from his position as Vice President, in a move attributed by Israeli intelligence to Saddam Hussein, and was assassinated in Kuwait a year later.[67] Furthermore, the Arab Liberation Front, an Iraqi supported Fedayeen group, was seriously weakened as its leader Munif ar-Razzaz resigned because of Iraqi passivity during the civil war.[68] Accounts of the Jordanian Civil War and evidence from participants illuminated the complexity of the situation; divisive power struggles within the Fedayeen, within Jordan and in Iraqi–Syrian Ba'ath rivalry. The White House view of the conflict as a proxy war informed US actions during September 1970 and also the subsequent promotion of Israel as stabilizing regional influence. Nixon and Kissinger's focus on the global balance of power was evident again, as events in 1972 prompted the White House to reassess the threat posed by Iraq.

The Iraqi–Soviet Treaty and the US response

Rogers and the State Department had tracked Soviet–Iraqi relations from 1969 through embassies in the Middle East, Iraqi exiles and regional newspaper reports. In January 1972, Rogers sent a telegram to the US embassies in Tehran, London and Moscow outlining the increased Soviet arms shipments to Iraq; they believed that they were made to placate the al-Bakr government rather than to pose a threat to Iran.[69] The State Department believed that Iraq's weakness was evident in the Kurdish challenge to the regime and Saddam Hussein's efforts to purge opposition from the Ba'athist Party for the al-Bakr government. They therefore concluded that Iraq did not pose a regional threat.[70]

The State Department view did not radically alter as a result of the Iraqi–Soviet Treaty of 9 April 1972 which introduced a 15-year agreement on political, economic, technical and military cooperation. Central Intelligence Agency (CIA) Director Richard Helms reported on 12 May that 'in the long run' the treaty would lead to 'a stronger Soviet political position and [that] a more obtrusive military posture can be expected through out the Persian Gulf'.[71] Both the State Department and the CIA agreed that as the Soviets currently enjoyed good relations with both Iraq and Iran they would be unlikely to jeopardize their considerable economic interests in Iran by provoking a conflict. Documents prepared by NSC staff Harold Saunders and Samuel Hoskinson for Kissinger in advance of his 30–31 May meetings with the Shah in Tehran described both Iraq and Syria as unreliable and 'not sure bets as firm Soviet client states or as protectors of Soviet interests in the area'.[72] The NSC staff thought that regional instability might be caused by an overreaction by the Shah to the Iraqi–Soviet Treaty and Iraqi overconfidence resulting from the agreement.[73]

For Nixon and Kissinger, the Iraqi–Soviet Treaty had disturbed the regional equilibrium which was considered vital for the preservation of moderate Middle Eastern regimes and Western access to oil.[74] In the now infamous and unprecedented agreements in Tehran, Nixon beseeched the Shah to protect US interests and promised to sell Iran any weapon in the US conventional arsenal.[75] This included the most advanced US aircraft, the F-14 and F-15 as well as laser guided bombs.[76] This decision went against the conventional wisdom in the Department of Defense because the aircraft had only recently emerged from the research phase and had yet to be operationally tested.[77] Deputy Secretary of Defense Kenneth Rush presciently maintained that no commitment should be made as 'we cannot foresee the world situation in the latter half of this decade' and that 'conditions in the region by the time of aircraft availability might make a sale counterproductive to USG interests'.[78] These arguments were ignored by the White House which emphasized Iran's vital contribution to current regional stability. Other considerations also played a part. US Ambassador to Iran Joseph Farland (1972–1973) relayed to the White House how the Military Assistance Advisory Group (MAAG) were hesitant in pushing US weapons as they believed that there was a point of view 'in certain echelons of the USG to the effect that we should do what is possible to prevent Iran, in our studied wisdom from overbuying'.[79] Faced with much competition from British, French and Italian arms salesmen, Farland argued that 'as long as

Iran can financially afford both guns and butter, there is no reason for us to lose the market, particularly when viewed over the red ink in our balance of payments ledger.'[80] Kissinger's response to Farland was to order no restrictions on Iranian arms purchases other than normal licensing and legal requirements. On 25 July Kissinger reiterated the arms sales position to the Departments of State and Defense: 'In general, decisions on the acquisition of military equipment should be left primarily to the government of Iran.'[81] Giving the Shah a carte blanche on military purchases was described as the 'application of the Nixon Doctrine with a vengeance'.[82]

Alternative explanations for the Iraqi–Soviet Treaty were overshadowed by the bipolar focus. Evidence from Soviet sources pointed to the domestic ambitions of the Iraqi government rather than regional aspirations as the motivating factor behind the Iraqi–Soviet Treaty.[83] Saddam Hussein al-Takriti, the rising star of the Ba'ath Party, sought external support to facilitate internal ambitions such as the long mooted nationalization of the IPC and the suppression of the Kurds.[84] Furthermore, Iraqi perceptions of the growing Iranian threat informed their decision to enlist Soviet support.[85] Ironically, Nixon and Kissinger's focus on the global level made them inclined to overlook negative reports on the internal Iranian situation in 1972. The arms agreement with the Shah was made at a time when numerous reports highlighted the growing domestic opposition to the Shah's rule resulting from poor living standards, repressive, unpopular secular policies and the brutal methods used by his intelligence and security service, SAVAK.[86] Evidence of Iranian financial difficulty brought about by excessive arms purchases were disregarded as the Shah's oil income increased and Iran was deemed an economic success.[87]

The May 1972 meetings with the Shah marked a further change in US policy because Nixon agreed to the Shah's request for US aid to the Kurds in Northern Iraq. The Kurds had sought US support for their claims for autonomy.[88] Nixon's earlier refusal to assist the Kurds was rooted in perceptions of US interests. Kurdish autonomy or independence could potentially destabilize US allies, particularly Iran and Turkey, both of which had larger Kurdish populations than Iraq. Moreover, the Nixon administration publicly maintained the policy of non-interference in the internal affairs of states. Furthermore, Washington did not wish to engage in activities that could be considered anti-Soviet and jeopardize détente especially as it was generally believed that the Kurds could receive aid through the long-standing channels of Iran and Israel. As part of the Iraqi–Soviet Treaty, Moscow attempted to win the Kurds over to the concept of a national unity government but previous Ba'athist attempts, apparently engineered by Saddam Hussein, to undermine and divide the Kurds and to assassinate their leader, Mullah Mustafa Barzani, ensured failure.[89]

The Shah and the White House did not wish to see a domestically consolidated Iraq exert regional influence and looked to the Kurdish insurgency which would be capable of preoccupying the Iraqi military.[90] The Kurds sought US involvement because they did not trust the Shah's intentions, and feared abandonment.[91] Responding to the Shah's request, they agreed to provide assistance to the Kurds in what a House Select Committee on Intelligence concluded, in what ultimately became known as the Pike Report, was a 'cynical enterprise' even in the context of covert action.[92] In a memorandum to Kissinger, Hal Saunders admitted that 'if the battle turns against the Kurds we would have neither the assets nor the interest to provide decisive support'.[93] From 1972–1975, the Kurds received $16 million in covert US aid through the CIA, in addition to the funds provided by Iran.[94] The battle did turn against the Kurds on 13 June 1975 with the signing of the Algiers agreement in Baghdad. The Shah reached an agreement with Saddam Hussein which stipulated that in return for a favourable resolution of the dispute over the Shatt-al-Arab waterway, Iran would seal the border and cease aid to the Kurds.[95] Although displeased by the Shah's agreement, Ford and Kissinger acquiesced and refused to pressure the Shah to reconsider.[96] The over-reliance on the Shah of Iran as a regional ally coupled with the emphasis on balance of power led the Nixon administration to covertly aid the Kurds and the Ford administration to brutally abandon them as the Shah's priorities shifted.

Oil and arms: the oil crisis and arms exports

The 1973 Arab–Israeli War[97] heralded profound changes in the Middle East and Persian Gulf. Nixon and Kissinger's confidence in the stability provided by the Israeli military deterrent proved misplaced as Egypt and Syria succeeded in launching an effective surprise attack in the Sinai and Golan Heights. Throughout the war, the US matched Soviet moves in the area to maintain the pre-war balance of power which favoured Israel while seeking to create post-war conditions conducive to a US-dominated peace initiative.[98] The US furnished Israel with war materials as the Soviets replenished Syrian and Egyptian arsenals. In response to the perceived Soviet threat of unilateral intervention resulting from Israeli ceasefire violations, Kissinger ordered a DEFCON 3 nuclear alert. Iraqi forces were deployed to Syria but had a limited impact; they arrived too late to thwart the successful Israeli counterattack.[99] The stated aim of the Nixon administration during the war was to diminish Soviet influence in the area, a goal ultimately made achievable by the pro-Western tilt of Egyptian President Anwar Sadat.[100] Kissinger pursued the same goal with his shuttle diplomacy: 'In six months, if we pull off this agreement, we'll have the Soviets hanging by their fingernails in the area.'[101] US support for Israel during the war was not without complications. Following the White House announcement of the airlift of military supplies to the Jewish state and the provision of $2.2 billion in military assistance, the Organisation of Arab Petroleum Exporting Countries (OAPEC) imposed an oil embargo on the US and the Netherlands. The embargo and the attending cutback in Arab oil production caused the price of crude oil to jump from $5.12 a barrel to $11.65 by the end of 1973.[102] The oil price increases raised the spectre of Western economic stagnation and balance of payments crises in Washington but ushered in a period of prosperity for oil producing states including Iran and Iraq. The increased prosperity of Persian Gulf states provided the pretext for an expansion of US economic interests in the Persian Gulf.

Iran did not participate in the oil embargo but the Shah was central to the OPEC push for higher revenue. Iran benefited considerably from the price rises with increased annual oil income from $4 to $20 million.[103] Gerald Ford, who succeeded Nixon on 9 August 1974, maintained the central importance of Iran; amongst talking points for Ford in preparation for a meeting with the Iranian Ambassador they noted: 'We view a strong and stable Iran as the key to the stability of the oil-rich Persian Gulf region.'[104] Economic and military cooperation expanded significantly during Ford's tenure. By the autumn of 1975 39 US arms, electronic and telecommunications companies had contracts with Iran.[105] Iranian military expenditure facilitated by the 1972 commitment continued apace with the Shah placing large multibillion dollar contracts for the most advanced US aircraft. From 1973–1976, the US sold more arms to Iran than to any other state with military sales totalling $8.3 billion.[106] The US economic penetration coupled with military sales placed strain on the Iranian economy which was now ever more reliant on oil revenues. By 1975, the strain on the economy was evident and Iran's revenues were not matching the Shah's ambitions so he once again agitated in Washington for more oil income.[107] Still the Shah and the White House persisted and arms deals for the advanced airborne radar AWACS system and the latest McDonnell Douglas jet F-16 were agreed.

Despite the warning signs Ford pursued the same line as Nixon and Johnson heralding the positive impact of the 'White Revolution' and Iranian economic growth. The White House myopically ignored the inflation generated by the Shah's military spending, which eroded the earnings of Iranian shop keepers, oil workers and tenant farmers.[108] The rise in anti-American sentiment in Iran fanned by middle class perceptions of the Shah as a US puppet and the endemic corruption of the regime was downplayed in Washington.[109] The seeds planted that led to an over-reliance on the Shah to defend US strategic interests would bear bitter fruit during the Carter administration.

A more 'sophisticated understanding': attempted US–Iraqi rapprochement

Economic relations also improved with Iraq during this period. The State Department noted Saddam Hussein's declaration that he would welcome better relations with the US in July 1973 and viewed it as an indication that Iraq was prepared to chart a more independent course in foreign relations.[110]

David Korn of the State Department's Bureau for Near Eastern and South Asian Affairs commented on the importance of US economic interests in Iraq particularly as the regime intended to significantly increase oil production by 1975. According to Korn's briefing, 'Iraq has indicated a strong and increasing interest in buying American and US businessmen are receiving a warm welcome.'[111] Korn reported that US exports to Iraq had increased 100 percent from 1972 and that large contracts for $62 million and $122 million had been agreed with Boeing and Brown and Root respectively.[112] In 1975 a joint State Department, CIA and Defense Intelligence Agency report examining the implications of the 1975 Iran–Iraq agreement mentioned the growing US–Iraqi economic ties citing a further contract with Boeing for $225 million and that Iraq was 'one of the fastest growing markets for US products in the Middle East'.[113]

In December 1975 seeking to build on the improved economic relations, Kissinger met with his Iraqi counterpart Sadun Hammadi in the Iraqi Ambassador's residence in Paris.[114] Having successfully reduced Soviet influence in Egypt and Syria and aware of the more moderate stance of Baghdad as seen in their willingness to peacefully resolve border disputes with Iran, Saudi Arabia and Kuwait, Kissinger turned his attention to Iraq.[115] In this meeting Kissinger professed to have a more 'sophisticated understanding' of Iraq than he had previously. He defined Iraq as a 'friend of the Soviet Union' who acted on their own principles.[116] Hammadi proved hostile to such assertions and enquired whether the US would revert to its previous view of Iraq as a Soviet satellite if Baghdad signed another economic agreement with Moscow. Hammadi took issue with the US support of the Kurds 'who wanted to cut Iraq to pieces'.[117] Ultimately US support for Israel within the Nixon Doctrine became the obstacle to the reinstatement of relations. Despite Kissinger's claims that US support for Israel would wane since the current $2–3 billion level of support was unsustainable, Hammadi was adamant: 'On a political level we broke relations for a reason and we think the reason stands.'[118] Although Kissinger's argument that there was not 'a basic clash in national interests between Iraq and the United States' floundered on the rock of Israel, the Iraqis welcomed commercial cooperation.[119] Washington had to wait until 1984 for a resumption of full diplomatic relations with Iraq.

From 1969–1977 the Nixon and Ford administrations pursued a narrowly focused policy in the Middle East. Interpretations of regional developments were viewed through Cold War prisms whose distorting gaze underplayed analysis of regional dynamics. The stage was set for upheaval in Iran by the policies inspired by Nixon and Kissinger's reductive focus on the US–Soviet balance of power. Every request made by the Shah for arms was accommodated to the detriment of domestic development. Even Carter with his adherence to the principles of human rights acceded to the Shah's requests and upheld the policies of his predecessors. Multibillion dollar deals for jet aircraft were approved despite growing dissent within the administration and Congress.[120]

The focus of successive administrations is neatly illustrated by Gary Sick, a member of Carter's NSC: 'Our intelligence in Iran was focused on the Soviet Union. We were using Iran as a location for looking at the Soviet Union and were paying virtually no attention to Iran's internal politics.'[121] The geopolitical focus that nurtured the Shah's ambitions turned out to be a poisoned chalice. With the Shah's exit and the rise of the Islamic Republic under Ayatollah Khomeini, the US had to renegotiate the balance of power in the Persian Gulf and despite the leading role played by Iraq in providing the rationale for Iranian militarization, Washington's focus turned to Saddam Hussein.

Notes

1 William Shawcross, *The Shah's Last Ride: The Story of the Exile, Misadventures and Death of the Emperor* (London: Pan Books, 1989), 23.
2 Robert Fisk, *The Great War for Civilisation. The Conquest of the Middle East* (London: Fourth Estate, 2005), 128–129.
3 Richard Clarke, *Against All Enemies: Inside America's War on Terror* (London: Simon & Schuster, 2004), 37.
4 David Ryan, *US Foreign Policy in World History* (London: Routledge, 2003), 163.
5 Briefing by Henry Kissinger, 7 March 1972, White House, Presidential/HAK Memcons, Box 1026, NSC Files, NPMS, 11.
6 Memorandum of Conversation, 5 January 1972, Dr. Henry A. Kissinger and a Group of Conservative Administration Supporters, Presidential/HAK Memcons, Box 1026, NSC Files, NPMS, 4; Memorandum of Conversation, 17 May 1972, White House, Dr. Henry A. Kissinger and Ivy League Presidents, Presidential/HAK Memcons, Box 1026, NSC Files, NPMS, 3.
7 Ryan, *US Foreign Policy*, 163.
8 For more detailed accounts of the worldviews of Nixon and Kissinger, see *Foreign Relations of the United States Volume 1 Foundations of Foreign Policy* (Washington, DC: Government Printing Office, 2003); Walter Isaacson, *Kissinger: A Biography* (London: Faber and Faber, 1992); Bruce Kuklick, *Blind Oracles: Intellectuals and War from Kennan to Kissinger* (Princeton: Princeton University Press, 2006).
9 Excellent accounts of détente and linkage are provided in Raymond Garthoff, *Détente and Confrontation American–Soviet Relations from Nixon to Reagan* (Washington, DC: Brookings Institution, 1994); Jussi Hanhimaki, *Flawed Architect, Henry Kissinger & American Foreign Policy* (New York: Oxford University Press, 2004); Jeremy Suri, *Power and Protest: Global Revolution and the Rise of Détente* (Cambridge: Harvard University Press, 2003).
10 Garthoff, *Détente and Confrontation*, 28–37.
11 Memorandum of Conversation, Henry Kissinger & Newsweek Group, 9 November 1971, Presidential/HAK Memcons, Box 1025, NSC Files, NPMP, 8.
12 Memorandum of Conversation, Washington, 1 March 1974, Memcons January–March 1973 Presidential/HAK, Box 1026, Presidential/HAK Memcons. NSC Files. NPMP.
13 Henry Kissinger, *White House Years* (Boston: Little Brown, 1979), 225.
14 Ryan, *US Foreign Policy*, 163.
15 The best account of the war is provided in Michael Oren, *Six Days of War: June 1967 and the Making of the Modern Middle East* (London: Penguin, 2003); see also

Jeremy Bowen, *Six Days: How the 1967 War Shaped the Middle East* (London: Pocket, 2004).

16 Briefing Paper, 'Major Problems and US Objectives', TAB C, US Relations with the Eastern Arab World, Box 4, HAK Administrative & Staff Files-Transition, HAK Office Files, NSC Files, Nixon Presidential Materials Staff, 6.

17 Ibid., 3.

18 Ibid., 6–7.

19 Ibid., 7.

20 Kissinger, *White House Years*, 347.

21 Briefing Paper, 'Major Problems and US Objectives', op. cit., 4.

22 Memorandum, Henry Kissinger to Richard Nixon, 7 January 1969, TAB B, NSDM 2, National Security Decision Memoranda, National Security Council Institutional 'H' Files Policy Papers 1969–1974, NPMS.

23 Hanhimaki, *Flawed Architect*, 94–95.

24 Telecon, The President/Mr. Kissinger, 12 July 1970, Home July 1970–October 1970, Home File, Box 29, Henry A. Kissinger Telephone Conversation Transcripts (Telecons), NPMS.

25 Briefing Paper, 'Major Problems and US Objectives', TAB E, Persian Gulf, Box 4, HAK Administrative & Staff Files-Transition, HAK Office Files, NSC Files, NPMS, 1.

26 Douglas Little, *American Orientalism: the United States and the Middle East since 1945* (Chapel Hill: University of North Carolina Press, 2002), 221.

27 Briefing Paper, 'Major Problems and US Objectives', TAB I, Iran, Box 4, HAK Administrative & Staff Files-Transition, HAK Office Files, NSC Files, NPMS, 3.

28 Telegram from Department of State to Embassy in Iran, Washington, 6 May 1968, *Foreign Relations of the United States 1964–1968, vol. XXII, Iran*, at www.state.gov/www/about_state/history/vol_xxii/zc.html.

29 Memorandum From the Executive Secretary of the Department of State (Read) to the President's Assistant for National Security Affairs (Kissinger), Washington, 30 January 1969, *Foreign Relations of the United States, 1969–1976, vol. E-4, Documents on Iran and Iraq, 1969–1972*, at www.state.gov/r/pa/ho/frus/nixon/e4/64774.htm.

30 Memorandum of Conversation with Iranian Delegation, 1 April 1969, *FRUS, vol. E-4*, at www.state.gov/r/pa/ho/frus/nixon/e4/69230.htm; Memorandum of Conversation, Washington, 1 April 1969, 10:00 a.m., *FRUS, vol. E-4*, at www.state.gov/r/pa/ho/frus/nixon/e4/69858.htm; Memorandum of Conversation, 1 April 1969, the Shah of Iran, Henry A. Kissinger, Hushang Ansary, Ambassador of Iran, Harold Saunders, Iran, volume II, 1 June 1970–Dec 1970 [1of 2], Box 601, Country Files-Middle East, NSC Files, NPMS, 2.

31 Memorandum of Conversation, 1 April 1969, the Shah of Iran, Henry A. Kissinger, Hushang Ansary, Ambassador of Iran, Harold Saunders, Iran, volume II, 1 June 1970–Dec 1970 [1of 2], Box 601, Country Files-Middle East, NSC Files, NPMS, 2.

32 Memorandum from Joseph J. Sisco, Chairman of NSC Interdepartmental Group Near East and South Asia to Henry A. Kissinger, Chairman NSC Review Group, 10 March 1970, 'US Policy in the Persian Gulf Response to NSSM 66' [2of 3], Box H-156, National Security Study Memorandums, Study Memorandums (1969–1974), NSC Institutional 'H' Files, NPMS, 15.

33 Ibid., 16.

34 Record of National Security Council Interdepartmental Group for Near East and South Asia Meeting, Washington, 3 April 1969, *FRUS, vol. E-4*, at www.state.gov/r/pa/ho/frus/nixon/e4/71747.htm.

35 Memorandum from President's Assistant for National Security Affairs

(Kissinger) to President Nixon, Washington, 29 April 1969, *FRUS, vol. E-4*, at www.state.gov/r/pa/ho/frus/nixon/e4/65009.htm.

36 Research Study Prepared in the Bureau of Intelligence and Research, Washington, 28 January 1972, *FRUS, vol. E-4*, at www.state.gov/r/pa/ho/frus/nixon/e4/69477.htm.

37 Record of National Security Council Interdepartmental Group for Near East and South Asia Meeting, Washington, 3 April 1969, *FRUS, vol. E-4*, at www.state.gov/r/pa/ho/frus/nixon/e4/71747.htm.

38 Harvey H. Smith *et al.*, *Area Handbook for Iraq* (Washington, DC: US Government Printing Office, 1971), x.

39 Telegram, 27 January 1969, Ambassador Barbour to Secretary of State Rogers, *FRUS, vol. E-4*, at www.state.gov/r/pa/ho/frus/nixon/e4/65181.htm.

40 Memorandum from John M. Leddy, European Bureau to William Rogers Secretary of State, 7 February 1969, *FRUS, vol. E-4*, at www.state.gov/r/pa/ho/frus/nixon/e4/65185.htm.

41 Research Memorandum RNA-6 from the Director of the Bureau of Intelligence and Research (Hughes) to Secretary Rogers, Washington, 14 February 1969, *FRUS, vol. E-4*, at www.state.gov/r/pa/ho/frus/nixon/e4/65186.htm.

42 Telegram from the Department of State to the Embassy in Lebanon, 10 December 1969, *FRUS, vol. E-4*, at www.state.gov/r/pa/ho/frus/nixon/e4/ 65198.htm.

43 Memorandum from Harold Saunders to Henry Kissinger, 20 October 1969, *FRUS, vol. E-4*, at www.state.gov/r/pa/ho/frus/nixon/e4/65021.htm.

44 Memorandum from Harold Saunders to Henry Kissinger, 2 September 1970, Iran, vol. II, 1 June–December 1970 [1 of 2], Box 601, Country Files-Middle East, NSC Files, NPMS.

45 Ibid.

46 Garthoff, *Détente and Confrontation*, 740–741; Kissinger, *White House Years*, 1255.

47 Avi Shlaim, *Lion of Jordan: The Life of King Hussein in War and Peace* (London: Allen Lane, 2007), 322.

48 Telegram from American Embassy, Moscow to Secretary of State, 2 September 1970, June Initiative 28 August–15 November 1970, Volume IV [1 of 5], Box 1156, Middle East Negotiation Files, Harold H. Saunders Files, NSC Files.

49 Kissinger, *White House Years*, 600.

50 Kissinger, *White House Years*, 600.

51 William Quandt, *Peace Process: American Diplomacy and the Arab-Israeli Conflict Since 1967* (Washington: Brookings Institution, 2001), 76–77.

52 Memorandum from Henry Kissinger to President Nixon, 16 September 1970, Jordan Volume 5, 1 July 1970–30 September 1970 [1 of 2], Box 615, Country Files-Middle East, NSC Files, NPMS.

53 Memorandum from Helmut Sonnenfeldt to Henry Kissinger, 18 September 1970, Jordan, Volume 5, NPMS.

54 Ibid.

55 Memorandum from Henry Kissinger to President Nixon, 16 September 1970, Jordan, Volume 5. Any reference to an Israeli attack on Iraqi forces Nixon strongly underlined and wrote no and in another instance 'We shall not support Israel if they attack Jordan on their own.' Telecon Richard Nixon and Henry Kissinger, 20 September 1970, 7.45pm, Home File, Box 29, HAK Telecons, NPMS.

56 Telecon, The President, Mr. Kissinger, 17 September 1970, 2.40pm, Chronological File, 12–17 September 1970, Box 6, HAK Telecons, NPMS.

57 Shlaim, *Lion of Jordan*, 334.

58 Telecon, Henry Kissinger, Melvin Laird, 17 September 1970, 7.45pm, Chronological File, 12–17 September 1970, Box 6, HAK Telecons, NPMS.

59 Ibid.
60 Quandt, *Peace Process*, 103.
61 Ibid., 103–104.
62 Memorandum of Conversation, Washington, 1 March 1974, Memcons, January–March 1973, Presidential/HAK, Box 1026, Presidential/HAK Memcons. NSC Files, NPMP.
63 Memorandum of Conversation, Dr. Kissinger, Liebman Group, 13 October 1971, Box 1025, Presidential/HAK Memcons, NSC Files, NPMS.
64 Shlaim, *Lion of Jordan*, 334.
65 Hanhimaki, *Flawed Architect*, 97.
66 Memorandum of Conversation, Damascus, 12.10am–3.25am, 25–26 February 1974, Memcons January, 1974–28 February 1974, HAK and Presidential [1of 3], Box 1028, Presidential/HAK Memcons, NSC Files, NPMP, 31.
67 Shlaim, *Lion of Jordan*, 334.
68 William Quandt, 'Political and Military Dimensions of Contemporary Palestinian Nationalism' in William Quandt, Fuad Jabber, Ann Mosley Lesch, *The Politics of Palestinian Nationalism* (Berkeley: University of California Press, 1973), 129–130.
69 Telegram from the Department of State to the Embassies in Iran, the United Kingdom and the Soviet Union, 22 January 1972, *FRUS, vol. E-4*, at www.state.gov/r/pa/ho/frus/nixon/e4/65600.htm.
70 Airgram from Embassy in Lebanon to Department of State, 2 February 1972, *FRUS, vol. E-4*, at www.state.gov/r/pa/ho/frus/nixon/e4/65602.htm.
71 Intelligence Memorandum, Washington, 12 April 1972, *FRUS, vol. E-4*, at www.state.gov/r/pa/ho/frus/Nixon/e4/69743.htm.
72 Memorandum from Harold Saunders and Samuel Hoskinson to Henry Kissinger, Washington, 17 May 1972, *FRUS, vol. E-4*, at www.state.gov/r/pa/ho/frus/nixon/e4/65148.htm.
73 Memorandum from Harold Saunders and Samuel Hoskinson to Henry Kissinger, Washington, 17 May 1972, *FRUS, vol. E-4*, at www.state.gov/r/pa/ho/frus/nixon/e4/65148.htm.
74 Kissinger, *White House Years*, 1263–1264.
75 Memorandum of Conversation, Tehran, 30 May 1972, *FRUS, vol. E-4*, at www.state.gov/r/pa/ho/frus/nixon/e4/65153.htm; Memorandum of Conversation, Tehran, 31 May 1972, *FRUS, vol. E-4*, at www.state.gov/r/pa/ho/frus/nixon/e4/69507.htm.
76 Memorandum from Henry Kissinger to Departments of State, Defense, 15 June 1972, Iran (2), Box 12, National Security Adviser, Presidential Country Files for Middle East and South Asia, Gerald R. Ford Library.
77 Memorandum from Deputy Secretary of Defense Rush to National Security Adviser Kissinger, Washington, 18 May 1972, *FRUS, vol. E-4*, at www.state.gov/r/pa/ho/frus/nixon/e4/69506.htm.
78 Ibid.
79 Memorandum form Harold Saunders to Henry Kissinger, Washington, 14 July 1972, *FRUS, vol. E-4*, at www.state.gov/r/pa/ho/frus/nixon/e4/69582.htm.
80 Ibid.
81 Memorandum from Henry Kissinger to Departments of State, Defense, 25 July 1972, Iran (2), Box 12, NSA, Presidential Country Files for Middle East and South Asia, GRFL.
82 James Bill, *The Eagle and the Lion: The Tragedy of American-Iranian Relations* (New Haven: Yale University Press, 1988), 203.
83 Marion Farouk-Sluglett and Peter Sluglett, 'The Historiography of Modern Iraq', *The American Historical Review* 96, No. 5 (December 1991): 1408–1421.

84 Oles Smolansky and Bettie Smolansky, *The USSR and Iraq: The Soviet Quest for Influence* (Durham, NC: Duke University Press, 1991), 17–18.

85 Haim Shemesh, *Soviet-Iraqi Relations, 1968–1988: In the Shadow of the Iraq–Iran Conflict* (Boulder, CO: Lynne Rienner, 1992), 60.

86 Little, *American Orientalism*, 220–227; Bill, *The Eagle and the Lion*, 213–215; Airgram from the Embassy in Iran to the Department of State, 15 April 1971, *FRUS, vol. E-4*, at www.state.gov/r/pa/ho/frus/nixon/e4/65104.htm; Situation Report, 28 February 1972, *FRUS, vol. E-4*, at www.state.gov/r/pa/ho/frus/nixon/e4/69577.htm.

87 Intelligence Memorandum, February, 1972, *FRUS, vol. E-4*, at www.state.gov/r/pa/ho/frus/nixon/e4/69478.htm; Telegram from the Embassy in Iran to the Department of State, 31 May 1972, at www.state.gov/r/pa/ho/frus/nixon/e4/69508.htm.

88 Memorandum of Conversation, 13 June 1969, *FRUS, vol. E-4*, at www.state.gov/r/pa/ho/frus/nixon/e4/65195.htm.

89 Memorandum from Harold Saunders to Henry Kissinger, 7 June 1972, Tab A, Research Study, 'The Kurds in Iraq Renewed Insurgency', 31 May 1972, NPMP Mandatory Review Documents, Online Sample, at http://nixon.archives.gov/virtuallibrary/documents/mr/060772_iraq.pdf.

90 Bill, *The Eagle and the Lion*, 205.

91 William Safire, 'Mr. Ford's Secret Sellout: What happened when our "Shah forsaken clients, the Kurds" turned to the US', *New York Times*, 5 February 1976.

92 Bill, *The Eagle and the Lion*, 205.

93 Memorandum from Harold Saunders to Henry Kissinger, 7 June 1972, NPMP Mandatory Review Documents, Online Sample, at http://nixon.archives.gov/virtuallibrary/documents/mr/060772_iraq.pdf.

94 Bill, *The Eagle and the Lion*, 207.

95 Bill, *The Eagle and the Lion*, 206.

96 Henry Kissinger, *Years of Renewal* (New York: Simon & Schuster, 1999), 595.

97 For a good account of the war see Abraham Rabinovich, *The Yom Kippur War: The Epic Encounter that Transformed the Middle East* (New York: Shocken Books, 2004).

98 Henry Kissinger, *Years of Upheaval* (Boston: Little Brown, 1982), 467–468; Robert Dallek, *Nixon and Kissinger: Partners in Power* (New York: Harper Collins, 2007), 521–522; Shlomo Ben-Ami, *Scars of War, Wounds of Peace: The Arab-Israeli Tragedy* (London: Phoenix, 2006), 145.

99 Memorandum of Conversation, Damascus, 12.10am–3.25am, 25–26 February 1974, Memcons January 1974–28 February 1974, HAK and Presidential [1of 3], Box 1028, Presidential/HAK Memcons, NSC Files, NPMP, 31.

100 Memorandum of Conversation, Bipartisan Leadership Meeting, Washington, 27 November 1973, Memcons, April–November 1973, HAK and Presidential [1 of 5], Box 1027, Presidential HAK Memcons, NSC Files, NPMP; Minutes, NSC Meeting, 28 March 1975, NSC Meeting 28 March 1975, Box 1, National Security Adviser, NSC Meeting File, 1974–1977, GRFL, 4.

101 Untitled, Undated, Memorandum of Conversation, Kissinger, Sisco, Dayan, Allon, Meir, General Gur, Memcon, 8 May–31 May 1974, HAK and Presidential [2 of 3], Box 1029, Presidential/HAK Memcons, NSC Files, NPMP, 47.

102 Stephen Randall, *United States Foreign Oil Policy Since World War I: For Profits and Security* (Toronto: McGill-Queens University Press, 2005), 288.

103 Bill, *The Eagle and the Lion*, 202.

104 Talking Points for Meeting with the Iranian Ambassador, Ardeshir Zahedi, 21 August 1974, Iran (1), Box 12, NSA Presidential Country Files for the Middle East and South Asia, GRFL.

105 Bill, *The Eagle and the Lion*, 209.
106 Leslie Pryor, 'Arms and the Shah', *Foreign Policy*, no. 31 (Summer, 1978), 56–71. This chapter was penned by a 'Western observer who has lived in Iran' under the pseudonym Leslie M. Pryor.
107 Memorandum from Henry Kissinger to President Ford, 14 August 1975, Iran (4), Box 13, NSA Presidential Country Files for Middle East and South Asia, GRFL; Talking Points for Meeting with Hushang Ansary, Minister of Economy and Finance, 29 March 1976, Iran (9), Box 13, NSA Presidential Country Files for Middle East and South Asia, GRFL.
108 Little, *American Orientalism*, 222.
109 Little, *American Orientalism*, 222; Bill, *The Eagle and the Lion*, 209–210.
110 Telegram from Department of State to US Embassy, Beirut, Undated, POL-Iraq, Iraq/US Policy, 1973, Box 1, Records Relating to Iraq, 1973–1975, Office of Lebanon, Jordan, Syria and Iraq Affairs, Bureau of Near Eastern and South Asian Affairs, RG 59, General Records of the Department of State, National Archives and Records Administration.
111 Memorandum, from David Korn to Roy Atherton, 22 April 1974, POL-13, Iraq 1974, Ethnic Groups-Kurds, Box 1 Records Relating to Iraq, 1973–1975, Office of Lebanon, Jordan, Syria and Iraq Affairs, Bureau of Near Eastern and South Asian Affairs, RG 59, NARA.
112 Ibid.
113 NIO/Middle East, 'The Implications of the Iran-Iraq Agreement', 1 May 1975, National Security Archive Electronic Briefing Book, no. 167 (18 October 2005), at www.gwu.edu/~nsarchiv/NSAEBB/NSAEBB16/01.pdf.
114 David Ryan, *Frustrated Empire: US Foreign Policy, 9/11 to Iraq* (London: Pluto Press, 2007), 79.
115 Ryan, *Frustrated Empire*, 78–79.
116 Memorandum of Conversation, Sadun Hammadi, Minister of Foreign Affairs of Iraq, Henry Kissinger, Secretary of State, Paris, 17 December 1985, National Security Archive Electronic Briefing Book, no. 192 (26 May 2006), at www.gwu.edu/~nsarchiv/NSAEBB193/HAK-12-17-75.pdf.
117 Ibid.
118 Ibid.
119 Ibid.
120 Seymour Hersh, 'Proposed Sale of Fighters to Iran Challenged Within the Administration', *New York Times*, 9 October 1977.
121 Gary Sick, 'Iran: A View from the White House', *World Affairs*, vol. 149 (1987), 209–213.

3 From the 'tilt' to the unintended 'transformation'

The United States and Iraq, 1975–1992

David Ryan

Across the spring of 2008 the United States had 160 000 troops in Iraq; the fifth anniversary of the war had passed and attention in the United States and elsewhere shifted to determine what the Iraq policies and options of the three remaining presidential candidates might be in early 2009 or beyond. All three senators had the opportunity to question General David H. Petraeus, Commander of the Multi-National Force – Iraq; one of them would have to deal with the morass. Despite his broadly positive assessment, when pushed by Senator Evan Bayh, the Democrat from Indiana, General Petraeus admitted: 'The Champagne bottle has been pushed to the back of the refrigerator.' He had characterised the situation in Iraq to the Senate Foreign Relations Committee as 'fragile and reversible'. Petraeus was clear that corners had not been turned and that 'we haven't seen any lights at the end of the tunnel'. Yet Senator John McCain envisaged the potential for 'the genuine prospect of success' indicating that the US was 'no longer staring into the abyss of defeat'. Senator Hilary Clinton made the prescient observation that it 'might well be irresponsible to continue the policy that has not produced the results that have been promised time and again', despite having voted for the war, she, perhaps unwittingly, tapped into the sentiments of failed ambition that drove policy makers towards Iraq across the 1990s and into the post-9/11 era. Senator Barack Obama, begging the indulgence of committee members, identified the 'massive strategic blunder' that would require a timetabled withdrawal and an intense regional diplomatic effort, including talks with Iran. It has been clear for some time that the situation would not resolve itself during the Bush administration, now it has been articulated. Petraeus recommended a drawdown of the surge combat forces to July 2008 which would be followed by a 45 day period of 'consolidation and evaluation'.[1] That identification of the massive strategic blunder punctuated years of US attempts to engage Iraq in various ways; first in attempts to rebuild relations after the 1967 War, courting Iraq diplomatically through the 1970s and 1980s, but especially after a pillar of the Nixon Doctrine, Iran, was 'lost'. The US victory in 1991 enhanced ideologies associated with a transformation of US power and 'strategic depth', yet Saddam Hussein's continued presence drew these strategists back to Iraq after 9/11. It is an irony of extraordinary proportions that this was supposed to be the location where the United States would demonstrate its power and move out of the world of realism and an international balance of power into a commanding and pre-eminent strategic position; this was the place Washington now struggled to find an effective exit strategy, with all the attendant narratives on the 'legacy' of Iraq and its implications for US power and prestige.[2]

Petraeus outlined a number of operational considerations, but it is the strategic considerations that provide a point of irony, not just for the five-year old war, but also for the post-Vietnam War decades in which US strategists have been preoccupied by US ground force capabilities, regional threats in the Gulf and the prospects of failure and increased terrorist violence. In moving towards his recommendations, Petraeus acknowledged that

> the strain on the US military, especially on its ground forces, has been considerable; a number of the security challenges inside Iraq are also related to significant regional and global threats; and a failed state in Iraq would pose serious consequences for the greater fight against Al Qaeda, for regional stability, for the already existing humanitarian crisis in Iraq, and for the effort to counter malign Iranian influence.[3]

These strategic issues might not have arisen had the Bush administration not invaded in 2003 or, for that matter, in 1991.

Yet in various ways the United States was in Iraq precisely because one element of the narrative on the capabilities of US ground forces and the strains under which they could operate and endure were considerations in 1991 and shaped the conclusion of that Gulf War. The regional and global threats that emanated especially in the late 1970s following the Iranian Revolution and a decade later following Saddam Hussein's invasion of Kuwait had indeed first shaped and then accelerated the US rapprochement with Iraq before the sharp turn against the regime in 1990. The overwhelming and decisive victory of 1991 produced a situation that cut two ways. On the one hand documents declassified in December 2007 reveal that certain strategists thought that the victory might act as a demonstration case to deter regional actors from aspiring to a greater local hegemonic role, yet some of these strategists were also chagrined by the way in which that very war ended, leaving Saddam Hussein in power, free to further annihilate opposition, particularly the Shia uprising in the south.

Over a decade of rapprochement across the 1970s and 1980s served US interests to the extent that such regional countries had to be ameliorated or isolated, especially in the post-Vietnam context and even more so after the Iranian Revolution. The Gulf War provided the United States with a new assertive posture. Yet, with the loss of the two pivotal Gulf regimes the 1990s was characterised as a decade of sanctions and isolation, while the US presence was increasingly resented and controversial, and simultaneously susceptible to Chinese competition.[4] The invasion of 2003, while attempting to address one set of issues, initiated the recent process of destabilisation and the inward migration of al Qaeda. As the situation fell apart in 2006 and the Iraq Study Group recommended regional negotiations,[5] the Bush administration responded otherwise. As President Bush sent General Petraeus off on the 'surge' he pointed out that 'most people recognize that failure would be a disaster for the United States'.[6] Failure of course would be a disaster for the United States; and by 2008 failure was inevitable. Even the most successful diplomatic strategy that produced an exit for Washington would fall far short of its original ambitions.

Rapprochement and reproachment

Washington's ambivalence on the Iraqi regime was placed in sharp relief in August 1990. Just days before Iraqi forces invaded Kuwait, Saddam Hussein summoned the US Ambassador to Iraq, April Glaspie, for a conversation in his office. Hussein outlined his grievances against Kuwait; they had according to his account been waging economic warfare against Iraq at a time when Iraq needed the dollar income to repay the debts following the Iran–Iraq War that lasted through most of the 1980s. Kuwait's production had pushed the international prices downward accentuating difficulties for Iraq. Moreover, Hussein had other concerns with Kuwait's practice of horizontal drilling and their occupation of the oil fields that were disputed between the two countries. Glaspie worried about the Iraqi military build-up on Kuwait's borders, but also indicated that she understood the difficulties associated with the Iraqi loss of revenue to the tune of $6–7 billion given that the price of a barrel of oil was holding at $12. In an extraordinary and controversial exchange she related that 'I know you need the funds. We understand that and our opinion is that you should have the opportunity to rebuild your country. But we have no opinion on the Arab–Arab conflicts, like your border disagreement with Kuwait.'[7] She had that message on specific instruction from the Secretary of State, James Baker. Yet within days, after Iraq invaded Kuwait in early August 1990, Washington mobilised an extensive range of states in diplomatic opposition, a sanctions regime and then ultimately a military expulsion of Iraq from Kuwait. Glaspie was later isolated and depicted as operating outside the policy framework. But that narrative was always problematic. Days after she delivered her message to Saddam Hussein, a similar message was put to a subcommittee of the Committee on Foreign Affairs in Washington. The Assistant Secretary of State for Near Eastern and South Asian Affairs, John Kelly, explained on 31 July 1990, that

> historically, the United States has taken no position on the border disputes in the area, nor on matters pertaining to integral OPEC deliberations, but the United States has taken a strong position in support of the sovereignty of all States in the area

When pressed by Lee Hamilton on US commitments to 'our friends in the Gulf', Kelly responded that they had 'no defense relationship with any of the countries'. The US position was one of extreme concern, but he argued that he could not get into the hypothetical scenarios on what the US response would be should an invasion occur.[8]

Human rights and a concern for Iraq's possession of WMD had crept back onto the agenda, having been muted for some time. But US commercial interests and its concern for its own prestige were also growing concerns. Earlier in 1990 Kelly testified before Hamilton's subcommittee on the importance of Gulf oil. He explained that the United States had experienced seven years of economic growth which necessitated increased oil consumption:

> since 1983 there has been a 66 percent increase in our annual net oil imports. [Moreover] net imports as a share of our total petroleum needs may grow from 42 percent in 1989 to the 50–60 percent range by the year 2000. Approximately 53 percent of the increase in total U.S. imports of crude and refined petroleum products since 1985 has come from the Persian Gulf.

Without the prospect of major new oil finds in the United States at the time, Kelly thought the trend of dependency would continue 'in the foreseeable future'. Finally he indicated that the Gulf producers account for about 65–70 percent of the world's excess production capacity. So despite the troubling aspects of the relationship, Iraq sought improved relations with the United States and there were 'important opportunities for American business in Iraq'. But Kelly concluded, 'this is not an easy relationship, but it is an important one in which we have made significant progress in recent years'.[9]

So there was the rub: Washington had no opinion on the border disputes of the region, a deep commitment to sovereignty of the countries, a growing dependence on Gulf oil and a reinvigorated concern for its own prestige coupled with an awareness of Saddam Hussein's 'increased military power and prestige in the Arab world to supplement its vast oil reserves'.[10] The prospects of balancing these various issues provided Washington with a deep predicament. Washington made various overtures to improve relations with Iraq across the 1970s and 1980s and it calculated an increased geo-strategic interest in Iraq after the collapse of the Shah's Iran, a pillar of US foreign policy under the Nixon Doctrine. Yet the combination of no opinion on the border disputes with the commitment to sovereignty could not be resolved so long as US prestige was also thrown into the bargain.

Iraq's border dispute with Kuwait was clearly an issue that could have been explored further through concerted diplomatic action. However the will to do so was missing in both Washington and initially in Baghdad. Frustrated with the ongoing negotiations across 1990 Iraq invaded Kuwait taking the entire country. Had they not taken the entire country the issue of Kuwaiti sovereignty might not have been as pressing. Washington had watched the growth of Iraqi power and prestige in the region and after the invasion found that its own calculus of resolve and prestige was on the line. The US decision to commit US forces to the region was taken very shortly after the invasion. Participants at the Camp David meeting had realised that the operation would be 'no wham-bam weekend excursion to Grenada, Libya or Panama'. It could possibly be messy, lengthy and potentially disastrous for the Bush administration. Yet inaction with the potential Iraqi threat to Saudi Arabia, the participants concluded, would be even more 'disastrous for US strategic and economic interests' and thus political fortunes. Bush had opted to do nothing as intelligence was gathered on the massing of Iraqi forces on the Kuwaiti border. Despite CIA analysis on the manoeuvres Bush was assured by Egyptian President Hosni Mubarak and Jordan's King Hussein that Iraq would not attack. After it did, the Camp David participants concluded that it was 'now strategically vital for the US to humiliate the Iraqi leader politically and economically and face him down militarily'.[11] Former President Richard Nixon reiterated the theme on the eve of war in 1991. Writing an op-ed piece in the *New York Times* he identified and justified the option of war on the grounds of national interests, especially oil and jobs. But given Hussein's strategic potential and the signal that if aggression against Kuwait did not go unanswered 'other potential aggressors in the world will be tempted to wage war against their neighbors'. Yet if the United States did remove Iraq from Kuwait, 'we will have the credibility to deter aggression elsewhere without sending American forces. The world will take seriously U.S. warnings against aggression.' This message was frequently echoed by George W. Bush across 2005, as pressure grew for US withdrawal from Iraq. Back in 1991 Nixon admonished through implicit analogy his readers to remember that when dealing with an insatiable aggressor 'a bad peace is worse than war because it will inevitably lead to a bigger war'. The war was therefore also about a demonstration effect to deter future aggression in regional conflict in the full knowledge that Washington was watching and *would* respond. It was consequently 'a war about peace – not just peace in our time, but peace for our children and grandchildren in the years ahead'.[12] (Those words are even more poignant as US troops, the children of the earlier generation were back in Iraq, perhaps in part because of the 'bad peace' concluded in 1991.)

A few years after Iraq broke diplomatic relations with the United States for its support of Israel in the 1967 War, Washington made efforts to mend them. Washington was well aware of Iraq's ambitions in the 1970s. In 1975 it reported that its recent actions had been 'rather phenomenal'; Hussein was meeting with the Shah, had made overtures to Saudi Arabia and discussed border disputes with Kuwait. They had moved closer to Jordan and Egypt and Washington expected them to play a 'dynamic' role in the region. They also concluded that Hussein was a remarkable character, he held no official position, but 'he is running the show; and he's a very ruthless and – very recently, obviously – pragmatic, intelligent power. I think we're going to see Iraq playing more of a role in the area than it has for many years.'[13] Henry Kissinger met the Iraqi Minister of Foreign Affairs, Sadun Hammadi, in Paris in December 1975. Their discussion meandered through Iraq's concerns with the earlier US support for the Kurds and its continued support for Israel. Kissinger tried to reassure Hammadi that Israel's power would be no more than that of Lebanon in 15 years, but Hammadi was still reluctant to move further. Ultimately, Kissinger suggested, 'You will see: Our attitude is not unsympathetic to Iraq. Don't believe; watch it.'[14]

The gist of these messages was maintained during the Reagan administration. With the loss of Iran the communication became even more strategically important. The US had simultaneously lost access to Iran's oil reserves and the Carter administration suffered further humiliation with the protracted hostage crisis that ended as Reagan entered the White House. Moreover, with the Soviet invasion of Afghanistan, Iraq's importance was accentuated.

Alexander Haig, Reagan's first Secretary of State, dispatched a deputy assistant, Morris Draper, to Iraq during his visit to the Middle East in April 1981. Haig was eager to keep the Iraqis, and Hammadi in particular, informed of his meetings. Haig viewed Iraq as a good bulwark against the Islamic Revolution in Iran. And though Iraq did not want to restore full diplomatic relations (ultimately restored in 1984 after the de-designation of Iraq from the list of countries supporting terrorism in 1982) till the US altered its Middle East policies, it sought closer relations and greater commercial ties. Officially, Washington maintained a neutral position on the Iran–Iraq War and Washington sent the signal that a swift end to the war would be in the interest of all concerned.[15]

Over the next few years Washington moved closer to Iraq building up its commercial, diplomatic and ultimately military assistance. The contacts between the two countries increased following an appreciative letter from Hammadi to Haig. In May 1981 Tariq Aziz, the most significant contact with a senior member of the Revolutionary Command Council (RCC) met with William Eagleton of the US interest section in Baghdad. While the US interlocutor spoke of the desire to contain Soviet influence in the region, Aziz emphasised the US–Israeli relationship. But importantly Aziz took the opportunity to characterise the Iraqi regime as nationalist, socialist and independent and 'hostile only to those who threaten Iraqi vital interests'. It was a stabilising force in the region according to his iteration. While they retained the right to maintain friendly relations with Moscow, they did not want to facilitate the extension of Soviet regional power. Moreover, they had made the realistic assessment that Europe and the United States were more affluent and technologically advanced and therefore Iraq had objective reasons to cultivate these relations.[16]

As the Iran–Iraq War persisted and given the US dependency on the region's oil, President Reagan signed National Security Decision Directive 114. The directive was concerned with maintaining US access to the oil supplies because 'of the real and psychological impact of a curtailment in the flow of oil from the Persian Gulf on the international economic system'.[17] Access was deemed so important that by October 1983 Washington began discussion on the 'tilt toward Iraq' and abandoning the stated position of neutrality. The State Department averred that US policies were designed to circumvent direct great power involvement, to contain the war within the two countries, to contribute to the stalemate leaving the opportunity open to subsequently develop relations with Iran and simultaneously curtail Soviet influence. Yet the tilt became even more pressing because of improved US–Iraqi relations and the potential for regime collapse in Baghdad brought on by Iranian attrition and financial strangulation. Washington recognised that in practice it had already initiated the 'tilt' 'for over a year' since Iran crossed into Iraq and Washington responded with tactical intelligence, financial, diplomatic and military assistance to Baghdad. Yet this aid had to be tempered so that the United States was not directly drawn into a conflict of such magnitude, especially after Vietnam.[18]

Donald Rumsfeld, special envoy for President Reagan, was sent to meet Saddam Hussein to facilitate the policy shift. Washington was well aware of Iraq's disadvantage in the war since Iran maintained access to the Gulf, whereas Iraq did not. In such circumstances Iraq's economy suffered and therefore its ability to wage war was compromised. While Washington was clear that it would be in the interest of all concerned to bring the war to an end, the cable from the US interests section in Baghdad to the US embassy in Amman dealing with 'talking points' for Rumsfeld's visit with Tariq Aziz, concluded that the US 'would regard any major reversal of Iraq's fortunes as a strategic defeat for the West'.[19] Stability and access were watch words for both parties as Iraq pursued access to lucrative markets, technology and assistance to bring the war to an end while the US desired access to the oil. Moreover, Rumsfeld emphasised the importance of rectifying the regional balance of power.[20]

Washington communicated a demarche to Baghdad for its use of chemical weapons against Iran. Their use had been resumed following the Iranian offensive of February 1984 after which Washington again sent a warning to Iraq; it recognised, in part, that the issue attracted 'greater media attention in the United States'.[21] Rumsfeld returned to Baghdad as Iraqi war efforts were flagging and its bilateral relationship with Washington was strained following the US condemnation on the use of chemical warfare.[22] US officials urged Iraqis to help 'in avoiding ... embarrassing situations' and reassured them that they did not want 'this issue to dominate our bilateral relationship'.[23] Soon after, National Security Decision Directive 139 instructed State, Defense and CIA to prepare plans 'of action designed to avert an Iraqi collapse'.[24]

The Defense Intelligence Agency (DIA) conducted an 'estimative' on Iraq just prior to the US resumption of diplomatic relations with Baghdad on 26 November 1984, during which Secretary of State, George Shultz, met with

Aziz. The DIA held few illusions on Hussein's power or capabilities. They recognised him as a 'ruthless but pragmatic leader' of a 'well-organized' party which dealt with its Shia opponents 'by executing, jailing and deporting suspected members' of the Dawa Party. Washington provided further assistance to Iraq in the war that ground on till 1988, despite Baghdad's use of gas against the Kurds in Halabja. The DIA accurately recognised that even though Hussein had reduced certain tensions with Arab countries, others were likely to be resumed after the war:

> Husayn most likely will resume fully his support toward the overthrow of Assad. Moreover, Iraq's intransigence in settling territorial claims to two islands (Bubiyan and Warbah) with Kuwait, despite Kuwaiti support during the war, suggests that Baghdad's relationship with the Arab Gulf states will continue to experience strains.

It estimated that Iraq would move to occupy one of the islands to gain access to the Gulf but that activity against moderate Arab countries was unlikely.[25]

The US tilt towards Iraq had certainly paid dividends for Baghdad. If it could secure a UN guaranteed peace, the DIA estimate argued, it would resume 'full-time pursuit of its international leadership ambitions'. Hussein would be reinvigorated in his pursuit of Arab world leadership and that of the Non-Aligned Movement. The size of its armed forces and the extent of its oil reserves placed it in a 'position of strength' and these would 'give Saddam enormous economic leverage in pursuit of his policy goals'. Yet they also concluded that a 'war weary Iraq probably will not undertake significant military adventures in the near to medium term'. It would however intensify efforts to obtain nuclear weapons following the war which had 'whetted its appetite for advanced technology'. Despite these fears the United States built on the lucrative commercial opportunities and by 1987 it had become Iraq's largest supplier of civilian goods to the tune of $700 million in exports.[26]

The border dispute between Iraq and Kuwait remained acute and a subject for US intelligence comment. Despite Baghdad settling disputes with Jordan and Saudi Arabia the one with Kuwait remained problematic. Despite Kuwait's support for Iraq during the war, US intelligence concluded that

> Iraq's need to finance rearmament, reconstruction of war damage, and economic and social development to fulfil the expectations of its populace will lead it to seek maximum oil revenues. Iraqi efforts to capture a larger share of any increase in demand for OPEC oil probably will worsen present frictions with other OPEC exporters, especially Iran.

It suggested that Baghdad would probably press Kuwait over control of the islands, including the option of building a military base on Bubiyan, 'as a price for formally settling the border dispute'.[27]

Outflanking talks

So, given this trend in improved relations, despite Halabja, Glaspie had reiterated established policy. The crux of the problem lay in the incompatibility with the policy of 'no opinion' and the commitment to sovereignty. Had Saddam Hussein's forces invaded Kuwait to restore Iraqi control over the northern Kuwaiti oil fields US foreign policy might have been placed in an acute dilemma; a limited invasion would have been about territory, resources and borders rather than questions of overall sovereignty. Despite the complete and brutal invasion of Kuwait there were prospects for a diplomatic solution. But these were precluded by the wording adopted in UN Security Council Resolution 660, which demanded 'that Iraq withdraw immediately and unconditionally all its forces to the positions in which they were located on 1 August 1990'. By 2 August 1990 Washington had condemned the invasion, mustered the necessary UN diplomatic opposition and declared that they stood 'shoulder to shoulder with Kuwait in this time of crisis'.[28]

The early diplomatic gambits initiated by Saddam Hussein were bound to fail as he linked the issue of Iraqi withdrawal to that of Israeli withdrawal from the Gaza Strip and the West Bank. Days later on 14 August King Hussein of Jordan flew from Baghdad to Washington in another failed attempt to mediate settlement. By the end of the month there were increasing questions on the possibility of a diplomatic solution. President Bush's position firmly supported the UN Secretary General, Javier Pérez de Cuéllar's attempts to find a peaceful solution based on UNSC resolution 660, but this was the sticking point that precluded compromise. Bush argued that it was abundantly clear that the world was demanding a withdrawal and the restoration of the Kuwaiti government and given Hussein's intransigence Bush responded to a question on the prospect for a diplomatic solution with the observation: 'I don't particularly see more hope now.' He was further questioned whether entering into negotiations might lead to 'small peace offerings' that could lead to protracted discussion and the potential that 'world resolve will crumble'. Ultimately Bush explained:

> I'm not saying we're not going to talk. But what, clearly, world opinion is saying and what the United Nations has said and what is now codified in international law is: Out, Saddam Hussein, Iraq, out of Kuwait, and restore the leaders! But you have to talk to get there. But that doesn't mean there is to be compromise. Clearly we would oppose any compromise on these fundamental principles that have been laid down by the United Nations.

When pressed on 'what's negotiable here?' Bush responded that 'certainly not the U.N. position' and that there was 'no flexibility on Iraq getting out of Kuwait...' The following day when Bush briefed congressional members in the Old Executive Office Building he reiterated the objectives: 'the

immediate, complete, and unconditional withdrawal of all Iraqi forces...'
and the restoration of the Kuwaiti government. He appealed to those assem-
bled to work in bipartisan unity and emphasised that no one at home ought
to doubt his commitment to work with Congress and that no one abroad
ought to doubt 'our national unity or staying power'.[29]

And while he identified the strong international condemnation of Iraq
there were clearly misgivings on the intransigent stance and a series of
attempts to find some diplomatic solution. But the yardstick had been set:
no negotiations on complete withdrawal. For his part Saddam Hussein had
indicated that he intended to hold Kuwait permanently, a position that
would subsequently change before the US led UN intervention. There were
small signs of a tentative shift in early September, just days after Bush's
strong statement. Pérez de Cuéllar met with Tariq Aziz in Amman. Following hours of talks Aziz emerged alone and reiterated the links between
Iraqi and Israeli withdrawal. But calling for 'quiet diplomacy' he hinted at
the option of working with Arab leaders to find a solution. Still nothing
definitive developed.[30]

The Soviet intervention was far more significant. While ultimately the
transcripts reveal a narrative of communion between Moscow and Washington
there were underlying tensions on the approach to Iraq. In essence the Soviets
also made the link between Iraq and Israel and proposed an international conference that would consider the two issues. Though Soviet Foreign Minister,
Eduard Shevardnadze, emphasised that they felt 'duty bound' by the UN resolutions, he emphasised the importance of a diplomatic settlement and
explained that the priority 'should unquestionably be given to non-military
means'. He indicated that both the Chinese and North Koreans shared the
view. A part of the concern was not just the earlier US stance on diplomacy,
but also the prospect that the United States might build up forces in
Saudi Arabia and leave them there. Some Soviet officials departed from the
Kremlin's script voicing concern on such prospects. Days later following the
extended meeting between Bush and Gorbachev in Helsinki the *New York
Times* reported the fundamental differences that underlay the US and Soviet
preferences on talks, but Gorbachev took the opportunity to emphasise a
message just delivered by Bush, when Gorbachev confirmed, 'that the United
States of America does not intend to leave their forces in the zone'. Nevertheless, James Baker had paved the way for a pre-emptive strike on the diplomatic option indicating that they would like to 'see a little bit more of what
the Soviets have in mind'.[31] The differences were clearly stark beneath the
surface unity. Days before, Tariq Aziz met with Gorbachev in the Kremlin
and while Moscow maintained its criticism of Iraq, it insisted that it would
maintain diplomatic relations and *Tass* reported that Soviet officials favoured
'exhaustive use of political means to settle the crisis...'[32]

In early October 1990 there were gestures towards further diplomatic
solution or potential, but none evolved. President François Mitterrand
suggested that it would suffice for Iraq to promise withdrawal to start

negotiations. But Hussein quickly indicated that he would not withdraw his forces until Western forces had been withdrawn from the region. In turn Bush quickly asserted that they required an unconditional withdrawal before negotiations could be held. He did however put a positive tone on his remarks to the United Nations in early October indicating that following withdrawal there would be an opportunity to explore a permanent settlement between the two countries. He even went so far as to implicitly link the Iraqi occupation of Kuwait with the Israeli occupation of land that Syria and Jordan lost in the 1967 War by mentioning the two issues in one sentence. (That linkage was subsequently rejected by Baker when the Soviets mooted it again in mid-November).[33] By mid-October the US and Kuwaiti officials rejected an offer by Saddam Hussein to pull his troops out of Kuwait in return for 'peace'. By that point, despite the positive statements on a negotiated solution, Brent Scowcroft, the National Security Advisor, had advanced an idea for a tougher UN resolution on the use of force.[34]

Ultimately the response was not just about bringing about an effective solution to this crisis, but also to demonstrate in the recently identified 'new world order' that such aggression could not stand. The Secretary of State, James Baker, told his audience at the Los Angeles World Affairs Council that Iraqi's aggression 'shatters the vision of a better world in the aftermath of the Cold War'. Even if a formula could have been found to kick-start negotiations, short of Iraq's complete compliance with UNSC resolution 660, there were other sentiments working against these options.

Munich and the derivative analogies had been used frequently by Bush administration officials throughout the autumn of 1990: that sense of history that the appeasement of a dictator for short term benefit only led to protracted and devastating war down the line. Though Baker worried more than Bush about the Vietnam analogies Munich was still influential. Baker outlined that at this point in time 'Iraq's invasion of Kuwait is a clear, indeed historic, challenge to the rest of the international community.' The US reversal of that aggression would define a post-Cold War world as a 'place where civilized rules of conduct apply'. In direct reference:

> The rest of the world is trying to go forward with the 1990s. But Saddam Hussein is trying to drag us all back into the 1930s. And we know what that means: The tempting path of appeasing dictators in the hope that they won't commit further aggression. The self-defeating path of pretending not to see what was really happening as small nations were conquered and larger nations endangered. And then finally, war at terrible cost.[35]

But if, by analogy, diplomacy was denigrated, it was not just about the international community and the potential lessons for the new era, it was also about a vision of world order dominated by US power that would soon be set out in the Defense Planning Guidance (DPG) documents.

On one level war was not inevitable; sanctions and diplomacy were not pursued to their logical conclusion. The sanctions regime was deemed to be working effectively. There were several violations but Iraq's isolation was increasingly severe. A range of speakers provided testimony in US Congressional hearings to the effect that the sanctions were indeed effective. Admiral William Crowe argued that US current attitudes toward Hussein 'crowded out many other considerations...' Sanctions ought to be given a 'fair chance' and that even if they took 12–18 months it would be worth pursuing them given the sacrifices that war would entail. Those who advocated war, according to Crowe, sold the US short:

> It is curious that just as our patience in Western Europe has paid off and furnished us the most graphic example in our history of how staunchness is sometimes the better course in dealing with thorny international problems, a few armchair strategists are counselling a near-term attack on Iraq.

General David Jones supported the position. William Webster, Director of the CIA, similarly testified that sanctions were effective, though it was uncertain when they might produce results. It was unlikely that they would be effective before the UN-imposed deadline for complete withdrawal of 15 January 1991. Former Secretary of Defense, James Schlesinger, informed Congress that sanctions would be far more cost effective even if pursued over 11 months than the resort to war. However, he argued, additional US motives were becoming apparent; these motives limited Iraq's ability to voluntarily withdraw. This not only related to the unconditional demand for complete withdrawal, but also to the US desire to undermine Iraq's capacity to intimidate, to eliminate its military capability and to remove Hussein from power. Schlesinger argued that these were counterproductive to US stated objectives:

> The general effect is to paint Iraq as a rogue or outlaw state, and that its menace to its neighbours and to the international order must be eliminated. To the extent that these additional objectives are embraced, either in appearance or reality, the prospect for a voluntary Iraqi withdrawal from Kuwait is sharply diminished. To achieve these objectives there is really no alternative but to resort to war.[36]

It is within the context of the discussion on sanctions and the emerging disagreements between the United States and some of its allies and within the United States that the Bush administration pushed for the UN to adopt the next stage: the authorisation to use 'all necessary means to uphold and implement Resolution 660'.[37] UN Security Council Resolution 678, adopted by 12 votes to 2, with an abstention from China set 15 January as a deadline for Iraq to withdraw from Kuwait. The resolution and accompanying statements reinforced the demand for a complete and unconditional withdrawal. The time frame was presented as a demonstration of resolve, but also as an indication that the subsequent 47 days could be used to search for a diplomatic solution; the timetable would force the issue. But the timetable also denigrated the possibility that sanctions might work in the mid to longer term. Moreover, Washington's credibility was also on the line. As the *New York Times* pointed out, if time were allowed to elapse after that date 'without using force they would seriously [undermine] the credibility of the American and allied military threat'. They speculated that Saddam Hussein might try to engage the United States in diplomacy by offering a partial withdrawal as the basis for further dialogue; and given the internal US opposition to the war and some Congressional wariness it would be difficult to avoid such negotiations.[38] Hussein's response was one of defiance, asserting that Iraq was prepared to fight and, playing on what he hoped would invoke memories of Vietnam, that they even had some mysterious technology that could detect US stealth bombers.[39]

Bush simultaneously dispelled any notions of diplomatic compromise or US inhibition brought on by invocations of Vietnam. In a lengthy opening statement at a press conference he advanced proposals for Aziz to travel to Washington and Baker to travel to Baghdad. Not to seek compromise, but to present the face of US resolution. He talked about going the extra mile to basically persuade Hussein to 'reconsider his position and to take the steps necessary for a peaceful resolution of the crisis. But it isn't a trip of concession.' While the talks were intended to invite Iraqi reconsideration, Saddam Hussein seemed to have more faith in the Vietnam syndrome than the members of the Bush administration and perhaps banked on their reconsideration. In a now infamous press conference Bush attempted to dispel the Vietnam analogy, in part to allay the remaining Congressional reticence. He argued:

> I know there are fears about another Vietnam. Let me assure you, should military action be required, this will not be another Vietnam. This will not be a protracted, drawn-out war. The forces arrayed are different. The opposition is different. The resupply of Saddam's military would be different. The countries united against him in the United Nations are different. The topography of Kuwait is different. And the motivation of our all-volunteer force is superb.

And he continued:

> we will not permit our troops to have their hands tied behind their backs. And I pledge to you: There will not be any murky ending. If one American soldier has to go to battle, that soldier will have enough force behind him to win. And then get out as soon as possible.[40]

Despite the numerous and limited attempts to find a diplomatic solution none could be secured. Washington's promise to go the extra mile to secure a diplomatic resolution needs to be placed within the context of maintaining consensus on military action. Just as it was necessary to demonstrate that sanctions were both effective (to maintain the coalition) and ineffective (to legitimate war), so too with the diplomatic track. There had to be strenuous efforts in pursuit of talks, but these were always choked by the condition for total and unconditional withdrawal; diplomacy had to be seen to be conducted *and* pursued to failure. Without the alternatives of sanctions and diplomacy and with the reassurances that the war would not be another Vietnam, Congress was far more likely to provide their consent for war. But diplomacy was still 'one final box that had to be checked'. James Baker was sent to Geneva to meet Tariq Aziz. After a lengthy meeting he emerged to inform those gathered: 'I met Mr. Aziz today not to negotiate, as we had made clear we would not do, that is, negotiate backwards from UN Security Council resolutions.' It was understood that the talks would not achieve desired results. James Schlesinger, dismissed the likelihood of their success in Congressional testimony because no effective communication could occur till Iraq left Kuwait, in effect producing the stated objective of US and UN policy. Technically, the middle ground for compromise was missing. Washington could not offer anything short of capitulation for fear of reviving the narratives on appeasement following the analogies with Munich that had been sown, and Baghdad, hoping that the balance of force would not be so uneven, banked on inflicting sufficient damage to caution the US hand; moreover, Hussein could not accept an unconditional ultimatum. The Long Island newspaper *Newsday* reported that US regional specialists considered that there were 'serious' possibilities for diplomacy. The *New York Times* reported that Washington 'intended to block the "diplomatic track", ... for fear that negotiations might "defuse the crisis"'.[41]

UN Secretary General Javier Pérez de Cuéllar met Saddam Hussein in Baghdad on 13 January 1991. Hussein characterised the UN resolutions as 'American resolutions'; they reflected US objectives not those of the Security Council. De Cuéllar conceded that 'I agree with you...' Hussein indicated that Washington complicated the situation because while they demanded total withdrawal, 'they do not say where to, irrespective of Iraq's views'. In fact resolution 660 was clear that it was the border line of 1 August 1990. Hussein traced Kuwait's expansion into Iraq on a map for de Cuéllar.

> Here were Kuwait's borders when it was a protectorate ... it then expanded to here, and then to this point in a place called Mitllah. I think you should write down this name. This is the way the Kuwaitis were until 1963. Mr. Yassar Arafat's passport is stamped in Mitllah ... so ... when someone says let Iraq withdraw, the question is where to?[42]

Hussein had been significantly influenced by his reading of the Vietnam War. He had told Glaspie, 'yours is a society which cannot accept 10 000 dead in one battle'. He knew that his could; they had no choice. Glaspie later affirmed that this effort to play on the Vietnam syndrome was frequent in Baghdad, pointing out in Congressional testimony that 'it was a very common misapprehension about us'.[43] Bush was determined that the syndrome would not inhibit the prosecution of war, but an administration study from February 1990 before the Iraqi invasion concluded that

> For small countries hostile to us, bleeding our forces in protracted or indecisive conflict or embarrassing us by inflicting damage on some conspicuous element of our forces may be victory enough, and could undercut political support for US efforts against them.

It was therefore necessary to defeat weaker regional enemies, according to the document, 'decisively and rapidly'. The war was not just about the limited and defined UN supported objectives, it was also now about US credibility and its emerging security agenda; it was not just about Iraq, it was also about US power. Bush asserted:

> When we win, and we will, we will have taught a dangerous dictator, and any tyrant tempted to follow in his footsteps that the U.S. has a new credibility, and that what we say goes, and that there is no place for lawless aggression in the Persian Gulf and in this new world order that we seek to create.[44]

Washington set out its rationale as the UN-imposed deadline for withdrawal passed on 15 January 1991. The National Security Directive asserted that 'access to Persian Gulf oil and the security of key friendly states in the area are vital to U.S. national security'. Sanctions had a 'measurable impact upon Iraq's economy but have not accomplished the intended objective of ending Iraq's occupation of Kuwait' and 'there is no persuasive evidence that they will do so in a timely manner'. It was imperative to take military action because

> prolonging the current situation would be detrimental to the United States in that it would increase the costs of eventual military action, threaten the political cohesion of the coalition of countries arrayed against Iraq, allow for the continued brutalization of the Kuwaiti people and destruction of their country, and cause added damage to the U.S. and world economies.

In addition the 'United States recognizes the territorial integrity of Iraq and will not support efforts to change current boundaries'. If Iraq attempted to use chemical, nuclear or biological weapons or lent its support to terrorism, NSD 54 indicated 'it shall become an explicit objective of the United States to replace the current leadership of Iraq'.[45]

Unintended consequences of transformation

The haste with which war was approached was matched by the haste with which it was brought to a temporary conclusion. Despite the narratives of justice and proportionality that attended the rhetoric prior to the 1991 war it was soon clear that the Iraqi navy was destroyed easily, its air force defected to Iran to preserve its machinery and the reference to Iraq's fourth largest army in the world focused on numbers rather than capability. What was clear was that this regional state engaged the US-led forces without Soviet backing in what Lawrence Freedman characterised as 'a ridiculously unequal contest'. Though Bush might have been confident that this would not be another Vietnam, that view was not shared by Powell. Indeed the potential Iraqi damage to US forces was a frequent theme in Iraqi meetings with US officials. April Glaspie testified that the argument on 10 000 US casualties was a frequent refrain, not just a line in her infamous meeting with Saddam Hussein on 25 July 1990. Freedman argues that 'given the litany of horrors widely expected to be inflicted on the allies, there was reason to question their readiness to sustain the conflict over an extended period. This was always Saddam's best hope.' Back in 1991 Freedman observed that the Gulf War would serve to illustrate the gap between the advanced powers and those who aspired to that status, but he added a pre-scient caveat that 'this is true so long as the war is fought on a wholly conventional basis'. Hitherto, during the Cold War the gap between these forces was somewhat masked by the engagement of the other superpower that had ultimately served to humble their opponent; witness the US defeat in Vietnam and the Soviet defeat in Afghanistan because 'an irregular enemy refus[ed] to engage regular forces on their own terms'.[46]

The restraints that Freedman had identified immediately became operative in the decision to end the war abruptly. Though there was subsequently considerable controversy over who was on board the decision was made to end the war after 100 hours, when they had in the words of Bush announced from the Oval Office at 9.02 pm EST: 'Kuwait is liberated. Iraq's army is defeated. Our military objectives are met.' Various positions have been rehearsed in the memoirs. For his part Powell asserts that all key players had been consulted and though some subsequently backed off the decision, that was their call at the time. Shortly after, Norman Schwarzkopf infamously retracted his earlier decision in an interview with David Frost when he in effect questioned why they had not continued 'the march'. Though he moderated his position in his memoir, It Doesn't Take A Hero, the sentiment that it was a mistake not to press the advantage and move on into Baghdad to capture Saddam Hussein soon spread. Though Powell had argued that the infliction of further casualties was unnecessary and pointed out that others, especially Secretary of State James Baker, worried about the 'effect on world opinion of pointless killing'. Scowcroft argued that after such a brilliant military operation, 'fighting beyond necessity would leave a bad taste...' Moreover, the objectives had been secured and US officials worried about the cohesion of the coalition should they expand war aims. Still, within the Pentagon it was soon reported that Desert Storm was regarded as 'unfinished business' and the fear as one army officer was quoted as saying in 1992, was that 'we're going to be back ... doing this again in three to five years'.[47]

Yet the obvious restraints were there. Robert Gates, Deputy National Security Adviser during the war, later Director of the CIA and currently Secretary of Defense, explained in 1993 why they had left Saddam Hussein alone. The issue was discussed at length; he frequently chaired the Deputies Committee, which comprised sub-cabinet level officials brought together to iron out department disagreements, and by and large they feared that Saddam Hussein might go into hiding as Noriega had done in Panama after the US invasion of 1989. Gates explained that it was feared that US casualties would mount in an extended drive on Baghdad and that ultimately: 'We specifically decided not to make it a war aim so that we would not set ourselves objectives that we were not confident we could accomplish.'[48]

It was those restraints that aggravated some of the strategic thinking in the Bush administration. Though the conclusive victory was supposed to have a demonstration effect, and act as a deterrent to regional hegemonic ambitions or challenges to US power, the Gulf War had not entirely provided that optimum scenario. First drafts of the now famous Defense Planning Guidance (DPG) document, originally leaked to the *New York Times*, were declassified in December 2007. In a memorandum by Dale Vesser to 'Scooter', the first draft of the DPG argued that the end of the Cold War might introduce a period of hegemonic instability in which either the Soviets or US 'may tend to watch the actions of clients less closely and put less pressure on them to refrain from provocative actions'. Iraq's intervention was referenced in this regard:

> The net result may be that serious regional challenges to US interests, while ultimately less dangerous, may in fact become more likely. For the near term, this tendency may be balanced somewhat by the high degree of political-military credibility the US gained as a result of Desert Storm.

Nevertheless, the Department of Defense would likely be called on to address regional challenges and 'various *ad hoc* command, communication and logistics arrangements, such as those created for Desert Shield/Storm will be necessary'.[49] Later drafts brought in the now familiar language associated with the pursuit of 'strategic depth'. Washington's first objective was to 'prevent the re-emergence of a new rival...' and that they should 'endeavor to prevent any hostile power from dominating a region whose resources would, under consolidated control, be sufficient to generate global power' (Western Europe, East Asia, the territory of the former Soviet Union and Southwest Asia). The document advocated a strong demonstration of US leadership; potential competitors should be actively deterred 'from even aspiring to a larger regional or global role'. The strategy argued that the US could not become the world's 'policeman', but selectively it would have to 'retain the pre-eminent respons-ibility' for addressing the wrongs that threaten US interests, including 'access to vital raw materials, primarily Persian Gulf oil; proliferation of weapons of mass destruction and ballistic missiles; threats to US citizens from terrorism or regional or local conflict...'[50] Of course, much of the sentiment of the stra-tegic documents reappeared in altered form in George Bush's 2002 National Security Strategy paper, but in 1992 its leak caused some embarrassment to the administration, who hastily redrafted the paper. Despite the controversy Cheney, then Secretary of Defense, was according to James Mann, 'effusive'. He told Zalmay Khalilzad, then a Wolfowitz aide, later ambassador to Afghanistan: 'You've discovered a new rationale for our role in the world.' The concept of strategic depth was formulated to place the United States in the position as 'the world's dominant superpower – not merely today, or ten years from now, or when a rival such as China appears, but permanently'. As Lewis I. Libby, then nominee for the position of Under Secretary of Defense for Policy, explained to a Congressional committee, the idea was to move beyond the balance of power configuration of international relations. Libby explained:

> It is not in our interest or those of other democracies to stand back and leave a vacuum in regions critical to our interests, and thereby increase the chances of returning to earlier periods when multiple military powers balanced one against another in what passed for security struc-tures while regional or even global peace hung in the balance. As in the past, such struggles might eventually force the United States to protect its interests at much higher costs and much higher risks.[51]

If in the 1970s and 1980s Washington's attempts to improve relations with Saddam Hussein represented a form of the realist attempts to balance power within the region, especially after the Iranian Revolution, and if the Gulf War (1991) generated two narratives (on decisive power and incomplete victory), it presaged a period across the 1990s that was characterised by a form of dual containment associated with punitive sanctions. Then the war in 2003, facilitated by the ideological structures after 9/11, was filled with the vision to move away from concepts of balance, into an era that would supposedly diminish risks the US had to face.

Notes

1 Steven Lee Myers and Thom Shanker, 'Petraeus Urges Halt in Weighing New Cut in Force', *New York Times*, 9 April 2008; General David H. Petraeus, Com-mander, Multi-National Force – Iraq, Report to Congress on the Situation in Iraq, US Senate Hearing, Committee on Foreign Relations, *Iraq After the Surge: What Next*, 110th Cong., 2nd sess., 8 April 2008.
2 John Dumbrell and David Ryan, 'Introduction' in their edited *Vietnam in Iraq: Tactics, Lessons, Legacies and Ghosts* (London: Routledge, 2007), 5; James Mann, *Rise of the Vulcans: The History of Bush's War Cabinet* (New York: Penguin, 2004).

3 General David H. Petraeus, Commander, Multi-National Force – Iraq, Report to Congress on the Situation in Iraq, US Senate Hearing, Committee on Foreign Relations, *Iraq after the Surge: What Next*, 110th Cong., 2nd sess., 8 April 2008.
4 See Cary Fraser's article in this collection.
5 James A. Baker and Lee H. Hamilton, *The Iraq Study Group Report* (New York: Vintage, 2006), 45.
6 President George W. Bush, President Bush Congratulates General Petraeus on Senate Confirmation, Discusses Way Forward in Iraq, The White House, 26 January 2007, at www.whitehouse.gov/news/releases/2007/01/print/20070126.html.
7 The Glaspie Transcript, 25 July 1990, in Micah L. Sifry and Christopher Cerf (eds), *The Gulf War Reader: History, Documents, Opinions* (New York: Random House, 1991), 122–133.
8 Assistant Secretary of State for Near Eastern and South Asian Affairs (Kelly), 31 July 1990, *Developments in the Middle East: July 1990*, Hearing before the Subcommittee on Europe and the Middle East of the Committee on Foreign Affairs, House of Representatives, 101st Cong., 2nd sess. (Washington, 1991), in Department of State, *American Foreign Policy Current Documents 1990* (Washington, DC: Department of State, 1991), 451–452.
9 Assistant Secretary of State for Near Eastern and South Asian Affairs (Kelly), 28 February 1990, *Developments in the Middle East: February 1990*, Hearing before the Subcommittee on Europe and the Middle East of the Committee on Foreign Affairs, House of Representatives, 101st Cong., 2nd sess. (Washington, 1990), in Department of State, *American Foreign Policy Current Documents 1990* (Washington, DC: Department of State, 1991), 431–432.
10 Kelly, 28 February 1990, *Current Documents 1990*, 432.
11 John Lichfield, 'How Bush Went From Weakness to Strength', *The Independent* (London), 10 August 1990.
12 Richard Nixon, 'Why', *New York Times*, 6 January 1991.
13 Meeting chaired by Henry Kissinger, 28 April 1975, declassified 7 June 2001, National Security Archive Briefing Book, no. 82 (25 February 2003). See also David Ryan, *Frustrated Empire: US Foreign Policy, 9/11 to Iraq* (London: Pluto, 2007), 77–96.
14 Memorandum of conversation, Sadun Hammadi, Minister of Foreign Affairs of Iraq, and Henry Kissinger, Secretary of State, Iraqi Ambassador's Residence, 17 December 1975, NSA, Book 82.
15 Alexander Haig, Secretary of State, Department of State telegram to USINT Baghdad, 8 April 1981, document 5, NSA, Book 82; USINT Baghdad to Secstate, Department of State telegram, Morris Draper meeting with Foreign Minister Hammadi, 12 April 1981, document 6, NSA, Book 82.
16 William L. Eagleton to Department of State, telegram, 'Meeting with Tariq Aziz', 28 May 1981, document 10, NSA, Book 82.
17 President Ronald Reagan, National Security Decision Directive 114, 'US Policy toward the Iran-Iraq War', 26 November 1983.
18 Nicholas A. Veliotes and Jonathan Howe information memorandum to Lawrence Eagleburger, 'Iran-Iraq War: Analysis of Possible US Shift from Position of Strict Neutrality', 7 October 1983, NSA, Book 82.
19 USINT Baghdad to American Embassy Amman, 'Talking points for Amb Rumsfeld's meeting with Tariq Aziz and Saddam Hussein', December 1983, NSA, Book 82.
20 American Embassy Rome to Secretary of State, Washington DC, telegram, Rumsfeld's larger meeting with Iraqi Deputy, December 1983, NSA, Book 82.
21 Secretary of State, Shultz to USINT Baghdad, telegram, US Chemical Shipment to Iraq, 3 March 1984, document 42, NSA, Book 82.

22 Secretary of State to American Embassy Khartoum, telegram, Briefing notes for Rumsfeld visit to Baghdad, March 1984, NSA, Book 82.

23 Joyce Battle, 'Shaking Hands with Saddam Hussein: The U.S. Tilts towards Iraq, 1980–1984', National Security Archive Briefing Book, no. 82 (25 February 2003).

24 President Ronald Reagan, National Security Decision Directive 139, 'Measures to Improve U.S. Posture and Readiness to Respond to Developments in the Iran-Iraq War', document 53, NSA, Book 82.

25 Defense Estimative Brief, 'Prospects for Iraq', DEB-85–84, 25 September 1984, NSA, Book 82.

26 An Intelligence Estimate, 'Iraq's National Security Goals', Central Intelligence Agency, December 1988, NSA, Book 82.

27 Ibid.

28 UN Security Council Resolution 660 (1990) adopted 2 August 1990 and Statement by the Permanent Representative to the United Nations, Thomas Pickering, before the UN Security Council, 2 August 1990 both in *Current Documents 1990*, 454–455.

29 George H.W. Bush, statement, Chances for diplomatic solution, Kennebunkport, Maine, 27 August 1990 and Bush, statement, Old Executive Office Building, 28 August 1990, both in *Current Documents*, 489–490.

30 John F. Burns, 'U.N. Chief's Talk With Iraqi Breaks Off Inconclusively', *New York Times*, 2 September 1990.

31 Francis X. Clines, 'Soviets Suggest Conference Combining Issues of Mideast', *New York Times*, 5 September 1990; Eduard A. Shevardnadze, address in Vladivostok, 4 September 1990 in *New York Times*, 5 September 1990; Bill Keller, 'Bush and Gorbachev says Iraqis Must Obey U.N. and Quit Kuwait', *New York Times*, 10 September 1990; Joint text George Bush and Mikhail Gorbachev, Helsinki, 9 September 1990, *New York Times*, 10 September 1990; Joint news conference Bush and Gorbachev, Helsinki, 9 September 1990, in *Congressional Quarterly*, 15 September 1990.

32 Francis X. Clines, 'Top Iraqi Aide Sees Gorbachev On Gulf Crisis', *New York Times*, 6 September 1990.

33 AP, 'Diplomatic Chronology of the Gulf War', *New York Times*, 22 February 1991.

34 Maureen Dowd, 'Bush at UN Sees Hope in Diplomacy in the Gulf Crisis', *New York Times*, 2 October 1990; Michael R. Gordon, 'Top Soviet General Tells U.S. Not to Attack in Gulf', *New York Times*, 3 October 1990.

35 James Baker, 'Why America Is in the Gulf', address before the Los Angeles World Affairs Council, 29 October 1990, in *Current Documents*, 524–525; Jeffrey Record, *Making War, Thinking History: Munich, Vietnam, and Presidential Uses of Force from Korea to Kosovo* (Annapolis: Naval Institute Press, 2002), 103.

36 Crowe, cited in Bob Woodward, *The Commanders* (New York: Simon and Schuster, 1991), 331–332; DCI William Webster, Statement to House Armed Services Committee, 5 December 1990, in James Ridgeway (ed.), *The March to War* (New York: Four Walls Eight Windows, 1991), 154–157; James Schlesinger, 'Crisis in the Persian Gulf Region: U.S. Policy Options and Implications', Hearings, Committee on Armed Services, US Senate, 101st Cong., 2nd sess., 11 September to 3 December, 1990, 118.

37 Thomas L. Friedman, 'Baker Trip Shows Coalition Discord on War with Iraq', *New York Times*, 11 November 1990; UN Security Council Resolution 678, 29 November 1990, in E. Lauterpacht *et al.*, *The Kuwait Crisis: Basic Documents*, Cambridge International Document Series (Cambridge: Grotius, 1991), 98.

38 Thomas L. Friedman, 'Lighting the Fuse', *New York Times*, 30 November 1990.

39 Philip Shenon, 'Defiant Iraqi President Declares He Is Ready for War Against U.S.', *New York Times*, 30 November 1990; Record, *Making War*, 107.

40 George H.W. Bush, U.S. Proposal for Direct Discussions With Iraq, press conference, 30 November 1990, *Current Documents*, 545–546.

41 Woodward, *Commanders*, 355; Schlesinger, Hearings, Committee on Armed Services, 118; Lawrence Freedman and Efraim Karsh, *The Gulf Conflict 1990–1991: Diplomacy and War in the New World Order* (London: Faber, 1993), 431; Noam Chomsky, *World Orders, Old and New* (New York: Columbia University Press, 1994), 10.

42 Transcript of Pérez de Cuéllar-Hussein meeting, 13 January 1991, as 'A Bitter Cup of Coffee in Baghdad', *The Independent* (London), 14 February 1991. De Cuéllar's office indicated that the release of the transcript was a breach of diplomatic protocol, and not the same as the version they had, though they did not have a problem with its substance. See also: Pierre Salinger with Eric Laurent, *Secret Dossier: The Hidden Agenda Behind the Gulf War* (London: Penguin, 1991), 212–221.

43 April Glaspie, testimony, *United States-Iraqi Relations*, Hearing, Subcommittee on Europe and the Middle East, Committee on Foreign Affairs, House of Representatives, 102nd Cong., 1st sess., 21 March 1991, 37.

44 Glaspie Transcript, 25 July 1990, in Sifry and Cerf, *Gulf War Reader*, 122–133; Bush cited by Jonathan Mirsky, 'Reconsidering Vietnam', *The New York Review of Books* 28, no. 15 (10 October 1991), 44; NSD document cited by, Maureen Dowd, *New York Times*, 23 February 1991; Robert W. Tucker and David C. Hendrickson, *The Imperial Temptation: The New World Order and America's Purpose* (New York: Council on Foreign Relations, 1992), 86–93, 152–159; Ryan, 'Asserting US Power', in Philip John Davies (ed.), *An American Quarter Century: US Politics from Vietnam to Clinton* (Manchester: Manchester University Press, 1995), 119.

45 George Bush, Responding to Iraqi Aggression in the Gulf, National Security Directive 54, White House, 15 January 1991.

46 Lawrence Freedman, 'A Superpower Victorious but Not Unrestrained', *The Independent* (London), 1 March 1991; Record, *Making War*, 105; April Glaspie, testimony, *United States-Iraqi Relations*, Hearing, Subcommittee on Europe and the Middle East, Committee on Foreign Affairs, House of Representatives, 102nd Cong., 1st sess., 21 March 1991, 37.

47 Colin Powell, *A Soldier's Way: An Autobiography* (London: Hutchinson, 1995), 519–525; Douglas Waller *et al.*, 'The Day Bush Stopped the War', *Newsweek*, 20 January 1992.

48 Jim Mann, 'Gates Tells Why US Left Saddam Alone', *Guardian* (London), 9 January 1993.

49 Dale A. Vesser to Scooter, Office of the Principal Deputy Under Secretary of Defense, First Draft DPG, 3 September, 1991, secret excised copy, document 2, The Making of the Cheney Regional Defense Strategy, 1991–1992, National Security Archive, at www.gwu.edu/~nsarchiv/nukevault/ebb245/ index.htm.

50 Dale A. Vesser, memorandum for Secretaries of the Military Departments, Chairman of the Joint Chiefs of Staff, Undersecretary of Defense for Acquisition, and others, 18 February 1992, document 3, The Making of the Cheney Regional Defense Strategy, 1991–1992, National Security Archive. Online at www.gwu.edu/~nsarchiv/nukevault/ebb245/index.htm.

51 James Mann, 'The True Rationale? It's a Decade Old', *The Washington Post*, 7 March 2004; Lewis I. Libby, testimony, *Defense Planning, Guidance and Security Issues*, Hearings, Committee on Armed Services, United States Senate, 102nd Cong., 2nd sess., 3 June 1992, 6; Mann, *Rise of the Vulcans*.

4 Lost in the desert

Lawrence and the theory and practice of counterinsurgency

Marilyn B. Young

When he was just 12, his father – a philosophy professor – gave [David Kilcullen] a copy of Lawrence's Seven Pillars of Wisdom, which he has carried ever since. 'It's fairly battered now!' he laughs. 'I do believe we can learn a great deal from him.'

David Kilcullen.[1]

This is the best training ground in the world. For the German troops it was Spain, right? Well, Iraq is ours.

Marine Lieutenant General James Mattis, March, 2006.[2]

Twice a week the Insider column of InsideDefense.com offers 'defense professionals' useful news and notes from Congress, the Department of Defense and the defence industry more generally. In early December 2004, the Insider ran a special report on the 'book picks' of US generals and intelligence experts. Among the 100 titles listed, T.E. Lawrence's *The Seven Pillars of Wisdom* was the second most recommended, along with his *Revolt in the Desert*, and Michael Asher's biography, *Lawrence: The Uncrowned King of Arabia*.[3] Lt. General James Mattis, who had served in Iraq, agreed with his colleagues that *Seven Pillars* was vital but added to the list a collection of Gertrude Bell's letters. She was, after all, the woman 'who practically invented modern Iraq'. Somewhat further down on the list was a book detailing Britain's colonial successes and America's imperial failures: Robert Thompson's *Defeating Communist Insurgency: Experiences from Malaya and Vietnam*. Following the Thompson recommendation, a natural connection, John Nagl's *Learning to Eat Soup with a Knife: Counterinsurgency Lessons from Malaya and Vietnam*. The title is a quotation from T.E. Lawrence, in his guise as rebel mentor: 'To make war upon rebellion is messy and slow, like eating soup with a knife.' Nagl's book was devoted to demonstrating that it could be done.

This chapter is about the American romance with the British Empire as expressed in an ongoing fascination, on the part of defence professionals of all sorts, with T.E. Lawrence.[4] I want to examine this romance of imperial counterinsurgency with some care because of the role it plays in current US policy in Iraq and Afghanistan. The gap between the theory of counterinsurgency and the practice of the US military in the Middle East, like the gap between theory and practice in Vietnam over 30 years ago, is an abyss into which US policymakers have carefully managed not to look.

It is only meat that Lawrence's name should crop up in so many American newspaper articles beginning with the American invasion of Iraq in 1990, given that his fame was in part the invention of the American journalist Lowell Thomas. Ambitious and convinced of the power of film to tell a story, in 1917 Thomas raised the money to take himself and a cameraman to Europe to film the war. He gathered material for some 18 months, sent not a single dispatch home, and when the war ended found no one particularly interested in what he had collected. Undaunted, Thomas put together several multi-media events, one on the American Expeditionary Force, a second on the Italian Front, a third on the British campaigns in the Middle East. No one seemed at all interested in the first two, but Allenby in Jerusalem and Lawrence in Arabia drew huge crowds.

For four years, Thomas toured the world with it, delivering his lecture 4000 times, while his 240 lantern slides filled the screen, along with some 30 film segments. Invited by a British impresario to bring his show to London, Thomas renamed it 'The Last Crusade' and presented it at the Royal Opera House, among other venues. (The cover of the programme described the show as 'America's Tribute to British Valour'.[5]) In an orchestra pit decorated with palm trees, the Welsh Guard played Oriental music and incense wafted through the hall. The curtain rose to reveal a painted backdrop of moonlight on the Nile before which a dance of the seven veils put the audience entirely in the mood as Thomas invited them to 'come with me to lands of mystery, history, and romance'. Among tens of thousands of others, Rudyard Kipling, George Bernard Shaw, Winston Churchill, and members of the royal family accepted the invitation and Lloyd George told the press that 'in my opinion, Lawrence is one of the most remarkable and romantic figures of modern times'.[6] Until Thomas finally put the performance to rest in 1928, he had been joined in those lands of mystery, history and romance by four million viewers.

Lawrence was the perfect antidote to the trenches and mass death of World War I. The desert, like Lawrence himself, was clean and white, blue skies and blue eyes and death was individual and honourable. Ronald Blythe explained what the English liked about him:

> his amateurism, his 'modesty' and his make-your-own-kingdoms kit. He reappeared on the scene when patriotism had become rather smudgy and before empire worship had been safely channeled off into royalty worship, which left quite a lot of emotion going begging.[7]

Americans loved him, according to Lowell Thomas, because they identified with the Arab struggle for self-determination. Lawrence, Thomas wrote, was the 'George Washington of Arabia'. They kept loving him as Lawrence's desert exploits morphed into Hollywood 'sun and sand' epics from Rudolph Valentino in 1921 to Peter O'Toole in 1962. And when the United States, in 1990, moved in force into Lawrence's old stomping grounds, he re-possessed the American imagination, camel, burnoose and all.[8]

Lawrence's example was, after all, geographically appropriate to the US effort in the Middle East. Russell Baker commented on this early in Gulf War I when he reflected on the way the TV evening news shows were reporting the war: 'He had been the first to get into Baghdad', he began his regular op-ed column in the late summer of 1990. 'That's why they called him Koppel of Arabia.' Soon Koppel was joined by Dan Rather and America became 'Number One in Anchors of Arabia'. Older audiences remembered when Peter O'Toole, Anthony Quinn and Omar Sharif 'all suited up at the same time for action in the deep sand'. They weren't newsmen but they might have done 'a terrific job of telling an America desperate for news – was the desert still hot?'[9] Given the tight restrictions placed on reporters by the government, informing the TV audience that the desert was still hot was about as much illumination as the news offered or the public seemed to want.

Norman Schwarzkopf, the commanding general in the first Gulf War, had Lawrence – or more exactly, Peter O'Toole – in mind as well. 'Turning self-consciously this way and that, I couldn't help but think of the film *Lawrence of Arabia*, in which Peter O'Toole dressed in Arab garb for the first time, swirls slowly around on sand dunes, admiring himself.'[10] Schwarzkopf as Peter O'Toole as Lawrence of Arabia: the white man in the desert, saving help-less Kuwaitis from the vicious legions of Saddam Hussein; Lawrence as the sign and symbol of American righteousness. Steven Caton has read the movie as an 'anti-imperialist Orientalist' epic; one might say the same of America's self-understanding of its Persian Gulf crusades.[11] As Rumsfeld put it shortly after the US took Baghdad: 'We don't do empire.' Colin Powell agreed: 'We are not an empire.... We come here as liberators.' An anonymous official of the Coalition Provisional Authority was more circumspect: 'Of course we are an empire', he told an American reporter, 'but we are different. Our empire is not defined by territorial ambitions but by ideas. A lot of ideas, like free trade, like democracy, like copyright laws.' And of course 'to help the Iraqi people build their own future'.[12]

Lawrence was not an inappropriate model for those who wished to build nations in the desert. He had, after all, helped to install the Hashemite dynasty in two countries carved out of the Ottoman Empire in Arabia – Mesopotamia and Transjordan. His next reincarnation was in the person of Paul Wolfowitz, aka Wolfowitz of Arabia. (One blogger has suggested it is a reasonable match: like Lawrence, Wolfowitz's dedication to the cause of democracy in the Middle East was inspired not by love for all Arabs but for just one very lovely Arab.)[13] Wolfowitz seems to have acquired his sobriquet at the very beginning of the war and it always appears without quotation marks. For most commentators it remained a cleverly demeaning nickname (especially the diminutive: Wolfie of Arabia).[14] But some took the title more literally, among them Richard Cummings, writing for *The American Conservative* in May 2003, who argued that Wolfowitz planned no less than the restoration of the Hashemite kingdom under the auspices of Sherif Ali bin al-Hussein, a descendant of Lawrence's old friend and ally.[15]

Few of those who delighted in calling Wolfowitz 'of Arabia', noted a signal difference between the two men. Not only did Wolfowitz not speak Arabic (even 'passably', as Lawrence was said to have done) but he was entirely ignorant of the country he urged his government to invade and conquer. In an appearance before the House Budget Committee shortly before the invasion, he derided the notion that a major commitment of US troops was required in Iraq. That country would pose none of the problems still at issue in the Balkans:

> There's been none of the record in Iraq of ethnic militias fighting one another that introduced so much bloodshed and permanent scars in Bosnia, along with a continuing requirement for large peacekeeping forces to separate those militias. And the horrors of Iraq are very different from the horrific ethnic cleansing of Kosovars by Serbs that took place in Kosovo and left scars that continue to require peacekeeping forces today in Kosovo. The slaughter in Iraq – and it's been substantial – has unfortunately been the slaughter of people of all ethnic and religious groups by the regime. It is equal opportunity terror.[16]

In an interview on National Public Radio in mid-February, 2003, Wolfowitz sharply corrected interviewer Melissa Block's suggestion that the 'the presence of U.S. troops in Saudi Arabia' had inflamed groups like al Qaeda who saw 'U.S. occupation or U.S. presence in that country as something that they must fight against. How would it be any different in Iraq?' For a start, Wolfowitz replied, once the 'Iraqi threat' was dissolved, there would no longer be any need for US troops in Saudi Arabia. But more significantly:

> The Iraqis are among the most educated people in the Arab world. They are by and large quite secular. They are overwhelmingly Shia which is different from the Wahabis of the peninsula, and they don't bring the sensitivity of having the holy cities of Islam being on their territory. They are totally different situations. But the most fundamental difference is that, let me put it this way. We're seeing today how much the people of Poland and Central and Eastern Europe appreciate what the United States did to help liberate them from the tyranny of the Soviet Union. I think you're going to see even more of that sentiment in Iraq.

As for the suggestion that there might be some hostility to the US military presence in the region, if not in Iraq itself, Wolfowitz responded firmly: 'It's hard to see how people externally can complain if the Iraqi people are saying these people came and liberated us.'[17]

Although Wolfowitz's knowledge of Iraq was minimal, he was, like Lawrence, a deft hand at Orientializing the country. 'America is on an orientalist rampage', Jonathan Raban observed. The abuse in Abu Ghraib prison only pointed to the larger context in which Arabs were systematically 'denatured, dehumanized, stripped of all human complexity...' In the 'perorations of Wolfowitz of Arabia', Raban recognized 'the ghostly voice of TE Lawrence....'[18] As the war in Iraq slid inexorably into the hellish stew with which we have all become familiar, Wolfowitz, like Robert McNamara when he left the Johnson administration, moved on to become President of the World Bank, briefly.

Meanwhile, back in Iraq, as the multiple insurgencies no one in the Bush administration had predicted gained force, the press, journals and TV filled with Vietnam era analogies. As was also the case during and after the Vietnam War itself, the call went out for an effective counterinsurgency strategy. Here, although few of those who are fond of citing him recognize it, Lawrence is an uncertain, even an untrustworthy guide. Whatever his ultimate relationship to British imperialism and Arab nationalism, during the war against the Turks Lawrence fought with and as a guerrilla, an insurgent, not a counterinsurgent.

A similar cognitive displacement and false identification plagued counterinsurgency experts in the Kennedy administration. Roger Hilsman, briefly one of Merrill's Marauders in the China–Burma–India theatre during World War II, later an officer in the OSS and finally head of the State Department's Bureau of Intelligence and Research, was very fond of Vo Nguyen Giap's account of the war against the French in Indochina, *People's War, People's Army*. He wrote the preface to its 1962 re-publication in English. The new nations, Hilsman wrote, are

> struggling toward freedom, and toward democracy. But in the villages of these nations, men live isolated from the men in the next village, as their fathers and grandfathers before them have lived for thousands of years.... In the village world we cannot win through H-bombs or through television networks. Even in the day of the missile and the bomber, the Southeast Asian fighting is frequently hand to hand. To counter it, we must understand the elements of man-to-man war as practiced by Lawrence of Arabia, Tito of Yugoslavia or the 'raiders' and 'rangers' of American history.[19]

Apart from Hilsman's ignorance of the actual organization of village life – threaded through with networks of all kinds – what is striking is his notion that the US in Vietnam could function as a people's army fighting a people's war.[20]

Lt.-Colonel John Nagl, now retired, also sought to learn Lawrence's lessons.[21] He was among a larger cadre of officers with combat experience and advanced degrees, most of whom have written dissertations about why the

US did not win in Vietnam.[22] Nagl had served in Iraq as Operations Officer of the First Battalion of the 34th Armored Regiment (aptly known as the 'Centurions') from September 2003 to September 2004. During that time, he was interviewed by Peter Maass of the *New York Times*. Maass, who had read his book – *Learning to Eat Soup with a Knife: Counterinsurgency Lessons from Malaya and Vietnam* – understood the reference to Lawrence, and reported with considerable sympathy the difficulties Nagl was having putting counterinsurgency doctrine into practice. What upset Nagl most was his inability to communicate to the hostile Iraqis in whose midst he led his patrols, that

> what we want for them is the right to make their own decisions, to live free lives. It's probably hard to understand that if you have lived your entire life under Saddam Hussein's rule. And it's hard for us to convey that message, particularly given the fact that few of us speak Arabic.

But what upset him even more was the fact that the Iraqis whose hearts and minds he sought to win were shooting at him. 'I'm not really all that concerned about their hearts right now', he told Maass. 'We're into the behavior-modification phase.'[23]

In 2005, Nagl's book was re-issued with a new preface, disarmingly called 'Spilling Soup on Myself', and reflecting on his battlefield experience. It had all proven to be far more difficult than he'd imagined. His admiration for Sir Gerald Templer's success in Malaya remained undimmed, but he realized that he had not sufficiently taken into account that 'when the insurgency began, [the British] had been in the country for well over a century, developing long-term relationships and cultural awareness that bore fruit in actionable intelligence'.[24] More significant was Nagl's conviction, shared by all those who write about counterinsurgency in Iraq, that most Iraqis have been intimidated into cooperation with the insurgents.[25] He was confident that the majority of Iraqis 'prefer the American vision of a democratic and free Iraq to the Salafist version of Iraq as Islamic theocracy'.[26] That not all insurgents are Salafist does not, and cannot be allowed, to enter into Nagl's analysis. Despite his experience in Iraq and his Oxford DPhil in International Relations, Nagl's understanding of the world has remained entirely ideological: 'The United States', he wrote in his new preface, 'is working diligently in Iraq, as it did in Vietnam, to improve the lives of the people.'[27]

Nagl quoted Lawrence only once. General David Petraeus, recently appointed to command all forces in Iraq, on the other hand, quotes Lawrence frequently. He is the latest in the long line of Lawrentian Americans in Arabia. Like Nagl, Petraeus earned a doctoral degree (his from Princeton) with a thesis on the lessons of Vietnam. He served in Bosnia and later commanded the 101st Airborne in Iraq. In mid-2004, he was put in charge of training Iraqi security forces.[28] In January 2007, he replaced General George W. Casey, Jr. as over-all commander in Iraq, and, despite the opposition of some senior military men, requested and was granted an additional 30 000 troops – a surge, the Bush administration insisted, not an escalation. In the words of an admiring article in *Esquire Magazine*, he is 'the closest thing the Army has to its own Lawrence of Arabia'. Petraeus does not discourage the comparison – in this a true avatar –

> as he seems to identify with the British colonel's experiences in the region ... and the enduring wisdom of his advice to those military officers caught in similar trying circumstances (Lawrence's legendary book, *Seven Pillars of Wisdom*), which Petraeus appears to know by heart.[29]

Once more, the oddness of the identification of counterinsurgents with insurgents goes unnoticed because, like Petraeus himself, the reporter takes it as self-evident that Americans are always and everywhere on the side of freedom, guerrillas for democracy.

Of course anyone would rather identify with Peter O'Toole than with his enemies. But the problem is national rather than individual. Americans have always been loath to see themselves in the position of the colonial power, the occupier, not the liberator; if as the occupier, only for the purpose of building an independent nation. This seems to be the way General Petraeus understands himself.

> 'Everyone does nation building', Petraeus insisted. All US field commanders have to do the hard work of 'drinking tea with the locals, delivering air conditioners to the mosques, meeting with the neighborhood units, getting to know the imams, and all the rest of that.'

He quoted, as does the new Field Manual on Counterinsurgency compiled under his aegis, Lawrence's unfortunately condescending aphorism: 'Better the Arabs do it tolerably than that you do it perfectly. It is their war, and you are to help them not to win it for them.' But neither Petraeus nor the manual continue to the next sentence: 'Actually, also, under the very odd conditions of Arabia, your practical work will not be as good as, perhaps, you think it is.'[30] Lawrence's relationship to the British Empire in the Middle East was at best ambivalent. Petraeus, by contrast, is very clear: 'I don't think we are an empire. We don't have imperial designs. I think we'd be happy to live and let live.... We aren't here to stay.'[31]

Marine Lieutenant General James Mattis is another Lawrence acolyte, but with a dash of General George S. Patton. Speaking on a panel at the Armed Forces Communications and Electronics Association, Mattis-as-Patton observed that it was 'quite fun to fight them, you know. It's a hell of a hoot'. As the audience laughed appreciatively, Mattis continued: 'It's fun to shoot some people. I'll be right up there with you. I like brawling. You go into Afghanistan, you got guys who slap women around for five years because they didn't wear a veil. You know, guys like that ain't got no manhood left anyway. So it's a hell of a lot of fun to shoot them.'[32] He says as much to his troops. 'The first time you blow someone away is not an insignificant event. That said, there are some assholes in the world that just need to be shot.... It's really a hell of a lot of fun. You're gonna have a blast out here!... I feel sorry for every son of a bitch that doesn't get to serve with you.' His motto: 'Be polite, be professional, but have a plan to kill everybody you meet.'[33]

Mattis takes history seriously. Before the 1st Marine Division returned to Iraq (they had been part of the initial assault) he assigned about 1000 pages of required reading to all the officers and provided written explanations of his choices. Among these were several newspaper articles detailing the dispropor- tionate violence of some Army units in Iraq. One concerned a battalion commander's mistreatment of a prisoner: 'this shows a commander who has lost his moral balance or has watched too many Hollywood movies. By our every act and statement, Marine leaders must set a legal, moral and ethical model....' Lawrence set the standard of proper behaviour. Mattis assigned his Twenty-Seven Articles, stressing the importance of local knowledge. His message, according to one officer, was 'Iraqis aren't your enemy, don't let the insurgents make you think that. *The people are the prize*' (emphasis in original).[34]

Ironically, Mattis commanded the Marines in the destruction of Fallujah in April 2004.[35] It was a mission of which he disapproved, convinced the best response to the mutilation of several private security guards, the proxi- mate cause of the attack on the city, should have been a police operation. Nevertheless, he followed orders and Operation Vigilant Resolve began on 5 April. On 9 April the city smoking in ruins, uncounted dead, injured, thousands made refugees, the attack was called off for reasons of bad public- ity. Mattis was enraged, convinced the Marines were on the verge of victory and that the retreat would only strengthen the insurgents. He did not command the Marines in the second battle of Fallujah in November 2004 during which what was left of the city was pulverized and a Carthaginian victory declared.

I want to discuss a third Lawrence devotee and then turn to a discussion of why Lawrence, 70 years after his exploits in a campaign that has been called a side-show of a side-show, continues to resonate for American military men and their journalist camp followers. David Kilcullen is a veteran of the Australian army (he served with the UN force in East Timor), holds a PhD in political anthropology from the University of New South Wales (his dissertation was on a separatist Muslim insurgency in West Java) and served as Senior Counter- Insurgency Adviser to Gen. Petraeus in 2007. Earlier, Wolfowitz had invited him to participate in the writing of the Pentagon's new Quadrennial Defense Review and when Wolfowitz left office, Kilcullen moved to Condoleeza Rice's counter-terrorism office. According to a breathless account of his thinking by George Packer, he was in part responsible for introducing the term 'the long war' into the Quadrennial Review. On the model of the Cold War, the term is now regularly used to describe the current conflict and seems to have replaced the Global War on Terror (GWOT).

Kilcullen's heroes, Packer wrote, 'are soldier-intellectuals, both real (T.E. Lawrence) and fictional (Robert Jordan, the flinty-self-reliant school-teacher turned guerrilla who is the protagonist of Hemingway's *For Whom the Bell Tolls.*)'[36] Like others who have fought against guerrillas whose fighting skills they admired, Kilcullen confided to Packer – as he showed him a knife he'd lifted off a militiaman he'd ambushed in East Timor – that he'd be a jihadist if he were a Muslim. After all, he too is driven by what he assumes to be the basic motivations of jihadists: 'a sense of adventure, wanting to be part of the moment, wanting to be in the big movement of history that's happening now...'

Packer was much taken with Kilcullen. He describes him sitting down one night with a bottle of single malt Scotch and writing his Twenty-Eight Articles, on the model of Lawrence's Twenty-Seven. In Kilcullen's view, counterinsurgency is basically 'armed social work; an attempt to redress basic social and political problems while being shot at'.[37] The local population need not like you; calculated self-interest will do.

There are many differences between Lawrence writing from a specific battlefield about a specific group of Arabs and Kilcullen imagining himself into a company commander's position and writing instructions for counterinsurgency as such. But the most striking difference is that Lawrence's reflections on guerrilla war were precisely instructions *to* guerrillas. As David Fromkin put it, Lawrence 'taught how to wear down an opponent: a strategy that will win only against an enemy that will surrender if tired, an enemy, therefore, fighting to hold on to something it can afford to give up'. It allowed a weaker force to 'sap the resources – and therefore the will to continue fighting – of a Great Power that cannot be defeated face-to-face in the field'. Perfect, therefore, for anti-colonial rebellions. 'And it is a typical paradox of [Lawrence's] career', Fromkin wrote, 'that he, the hero of British imperialism, should have become an inspirer of the Third World's revolt against the imperial West'. Once again, it is an unrecognized paradox for Lawrence's American admirers that his lessons are basically about how to defeat the US in Iraq.[38]

Kilcullen sounds sensible. He is clear on the importance of disaggregating the various insurgencies around the world so that local grievances are addressed rather than being lumped together as examples of terrorism. Yet, at the same time, he is convinced that classic counterinsurgency, 'designed to defeat insurgency in one country', will no longer do. The long war, in his view, is about 'global counterinsurgency'. There is a lurking contradiction here which Kilcullen does not recognize; nor did Packer push the point. And the contradictions multiply. Kilcullen is full of praise for American civic action in Afghanistan. 'Before conducting operations in a given area', Kilcullen told Packer, 'soldiers sit down over bread and tea with tribal leaders and find out what they need – Korans, cold-weather gear, a hydroelectric dynamo.' In exchange for local support, the Americans then produce the desired goods, demonstrating 'what can be gained from cooperating'. (Let us leave aside widespread reports of US bombing and wanton firing on civilians.)

Yet he thoroughly disapproves of NATO's 'development model' of counterinsurgency, which seems to be based on the futile hope 'that gratitude for good work would bring the Afghans over to their side.' Nonsense, Kilcullen insists.

> In a counterinsurgency, the gratitude effect will last until the sun goes down and the insurgents show up and say, 'You're on our side, aren't you? Otherwise, we're going to kill you.' If only one side is ready to apply lethal force to bring the population to its side and the other side isn't, ultimately you're going to find yourself losing.[39]

In *Seven Pillars* Lawrence offered two contradictory accounts of the meaning of his time in the desert. In one he is the guilty deceiver of the Arabs with whom he fought; in the other, he shared their longing for freedom and independence. The contradiction was resolved in his post-war efforts to make the 'Arabs ... our first brown dominion, and not our last brown colony'.[40] As a member of Churchill's Colonial Office, Lawrence played a role in the ultimate disposition of Iraq and Transjordan, both of which, as I mentioned earlier, would be governed by Hashemite monarchs friendly to and dependent upon Great Britain. Here Lawrence *is* an appropriate mentor for Americans: like them, an aspiring nation-builder; like them, building nations whose sovereignty, having been granted them by an outside power, would always be less than full. Winston Churchill, Lawrence's boss, added another element relevant to the contemporary US effort: a determination to build airbases in Iraq so that – in his words – the Royal Air Force could 'operate in every part of the protectorate and to enforce control, now here, now there, without the need of maintaining long lines of communications eating up troops and money'.[41] For his part, Lawrence believed that with the establishment of Palestine, Transjordan and Iraq, 'England is out of the Arab affair with clean hands'.[42] Leaving the US with two out of the three.

It may be that at some point the US goal of establishing permanent bases in Iraq under the benevolent eye of a pliant, stable government will be realized. At the moment the contradictions in US policy exist in another realm and are perhaps best illustrated by the fact that General Petraeus, the apostle of 'nonkinetic' counterinsurgency has had, until recently, Raymond Odierno as his second in command. Odierno was well known in Iraq for the aggressive conduct he encouraged in the troops under his command in Iraq in 2003–2004. 'The 4th ID [infantry division] was bad', Tom Ricks quotes an Army intelligence officer remarking: 'These guys are looking for a fight ... I saw so many instances of abuses of civilians, intimidating civilians, our jaws dropped.'[43] By contrast, when Petraeus commanded the 101st Airborne during that same year, he abandoned abusive 'cordon and search' operations. In light of events like Haditha, Petraeus wrote a letter addressed to all 'Soldiers, Sailors, Airmen, Marines, and Coast Guardsmen serving in the Multi-National Force-Iraq'. He pointed out that:

> Our values and the laws governing warfare teach us to respect human
> dignity, maintain our integrity, and do what's right. Adherence to our
> values distinguishes us from our enemy. This fight depends on securing
> the population, which must understand that we – not our enemies –
> occupy the moral high ground.

He appealed to the troops to report abuses, to confess to combat stress if
they experienced it, to treat all Iraqis with respect and dignity.[44]

Yet the reality of combat in Iraq, of occupation, of the assiduously
uncounted deaths of Iraqi civilians at the hands of American troops, of the
invisible air war, makes Petraeus's plea hollow. Examples abound. In mid-
March, 2008, American soldiers 'accidentally shot and killed a young girl'.
Observing a woman they deemed 'suspicious', troops fired a warning shot – and
the girl was hit. Military officials referred to this as an 'escalation of force incident', explaining that an improvised explosive device had been found 'in the
region where the shooting occurred'.[45] The more American troops on the streets
– which is part of the current counterinsurgency surge – the more likely such
deaths. Yet another counterinsurgency expert, Kalev Sepp, 'doubts there are
enough mid-level Army officers who fully understand the complex tactics
needed to win over local populations when US units move into neighborhoods
en masse'. The sentence is oxymoronic: no amount of understanding on the part
of mid-level Army officers can transform a foreign army moving into neighborhoods en masse into the armed social workers of Kilcullen's dreams.[46]

Lawrence, probably embraced by most of his American admirers in the shape
of Peter O'Toole, seems to be the opposite of all that. He offers the US military
men who adore him the possibility of a fighting unambiguously on the right
side, a friend of the people, a hero to Arabs and American audiences alike.
Moreover, he was a warrior. He *had been there* – in the ubiquitous phrase of all
veterans. The romance of Lawrence is the romance of America the Good, as first
presented to both Americans and Englishmen in Lowell Thomas' travelogue.

I referred earlier to General Mattis' schizophrenic combination of Patton
and Lawrence, a combination I think marks the entire American enterprise
in Iraq – and perhaps the American empire as such. An insistence on
concern for the population, a deep conviction that force must be judiciously
mixed with politics, a cult-like devotion to the benefits of democracy, and in
practice an indifference to the results of democratic elections should they not
suit American needs, a cult-like devotion to the free market, and a ferocious
military machine intent on imposing the will of the US on the Middle East
or any other area of the world considered necessary to the security of the
American system. Petraeus has not yet found his Lowell Thomas, but Mattis
may soon command movie screens in the person of Harrison Ford, who is
slated to play him in a movie based on the book written by Bing West, *No
True Glory: The Battle for Fallujah*.[47]

There has been one officer in Iraq so torn by the contradictions of the US
war in Iraq that he might be compared to Lawrence – or at least to David

Lean's Lawrence. Ted Westhusing committed suicide in Baghdad in May 2005, one month before he was due to return home from his six-month tour in Iraq. (Or – similar rumours surround Lawrence's death – perhaps he was murdered.) After completing a dissertation on the notion of honour in war, Westhusing taught military ethics at West Point until, impelled by his conviction that the war in Iraq was just and convinced that going there would make him a better teacher of his subject, he volunteered for service.[48] A friend recalled: 'He wanted to serve, he wanted to use his skills, maybe he wanted some glory.'[49] Instead, according to his friends, what he saw in Iraq 'drove him to this.... It's because he believed in duty, honour, country that he's dead.'[50]

In Iraq, Westhusing was assigned to train Iraqi security forces under the general supervision of two senior officers – Joseph Fil and David Petraeus. Part of his job was to oversee the work of USIS, a private firm with multimillion dollar contracts. Within a short time, Westhusing was convinced that USIS was both corrupt and in violation of the restrictions on security firms engaging in combat (members of USIS had boasted of the killing they did during the first battle of Fallujah). He sent increasingly despondent emails to his family. On the afternoon of 5 June 2005, Westhusing shot himself to death (though the circumstances remain murky), leaving behind an angry note addressed to Petraeus and Fil:

> Thanks for telling me it was a good day until I briefed you. [Redacted name] – You are only interested in your career.... I cannot support a msn [mission] that leads to corruption, human rights abuses and liars. I am sullied – no more.... I came to serve honorably and feel dishonored. I trust no Iraqi. I cannot live this way.... Death before being dishonored any more.... Why serve when you cannot accomplish the mission, when you no longer believe in the cause.... Reevalute yourselves, cdrs [commanders]. You are not what you think you are and I know it.[51]

An Army psychologist concluded that despite

> his intelligence, his ability to grasp the idea that profit is an important goal for people working in the private sector was surprisingly limited ... nor could he change his belief that doing the right thing because it was the right thing to do should be the sole motivator for businesses.[52]

Months later, an Army investigation into Westhusing's charges that human rights abuses and corruption had been ignored found that 'commands and commanders [i.e. Fils and Petraeus] operated in an Iraqi cultural and ethical environment often at odds with Western practices'. When Westhusing's wife was asked what had happened to him, she answered, 'Iraq.' In the movie version of his life, at least, the same was true of T.E. Lawrence. In the real world of the present, Iraq is definitely what is happening to the US; even worse, as Westhusing knew, the US has happened to Iraq.

Notes

1 Christina Lamb, 'Lawrence of Arabia Takes on the Taliban', *Sunday Times* (London), 11 March 2007. The article, accessed 6 June 2007 from *Timesonline.com*, is about David Kilcullen, an Australian anthropologist currently serving as chief adviser to General Petraeus.

2 Quoted in Thomas P.M. Barnett, 'The Monks of War', *Esquire*, March, 2006.

3 Elaine M. Grossman, 'To Understand Insurgency in Iraq: Read Something Old, Something New', The Insider, Insidedefense.com, 2 December 2004. The most recommended book was by Col. Thomas Hammes' *The Sling and the Stone: On War in the 21st Century*. Ryan Dilley reported that sales of *Seven Pillars* had doubled in the UK with the start of the Iraq war. Dennis Hart of Wordsworth Editions considered this a 'significant increase for a title such as this'. Ryan Dilley, 'Lessons from Lawrence of Arabia', BBC News Online Magazine, 9 April 2004.

4 In addition to Lawrence and Malaya, the third most popular reference for counterinsurgency theorists is the French empire and in particular, Algeria. Early on in the Iraq War, the Pentagon offered free showings of 'The Battle of Algiers', and David Galula's book on counterinsurgency in Algeria is on all the Pentagon reading lists. The French, at least as represented by David Galula's book on Algeria, are also much on the minds of contemporary counterinsurgency experts. Galula makes the top 100 cut and the note on his book, *Counterinsurgency Warfare: Theory and Practice*: reads

> 'May I suggest that you run – not walk – to the Pentagon library and get in line' for this book, says one retired CIA officer with counterinsurgency experience in Vietnam, who asked not to be named. Finding a copy ... is 'almost impossible', but Galula's writing should be regarded as a 'primer for how to win in Iraq', says this source.

5 L. Robert Morris and Lawrence Raskin, *Lawrence of Arabia: The 30th Anniversary Pictorial History* (New York: Doubleday, 1992), 9. Morris and Raskin have an interesting chapter on the many attempts to make a movie out of *Seven Pillars*.

6 Ibid., 8.

7 Quoted in Joel Hodson, *Lawrence of Arabia and American Culture* (Westport, Conn.: Greenwood Press, 1995), 60.

8 David Fromkin adds another element: the delight of Englishmen in the possibility of 'perpetual boyhood', as exemplified by the literature of Lawrence's time and after: Peter Pan and the Wind in the Willows among others. I would suggest the sentiment was shared by American men then and since. See, 'The Importance of T.E. Lawrence', *The New Criterion* (newcriterion.com), 10:1 (September 1991).

9 Russell Baker, 'The Oasis Crowd', *New York Times*, 25 August 1990, p. 23.

10 Quoted in Steven C. Caton, *Lawrence of Arabia: A Film's Anthropology* (Berkeley, CA: University of California Press, 1999), 172.

11 In several early essays I wrote on the Gulf War, like many other commentators, I remarked on the alacrity with which conservative critics were embracing the word empire as a description of the US in the twenty-first century. A few, like Richard Haas, who served briefly in Colin Powell's State Department, allowed as how the US was an empire, but denied it was 'imperialist'. Outside observers, most prominently Niall Ferguson, berated the country for its reluctance to go all the way and govern its empire, as the British had so ably done in the past. What's interesting is how completely all the empire talk disappeared as the war in Iraq went sour.

12 Charles M. Sennott, 'The Imperial Imperative', *Boston Globe* (boston.com), 8 February 2004.
13 Steve Sailer (iSteve.com), 18 March 2005. Sailer quotes from an interview with Lawrence about why he had fought for Arab independence. His answer: 'Personal: I liked a particular Arab, and I thought that freedom for the race would be an acceptable present.' Sailer suggested that Shaha Riza played a similar role in inspiring Wolfowitz's dedication to democratizing the Middle East.
14 See, for example, Jane Perlez, 'A Nation at War', 3 April 2003, *New York Times*, who uses the phrase as if it were already in circulation. She was reporting from Kuwait about the group of experts around Jay Garner still awaiting the order to move on to Baghdad.
15 Richard Cummings, 'Wolfowitz of Arabia', *The American Conservative*, 5 May 2003.
16 Juan Cole, 'Awful Crap from Wolfowitz', Informed Consent, 9 March 2005 (juancole.com/archive).
17 Transcript of Wolfowitz interview with Melissa Block, NPR radio, available on the US Department of Defense Office of the Assistant Secretary of Defense (Public Affairs), www.defenselink.mil/transcripts. 19 February 2003.
18 Jonathan Raban, 'Emasculating Arabia', *Guardian* (London), 13 May 2004.
19 Preface to *People's War, People's Army*, vii–ix.
20 Of course, as Edward Luttwak has pointed out, the Romans, Ottomans and the Wehrmacht did figure out how to defeat insurgencies through the implacable and ruthless exercise of force for as long as it took to wipe out the rebels. He could have added the US in the Philippines at the turn of the twentieth century. Luttwak imagines the US loathe to employ such means. See Edward N. Luttwak, 'Dead End: Counterinsurgency Warfare as Military Malpractice', *Harper's Magazine*, February 2007.
21 His book, *Learning to Eat Soup with a Knife: Counterinsurgency Lessons from Malaya and Vietnam*, originally published by Praeger (an old CIA outlet) in 2002 for a hefty $97.95, was re-published by Chicago University Press as a handsome paperback with a new preface for a modest $17.00 in 2005, and sells briskly on Amazon.com.
22 A few, like Andrew Bacevich, left the military for the academy and have written extensively in opposition to American militarism and the war in Iraq. Lawrence, of course, moved in the opposite direction, from the world of scholarship to the military. Lt.-Col. Ralph Peters wrote a vitriolic attack on the practice of officers going to civilian universities for anything other than language training. They emerged 'diseased with theory', and in danger of losing their ability to 'become the visceral killer any battlefield demands'. He was particularly contemptuous of an officer whose writings were all about hearts and minds but whose practice in Iraq was, quite properly in Peters' view, to strap dead insurgents to their tanks and drive around the neighborhood 'for the locals to get a good look at'. Ralph Peters, 'Learning to Lose', *American Interest Online*, July–August 2007. The same issue has an article by David Petraeus, 'Beyond the Cloister', full of praise for graduate education for officers.
23 Peter Maass, 'Professor Nagl's War', *New York Times Magazine*, 11 January 2004, 30.
24 John Nagl, *Learning to Eat Soup*, xiii.
25 Andrew Krepinevich reached similar conclusions about the National Liberation Front. In his account of the failure of the US to pursue counterinsurgency properly in Vietnam, he wrote: 'The support of the people does not, however, necessarily imply their support for the aims and goals of the insurgent, although this is, of course, desirable. Rather, the support of the people is a measure of the insurgents' ability to control the people, whether through their willing

cooperation or as the result of threats, acts of terrorism, or the physical occupation of their community. T.E. Lawrence recognized this when he stated that "rebellions can be made by 2 percent active in a striking force, and 98 percent passively sympathetic". Thus, the insurgent need not possess the hearts and minds of the population, only the minds – the people's acquiescence, willing or unwilling, in the revolutionary cause.' Note the transformation of Lawrence's 98 percent sympathetic acquiescence to 'willing or unwilling acquiescence'. Andrew Krepinevich, *The Army and Vietnam* (Baltimore: Hopkins Press, 1986), 9.

26 Ibid., xiv.
27 Ibid., xiii.
28 See Michael Moss and David Rohde, 'Misjudgments Marred U.S. Plans for Iraqi Police', *New York Times*, 21 May 2006. Moss and Rohde did a series on the subject, tracking the disaster of police training in Iraq.
29 Thomas P.M. Barnett, 'The Monks of War', *Esquire*, March 2006. He worked as a 'strategic consultant' for Rumsfeld's Department of Defense from 2001–2003.
30 T.E. Lawrence, 'Twenty-Seven Articles', *The Arab Bulletin*, 20 August 1917. Available online from the U.S. Army Command and General Staff College Combined Arms Research Library. The other 26 articles are equally interesting and rarely quoted. Lawrence is explicit. His notes refer only 'to Bedu; townspeople or Syrians require totally different treatment.... Handling Hejaz Arabs is an art, not a science, with exceptions and no obvious rules'.
31 Quoted in Sennott, 'The Imperial Imperative...'
32 'General: It's fun to shoot some people', CNN.com, 4 February 2005; streaming video still available 14 June 2007 at CNN.com.
33 Thomas E. Ricks, *Fiasco: The American Military Adventure in Iraq* (London: Allan Lane, 2006), 313.
34 Ibid., 318.
35 This account comes from Ricks, 330–346 *passim*.
36 George Packer, 'Knowing the Enemy', *The New Yorker*, 18 December 2006, 62. See also Joel Hodson, *Lawrence of Arabia and American Culture*, which makes a similar connection, 96 ff.
37 David Kilcullen, 'Twenty-eight Articles: Fundamentals of Company-level Counterinsurgency', March, 2006, 8.
38 David Fromkin, 'The importance of T.E. Lawrence', *The New Criterion*, 10:1, September 1991 (accessed from www.newcriterion.com/archive/10/sept91).
39 George Packer, *Assassins' Gate: America in Iraq* (New York: Farrar, Straus and Giroux, 2005), 63–64. One of the articles observes that in an ideal world each company would have a political/cultural adviser attached to it. Apparently a pilot programme to make this happen has been launched. According to Packer, the Pentagon is currently recruiting social scientists who will form five person 'human terrain' teams and be attached to combat brigades.
40 David Fromkin, *A Peace to End All Peace* (New York: Henry Holt, 1989), 501.
41 Ibid., 500.
42 Ibid., 529.
43 See Ricks, *Fiasco*, 232–233.
44 Petraeus Letter, 10 May 2007.
45 The same story in the *New York Times* records the death of 16 Iraqi bus passengers in Basra. The US military claimed a roadside bomb had killed them; Iraqi survivors said the deaths were due to US troops firing after the bomb had exploded. Erica Goode, 'U.S. Troops Kill Iraqi Girl; 3 Soldiers Die in Attack', *New York Times*, 13 March 2008, accessed online 15 March 2008.
46 Sepp goes on to say that without these officers, 'you just end up with another group of foreign occupation troops shooting civilians who they feel threaten

them when their car drives too close to them'. Or, as soldiers used to say in Vietnam, 'shit happens'. Tina Susman, 'Close and deadly contact: the killing of an Iraqi teen offers a rare look at how US military action in an urban setting can be fatal to civilians', *Los Angeles Times*, 12 June 2007. Perhaps predictably, as counterinsurgency has begun to dominate US military planning and training, there has been a growing debate within the military over both its efficacy and its wisdom. One retired colonel, Douglas Macgregor, warned that its popularity has made military intervention more likely in the future. 'I think it's downright dangerous', he told an interviewer,

> because it suggests that we can repeat the folly of Iraq. That somehow or another, next time we can get it right without understanding that if the population is living within a social structure that doesn't want change, if the population doesn't want you in the country, if there is no legitimate government to begin with, your intervention is doomed to inevitable failure.
> (Guy Raz, 'Army Focus on Counterinsurgency Debated Within', National Public Radio report, 8 May 2008 (at www.npr.org/templates/ story/story.php?storyID=90200038))

47 Darrin Mortenson, 'Indiana Jones actor may play Mattis in Fallujah film', *North Country Times: The Californian*, 21 December 2004. NCTimes.com. Bing West is a Marine who served as Assistant Secretary of State under Reagan. He recently wrote an op-ed piece for the *New York Times* with his son, Owen, a stock broker in New York who has served in Iraq. The Wests believe the answer to the insurgency is biometric identification of every man, woman and child in Iraq – and troops equipped with laptops that can check them out. They are also upset at the number of Iraqi detainees who are regularly released from prison. There are only 40 000 people in Iraqi prisons at the moment. 'Texas, with a smaller population, has more than 170 000 in jail.' The problem lies with the 'vastly excessive civil rights protections for detainees'. Thus far, 'to his credit', Petraeus has resisted calls for a mass release of detainees and 'the result is prison over-crowding since the surge began'. The Wests do not comment on it and presumably they would be for it, but the crowded prisons are a direct result of how liberally Iraqis are swept into US and Iraqi prisons. See Owen and Bing West, 'The Laptop is Mightier than the Sword', *New York Times*, 15 June 2007.
48 See Robert Bryce, 'I am Sullied-No More', *Texas Observer*, 9 March 2007 for an account of Westhusing as a 'true Believer'.
49 Quoted in T. Christian Miller, 'The Conflict in Iraq', *Los Angeles Times*, 27 November 2005. Westhusing received his PhD in philosophy from Emory University for a thesis that focused on the notion of honour in war, using examples that ranged from Robert E. Lee to the Israel Defense Force.
50 Bryce, 'I am Sullied-No More'.
51 Ibid.
52 Quotes are from Lt. Col. Lisa Brietenbach, Miller, *Los Angeles Times*.

5 Grand ambitions and far-reaching failures

The United States in Iraq

Toby Dodge

Introduction

The United States' invasion of Iraq in 2003 was the centre-piece of a far-reaching and ambitious plan to re-work post-Cold War international relations.[1] The removal of Saddam Hussein was designed to send an unmistakable message not only to the ruling elites of the Middle East but to the post-colonial world more generally. The right to sovereign non-intervention born of decolonisation was now only to be granted if a new set of responsibilities were met. A new democratic regime in Iraq was meant to signal the lengths America would go to in a post-9/11 world to impose the Bush doctrine on recalcitrant regimes. However, what the neoconservatives at the heart of the Bush administration planned as a short sharp demonstration of America's unrivalled hegemony turned out to be a bloody occupation mired in state collapse and civil war. After two terms in the White House, George W. Bush will leave the quagmire that Iraq has become to his successor to sort out. Far from being a triumph, the invasion has highlighted profound short-comings in the projection of American power out of area. Tragically it has been the long-suffering people of Iraq who have had to pay the greatest price for this exercise in neoconservative hubris. After suffering 35 years of brutal dictatorship and over a decade of the harshest sanctions ever imposed, they now face a violent and profoundly uncertain future. As US public opinion increasingly demands that the US severs its ties with Iraq, the costs will be borne by the Iraqi people as they face continued inter-communal strife, civil war and state collapse.

Grand ambitions: Iraq and the Bush doctrine

The United States' goals for post-regime change Iraq were nothing if not ambitious. For the President's foreign policy team, 9/11 had 'ended the decade of complacency'.[2] The aftermath of al Qaeda's attacks on the twin towers and the Pentagon were seen as an opportunity to rework the envelope within which previous American foreign policy had been conducted. The domestic mood after 9/11 gave the Bush administration the opportunity to move away from the 'soft power' that the US had deployed since the end of the Cold War[3] to a much more coercive war of manoeuvre.[4] The US administration felt it could now use violence to deal with obstacles that had dogged the Clinton presidency. They, temporarily at least, managed to overcome public scepticism about US military action overseas to develop the 'forward leaning' approach to reordering world politics that key members of the administration had been advocating for more than a decade.[5]

Leading hawks, most notably Richard Cheney and Donald Rumsfeld, made the case for defining post-9/11 terrorism in the broadest possible way, going well beyond the immediate hunt for al Qaeda.[6] Although Bush appeared initially reluctant to pursue this grand vision, by the time of the State of the Union Address on 29 January 2002, the notion of terrorism had been stretched to include the 'axis of evil' facing America: Iraq, Iran, North Korea 'and their terrorist allies'. The State of the Union Address and more overtly *The National Security Strategy of the United States*, published that September, forged the issues of rogue states, Weapons of Mass Destruction and terrorism into one homogenous threat to the continued security of the American people. The foreign policy agenda that sprung from such a broad and wide-ranging definition focused on the unilateral and pre-emptive deployment of US military might as the only solution to these supposed new and increasingly pervasive threats.[7]

This new 'grand strategy' attempted to develop an answer to the problems posed by the more troublesome or unstable creations of decolonisation.[8] Their 'right' to sovereignty would now only be granted when post-colonial states had met their 'responsibilities' to the international community.[9] All means necessary, diplomatic, financial and, after 9/11, military would be deployed to convince the ruling elites of errant states that it was in their interests to conform to these new demands.

However, for the Bush administration, as it set about applying its new doctrine in the aftermath of 9/11, the Ba'athist regime in Baghdad stood as a glaring example of the previous limits of US hegemony. First it was a defiant third world state. Over the 1990s despite invasion, continuous bombing and over a decade of the harshest sanctions in diplomatic history, it had continued to reject the demands of the US and the international community. It was proof for those states of a rebellious disposition that autonomy could be indigenously defended in a world dominated by a single hegemon. After 1997, as the Ba'athist regime came to realise that it could survive under sanctions, it set about courting radicals from across the developing world. Baghdad begun to host a series of conferences, designed not only to organise the international campaign against its own isolation but also to create a more general anti-American coalition. For Saddam Hussein at least Baghdad was to become the new Bandung.

Second the stalemate with Iraq personified the problems, writ large, faced by US hegemony in the Middle East. The autonomy built up by the Ba'athist regime over 35 years of rule allowed it to defy the institutions of the international community and resist the application of 13 years of coercive diplomacy. Conversely if it could be removed, if the full force of US military might could be displayed in one of the most important states in the region, then the rest of the Arab regimes could be made to submit fully to US hegemony.[10]

It is indicative of the importance of the Middle East and the problems that Iraq posed for US hegemony that both dominated the first meeting of George W. Bush's National Security Council (NSC), a mere ten days after his inauguration. Condoleezza Rice, in the chair, explained 'How Iraq is destabilising the region' and how it might be the key to reshaping the Middle East. To quote Rumsfeld during the second NSC meeting of the new administration: 'Imagine what the region would look like without Saddam and with a regime that's aligned with US interests ... It would change everything in the region and beyond it. It would demonstrate what US policy is all about.'[11]

In the aftermath of 9/11 and what was seen at the time to have been a successful war in Afghanistan, Iraq was invaded to remove a decade long obstacle to US power in the Middle East but also as a direct result of the limits hegemony had faced in the wider region. The ideational war of position was traded for a coercive war of manoeuvre.[12]

US failure in Iraq: the dynamics of state collapse

The scope of the grand ambitions brought together in the Bush doctrine have only been matched by the extent of their failure when applied to Iraq. Iraq did not have the extensive network of non-conventional weapons procurement or indigenous WMD development that US Secretary of State Colin Powell put at the centre of the case for war at the United Nations in the run up to the invasion in 2003. This combined with the Abu Ghraib torture scandal has not only undermined the justification for war but seriously damaged the United States' long-term credibility as both a defender of international law and a promoter of universal human rights. Potentially, however, it is the US government's inability to implement its policy aims in Iraq itself that will inflict much longer lasting damage on its capacity to project state power out of area and specifically into the Middle East.

For all its ideological ambitions the United States' intervention in Iraq was perceived within very narrow logistical parameters. Occupation would entail the limited reform of a dictatorial state, a form of coercive structural adjustment. US forces would race to Baghdad and seize the coercive and political institutions of the Iraqi state. It would then use the capacity of the Ba'athist state to impose stability on the country. Once order had been achieved, the occupiers would then move to impose neo-liberal reform on the state they had seized. The restricted nature of the planned intervention negated the need for large numbers of US troops, detailed knowledge of the country or indeed an extended occupation. This ideologically structured understanding of a post-Saddam Iraq allowed the Pentagon under Donald Rumsfeld to budget for modest post-war expenditure and led to the presumption that US troops would be on the ground for a short period of time. To quote Condoleezza Rice, the then US National Security Advisor: 'The concept was that we would defeat the army, but the institutions would hold, everything from ministries to police forces.'[13]

However, US forces proved unable to impose order on Iraq in the immediate aftermath of the first stage of the war in April 2003. The speed with which US and coalition forces removed Saddam's regime initially left little doubt that American military superiority appeared absolute. This impression quickly dissipated. Studies of previous peacekeeping operations highlight the 'security vacuum that has confronted virtually every transitional administration-type operation'.[14] It stresses that the imposition of law and order within the first six to 12 weeks of any occupation is crucial for the credibility and legitimacy of the occupier. In the aftermath of regime change, the US military proved unable to impose order in any meaningful sense across Iraq.

What had began in April 2003 as a lawless celebration of the demise of Saddam's regime, grew into uncontrolled looting and violence. After three weeks the state's administrative capacity had been destroyed. Seventeen of Baghdad's 23 ministry buildings were completely gutted.[15] Looters first took portable items of value such as computers, then furniture and fittings. By the time I reached Baghdad, a month after US forces, looters were systematically stripping the electric wiring from the walls of former government buildings, to sell for scrap.

In May 2003 the United States added to the destruction of the state with two acts of almost wilful recklessness. On 16 May after only four days in the country, the US pro-consul in charge of Iraq Paul Bremer issued Coalition Provisional Authority Order No. 1: 'The De-Ba'athification of Iraqi Society.' This sacked all Ba'ath Party members in the top four ranks of the party in government employment. For Bremer the purpose of Order No. 1 was 'to rid the Iraqi government of the small group of true believers at the top of the party and those who had committed crimes in its name, and to wipe the country clean of the Ba'ath Party ideology'.[16] However CPA Order No. 1 purged the civil service of its top layer of management, making between 20 000 and 120 000 people unemployed.[17] Following the destruction of government infrastructure across the country, de-Ba'athification removed what was left, tens of thousands of senior civil servants and the state's institutional memory.

The second decision Bremer took during his first fortnight in Baghdad was even more damaging for law and order, the disbanding of the Iraqi army. The compulsory redundancy of 400 000 trained and armed men following hard on the heels of de-Ba'athification, created a very large pool of resentment across southern and central Iraq.

The looting combined with de-Ba'athification resulted in the partial collapse of the Iraqi state. Iraq's governing institutions and civil service had faced over a decade of sanctions, three wars in 20 years and then the growth of a violent anti-occupation insurgency. All these events combined to destroy the administrative coherence of the Iraqi state. The American occupation from 2003 onwards simply did not have the detailed knowledge needed to reconstitute the state it had worked so hard to destroy. What had been planned in Washington in 2002 as a short sharp exercise in regime change quickly expanded in Baghdad in 2003 into a long-term commitment to occupation.

State collapse leads to civil war

The United States' inability to impose order on Iraq combined with the disbanding of the army and the collapse of the state directly caused a profound security vacuum across central and southern parts of the country. The growing realisation amongst Iraqis that US troops were not in control of the situation helped turn criminal violence and looting into an organised and politically motivated insurgency. Former members of the security services, Ba'ath Party loyalists and then a wider and more diverse group of those opposed to the occupation began to mobilise as the US military failed to impose order.[18] Taking advantage of the coalition's vulnerability, they began to launch hit-and-run attacks on US troops, with increasing frequency and skill.

The organisation of a low-level military campaign against US occupation proved to be comparatively straightforward. The collapse of Saddam Hussein's regime allowed tens of thousands of Iraqi troops to make their own way home, untroubled by managed demobilisation or disarmament. They simply merged back into their own communities, taking their small arms with them. The stockpiling of weapons by the Ba'athist regime in numerous dumps across the country provided further munitions. The rapid collapse of the regime allowed ammunition to become widely available at very low prices. Historically, private gun ownership in Iraq has been high with the majority of adult males having received basic military training and a large minority having seen active service.

These factors combined with rising popular disenchantment with the occupation fuelled the increase in politically motivated violence. Small groups of highly mobile assailants, making use of their local knowledge, inflicted increasing fatalities on US troops. The genesis of the insurgency emerged in late May 2003, by July it was beginning to show signs of greater professionalism. By using widely available Russian-designed rocket-propelled grenades and improvised but highly effective roadside bombs the insurgents made the US military's technological superiority largely irrelevant. By October, US forces had recognised the increased geographical spread of the insurgency, better coordination between the different groups and a wider range of arms, including mortars and mines. The growing violence, both political and criminal, encouraged a deep sense of insecurity in the wider population, in turn fuelling increasing resentment against the occupation. Beginning in August 2003, car bombs became a key insurgent weapon.

It was this security vacuum that by 2006–2007 had driven Iraq into civil war. This internecine conflict has created, or at least empowered, three distinct sets of groups deploying violence for their own ends. The first are the 'industrial-strength' criminal gangs that terrorise what is left of Iraq's middle class. Although there is clear overlap between simple criminality and politically motivated violence, especially where kidnapping is concerned, the continuing crime wave is a glaring example of state incapacity. The persistent reports that crime is as big a problem for the citizens of Basra as Baghdad indicate that the state's inability to impose and guarantee order is a general problem across large swathes of southern and central Iraq. The high levels of criminal activity indicate that violence is driven primarily by opportunity springing from state weakness, not the antipathy of competing groups within Iraqi society. Crime is instrumentally driven, primarily non-communal and a key factor de-legitimising the new Iraqi ruling elite. Going well beyond the government's inability to increase electrical output or stimulate the job market, the continued freedom of criminal gangs to operate is indicative of a failing state.

The second type of organisation comprises the myriad groups making up the Iraqi insurgency. From 2005 onwards the insurgency consolidated around four or five main groups: the Islamic Army in Iraq, the Partisans of the Sunna Army, the Mujahadeen's Army, Muhammad's Army and the Islamic Resistance Movement in Iraq.[19] As the names suggest, political violence was by 2005 being increasingly justified in religious and sectarian terms. The main insurgent groups found ideological coherence by fusing a powerful appeal to Iraqi nationalism with an austere and extreme Salafism. The attraction of the Salafist doctrine for the insurgents was that it allows a distinction to be drawn between those involved in the jihad or struggle (the true believers) and those who are not. Those not backing the struggle could be branded non-believers and as such be killed. This approach has also lent itself to the increased use of sectarian violence. Shiites can be murdered both because they do not follow the 'true path of Islam' and because they formed the majority of those staffing the security forces against whom the violence is directed.[20]

The numbers of and role played by Arabs from neighbouring countries is estimated by the US military to be between 5–10 per cent of the total.[21] These foreign fighters played a disproportionately large role in the insurgency's ideological coherence. The group al Qaeda in Mesopotamia has driven the rising influence of Salafist doctrine and claimed responsibility or has been blamed for the majority of the violence that has increased sectarian tensions in the country. This dynamic reached its peak with the destruction of one of Shia Islam's holiest shrines, the al-Askariyya mosque in Samarra. Although the city of Samarra had long been dominated by the insurgency, the destruction of the mosque in February 2006 was an act calculated to outrage Shia opinion and drive Iraq into civil war.

The violence that erupted following the destruction of the al-Askariyya mosque saw the insurgency combine with a third type of organisation to drive violence forward. The plethora of independent militias is estimated to total 60 000–102 000 fighters.[22] They have overtly organised and legitimised themselves by reference to sectarian ideology. Their existence is testament to the inability of the Iraqi government to guarantee the personal safety of Iraqis on the basis of equal citizenship, not sectarian identity.

The militias themselves can be divided into three broad groups, depending on their organisational coherence and relationship to national politics. The first and most disciplined consists of the Kurdish militias of the Kurdistan Democratic Party (KDP) and the Patriotic Union of Kurdistan (PUK). The second includes those created in exile and brought back to Iraq in the wake of Saddam's fall. The most powerful of these is the Badr Brigade, the military arm of the Islamic Supreme Council of Iraq (ISCI), estimated at 15 000 fighters. The Badr Brigade, along with ISCI itself, was set up as a foreign-policy vehicle for the Iranian government. Indeed, the Badr Brigade was trained and officered by the Iranian Revolutionary Guard Corps, at least until its return to Iraq. It remains comparatively disciplined and responsive to its senior commanders.[23] But the Badr Brigade's colonisation of large swathes of the security forces, notably the police and paramilitary units associated with the Ministry of Interior, has done much to de-legitimise the already limited power of the state-controlled forces of law and order. The brigade's dominance of the Ministry of Interior reached its peak when one of its former commanders, Bayan Jabr, served as minister in Ibrahim al-Jaafari's government. The Ministry's Wolf Brigade commandos were repeatedly accused of acting as a death squad, frequently resorting to extra-judicial execution and torture.[24] Complaints reached their peak in November 2005, when US forces raided a Ministry of Interior detention facility and found 170 detainees 'who had been held in appalling conditions'.[25] ISCI's dominance of government, though, was such that Jabr was not removed from the Interior Ministry until the end of May 2006 and even then he was, in effect, promoted to become the Minister of Finance. His replacement, Jawad al-Bolani, a non-aligned politician, has struggled to reform the ministry.

The third group comprises militias created in Iraq since regime change. They vary in size, organisation and discipline, from a few thugs with guns controlling a street or a neighbourhood to militias capable of running whole towns. The largest and most coherent is the 50 000-strong Jaish al-Mahdi, set up by Moqtada al-Sadr. The speed with which the militia was built after regime change and the prolonged conflicts it has had with the US military have taken a toll on its organisational coherence. Mahdi Army commanders have become more financially independent of Sadr through the diversion of government resources, hostage-taking, ransom and the smuggling of antiquities and petroleum. In spite of al-Sadr's repeated calls for calm, the Mahdi Army was blamed for the majority of violence in and around Baghdad following the al-Askariyya bombing.

Once a state has failed, the population has to seek new, local ways to survive, to gain some degree of day-to-day predictability. This quest has haunted the majority of Iraq's population since regime change. The quality of an individual Iraqi's life depends on the discipline, organisational coherence and central control of the militias that dominate their streets, neighbourhoods and towns. In northern Iraq, the Kurdish militias of the KDP and PUK have centralised and largely institutionalised their military forces since fighting a civil war against each other in the mid-1990s.[26] Elsewhere in Iraq, the militias that arose after regime change are far more unstable, prone to criminality and divided loyalties. Although they were formed as a response to the security vacuum, they have attempted to legitimise themselves by the deployment of hybrid ideologies – sectarian, religious and nationalist. This has caused ethnic and religious cleansing across the country from Kirkuk in the north to Basra in the south, but most notably in Baghdad. This was not an inevitable result of regime change but a direct response to the collapse of the state. If Iraq is to be stabilised, a central government with a monopoly on coercion must be rebuilt with the administrative capacity to give it legitimacy. There is, sadly, no shortcut to this end, if it is possible, it will take many years and a great deal of resources to achieve.

Conclusions: United States power after failure in Iraq

Success in Iraq was placed at the centre of an ambitious plan to transform the political and economic trajectory of the region as a whole. A democratic and prosperously free-market Iraq would, it was argued, act as a beacon of light leading the way to the transformation of the region as a whole. However, once the post-Saddam electoral process finally got underway in January 2005 the results were not what were hoped for. Instead of producing a government of Jeffersonian democrats the polls were dominated by the United Iraqi Alliance, an electoral grouping specifically created to ensure the triumph of political parties formed to promote Islamic observance at the heart of the state. The dominant party of the alliance, ISCI, was built around the promotion of a radical Islamist philosophy. More worrying still for the US government and its regional ambitions, ISCI was formed in Tehran in 1982 at the height of the Iranian Revolution.[27] Designed as a vehicle to promote Iranian foreign policy in Iraq, the party still maintains very close ties to the Iranian regime, the second member of George W. Bush's axis of evil. Another marker of the unintended consequences of the invasion and its aftermath is how the Iraqi exiles that played such a central part in cheer leading for regime change have fared. Ahmed Chalabi, a politician of mercurial skill and unbounded flexibility, took the temperature of Iraqi politics after being flown back to the country by the US air force, and then radically transformed his previous commitment to neoconservatism. In an unsuccessful attempt to gain some degree of popularity and shake off his reputation as an American client he first aligned himself with

Shia Islam and when that did not deliver electoral support become a militant Iraqi nationalist. His capacity to act as a tool of US policy reached its nadir when American troops raided his Baghdad residence looking for evidence of his alleged intelligence links with Iran.

Beyond the ideological shortcomings of the US administration's visions for post-war Iraq, it is the US military's inability to control the country that continues to cause greatest damage to the potential for American hegemony in the region. The Bush administration convinced its electorate that the invasion would curtail the threat of asymmetrical warfare personified by 9/11. With this in mind it is tragically ironic that to date over 4 000 US soldiers have been killed in Iraq by a set of disparate Iraqi insurgents who have deployed hit-and-run techniques and low technology weapons to humble the US coercive capacity on the ground.[28] The insurgency's ability to innovate technologically and deploy increasing levels of violence is indicative of the severe limitations of the much-touted revolution in military affairs and the vast array of air power that the US has at its disposal.

Against a background of continued American casualties in Iraq and a collapse of support for the occupation at home, the issue is now how the US is going to extract itself from Iraq, not if it can afford geo-politically to do so. Comparative historical studies of military interventions suggest that governments who take troops in find it far too difficult, in terms of both ideology and prestige, to take them out after an unsuccessful occupation.[29] If correct this means the next presidential term will be dominated by how to pull the US out of this ill-judged quagmire. However, of longer term significance is the effect that this defeat, however explained and curtailed, will have on both US domestic politics and foreign policy. The fact that President Bush placed regime change and transition in Iraq on the front line of the global war against terrorism means that continuing failure and eventual withdrawal will greatly damage US power projection overseas, both ideationally and militarily.

The US occupation has been dogged by the collapse of the Iraqi state and then undermined by the rise of an insurgency driven by disparate groups combining Iraqi nationalism with Islamic radicalism.[30] But the invasion itself and its catastrophic aftermath have given rise to a series of interesting questions about the creation, expansion and defence of US hegemony. The invasion signalled the Bush administration's shift from a war of position back to one of manoeuvre, a move back to the overt deployment of violence from the ideology promotion of US dominance. The need to deploy coercion was indicative of the geographic limits of ideational hegemony. The Middle East became such a central concern for the administration and ultimately Iraq was invaded because the region had managed to retain a comparative autonomy from neo-liberal policy prescriptions and the universal promotion of polyarchy.[31] Coercion was deployed because consent did not work. The example of the Middle East highlights the geo-political limitations of ideational hegemony in the international sphere. The failure of regime change in Baghdad to deliver the government desired by the US administration and the humbling of the US military across Iraq indicates both the propensity of the hegemon internationally to resort to violence but also the limitations of coercion for delivering political transformation.

Notes

1 Toby Dodge, 'The invasion of Iraq and the reordering of the post colonial word', *Newsletter of the British International Studies Association*, no. 79 (January 2004).
2 Richard N. Haass, 'The 2002 Arthur Ross Lecture, Remarks to Foreign Policy Association', New York, 22 April 2002.
3 William I. Robinson, *Promoting Polyarchy, Globalization, US Intervention and Hegemony* (Cambridge: Cambridge University Press, 1996).
4 Toby Dodge, 'The Sardinian, the Texan and the Tikriti: Gramsci, the comparative autonomy of the Middle Eastern state and regime change in Iraq', *International Politics*, vol. 43, no. 4 (2006), 453–473.
5 Toby Dodge, *Inventing Iraq, the Failure of Nation-building and a History Denied* (New York: Columbia University Press, 2003), xvi–xvii; Patrick Tyler, 'US strategy plan calls for insuring no rivals develop', *The New York Times*, 8 March 1992; N. Leman, 'The next world order. The Bush Administration may have a brand-new doctrine of power', *The New Yorker Magazine*, 1 April 2002.
6 See Bob Woodward's description of the National Security Council meeting on 12 September 2001 in Bob Woodward, *Bush at War* (New York: Simon and Schuster, 2002), 43, 48.
7 R.S. Litwak, 'The New Calculus of Pre-emption', *Survival*, vol. 44, no. 4 (2002); United States Government, *The National Security Strategy of the United States of America*, www.whitehouse.gov/nsc/nss.html, September 2002. This was made even more explicit in the President's 2003 State of the Union address,

> Today, the gravest danger in the war on terror, the gravest danger facing America and the world, is outlaw regimes that seek and possess nuclear, chemical, and biological weapons. These regimes could use such weapons for blackmail, terror, and mass murder. They could also give or sell those weapons to terrorist allies, who would use them without the least hesitation.
> (George W. Bush, 'State of the Union Address',
> Washington DC, January 2003)

8 John Lewis Gaddis, 'A Grand Strategy of Transformation', *Foreign Policy* (November/December 2002).
9 George W. Bush, Remarks by the President at 2002 Graduation Exercise of the United States Military Academy West Point, New York, 1 June 2002; United States Government, *The National Security Strategy of the United States of America*, www.whitehouse.gov/nsc/nss.html, September 2002; R.N. Haass, 'The 2002 Arthur Ross Lecture, Remarks to Foreign Policy Association', New York, 22 April 2002; G. John Ikenberry, 'America's Imperial Ambition', *Foreign Affairs* (September/October 2002).
10 Dodge, 'The Sardinian, the Texan and the Tikriti', *International Politics*, 453–473.
11 Ron Suskind, *The Price of Loyalty: George W. Bush, the White House, and the Education of Paul O'Neill* (New York: Simon & Shuster, 2004), 72, 85.
12 Dodge, 'The Sardinian, the Texan and the Tikriti', *International Politics*, 453–473.

13 Michael Gordon, '"Catastrophic success": The strategy to secure Iraq did not foresee a 2nd war', *New York Times*, 19 October 2004.

14 Simon Chesterman, *You, the People: The United Nations, Transitional Administrations, and State-building* (Oxford: Oxford University Press, 2004), 100, 112.

15 David L. Phillips, *Losing Iraq: Inside the Post-war Reconstruction Fiasco* (New York: Basic Books, 2005), 135.

16 Paul L. Bremer with Malcolm McConnell, *My Year in Iraq. The Struggle to Build a Future of Hope* (New York: Simon & Schuster, 2006), 39; Toby Dodge, 'Review essay. How Iraq was lost', *Survival*, vol. 48. no. 4 (Winter 2006–2007), 157–172.

17 Phillips estimates it made 120 000 unemployed out of a total party membership of two million. Paul Bremer cites intelligence estimates that it affected 1 per cent of the party membership, 20 000 people. George Packer estimates 'at least thirty-five thousand'. The large variation in estimates indicates the paucity of reliable intelligence on the ramifications of such an important policy decision. See Phillips, *Losing Iraq*, 145–146; Bremer, *My Year in Iraq*, 40; George Packer, *Assassins' Gate: America in Iraq* (New York: Farrar, Straus and Giroux, 2005), 191.

18 Toby Dodge, *Iraq's Future: The Aftermath of Regime Change*, Adelphi Paper 372 (Abingdon: Routledge for the International Institute for Strategic Studies, 2005), 11–19.

19 International Crisis Group, 'In their Own Words: Reading the Iraqi Insurgency', *Middle East Report*, no. 50, 15 February 2006, 1–3.

20 Roel Meijer, 'The Sunni Resistance and the "Political Process"', in Markus Bouillon, David Malone and Ben Rowsell (eds), *Preventing Another Generation of Conflict* (Boulder, CO: Lynne Rienner Publishers, 2007).

21 Dexter Filkins, 'Foreign Fighters Captured in Iraq come from 27, mostly Arab, Lands', *New York Times*, October, 21, 2005.

22 Bremer, *My Year in Iraq*, 274; Larry Diamond, *Squandered Victory: The American Occupation and the Bungled Effort to Bring Democracy to Iraq* (New York: Times Books, 2005), 222.

23 Solomon Moore, 'Militias Seen as Spinning Out of Control. Growing Extremism among Splintering Groups and Recent Clashes have Cast Doubt on Paramilitary Leaders' Authority over Fighters', *Los Angels Times*, September, 12, 2006.

24 Hannah Allam, 'Wolf Brigade the Most Loved and Feared of Iraqi Security Forces', Knight Ridder Newspapers, 21 May 2005.

25 Amnesty International, *Beyond Abu Ghraib: Detention and Torture in Iraq* (London, 2006), 4.

26 Dodge, *Iraq's Future*, 4.

27 F. A. Jabar, *The Shi'ite Movement in Iraq* (London: Saqi, 2003), 235.

28 Dodge, *Iraq's Future*, 9–23.

29 A. E. Levite, B. W. Jentleson, L. Berman, (eds), *Foreign Military Intervention. The Dynamics of Protracted Conflict* (New York: Columbia University Press, 1992).

30 Toby Dodge, 'Iraqi transitions: from regime change to state collapse', *Third World Quarterly*, vol. 26, no. 4 (2005), 699–715.

31 Dodge, 'The Sardinian, the Texan and the Tikriti', *International Politics*, 459–461.

6 The geoeconomic pivot of the global war on terror

US Central Command and the war in Iraq

*John Morrissey**

> Let our position be absolutely clear: an attempt by any outside force to gain control of the Persian Gulf region will be regarded as an assault on the vital interests of the United States of America, and such an assault will be repelled by any means necessary, including military force.
>
> President Jimmy Carter, State of the Union Address,
> January 20, 1980[1]

Introduction

In January 1980, President Jimmy Carter affirmed his administration's commitment to protecting vital energy assets in the Middle East in a State of the Union address that spoke of America's challenge in securing a region his National Security Advisor, Zbigniew Brzezinski, had termed an *arc of* *crisis*. Over 25 years later, the *arc of crisis* has become part of an *axis of evil*, yet its geoeconomic importance remains precisely the same. In 1980, what was at stake in the Persian Gulf, according to then Defense Secretary, Harold Brown, was 'the economic and political well-being of the United States and its allies,' and if they were 'deprived of access to the energy resources of the Gulf,' the result would be 'collapse of our allies and the world economy.'[2] In 2006, the bipartisan Council on Foreign Relations report, *National Security Consequences of U.S. Oil Dependency*, concluded that because 'the United States alone has the capacity to protect the global oil trade against the threat of violent obstruction,' there is a perennial need for 'a strong US military presence in key producing areas and in the sea lanes that carry foreign oil to American shores.'[3]

The ongoing war in Iraq is part of a much longer American military involvement in the Middle East that, since the late 1970s, has revolved around the United States' positing of the Persian Gulf as a *geoeconomic pivot*,[4] vital to US and global economic health.[5] The defense of this pivotal region was entrusted to a newly-created unified command, United States Central Command (CENTCOM), and the story of its initiation, mission and deployment is critical to our understanding of the current war in Iraq, and to recognizing why even the US withdrawal of ground troops there will not end America's long war in the Middle East. Despite much crucial work that has focused on the cultural logics and imperial ideologies of US involvement in Iraq, there has been remarkably little interrogation of the underlying political economy of the Iraq War and broader war on terror, and few have documented the historical political economy of the United States military presence in the Middle East in detail. To this end, this chapter offers a critical reading of the historical political economy of CENTCOM, the chief body responsible for the US 'shaping of the Middle East' since the emergence of the Persian Gulf region as an area of *vital interest* for US and global capitalism in the late 1970s.[6] In providing historical context to recent American intervention in the Middle East, the chapter seeks to shed light upon some of the key strategic and geoeconomic priorities that underlie the current war on terrorism and its geographic focus on Iraq.

The rapid deployment force concept: Southwest Asia and the Carter doctrine

US concerns for safeguarding energy resources in the Middle East has been a component of US foreign policy for successive administrations since 1945, when President Franklin D. Roosevelt committed to backing King Abdul Aziz ibn Saud's reign in Saudi Arabia in return for 'assuring the flow of Persian Gulf oil.'[7] It was a 'promise that has been reaffirmed by every succeeding President, without regard to party,' and support for the use of military force to protect the flow of imported petroleum from the region has enjoyed bipartisan support in Washington since that period.[8] However, it was the turbulent 1970s – marked by oil crises, the collapse of the US-supported Shah in Iran and the Soviet invasion of Afghanistan – that precipitated the designation of the Gulf region as an area of *vital interest* to the United States and its allies, and prompted the establishment of a suitable military force for its defense. That force would become known as the Rapid Deployment Joint Task Force (and later as US Central Command), and would be the chosen instrument to implement the Carter Doctrine.[9]

In the 1970s, the idea of a rapidly deployable force that could be efficiently dispatched to a crisis region was not new to the US military; historically, the Marine Corps had occupied that role and indeed had intervened in the Middle East in the post-World War II period.[10] In 1961, US Strike Command was set up at MacDill Air Force Base in Tampa, Florida.[11] Formed from amalgamating various Army and Air Force units, Strike Command was the first attempt at building a unified command to 'provide an integrated, mobile, highly combat-ready force' for military deployment in critical 'remote areas.'[12] The development of a new strategic transport aircraft, the C-5A, and a new sealift vessel, the Fast Deployment Logistics ship, facilitated the deploying of such a force directly from MacDill Air Force Base.[13] Strike Command failed, however, as an effective unified command for two main reasons: first, the US military was overstretched significantly during the

Vietnam War; and, second, the non-involvement of the Marine Corps and Navy inhibited its unified command potential.[14] It was replaced in 1971 by US Readiness Command, but this command too met with a series of military bureaucratic impediments that rendered it effectively a non-combatant command, occupied mostly with planning and training.[15]

The 1970s proved to be a watershed for US foreign policy in the Middle East. The oil crises of 1973 and 1974 brought into sharp relief the region's key geoeconomic importance, and calls for US military intervention to solve such crises slowly began to discursively air in influential Washington circles.[16] US commitment to militarily safeguarding access to the region was subsequently refocused from the outset of the new Democratic administration of Jimmy Carter in 1977. An influential National Security Council review of American foreign policy and national security, carried out in mid-1977, identified the Persian Gulf region as the new frontier in Cold War relations. The review was conducted in the light of nuclear *strategic equivalence* with the USSR, and National Security Advisor, Zbigniew Brzezinski, saw countering the Soviet threat in the region as central to reasserting American power overseas in the aftermath of defeat in the Vietnam War.[17] To that end, a specific challenge for US military posture was envisaged as the safeguarding of access to energy assets in the region, and this key concern was mirrored in a simultaneous Presidential Review Memorandum 10 (PRM-10) from the Office of the Secretary of Defense. Several subsequent National Security Council decisions culminated in Presidential Decision 18 (PD-18) in August 1977, which recommended the establishment of a *quick-reaction* force composed of mobile light infantry and backed by strategic air- and sea-lift capabilities.[18] The US withdrawal from Wheelus Air Force Base in Libya in 1969 meant that the US had lost the 'last of its great Middle Eastern air bases';[19] therefore, the new tactical force was designed for 'strategic mobility independent of overseas bases and logistical support.'[20]

In March 1978, President Carter announced that he had instructed his Secretary of Defense to initiate a new Rapid Deployment Force to 'defend our interests throughout the world.'[21] Leaked press reports of PD-18, four months later, confirmed that 'world' as specifically the Gulf region, and for its defense the US had committed 100000 troops, four aircraft carriers and three Air Force wings totalling 200 planes.[22] No budgetary support for PD-18, however, came until early 1980, in the aftermath of President Carter's defiant State of the Union Address, which spelt out US intentions to use military force in defense of the Gulf region. A number of developments in a turbulent 1979 had raised the Rapid Deployment Force to the status of an urgent geopolitical project: the removal of the Shah in Iran; growing unease of the other US pillar in the region, Saudi Arabia (over ongoing crises in the Horn of Africa); the Tehran hostage crisis; and finally the Soviet invasion of Afghanistan. On March 1, 1980, the Rapid Deployment Joint Task Force (RDJTF) became officially operational. New strategic and logistic ships and transport aircraft were commissioned, and the RDJTF Headquarters was set up at MacDill Air Force Base and assigned the following mission: 'to plan, jointly train, exercise and be prepared to deploy and employ designated forces in response to contingencies threatening US vital interests.'[23] President Carter's earlier announcement that the new rapid-reaction force was devised for deployment throughout the world was quickly revised once the force was actually established; the Persian Gulf region became the stated exclusive focus. The *area of concern* of the new RDJTF, seen in Figure 1, mirrored geographically the various crises that had developed across the Middle East and Horn of Africa in the late 1970s, and refocused US foreign policy in the region.

As with its predecessor, Strike Command, the RDJTF was laden with bureaucratic command issues from the beginning, as its assigned forces would have to come from other commands worldwide (albeit from all four armed services). By 1981, the chief specialist on the Middle East at the Institute for Foreign Policy Analysis in Washington, Jeffrey Record, had concluded that the RDJTF was a 'fatally flawed military instrument for the preservation of uninterrupted U.S. access to vital Persian Gulf oil – the prin-

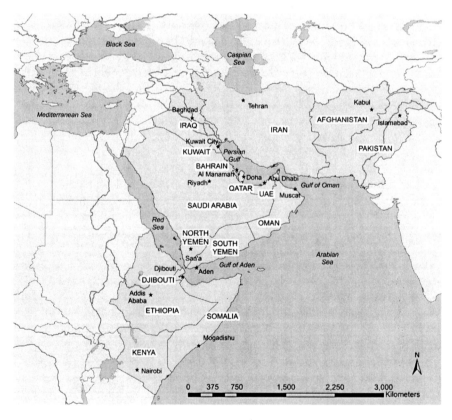

Figure 1 RDJTF, area of concern, 1980 (source: adapted from: US Department of Defense, Annual Report, FY 1982).

cipal rationale underlying the force.'[24] For Record, without its urgent reform, 'the uninterrupted flow of oil from the Persian Gulf' would continue to constitute a 'threatened and inadequately defended vital U.S. interest in the region.'[25] Record's concerns were addressed immediately by the new Republican administration of Ronald Reagan, which committed a budget increase for the RDJTF of 85 percent for the Fiscal Year (FY) 1982, and proposed spending an additional $17.5 billion on its reform over the next five years.[26] The Democrats may have established the idea of the RDJTF but the Republicans were keen to make it work, and work effectively, as the central instrument of US foreign policy in the Gulf. In April 1981, Secretary of Defense Caspar Weinberger announced that the RDJTF would be converted into a separate regional geographic command, with full responsibility concentrated on Southwest Asia.[27] He argued before the House Committee on the Budget later that year that the US faced a greater threat in Southwest Asia than in NATO Europe and Northeast Asia combined.[28] This new geographic focus culminated in the RDJTF being converted into United States Central Command on January 1, 1983.[29] The US military's Unified Command Plan, the codification of its global ambition of *full-spectrum dominance*, was changed accordingly, with 19 countries being incorporated into the new CENTCOM Area of Responsibility (AOR), seen in Figure 2.[30]

CENTCOM's mission from the outset was to carry on from the RDJTF in acting as the military, geopolitical instrument of the Carter Doctrine. In its own words, it had 'evolved as a practical solution to the problem of projecting U.S. military power to the Gulf region from halfway around the world,' and its central function was to 'project American power in the Middle East and East Africa.'[31] I have examined elsewhere the pervasive politico-cultural discourses that actively posit the United States military in the global role of policing and protecting the world from terror and threat.[32] The Department of Defense's 2005 *National Defense Strategy*, for example, refers unproblematically to America's central role in the world in envisioning and securing an 'international order' fashioned in its interests.[33] Such discourses of liberal empire enable the kinds of unreflective assumptions inherent in US military mission statements that speak of solutions to the 'problem' of 'projecting power' to regions 'halfway around the world.' Forming part, too, of a broader popular imaginary that defines the Middle East via essentialist equations of geography, identity, difference and terror, such geopolitical discourses have a profoundly exertive power in legitimating and allowing for geopolitical action and the exercise of military violence.[34] However, additionally, they function to take our attention away from the hard story: what can *not* be neatly abstracted and popularly packaged (such as the elite interests being served by aggressive geopolitics in *our* interests). What follows below is a reflection on the 'critical economic interests' that are both propelling and being served by CENTCOM's geopolitical project in the Middle East.

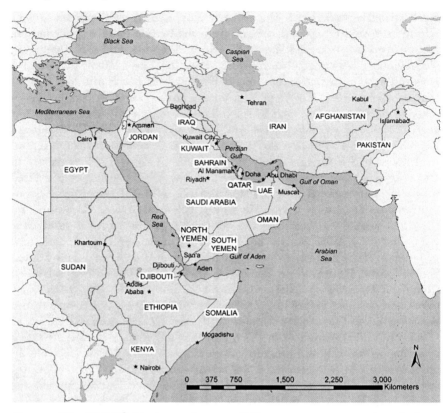

Figure 2 US CENTCOM Area of responsibility, 1983 (source: adapted from: CENTCOM CINC General George Crist *Statement before the Senate Armed Services Committee on the Posture of United States Central Command*, Washington, DC: Senate Armed Services Committee, 11 March 1986).

CENTCOM's world: defending vital interests

Stretching from the Horn of Africa, across the Yemens and the Arabian Gulf to Iraq, Iran and Afghanistan, CENTCOM's AOR is focused on the most energy-rich region in the world. Since 1983, each commander of CENTCOM has affirmed to Congress the pivotally important role CENTCOM plays in safeguarding US and World economic strength by guarding, patrolling, and maintaining forward deployment in the Persian Gulf region.[35] In 1999, for example, CENTCOM CINC,[36] General Anthony Zinni, told the Senate Armed Service Committee that 'with over 65 percent of the world's oil reserves located within the Gulf states,' the US and the West 'must have free access to the region's resources.'[37] CENTCOM Commander General John Abizaid reminded the Senate Armed Services Committee in 2006 of the region's *vital interests* to the United States:

It incorporates a nexus of vital transportation and trade routes, including the Red Sea, the Northern Indian Ocean, and the Arabian Gulf. It is home to the strategic maritime choke points of the Suez Canal, the Bab el Mandeb, and the Strait of Hormuz. It encompasses the world's most energy-rich region – the Arabian Gulf alone accounts for 57% of the world's crude oil reserves, 28% of the world's oil production, and 41% of the world's natural gas reserves.[38]

The Persian Gulf has long been posited as a special region, and the United States, and Britain before that, have consistently demonstrated a clear-cut economic logic of intervention when the free flow of petroleum has been threatened.[39] In 1981, Jeffrey Record, at the Institute for Foreign Policy Analysis in Washington, urgently advised the Pentagon of the 'need for military action in the event of disruption.'[40] In 1985, Thomas McNaugher, Gulf expert at the Brookings Institution, argued that protecting the oil-rich states from external threat and deterring Soviet encroachment would require greater military assertion and agility.[41] When General George Crist assumed CENTCOM command in November 1985, he noted that it was regarded by many nations in the region as 'little more than a major intervention force designed to operate solely for U.S. purposes without their consultation or participation.'[42] This is hardly surprising when you consider CENTCOM's stated theater strategy.[43]

At the outset, CENTCOM had 222 000 troops at its disposal but the Reagan administration actioned immediate plans to increase this number in 1983.[44] By 1986, CENTCOM could call upon 400 000 troops.[45] In 1987, President Reagan issued CENTCOM with its first forward deployment order: to protect Kuwaiti oil tankers with US warships in the Persian Gulf. Reflagging them with the American ensign and escorting them through the Gulf was to protect them against possible attack from Iran or Iraq, then in the final stages of a brutal eight-year war. CENTCOM's foundational mission, according to Reagan, was to demonstrate 'U.S. commitment to the flow of oil through the Gulf.'[46] After the Iraqi invasion of Kuwait in August 1990, CENTCOM quickly amassed a 500 000-strong defensive force to create a Desert Shield against the possible invasion of its key, oil-exporting ally in the region, Saudi Arabia. The swift passing of 12 UN Security Council resolutions against Iraq in only a few months was unprecedented in the 45-year history of the UN, and just seven months after the invasion, the US-led Desert Storm quickly restored the economic status quo and left the US in a stronger military position than ever before. Meanwhile, Iraq's and Kuwait's ecosystems lay in ruins, hundreds of thousands Iraqi soldiers and civilians had been killed, and the Middle East 'would never be the same again.'[47] The George F. Kennan Chair in National Security Strategy at the National War College of the National Defense University in Washington commented in 1994 that the war 'transformed the security structure of the Persian Gulf – a region that will remain the principal source of energy needs well into the next century.'[48] This expert in national security revelled in the reinvigorated US ascendancy brought about by CENTCOM's war, which had 'prevented something truly terrible': a 'nuclear war by a tyrant in control of most of the energy supplies that are the lifeblood of the industrialized democracies of the world.'[49] The National Defense University Chair in question was Paul Wolfowitz, and ten years later, he would be a key architect and advocate in the Bush administration's extension of CENTCOM's war in the Middle East into the new century.

Since 1983, CENTCOM's perennial focus on the geopolitics of energy explains why its AOR did not include Israel, the Occupied Territories, Lebanon and Syria.[50] The traditional strategy of separating Persian Gulf issues from Palestinian ones underlines US foreign policy in the region as primarily a geoeconomic project in which the concerns of the State Department are dwarfed by the concerns of the Department of Defense.[51] President Bush's Defense budget for FY 2009, released in early February 2008, 'provides $515.4 billion in discretionary authority' for the Defense Department, and an additional $70 billion as 'an emergency allowance for the Global War on Terror.'[52] By comparison, the FY 2009 International Affairs budget for the Department of State, the US Agency for International Development and other foreign affairs agencies totals approximately $39.5 billion.[53] Such numbers point to the Defense Department always winning out 'in any power struggle with the Department of State on Capitol Hill.'[54] Even General John Shalikashvili, as Chairman of the Joint Chiefs of Staff during the Clinton administration, pleaded in 1999 for more funding for the State Department: 'what we are doing to our diplomatic capabilities is criminal [...] we will be obliged to use military force still more often.'[55]

The emphasis on military force, rather than diplomacy, in dealing with the Middle East, was present from the beginning, as expounded by Pentagon advisor, Jeffrey Record: '[i]t should go without saying that military reputation, or the ability to use force successfully in defense of declared national interests, is desirable in a world where force remains the final arbiter of international disputes.'[56] The Goldwater-Nichols Defense Reform Act in 1986 was particularly important for CENTCOM CINCs, as, from thereon, all combatant commanders 'had a unique chain of command arrangement, reporting directly to the Secretary of Defense rather than through the Joint Chiefs of Staff.'[57] This is not to suggest that CENTCOM commanders have been autonomous since 1986; however, they have played a much more active, rather than adjuvant, role in effecting US foreign policy in the Middle East, in comparison with their diplomatic counterparts in the State Department. Former CENTCOM CINC, General Norman Schwarzkopf, recalls revelling in a military–diplomatic role in which he felt like 'a kind of military ombudsman [...] overseeing advisors' work, administering $1.6 billion a year in military programs, and solidifying relations with rulers and generals.'[58] In various ways, unified commanders have historically acted as 'America's viceroys';[59] and, indeed, the US military have even considered the lessons for a Pax Americana afforded by comparisons between US CINCs and the Roman Republic's proconsuls.[60]

Other than resources and access to the top channels of American power, CENTCOM CINCs have always had one additional advantage over their State Department counterparts in negotiating and effecting US national security policy on foreign shores: their political–military brief does not compel them to 'implicitly or explicitly pass judgment on the internal politics or regimes with which they do business.'[61] As James Robbins puts it, the 'broader promotion of human rights or political change' is not the 'primary province of the combatant commander.'[62] This, of course, accounts for CENTCOM's entirely pragmatic alliance with a host of brutal leaders in its AOR since 1983, from Saddam Hussein in Iraq to the current Northern Alliance in Afghanistan. For CENTCOM, human rights are way down its list of priorities.

A 1992 CENTCOM-commissioned report by Stephen Pelletiere and Douglas Johnson II, both then Professors of National Security Affairs at the Strategic Studies Institute of the US Army War College, is acutely revealing of what kind of interventionary practices CENTCOM would henceforth pursue. Their report, *Oil and the New World System: CENTCOM rethinks its Mission*, formed part of the CENTCOM 2000 project, run by the Strategy, Plans, and Policy Directorate of CENTCOM at MacDill Air Force Base. The report came out a year before the CENTCOM incursion into Somalia had failed, with the loss of 18 Army Rangers (including Master Sergeant Gary Gordon, whose half-naked body was dragged horrifically through the streets of Mogadishu). Yet even before this, Pelletiere and Johnson warned of Somalia-type operations taking CENTCOM's focus away from its long-term mission:

> at a time of shrinking financial resources, things cannot go on as before – economies must be made. The solution is to focus all of CENTCOM's efforts on the Gulf, abandoning practically all other responsibilities [...] missions like Somalia conflict with CENTCOM's main mission which is guarding Gulf oil. Thus Somalia type operations should be approached with extreme caution, and under no circumstances should they be allowed to escalate because they have the potential to wreck the system. [CENTCOM] has a crucial mission to perform – guarding the flow of oil. It cannot waste itself in non-essential operations, especially where it could at any time become bogged down.[63]

This clinical positing of what should constitute CENTCOM missions, and what should not, encapsulates the abstracted and indifferent US military outlook on the terrains, not worlds, it finds under its radar. For Pelletiere and Johnson, humanitarianism (however that would look with CENTCOM) should simply never be on the agenda.[64]

Guarding the Gulf: CENTCOM theater strategy for a global political economy

To return to what has always been firmly *on* the agenda, consider CENTCOM CINC General Norman Schwarzkopf's statement to the Senate

Armed Services Committee, six months prior to Saddam Hussein's invasion of Kuwait in 1990:

> the greatest threat to U.S. interests in the area is the spillover of regional conflict which could endanger American lives, threaten U.S. interests in the area or interrupt the flow of oil, thereby requiring the commitment of U.S. combat forces.[65]

In February 1990, Schwarzkopf had already scripted the Gulf War. CENTCOM's geoeconomic mission to protect US vital economic interests in the Gulf compelled it to intervene. CENTCOM's success in its execution of the war confirmed it in its role as 'Guardian of the Gulf,' and, in the war's aftermath, a series of CENTCOM-commissioned studies recommended a focused mission for the command henceforth, which neatly defined CENTCOM's mission around two concepts: *critical economic interests*, and *forward deterrence* of regional rivals.[66] Stephen Pelletiere's and Douglas Johnson II's 1992 report cited above offered the following recommendations to this end:

> This study rejects the argument that Saudi Arabia and the Gulf Cooperation Council (GCC) states can defend themselves. Only CENTCOM can do that [...] In effect, CENTCOM must become the Gulf's policemen, a function it will perform with mounting patrols.[67]

The 'free' market system, as ever, was to be patrolled, and CENTCOM would perennially be given the mission to do it.

A Democrat in the White House from 1993 did not alter CENTCOM's mission. The Clinton administration's chief defense policy document for the Gulf region, *United States Security Strategy for the Middle East*, which came out in mid-1995, defined 'America's enduring interest in the security of the Middle East' around the following key components: assured access to Gulf oil (which is outlined in three pages); security of key regional partners (outlined in two pages); and a durable Arab–Israeli peace (outlined in one paragraph).[68] Secretary of Defense William Perry introduced the strategy document thus:

> One of the most controversial questions the United States faces in the aftermath of the Cold War is when to use military force in this complex world. But there is little dispute that we must be prepared to use force to defend our vital interests: when the survival of the United States or its key allies is in danger, when our critical economic interests are threatened, or when dealing with the emergence of a future nuclear threat. Nowhere are these criteria met more clearly than in the Middle East.[69]

Later that year, CENTCOM CINC General James Binford Peay III outlined to the *Joint Force Quarterly* both CENTCOM's clear-cut geoeconomic mission and its military capabilities by citing the unprecedented rapid deployment of CENTCOM troops during Operation Vigilant Warrior in 1994:

> On October 6, 1994, reports poured into the command center at [CENTCOM] that two Iraqi Republican Guard divisions were moving by both rail and heavy equipment transporters southward from their garrisons near Baghdad to assembly areas south of the Euphrates. Eight divisions threatened Kuwait with lead brigades located only fifteen miles from the border [...] CENTCOM at once modified on-the-shelf operational plans and orchestrated the deployment of units from all services in what became known as Operation Vigilant Warrior. Postured to prevent Iraqi aggression against Kuwait and Saudi Arabia, the command built both on the combat power of U.S. forward deployed and coalition forces and on American prepositioned equipment ashore and afloat to emplace a defensive force. On October 10, as the first U.S.-based aircraft began landing at airfields in the Persian Gulf and lead companies of the 24th Infantry Division began moving to tactical assembly areas, Iraq announced the withdrawal of reinforcing Republican Guard divisions thus defusing the situation.[70]

For General Peay, CENTCOM's mission in the mid-1990s was vitally important, precisely because maintaining 'regional stability and security in the Persian Gulf [was] integral to the political and economic wellbeing of the international community.'[71]

The Clinton administration saw the orientation of an effective national security posture as coinciding with a dominant global economic posture.[72] In 1999, for example, a Defense Department-sponsored Institute for National Security Studies review underlined that 'national security depends on successful engagement in the global economy.'[73] Deterrence of enemies in defense of critical economic interests was also an integral component of national security strategy during the Clinton presidency, and this was reflected in CENTCOM theater strategy. By the late 1990s, CENTCOM's Operation Desert Spring involved frequent training exercises each year, resulting in a 'near continuous presence' south of the Iraqi border in Saudi Arabia, which could better 'deter conflict, promote stability, and facilitate a seamless transition to war, if required.'[74] Throughout the 1990s, CENTCOM's self-declared purpose, espoused in its annual posture statements, echoed closely the Clinton administration's vision of when to use force 'to protect the United States' vital interest in the region – uninterrupted, secure U.S./Allied access to Gulf oil.'[75] CENTCOM CINC General James Binford Peay III told the House Appropriations Committee Subcommittee on National Security in 1997 that any disruption in the flow of petroleum from the Persian Gulf would 'precipitate economic calamity for developed and developing nations alike.'[76] His successor as CENTCOM CINC, General Anthony Zinni, echoed these sentiments and located CENTCOM's geoeconomic mission precisely in his 1998 report to the Senate Armed Services Committee:

America's interests in [the Central Region] reflect our beliefs in access to free markets, the Middle East Peace Process, protection of and access to regional energy resources, and reduce the proliferation of conventional and mass destruction weapons. The vast quantities of oil, gas, and other resources present in the gulf region, which includes 69 percent of the world's known oil reserves plus significant natural gas fields, are essential to today's global economies. Much of the oil exported from the Arabian Gulf countries passes through at least one of three important maritime choke points: the Strait of Hormuz, the Suez Canal, or the Bab el Mandeb between Yemen and Eritrea. When the Central Asian States are added to CENTCOM's AOR in 1999, the addition of their energy resources, currently estimated at 15–25 billion dollars of oil, will only increase the importance of the region to economies worldwide.[77]

The Bush administration's arrival in 2001 once again did not alter CENTCOM's theater strategy of forward deterrence in defense of vital energy assets for the US and global economy. As Secretary of Energy Spencer Graham declared to the House International Relations Committee in 2002, 'energy security' was, after all, 'national security.'[78] Moreover, the administration's aggressive geopolitics in CENTCOM's AOR in the wake of the September 11 attacks did not occlude an ongoing and simultaneous security strategy of reform via 'economic liberalization and integration.'[79] Coinciding with the militarism of President Bush's war on terror in the Middle East, for example, is a little-discussed geopolitical and geoeconomic strategy of securing Free Trade Agreements with key Gulf States. Free Trade Agreements were signed with Bahrain in 2004 and Oman in 2005 (both of which had the additional provisos of dropping all boycotts of Israel), and negotiations to secure similar Free Trade Agreements with UAE, Kuwait and Qatar are underway.[80] These agreements have already opened up the market for a host of foreign oil and gas companies, such as Exxon Mobil, Totalfina Elf and Royal Dutch Shell.[81] The Bush administration's *National Defense Strategy* in 2005 further illustrates a dual strategy of securing militarily 'strategic access' and extending 'global freedom of action.'[82] Its policy objective incorporated four interrelated strategic and geoeconomic concerns: promoting 'the security of the United States'; ensuring 'freedom of action'; helping 'secure our partners'; and protecting 'the integrity of the international economic system.'[83]

In CENTCOM's world, the hard economic discourse of vital interests has always been accompanied by a more pervasive and softer cultural discourse of bringing stability, freedom and democracy in the face of evil, barbarity and fundamentalism. This is not new, of course; the world has a depressingly long history of colonial discourse vilifying whole nations and securing the moral compass for their social and economic correction. From the English in sixteenth-century Ireland to the French in twentieth-century Algeria, colonial discourse has not only furnished us with abounding examples of the circulation of imaginative geographical knowledges of *othered* peoples, but has always been mobilized in tandem with geoeconomic interests.[84] For CENTCOM's war in Iraq (neatly situated within a broader war on terror), when we peel away the affective imaginative geographies of *us* versus *them* that legitimize the use of military force and perform the discursive trick of monopolizing our attention, ethics and conception of humanity, we are left with an overt geoeconomic project, which reveals ultimately that maintaining the conditions for a US-centered global economy, defined by a neoliberal political economic doctrine, is CENTCOM's central geostrategic priority.[85] CENTCOM has always equated *security needs* with *economic interests*; the orientation of a culturally-nuanced foreign policy has never been the agenda, which perhaps critics of US foreign policy that focus exclusively on its lack of cultural sensitivity and nous fail to acknowledge. In 2003, bringing Iraq back into the global political economy was an immediate imperative of US occupation. Consider, for example, the first news briefing on the progress on reconstructing and stabilizing Iraq, given by Paul Bremer as head of the Coalition Provisional Authority (CPA):

> Now that [our] sanctions have been lifted, it's important for Iraq to reenter the world economy. The most obvious example of that is the sale of Iraqi oil, the first sale of Iraqi oil directly into the world market by the Iraqis. The bids went out about five days ago. They have been received yesterday. And I expect they will be opened announced [sic] here in the next 48 hours or so. And that is good news; it means Iraq will have reentered the world petroleum market.[86]

For Bremer, the 'main emphasis' was 'restoring economic activity,' and this would have the effect of not only enhancing global economic health but simultaneously showing the Iraqis that they were now better off.[87]

Conclusion

By way of conclusion, I want to return to a pivotal moment that set CENTCOM in motion: President Carter's State of the Union Address in 1980. In it, the scripting of the geoeconomic and geostrategic import of the Persian Gulf region could not be clearer:

> The region which is now threatened by Soviet troops in Afghanistan is of great strategic importance: it contains more than two-thirds of the world's exportable oil. The Soviet effort to dominate Afghanistan has brought Soviet military forces to within 300 miles of the Indian Ocean and close to the Straits of Hormuz, a waterway through which most of the world's oil must flow. The Soviet Union is now attempting to consolidate a strategic position, therefore, that poses a grave threat to the free movement of Middle East oil.[88]

And how correct he was in his declaration that the situation demanded 'resolute action, not only for this year but for many years to come.'[89] In this chapter, I have placed the war in Iraq in the wider picture of US involvement in the Middle East since the late 1970s that has now culminated in the so-called global war on terror. No other region has been afforded more Defense Department budgetary support or has seen greater numbers of troops deployed in the last 30 years. It has been the primary focus of US military activity and the region where most US armed service personnel have been killed or injured in forward-deployed areas. So why so few contemporary concerns? The expansion of US nuclear capabilities and satellite-based missile defense programs during the same period received considerable attention due to a surge in peace movements, especially in Europe. As Elizabeth Gamlen observes, '[l]ess widely recognized is the equally dramatic expansion in U.S. conventional capabilities, much of which was directed toward interventionist strategies,' such as those of CENTCOM.[90] Of course, the reason for the lack of attention is arguably two-fold: first, CENTCOM has always projected its protection of US interests in conjunction with the defense of broader Western and global economic health – CENTCOM was defending global capitalism, free markets and a neoliberal order that the Europeans or Japan simply were never going to challenge; and, second, an enduring imperial register at the heart of the Western world-view of the Middle East has allowed for an abstracted geopolitical rationale for CENTCOM interventions in regions still beyond the pale – whose histories, whose cultures, and whose citizens simply do not count.

In the late 1970s, the development of the RDJTF concept and subsequent initiation of United States Central Command signalled the beginnings of a new moment of US global ambition that emerged from the ashes of US military defeat in Vietnam and the 'burden of a sagging military reputation.'[91] CENTCOM's much-heralded military successes prior to, during, and after the Gulf War, served to banish the Vietnam Syndrome from the lexicon of US policymakers and strategists in Washington, and invigorated a defiant and confident Pentagon, which was augmented further under the current Bush administration. CENTCOM's long war in the Middle East did not begin on March 19, 2003; it began over 20 years before, and has been sustained by the careful designation of its AOR as a strategic space in the world – a *geoeconomic pivot*, vital to global economic health. Since its inception, its strategy has been about closing the gaps of global neoliberal order through military force, and its mission has always been defined by a geoeconomic logic that has never been challenged on Capitol Hill, by either the Republicans or Democrats. CENTCOM CINC after CENTCOM CINC affirmed the equation between vital security interests and safeguarding global capitalism in their yearly reports to Congress; their self-defined role being the effective military maintenance of a US-centered global political economy. To this end, CENTCOM CINCs tailored and directed a theater strategy of forward presence, military deterrence and warfighting;

and the ongoing war in Iraq can be read as the spearhead of US attempts to maintain global hegemony under the auspices of a global war on terror.

Notes

* Acknowledgements: My thanks to Carl Bon Tempo, Bruce Braun, Colin Flint, Peter Hitchcock, David Ryan, Neil Smith and the 2007–2008 fellows at the Center for Place, Culture and Politics at CUNY Graduate Center for their insightful comments at various stages. My thanks too to Jochen Albrecht for expertly drawing Figures 1 and 2.
1 President Jimmy Carter, *State of the Union Address 1980*, Atlanta, GA: Jimmy Carter Library and Museum, at www.jimmycarterlibrary.gov/documents/speeches/su80jec.phtml.
2 Secretary of Defense Harold Brown, *Statement before the House Foreign Affairs Committee*, Washington, DC: House Foreign Affairs Committee, 20 February 1980.
3 Quoted in Klare, M.T. 'Beyond the age of petroleum,' *The Nation*, November 12, 2007, 20.
4 I provocatively use the Halford Mackinder term *pivot* to indicate the strong echoes of Mackinder at the heart of CENTCOM geopolitical discourse. On this point, see also the work of Gerry Kearns: Kearns, G., 'Naturalising empire: echoes of Mackinder for the next American century?' *Geopolitics*, vol. 11, no. 1 (2006), 74–98; and Kearns, G., 'The political pivot of geography,' *The Geographical Journal*, vol. 170, no. 4 (2004), 337–346.
5 I use the terms *geoeconomic* and *geoeconomic pivot* less as an exercise in Luttwakian-style *geo-economics* but more as a way to signal the political economy logic of US involvement in the Middle East, which I am arguing has underpinned evolving ideological and geopolitical logics of intervention, especially since the 1970s. Cf.: Luttwak, E.N., 'From geopolitics to geo-economics: logic of conflict, grammar of commerce,' *The National Interest*, vol. 20 (1990), 17–23; and Cowen, D. and Smith, N. (forthcoming) 'After geopolitics? Geoeconomics and the territorial politics of security,' *Antipode*.
6 For a coherent reading of the historical trajectory of US involvement in the Middle East after World War II (from the initial *advancement of US naval power* under the Truman Doctrine, through to the *limited war strategy* of the Eisenhower Doctrine, to the *twin pillar regional security policy* of the Nixon Doctrine), see Gold, D., *America, the Gulf and Israel: CENTCOM (Central Command) and Emerging US Regional Security Policies in the Middle East* (Jerusalem: Jaffee Center for Strategic Studies, 1988), 8–28. See also Painter, D., *Oil and the American Century: The Political Economy of U.S. Foreign Oil Policy, 1941–1954* (Baltimore: John Hopkins University Press, 1986).
7 President of the National Defense Council Foundation, Milton R. Copulos, *Statement before the Senate Foreign Relations Committee*, Washington, DC: Senate Foreign Relations Committee, March 30, 2006, 4.
8 Ibid. This point is often forgotten in debates concerning the difficulties the Democrats have faced in contesting the ongoing war in Iraq. Zbigniew Brzezinski, one of the central architects of refocusing US foreign policy on the Middle East in the late 1970s, is now a senior foreign policy advisor to Barack Obama.
9 President Carter's State of the Union Address in 1980 set out the Carter Doctrine, which explicitly signalled a new US foreign policy of defending by 'any means necessary' the Persian Gulf region.
10 For example, in Lebanon in 1958.
11 MacDill Air Force Base, located at the southern tip of the Interbay Peninsula in

118   *J. Morrissey*

Tampa Bay, had been proposed for decommissioning in 1960, though only open since 1941. The Cuban Missile Crisis and the Bay of Pigs invasion, however, soon reaffirmed its geostrategic importance.

12 *Hearings on Military Posture and HR 9751, Fiscal Year (FY) 1963*, Washington, DC: House Armed Services Committee, 3296.

13 Record, J., *The Rapid Deployment Force and U.S. Military Intervention in the Persian Gulf* (Washington, DC: Institute for Foreign Policy Analysis, 1981).

14 Acharya, A., 'US Strategy in the Persian Gulf: The Rapid Deployment Force as an Instrument of Policy,' unpublished thesis, Murdoch University, 1986.

15 Gamlen, E.J., 'United States strategic policy toward the Middle East: Central Command and the reflagging of Kuwait's tankers,' in H. Amirahmadi (ed.) *The United States and the Middle East: A Search for New Perspectives* (Albany: State University of New York, 1993), 213–249; The Persian Gulf region was incorporated into US European Command's *Area of Responsibility* in 1972.

16 Record, *The Rapid Deployment Force.*

17 Brzezinski's memoirs, and contemporary commentaries of influential strategists such as Dr. Jeffrey Record at the Institute for Foreign Policy Analysis in Washington, are underscored by an anxious masculinity concerned with reasserting *pride* and *global forward presence* in the aftermath of a series of US military failures in the 1970s. See: Brzezinski, Z., *Power and Principle: Memoirs of the National Security Adviser, 1977–1981* (New York: Farrar, Straus, Giroux, 1983); and Record, *The Rapid Deployment Force.*

18 US Joint Chiefs of Staff, *Military Posture FY 1982*, Washington, DC: Department of Defense.

19 Gold, *America, the Gulf and Israel*, 26.

20 Ibid., 55.

21 President Jimmy Carter, (1978) 'Wake Forest Speech,' quoted in Gamlen, E.J., 'United States strategic policy toward the Middle East: Central Command and the reflagging of Kuwait's tankers,' in Amirahmadi, *The United States and the Middle East*, 218.

22 Acharya, 'US Strategy in the Persian Gulf.'

23 RDJTF Headquarters (1981) *Fact Sheet*, MacDill Air Force Base, Tampa, FL: Public Affairs Office.

24 Record, *The Rapid Deployment Force*, vii.

25 Ibid., 1.

26 See Gamlen, E.J. (1993) 'United States strategic policy toward the Middle East: Central Command and the reflagging of Kuwait's tankers,' in Amirahmadi, *The United States and the Middle East*, 244.

27 US Congressional Budget Office, *Rapid Deployment Forces: Policy and Budgetary Implications* (Washington, DC: US Congressional Budget Office, 1983), 4. The renaming of a vast, culturally diverse area, stretching from Central Asia to East Africa, reprised the long-established colonial practice of remapping the world in the interests of empire. *Southwest Asia* in Pentagonese later became known as the *Central Region.*

28 Secretary of Defense Caspar Weinberger, *Statement before the House Committee on the Budget*, Washington, DC: House Committee on the Budget, September 23, 1981, 9.

29 CENTCOM was the 'first new unified command with specific geographic responsibilities to be created in thirty-five years': see Gamlen, E.J. (1993) 'United States strategic policy toward the Middle East: Central Command and the reflagging of Kuwait's tankers,' in Amirahmadi, *The United States and the Middle East*, 219.

30 The original 19 countries in the CENTCOM AOR were: Afghanistan, Bahrain, Djibouti, Egypt, Ethiopia, Iran, Iraq, Jordan, Kenya, Kuwait, Oman, Pakistan,

Qatar, Saudi Arabia, Somalia, Sudan, United Arab Emirates, South Yemen and North Yemen. After Yemen's unification in 1990 and Eritrea's independence from Ethiopia in 1991, CENTCOM's AOR remained at 19 countries until the Seychelles was added in 1996. The five Central Asian states of Kazakhstan, the Kyrgyz Republic, Tajikistan, Turkmenistan and Uzbekistan were added in 1999 to bring the AOR to 25 countries, while, in 2004, the addition of Lebanon and Syria brought that number to 27, its current AOR. On October 1, 2008, seven CENTCOM countries are scheduled to officially become part of the new Africa Command (AFRICOM) when it reaches 'full operational capability': Djibouti, Eritrea, Ethiopia, Kenya, Seychelles, Somalia and Sudan (Egypt will be the sole African country to remain in CENTCOM's AOR for long-standing geostrategic reasons).

31 US CENTCOM, *US CENTCOM Histor*, at www.centcom.mil (accessed October 30, 2007).
32 Morrissey, J. (forthcoming) 'War, geopolitics and imaginative geographies,' in J. Morrissey, U. Strohmayer, Y. Whelan and B. Yeoh, *Key Concepts in Historical Geography* (London: Sage). See also: Gregory, D., *The Colonial Present: Afghanistan, Palestine, Iraq* (Oxford: Blackwell, 2004); Melling, P., 'War and memory in the New World Order,' in M. Evans and K. Lunn (eds), *War and Memory in the Twentieth Century* (Berg, Oxford, 1997), 255–267; and Smith, N., *The Endgame of Globalization* (New York: Routledge, 2005).
33 *The National Defense Strategy of the United States of America 2005*, Washington, DC: Department of Defense, March 2005, 1.
34 See: Said, E., *Covering Islam: How the Media and the Experts Determine How We See the Rest of the World*, 2nd edn (London: Vintage, 1997); and Shapiro, M.J., *Violent Cartographies: Mapping Cultures of War* (Minneapolis: University of Minnesota Press, 1997).
35 US CENTCOM, *United States Central Command Posture Statement* (MacDill Air Force Base, FL: Office of the Commander-in-Chief, 1995), 8–9; US CENTCOM, *United States Central Command Posture Statement* (MacDill Air Force Base, FL: Office of the Commander-in-Chief, 1997), 6–8; CENTCOM CINC General Anthony C. Zinni, *Statement before the Senate Armed Services Committee on the Posture of United States Central Command*, Washington, DC: Senate Armed Services Committee, March 3, 1998; CENTCOM CINC General Anthony C. Zinni, *Statement before the Senate Armed Services Committee on the Posture of United States Central Command*, Washington, DC: Senate Armed Services Committee, February 29, 2000.
36 Since before World War II, US military personnel had commonly used CINC as the shortened version of *Commander-in-Chief* when referring to commanders of unified commands. However, in 2002, Secretary of Defense Donald Rumsfeld, cited Article II, Section 2 of the US Constitution, which states that the 'President shall be Commander in Chief of the Army and Navy of the United States,' to officially strip commanders of their CINC title and replace it with *Commander*. The CINC title is used here for all references to combatant commanders serving prior to this formal adjustment.
37 CENTCOM CINC General Anthony C. Zinni, *Statement before the Senate Armed Services Committee on the Posture of United States Central Command*, Washington, DC: Senate Armed Services Committee, April 13, 1999.
38 CENTCOM Commander General John P. Abizaid, *Statement before the Senate Armed Services Committee on the Posture of United States Central Command*, Washington, DC: Senate Armed Services Committee, March 16, 2006.
39 Klare, M.T., *Resource Wars: The New Landscape of Global Conflict* (New York: Owl Books, 2002).
40 Record, *The Rapid Deployment Force*, 5.

41 McNaugher, T.L., *Arms and Oil: U.S. Strategy and the Persian Gulf* (Washington, DC: Brookings Institution, 1985).

42 Quoted in Hines, J., 'From Desert One to Southern Watch: the evolution of U.S. Central Command,' *Joint Forces Quarterly*, vol. 24 (2000), 44.

43 For a critical reading of Arab and Muslim world-views of the United States in the post 9/11 period, see Telhami, S., *The Stakes: America and the Middle East* (Boulder, CO: Westview Press, 2002).

44 US Congressional Budget Office, *Rapid Deployment Forces: Policy and Budgetary Implications* (Washington, DC: US Congressional Budget Office, 1983), xiii.

45 CENTCOM CINC General George Crist, *Statement before the Senate Armed Services Committee on the Posture of United States Central Command*, Washington, DC: Senate Armed Services Committee, March 11, 1986.

46 Quoted in Klare, M.T., *Blood and Oil: The Dangers and Consequences of America's Growing Dependency on Imported Petroleum* (New York: Owl Books, 2004), 4.

47 Amirahmadi, 'Global restructuring, the Persian Gulf War, and the U.S. quest for world leadership,' in Amirahmadi, *The United States and the Middle East*, 363–364.

48 Wolfowitz, P.D., 'Book Review. Crusade: The Untold Story of the Persian Gulf War by Rick Atkinson,' *Joint Force Quarterly*, vol. 3 (1994), 123.

49 Ibid., 124.

50 Lebanon and Syria were not incorporated into CENTCOM until 2004; Israel and the Occupied Territories remain in the AOR of US European Command.

51 For more on this, see Gamlen, 'United States strategic policy,' in Amirahmadi, *The United States and the Middle East*, 219.

52 US Department of Defense, 'Fiscal 2009 Department of Defense budget released,' News Release, February 4, 2008, at www.defenselink.mil/comptroller/defbudget/fy2009/2009_Budget_Rollout_Release.pdf (accessed February 6, 2008). The combined Defense Department budget has more than doubled in the last ten years; see *National Defense Budget Estimates for FY 1999*, Washington, DC: Office of the Undersecretary of Defense, March 1998, 4–13.

53 US Department of State, 'International Affairs FY 2009 Budget,' Fact Sheet, February 4, 2008, at www.state.gov/f/releases/factsheets2008/99981.htm (accessed February 6, 2008).

54 Reveron, D.S. and Gavin, M.D., 'America's viceroys,' in D.S. Reveron (ed.) *America's Viceroys: The Military and U.S. Foreign Policy* (New York: Palgrave Macmillan, 2004), 3. The Defense Department proclaims itself as America's oldest, biggest and most flourishing business: 'if you look at us in business terms, many would say we are not only America's largest company, but its busiest and most successful' (DoD 101: An Introductory Overview of the Department of Defense, at www.defenselink.mil/pubs/dod101 – accessed 11 February 2008).

55 Quoted in Wrage, S.D., 'US combatant commander: the man in the middle,' in D.S. Reveron (ed.) *America's Viceroys*, 190–191.

56 Record, *The Rapid Deployment Force*, 39.

57 Wrage, 'US combatant commander,' in Reveron, *America's Viceroys*, 186.

58 Schwarzkopf, N.H., *It Doesn't Take a Hero* (New York: Bantam Books, 1992), 271.

59 Reveron, and Gavin, M.D. (2004) 'America's viceroys,' in Reveron, *America's Viceroys*, 1.

60 See the detailed School of Advanced Military Studies monograph by Major Jeffrey Bradford: Bradford, J.A., *Proconsuls and CINCs from the Roman Republic to the Republic of the United States of America: Lessons for the Pax Americana* (Fort Leavenworth, US: School of Advanced Military Studies, 2001).

61 Robbins, J.S., 'U.S. Central Command: where history is made,' in Reveron, *America's Viceroys*, 172.

62 Ibid.
63 Pelletiere, S.C. and Johnson D.V., II, *Oil and the New World System: CENTCOM rethinks its Mission* (Carlisle, PA: Strategic Studies Institute, U.S. Army War College, 1992), v, 26.
64 It has been argued that CENTCOM forces intervening in Mogadishu in December 1992, as part of the broader UN humanitarian force, also had a geopolitical, military mission from Washington – to take out anti-American warlord General Mohammed Fareh Aideed, who had ousted the previous US-backed dictator, General Siad Barre.
65 CENTCOM CINC General H. Norman Schwarzkopf, *Statement before the Senate Armed Services Committee on the Posture of United States Central Command*, Washington, DC: Senate Armed Services Committee, February 8, 1990.
66 See, for example, Ian Lesser's 1991 study, *Oil, the Persian Gulf, and Grand Strategy: Contemporary Issues in Historical Perspective*, which was part of a larger RAND project, sponsored by CENTCOM and the Joint Chiefs, on US grand strategy for the Persian Gulf region (Lesser, I.O., *Oil, the Persian Gulf, and Grand Strategy: Contemporary Issues in Historical Perspective*, [Santa Monica, CA: RAND Corporation, 1991]).
67 Pelletiere and Johnson, *Oil and the New World System*, v.
68 Secretary of Defense William J. Perry, *United States Security Strategy for the Middle East* (Washington, DC: Department of Defense, Office of International Security Affairs, 1995), 5–8. The other components outlined are: protection of US citizens and property; freedom of navigation; successful reform in the former Soviet Union; human rights and democratic development; and access to regional markets – see pp. 8–10.
69 Ibid., ii.
70 Binford Peay J.H., III, 'The five pillars of peace in the Central Region,' *Joint Force Quarterly*, vol. 9 (1995), 32.
71 Ibid.
72 See, for example: Energy Information Administration, *Privatization and the Globalization of Energy Markets* (Washington, DC: Department of Energy, 1996).
73 Institute for National Security Studies, *Strategic Assessment 1999* (Washington, DC: Institute for National Strategic Studies, National Defense University, 1999).
74 US CENTCOM, 'Shaping U.S. Central Command for the 21st Century,' *Strategic Plan II, 1997–1999* (MacDill Air Force Base, FL: Office of the Commander-in-Chief, 1997), 5.
75 US CENTCOM, *United States Central Command Posture Statement* (MacDill Air Force Base, FL: Office of the Commander-in-Chief, 1995), 1. See pp. 8–9 for an elaboration on the dual focus on oil and access.
76 CENTCOM CINC General James H. Binford Peay III, 'Promoting peace and stability in the Central Region,' *Report to the House Appropriations Committee Subcommittee on National Security*, Washington, DC: House Appropriations Committee Subcommittee on National Security, March 17, 1997.
77 CENTCOM CINC General Anthony C. Zinni, *Statement before the Senate Armed Services Committee on the Posture of United States Central Command*, Washington, DC: Senate Armed Services Committee, March 3, 1998.
78 Secretary of Energy Spencer Graham, *Statement before the House International Relations Committee*, Washington, DC: House International Relations Committee, June 20, 2002.
79 See Katzman, K., *The Persian Gulf States: Issues for U.S. Policy, 2006* (Washington, DC: Congressional Research Service Report for Congress, 2006), 26–29,
80 Ibid., 28–29.
81 Ibid., 28.
82 *The National Defense Strategy of the United States of America 2005* (Washington, DC:

Department of Defense, March 2005), 6. With the so-called global war on terror focused exclusively on its AOR, CENTCOM was given foremost responsibility for enacting this national defense strategy. For further reflection on the geoeconomic imperative of the global war on terror, see: Dalby, S., 'Regions, strategies and empire in the global war on terror,' *Geopolitics*, vol. 12, no. 4 (2007), 586–606; Klein, N., *The Shock Doctrine: The Rise of Disaster Capitalism* (New York: Metropolitan Books, 2007); Martin, R., *An Empire of Indifference: American War and the Financial Logic of Risk Management* (Durham: Duke University Press, 2007); Smith, N., *The Endgame of Globalization* (New York: Routledge, 2005); and Le Billon, P. and El Khatib, F., 'From free oil to "freedom oil": terrorism, war and US geopolitics in the Persian Gulf,' *Geopolitics*, vol. 9, no. 1 (2004), 109–137.

83 *The National Defense Strategy of the United States of America 2005* (Washington, DC: Department of Defense, March 2005), 6.

84 Morrissey, J., *Negotiating Colonialism* (London: HGRG, Royal Geographical Society, 2003).

85 See: Harvey, D., *The New Imperialism* (Oxford: Oxford University Press, 2005); Gregory, D., *The Colonial Present: Afghanistan, Palestine, Iraq* (Oxford: Blackwell, 2004); and Graham, S., 'Remember Fallujah: demonising place, constructing atrocity,' *Environment and Planning D: Society and Space*, vol. 23 (2005), 1–10.

86 US Department of Defense, 'Briefing on coalition post-war reconstruction and stabilization efforts,' News Transcript, June 12, 2003, at www.defense link.mil/transcripts/index.aspx?mo=6&yr=2003 (accessed February 9, 2008).

87 As urgent as Charles Ferguson's 2007 film, *No End in Sight*, is, in terms of demonstrating the power of President Bush's inner circle in key decision-making after the invasion, and showing the ineptitude of the CPA, he does not, at any point, critique the neoliberal agenda that was prioritized and not so badly served; see Ferguson, C., *No End in Sight: Iraq's Descent into Chaos* (DVD) (Los Angeles: Magnolia Pictures, 2007).

88 President Jimmy Carter, *State of the Union Address 1980*, Atlanta, GA: Jimmy Carter Library and Museum, at www.jimmycarterlibrary.gov/documents/speeches/su80jec.phtml (accessed February 12, 2008).

89 Ibid.

90 Gamlen, 'United States strategic policy toward the Middle East,' in Amirahmadi, *The United States and the Middle East*, 220.

91 Record, *The Rapid Deployment Force*, 38.

7 What would Jesus do?

Evangelicals, the Iraq War, and the struggle for position

Melani McAlister

On March 11, 2003, the eve of the Iraq war, Larry King hosted a live debate among a group of Christian pastors and authors, posing the question: 'What would Jesus do in Iraq?' The group included a Catholic priest and a theologically diverse group of Protestants who were invited to spar with each other and the audience over the relationship between faith and politics. The question they were asked – 'what would Jesus do?' – referenced a pop culture phenomenon among younger evangelicals, who in the 1990s had taken to wearing bracelets and T-shirts with the (then) insiderish moniker: WWJD? The WWJD movement was perhaps a particularly evangelical gesture, invoking the presence of Jesus as so immediate, so accessible, that a believer could ask herself in any situation, 'what would Jesus do?' – and then presumably do likewise. But by 2003, the WWJD questions had a new urgency, as religious people in the United States, leaders and ordinary lay people alike, debated the Iraq war.

Certainly, the Larry King interview made for a lively debate. The priest Michael Manning opposed the war with traditional Catholic doctrine, calling for Christians to search first for peace. The presiding Bishop of the United Methodist Church, Melvin Talbert, also spoke strongly against the war. Talbert, the only African American in the group, had also been featured on a television ad sponsored by the National Council of Churches. The pending war, he said in that ad, 'violates God's law and the teachings of Jesus Christ.'[1]

The conservative white evangelicals, on the other hand (and they were three out of six guests on the panel) all argued in support of the war. Pastor and author John MacArthur was the most outspoken. 'Jesus himself spoke out for the possibility of a just war,' MacArthur insisted.

> He said, 'He who has no sword,' to his disciples, 'let him sell his garment and buy one.' Because he was sending his apostles out ... He knew there would be persecution ... And told them, get a sword because you may have to protect yourself.

Larry King appeared taken aback by this argument: 'So he endorsed war. He endorsed...' And MacArthur replied: 'He endorsed the fact of protection and just war.'[2]

The debate continued, with each side quoting scripture while mixing in more worldly arguments. The calls flooded in, with callers demanding to know how the panel saw Islam, whether the war was imperialist, and why Christians around the world were condemning the war while American Christians were largely supporting it. Throughout, the white evangelicals offered variations of the pro-war view, while the Catholic and mainline Protestant spoke for liberal opposition. Therein lay the problem.

While King's show highlighted the intensity of religious debate, it presented a vision of American evangelicals that simply reproduced a common, and erroneous, journalistic frame — one that constructed the definition of evangelicals as universally white and conservative. Thus, there were no black or Latino evangelicals on the panel, no liberals or even genuine moderates, and, typically, no women of any denomination.

This chapter advances a larger view of the role of US evangelicals in the debate over the Iraq war — one that accounts for the racial and regional diversity, political differences, and global consciousness of US-based evangelicals. My argument is three-fold. First, I assert that evangelical positions on the war were diverse, rooted in multiple and sometimes conflicting motivations and values. That is, I make the rather straightforward point that evangelicals who shared many basic religious beliefs were nonetheless frequently divided politically — theology is not destiny. Much of the public discussion of religion and the war has insisted on seeing 'evangelicals' as uniformly war-mongering. In fact, US evangelicals have held a variety of views about Iraq, and those views have changed over time.

Second, I argue that although there is no *one* politics that emerges from shared religious beliefs, an appreciation of the specific language and logic of evangelical faith is nonetheless crucial. While evangelicals talked about many issues in secular terms — questions about weapons of mass destruction or the number of troops needed in Iraq were not seen as theologically significant — they engaged many key issues at least partially in religious terms. Whether or not to go to war, whether and how to evangelize Muslims, how to respond to abuses at Abu Ghraib, the long-term future of the United States in Iraq — these were all debated in the emotionally and theologically rich terms of evangelical conviction.

Finally, this chapter makes the argument that the debates over Iraq would ultimately play a role in strengthening the hand of evangelical liberals, paving the way for important changes in evangelical political identity in the United States. Although the religious right is far from over, despite the enthusiasms of some commentators, there has definitely been a shift, an increasing willingness of evangelicals to critique the most hard-line assumptions of the old religious right. The battles among evangelicals about Iraq have played a largely unrecognized role in that shift.[3]

Examining the discussions about Iraq, I use Pierre Bourdieu's concept of 'position-taking,' articulated most clearly in *The Field of Cultural Production*. Bourdieu argues that in any given 'field' or arena, individuals and social groups are inevitably engaged in multiple actions – from policy statements to sartorial choices – that position them in relation to other actors and to the structures of power. For Bourdieu, the act of 'position-taking' is not just one of taking an intellectual position in a debate, nor it is just about positioning oneself on a cultural chess board, trying to outwit an opponent in a struggle for recognition or power. It is a combination of both of these things and more – a mixture of morally or socially derived behavior (practices and habits), individual belief, and political or social calculation.[4]

Bourdieu's model is designed to explore the ways that individuals operate as agents in a larger cultural or social field, but it also allows, indeed requires, that we examine the constitution of the field itself – the 'structuring structures' of power and sedimented social norms. In this chapter, I explore the evangelical public sphere as a social field, and the debate over Iraq as multiple instances of position-taking. My sources are the statements of religious opinion leaders, news accounts in evangelical media, and a range of cultural productions, including books, movies, advertisements, and web sites.

There is some danger in this approach, since it does restrict itself to religious and political *debate*. As scholars of religion have shown, people do not just 'think' religion, they live it – through its rituals, performances, and practices. You do not understand religion as an experience by following the details of debates over doctrine.[5] Still, the religious experiences of everyday people are not separated from the constructions of theology, negotiations of contending views, or proclamations of the obvious that structure any given religious field. As Laurie Maffly-Kipp, Leigh E. Schmidt, and Mark Valeri have argued, there is always a complex and rich relationship among 'theology, community structures, and individual agency.'[6] For evangelicals in particular, the Iraq war has served as the source of political debate and an occasion for spiritual reflection. It has also been the site of fierce competition for the right to define American evangelicalism in its national and global context.

This chapter is organized into four sections. The first examines the contours of the evangelical community today, arguing for an inclusive definition that accounts for evangelical diversity, particularly racial diversity. The second section surveys the evangelical debates about the beginning of the Iraq war, focusing particularly on the theological/political issue of whether or not Iraq was a 'just war.' The third section traces the impact that evangelicals' commitment to missionary work in the Middle East had on the Iraq war debate. Nothing was as charged, as religiously significant, or as deeply contentious as the question of when and how to evangelize in Iraq. The question galvanized evangelicals around the world, and horrified some secular observers. But a great deal was at stake, since 'missionary' work included not only evangelization, but social service and humanitarian work as well. This section on missionary work includes a discussion of evangelical views of Islam.

The fourth section focuses on evangelical reaction to Abu Ghraib in 2004 and subsequent revelations of torture or near-torture at Guantanamo. Evangelical observers were appalled by the vision of Americans and

Christians as torturers, and engaged in a multifaceted debate about the nature of sin. That debate, I argue, ultimately empowered the liberal wing of American evangelicals in ways that few other things had done. In the conclusion, I briefly explore how the impending 2008 elections prompted another discourse – at least for some evangelicals – about the problem of excessive (national) pride and the need for repentance.

I The evangelical community today

Evangelicals comprise between 25 percent and 40 percent of the US population, depending on how you define the terms and how pollsters phrase their questions. Perhaps the most useful framework is a theological one: evangelicals are those who themselves believe or whose churches and/or denominations assert the following: the inerrancy and completeness of the Bible; the centrality of the death and resurrection of Jesus; a belief that Christianity is the only route to salvation; and the importance of evangelizing others.[7] By that definition, the numbers are high: 33 percent to 38 percent of the US population, including the vast majority of African American and Latino Protestants.[8]

Questions about race are central here, in part because most analyses have actually misrepresented the evangelical public sphere by separating out African American evangelicals from the larger community. Of course it is the case that African Americans, and to a lesser degree Latinos, very often track differently on social and political issues than white evangelicals. Analysts and pollsters, trying to make clear this distinction, have generally instituted (at least) two categories: (white) evangelicals, on the one hand, and 'black Protestants,' on the other. The problem is, these divisions are actually producing the categories they claim to be analyzing: by deciding that African Americans who hold similar theological positions are not 'evangelical,' surveys themselves construct in advance what they are likely to find: we have some idea of what 'evangelical politics' will look like. In addition, African Americans are often not counted fully in this formulation, since they are also involved in many of the racially mixed evangelical and Pentecostal churches that are often defined as part of 'white' evangelicalism.[9] Latino evangelicals, on the other hand, are usually not separated out in survey data; about 15 percent of Latinos are evangelical, and they make up about 7 percent of the national evangelical population.[10]

Beyond the numbers, there is every reason to retain an inclusive definition of the term 'evangelical,' which is already and admittedly a slippery category, simply because it is clear that theologically conservative African American, Latino, Asian American and white Protestants are very much involved in a set of conversations *with each other* about faith and politics. The evangelicals who write in the pages of journals like the moderately conservative *Christianity Today*, the left liberal *Sojourners*, or the Pentecostal journal *Charisma* are at least somewhat diverse. And if we look at the representation of theologically conservative Christians on television or radio broadcasts, at national conferences and leadership seminars, or in book and DVD sales, African American mega-church pastors like TD Jakes, Creflo Dollar, and Freddie Haynes, and Latinos like Sam Rodriguez or Luis Palau are quite visible.

Of course, the involvement of people of color does *not* mean that race and racism are not issues among evangelicals – they very much are.[11] Traditionally African American denominations like the African Methodist Episcopal (AME) church certainly retain their distinct identities. But the division of evangelicals into black, white, and invisible 'others,' while useful at times, fails to account for the dynamism and border crossing within this community. Across and within lines of race, US evangelicals agree on many political and social issues, including opposition to abortion and gay marriage, support for Israel, and a commitment to missionary work globally and locally. (This agreement has in fact led to some increase, albeit small, in African American support for Republican candidates. Latinos were also moving toward more support for Republicans in the 2004 elections, although immigration battles have lessened that trend).[12] But white, black, and Latino evangelicals also disagree on many issues, including government involvement in social welfare, immigration, and – very profoundly – the Iraq war.

II Early views of the war: what makes a 'just war'?

In the spring of 2003, just before the invasion of Iraq, American churches were deeply divided, as the Larry King Live debate made clear. At the top, the liberal churches were outspoken, and the leadership of nearly every major mainline Protestant denomination (that is, non-evangelical Protestants like Episcopalians and Presbyterians) took a position that opposed or seriously questioned the war. The Catholic Church did the same. These denominations joined with Jews, Muslims, and others to form the heart of the Win without War Coalition, which was the center of much of the activism against the war in 2002 and 2003.[13]

Internationally, Christian leaders from around the world denounced the war, or at least raised serious doubts. Among others, the head of the Middle East Council of Churches, Riad Jarjour, argued that the US-led invasion 'lacks justification and has no discernible or constructive goal.'[14] At home, the National Council of Churches, which has sponsored Bishop Talbert's television ad, also took out a full page ad in the *New York Times* directed at President Bush. Referring to the President's public affirmations of his faith, the ad admonished: 'President Bush, Jesus changed your heart. Now let him change your mind.'[15] Others in the anti-war camp were less gentle. One popular bumper sticker read: 'Who would Jesus bomb?'

On the other hand, the local clergy and the people in the pews of the mainline Protestant churches were not nearly so anti-war. When polled, churchgoers said they had heard some about the war from the pulpit, but that their ministers generally had not taken a clear position. Certainly, the strong anti-war stances of the national leadership seemed to have relatively little effect: in March 2003, 62 percent of mainline Protestants supported the war, and the vast majority said that religion was a small part of how they reached their decision.[16]

One clear exception here were African American churchgoers, who, no matter their denomination, said they had heard more talk of the war from their ministers, and that the sermons were far more frequently opposed to the war – 38 percent of black Christians (Protestant and Catholic) said they had heard sermons opposing the war, versus only 5 percent of white evangelical Protestants. In the months leading up to the war, African Americans in general were opposed 56 percent to 37 percent, according to Gallup.[17] Latinos supported the war at levels similar to the US population overall, at about 75 percent in favor.[18]

Leaders in largely white evangelical churches and organizations supported the war at even higher levels, and their views tracked closely with those of their constituents. Among the most visible was the Southern Baptist Convention's Richard Land, whose argument in favor of the war was widely quoted. 'Romans 13 makes it very clear,' he argued, that 'God ordained the civil magistrate to punish those who do evil and to reward those who do right.' On a more secular note, Land also commented that the war was justified by the 'Hitleresque' nature of Saddam's regime: 'If it has to be Britain and America alone defending civilization against a ganger masquerading as a government leader for the second time in a century, then so be it.'[19] Various other evangelical leaders also reliably offered up support for the war: Rich Cizik of the National Association of Evangelicals; Charles Colson of the Prison Fellowship; James Dobson of Focus on the Family; right-wing publisher Marvin Olansky; and evangelist Franklin Graham were among the chorus.[20] Most liberal evangelicals, who I discuss in some detail below, were outspoken against the war from the start of the build-up in 2002, but at this point they were a distinctly minority voice.[21]

The views were generally not surprising: liberals and conservatives lined up fairly reliably in their positions on the war. But most evangelicals' arguments were not established merely in secular terms. Across the political spectrum, evangelical leaders drew heavily on the newly revitalized discourse of 'just war,' even as they also commented in detail about entirely factual and/or tactical questions about weapons of mass destruction, UN resolutions, and funding for terrorism.

'Just war theory,' originally developed by Augustine, Thomas Aquinas and others, was an attempt to challenge the pacifism of some Christian traditions with an argument that war might, sometimes, be acceptable. Although there are some disagreements among theorists, it is generally understood that a 'just war' must be both justified in its cause and 'just' in the way it is carried out. To launch a war, there must be a reasonable and just cause; the war must be carried out by a legitimate authority acting with 'right intentions' and with a reasonable probability of success. Once begun, the war must be fought with proportional force and avoid civilian casualties.

Did the theory of 'just war,' then, enable Christians to support wars, countering pacifist trends? Or was it designed to severely limit Christians to supporting only defensive wars? *World* magazine editor Olansky enthusiastically described the 'just war' tradition as an enabling one for Iraq war supporters:

> Theologians such as Augustine, Aquinas, Luther, and Calvin all saw some form of war as inevitable, due to the depravity of human nature ... [Thus] Christians developed codes of 'just war' that emphasized the use of necessary means of warfare but the avoidance of savagery.[22]

Just war was a moral opposition to pacifism, as well as a kind of muscular tool for Christians who might want to support a pre-emptive war.

On the other end of the spectrum, the international relations scholar George Lopez laid out the terms of a 'just war' in the left-liberal *Sojourners*. Lopez rather slyly contrasted 'traditionalists' like himself with the 'permissive school,' exemplified by Elstain and Michael Ignatieff. In writing for an evangelical audience, Lopez's act of claiming the moniker of traditionalist for himself – and describing as 'permissive' the pro-war crowd – was a savvy act of position-taking. However, Lopez was fair in his summaries of the views of the 'permissive school.' For them, he explained, the doctrine of 'just war' pivoted around the question of what constituted war as a 'last resort.' If defined too narrowly, 'last resort' gave too much leeway to norms violators and allowed rogue nations to inflict damage on innocents. For Lopez, however, 'last resort actually means *last*, with all other options exhausted.'[23]

In practice, the just war frame was remarkably flexible in the hands of Christian thinkers; it suited all comers (except for pacifists like Stanley Hauerwas at Duke), since criteria like 'legitimate authority' and 'last resort' were so vague. In some ways what was most interesting about just war theory was that it was used by evangelicals at all. After all, the question of whether or not Iraq was a 'just war' was not the same question as 'what would Jesus do?' Just war doctrine required drawing on traditions of Christian, specifically Catholic, thought, whereas the more common evangelical move would be to turn to scripture. Of course, many people did both. But the use of 'just war' doctrine was an addition – a position-taking that linked evangelicals to Catholic and mainline thinkers who were also using the frame. (This link between evangelicals and Catholics would emerge again, with the question of torture).

The interest in just war among evangelicals could be traced in part to the first war against Iraq, when an important Southern Baptist theologian, Daniel Heimbach, drafted a memo for George H.W. Bush that convinced the President to use 'just war' language in his defense of the 1991 attack. Heimbach then emerged as one of the most outspoken evangelical supporters of the 2003 war.[24] Then, as now, the term was useful precisely because it was so capacious: it signalled a specific Christian tradition, but it also seemed to speak to secular common sense: a 'just war' was one that was justifiable, in whatever moral and political terms were at hand. Charles Colson, for example, wrote an oft-cited article on 'Just War in Iraq' that primarily cited the obligation to love one's neighbor: if a Christian failed to use force to protect his neighbor, he was failing to love that neighbor. Thus, Colson argued, 'sometimes going to war is the charitable thing to do.'[25]

A small but outspoken group of evangelicals used the language of just war to very different ends. President Jimmy Carter, for example, penned an editorial in the *New York Times* saying that 'as a Christian and a president who was severely tested by international crises,' he was appalled: the United States was not directly threatened, the war was not proportional to the offence, the weapons would not discriminate between civilians and combatants, and the outcome of success quite unlikely. Still, the United States was 'determined to carry out military and diplomatic action that is almost unprecedented in the history of civilized nations.'[26] At about the same time, a group of religious leaders in the United States and the United Kingdom, including a number of American evangelicals, issued a statement saying they were 'compelled by the prophetic vision of peace' to speak out against the war.[27] In January 2003, Bishop Gilbert Paterson, Presiding Bishop of the Church of God in Christ, a historically black Pentecostal denomination, sent a letter to President Bush opposing the war. Without the proper justification for war, the 'aims, strategies, and tactics' became 'at a minimum, morally suspect and perhaps morally unacceptable in the eyes of the church universal and under the gaze of a just and holy God.'[28]

Despite the claims to 'prophetic vision' and the invocations of King, however, the general tenor of the early evangelical opposition to the war was rather defensive; they knew they were in the minority, in the country and among evangelicals more generally, and so frequently felt called to explain that in fact they were patriotic, were not trying to undermine people in uniform. One Memphis newspaper ran a column by a local Christian who explained his opposition to the war in 'just war' terms, saying that he was not unpatriotic. 'Christians who oppose the war,' he complained, 'should be respected instead of attacked.'[29] Perhaps he was right to be worried; when in the summer of 2003, one of the pastors at an evangelical church in Portland (OR) wrote a blog-post about the excessive patriotism at the church's July 4th service, the essay was enthusiastically received and widely re-posted, but he soon found himself out of a job.[30]

There was one group of evangelical observers, however, whose musings on the justness of the war generally did not appear – at least not often – in the organs of respectable opinion. The 'prophecy-watchers,' whom I have discussed elsewhere in detail, carefully parsed political events in the Middle East in term of their relation to the 'end-times' and the coming of Armageddon. For decades, well-known speakers or writers like Tim LaHaye (author of dozens of books on prophecy, including the remarkably successful *Left Behind* series) or John Hagee (whose books included *The Beginning of the End* and *Final Dawn over Jerusalem*) had offered up commentary on nearly every global political event as some kind of a sign of the 'end-times' approaching. One nationally-known African American minister, Tony Evans (who had been a leader in the Promise Keepers movement of the 1990s) supported the Iraq war on the basis of biblical prophecy.[31] End-times enthusiasm was not for experts only, however, and around the web, lay people – many of whom would probably not bristle at the term 'prophecy geek' – analyzed events as they happened, taking strongly argued positions for one or another school of interpretation. In this world of esoteric knowledge, the Iraq war engaged eager participants in heated debates over topics large and small: 'Is the Iraq war the start of Armageddon' or 'Is Bush the Antichrist?'[32]

Christianity Today insisted that, in fact, not that many of the key prophecy thinkers had jumped on the bandwagon; neither the princes of prophecy at Dallas Theological Seminary, nor the writers at RaptureReady.com, for example, were inclined to see the Iraq war as prophetically significant event.[33] And when the Iraq war did not turn out to be a conflagration, prophecy-watching returned to the sub-subcultural status that it generally occupies in evangelical life – at least until the next major Middle East crisis.

III Opportunities: missions to Muslims

The debate about just war positioned evangelical actors as liberal or conservative, nationalist or internationalist, in fairly straightforward ways. But a second major issue – perhaps even more significant as a specifically evangelical concern – was the war's impact on missionaries, in the Middle East and elsewhere. In the early phases of the war, no opportunity seemed riper, but few dangers were more immediate. At some level, it might seem like a practical question – how would US military action enable or threaten evangelical and/or social service work, and how should evangelicals respond to the situation on the ground? But in practice this problem would profoundly disturb the field of evangelical action, since individuals who agreed very closely on theology or politics might well part ways quickly on the topic of how to structure and support missionary work. Some evangelicals saw others' commitment to certain types of aggressive evangelism as a threat to Christians around the region, and perhaps around the world; for those committed to evangelism without limits, what was at stake was nothing less than the fate of the gospel itself. And so, on this issue, as much as any facing evangelicals in the post-9/11 period, pragmatic concerns and theological commitments were often dangerously in each other's way.

In the gospel of Matthew, Jesus tells his followers to 'Go therefore and make disciples of all nations.' This injunction was the impetus for the first great wave of American evangelical missionary fervor at the end of the nineteenth century, when 'evangelizing the world in this generation' was a broadly shared Protestant ambition. Today, that enthusiasm continues to form evangelical commitments, although now in a 'mission field' that has been dramatically transformed. The traditional areas of missionary activity for American evangelicals – Asia, Africa, Latin America – are now home to the largest and fastest growing Christian communities in the world. Within ten years, Africa, Asia, the Caribbean, and Latin America, and not Europe or the United States, will be the numerical and social centers of the 'next Christendom.'[34]

Debates about the goals and practices of 'missions' are one of the most politically and theologically significant issues in evangelism today.[35] The discussions among believers center on the changing relationship between the 'senders' (missionaries and their backers) and local 'receivers.' These days, those traditional power relationships are challenged. An international missionary from the United States to, say, Nigeria, is not likely to head out to the hinterlands as a lone believer in a native population, but instead may work closely with one of the Nigerian mega-churches, which likely already has multiple outreach programs throughout the country. And Nigerians – and Koreans, Brazilians, Indians, etc. – are sending out their own missionaries, to the Middle East and Asia, to Europe, and to the United States.

Within that changing context, certain types of power relationships are unsettled, although not entirely upended. Missionaries from whatever country, and the local churches they support, can still offer food, medical supplies, and other material goods. And, as in the past, pleasing the Christian missionaries can have real material benefits. Missionaries are generally quite cognizant of the issue of 'rice Christians' (the nineteenth century missionary term for Chinese who 'became' Christians in order to receive rice from the local missionaries). They continue to examine and debate their own strategies for mixing material goods and evangelism.

In general, there are three types of missionary projects: those focused on proselytizing, programs that are social-service oriented, or those that believe humanitarian aid will only work in the context of a total (Christian) remaking of a society. In the language of evangelicals, we might describe these as focused on, respectively, salvation, incarnation, or transformation.[36] All three were crucial to missions work in Iraq. There, however, the political valence of these approaches was intensified, due to the combination of the war and the particular difficulties of missionary work in a Muslim country.

The first model, proselytizing or salvation-focused, puts evangelism first and foremost. It focuses on proclaiming the gospel and starting churches. For mission groups working on this model, there is little excuse for *not* prioritizing the saving of souls: It is not that such organizations do not provide humanitarian aid; many do. But the aid is clearly secondary, usually a strategy to bring in people for evangelization. Southern Baptists, for example, sent thousands of boxes of dry food to Iraq. Each box contained a passage from the Gospel of John translated into Arabic. Other organizations, like Franklin Graham's Samaritan's Purse, do the same type of thing.[37]

Practitioners of the second model, incarnation, argue that humanitarian assistance has a purpose all of its own, in carrying out the Christian admonition to show God's love to others, even if it never leads to any conversions. This duty to incarnate the love of Jesus is a position traditionally taken by left-liberal Catholics and many mainline Protestant churches, but it is now heard among evangelicals as well.[38]

The 'transformation' model is more explicit about the requirement for evangelism: missions organizations can and should provide assistance, but real social and economic change can occur only through Christianity. At a 2007 conference on the global dimensions of faith-based organizations, Deborah Dortzbach of World Relief (an arm of the National Association of Evangelicals) argued: '[In the countries we work in] faith fuels behavior change – bringing foundational principles and standards, common language, impersonal accountability, and [the ability] to impact change.'[39]

The vast majority of mission organizations take some position that mixes the three models, combining evangelism with humanitarianism and some kind of commitment to 'social change' (of varying definitions).[40] World Vision, for example, the largest Christian aid organization in the world, sometimes provides humanitarian aid only, with no evangelical content. However, when it can – when funding and local conditions allow – it combines humanitarian aid with evangelism: a hospital clinic, for example, might be attached to a chapel.

In Iraq proselytizing of any kind was deeply problematic, and became more so as the war went on. Many religious leaders and evangelical organizations, especially those who had workers on the ground in Middle Eastern or Muslim countries, were quite worried about how Christians might be affected by the war and the general climate of hostility. In January of 2003, a group of Southern Baptists sent an open letter to their own community, highlighting the ways in which negative comments about Islam were endangering missionaries.[41] Similarly, as the Iraq war began, the leadership of the National Association of Evangelicals (NAE) found itself unable to issue a statement about the war, despite significant pro-war sentiment in the organization, because of fears about the response in the Middle East. As the NAE's Richard Cizik told an interviewer:

> [I]n many Middle Eastern countries, the word 'American' and 'Christian' are synonymous, and those angry with the United States might say, 'We can't do anything about the planes up there, but here's people [local Christians or missionaries] who are linked to Americans.'[42]

Not surprisingly, however, some prominent evangelical groups – especially those committed to a proselytizing model – saw the invasion of Iraq as providing an extraordinary opportunity to do mission work in a country that had previously been extremely difficult to access. Iraq, like most Muslim countries, had not allowed foreign missionaries into the country. That changed with the US-led invasion, and Iraq became the frontline, a kind of proving-ground, for the larger project of reaching Muslims everywhere with the gospel.[43]

Evangelicals around the world had been prioritizing missions to Muslims for more than a decade. In the 1990s, Argentinian evangelist Luis Bush founded the 'AD 2000 and Beyond' movement, which proclaimed as its goal 'a church for every people and a gospel for every person by AD 2000.' The movement's more specific target was the '10/40 Window,' that is, the rectangular region on the world map between 10° and 40° north latitude, encompassing North Africa, most of the Middle East, and Southeast Asia.[44] In 1997, the Southern Baptist Convention responded to the AD 2000 and Beyond movement by restructuring its large and well-funded missions program to focus more energetically on the 'Final Frontier' – un-reached peoples in the Middle East and South Asia. Since the 1980s, the number of missionaries in Islamic countries has quadrupled.[45]

In both Afghanistan and Iraq, a number of evangelical organizations simply followed behind the troops into these formerly 'closed' countries. For example, Franklin Graham's missionary and aid organization, Samaritan's Purse, had relief workers/missionaries massed over the border in Jordan as the US invasion of Iraq began. As the battles were won, they moved in, bringing both humanitarian assistance and the gospel message into Iraq. Graham, who after 9/11 had infamously called Islam 'an evil and wicked religion,' was the most incendiary of the wartime missionaries in Iraq, but he was far from alone: the Southern Baptist Convention also had an early program, as did scores of individual churches, from the United States and around the world.[46]

Proselytizing believers were quite clear on the stakes. As evangelicals were pouring into Iraq in the spring and summer of 2003, Albert Mohler, president of the Southern Baptist Theological Seminary, countered charges of Christian imperialism:

> The secular world tends to look at Islam as a function of ethnicity, which means seeking to convert these people to Christianity is an insult to them. But ... the Christian has to look at Iraq and see persons desperately in need of the gospel. Compelled by the love and command of Christ, the Christian will seek to take that gospel in loving and sensitive, but very direct, ways to the people of Iraq.[47]

This view was certainly not confined to Americans; in fact, many evangelists from the global south, with relatively little to offer in terms of financial assistance, had a similar focus on starting churches in Iraq. Although many evangelicals outside the United States had been quite outspoken about their opposition to the war, others were very involved in the post-war proselytizing activities. One Lebanese church pastor who helped start several churches in Iraq, especially in the Kurdish areas, told me in a personal interview: 'We are very grateful to your soldiers, who made it possible to bring the word of Christ to Iraq.'[48]

The idea of a 'clash of civilizations' loomed in all of the debates about the status of missionaries, either as a presumed reality or a fearful concern. In the DVDs, films, web-pages, and multiple books that examined Islam from an evangelical perspective, evangelical views were diverse – they traversed the spectrum from furious hatred to determined dialogue. On the right, Marvin Olansky, editor of the right-wing *World* magazine, called for a tougher policy in Iraq since military might was all Muslims would understand: 'Islam is a works-based religion that emphasizes winning: Muhammad and his successors spread the faith by wielding the sword.'[49] The relatively liberal evangelicals at Fuller Theological Seminary, on the other hand, started a one million dollar program to develop greater and more respectful understandings of Islam.[50] And the diplomacy-oriented moderates at the Institute for Global Engagement set up conferences, held workshops, and travelled to the Muslim world to try to create dialogue. 'As evangelicals,' one workshop leader said, 'we need to hear from Islamic voices so that the "CNN moments" – the flashes of something "newsworthy" that enter our experience and then vanish – don't blind us to the diversity and vitality of the Muslim tradition.'[51] These more moderate voices gain some influence, over time, but as the Iraq war began, the general climate was hostile. In one 2002 survey sponsored by the Ethics and Public Policy Center, a Christian think tank, and Beliefnet, 77 percent of evangelicals said their overall view of Islam was 'negative.' When asked if Muslims and Christians pray to the same God, 79 percent said no. Evangelicals also gave a high priority to missionary work: 97 percent thought it was 'very important' or 'somewhat important' to evangelize Muslims at home and abroad.[52]

In the field of missions, the question of how evangelicals should or could relate to Islam carried special weight: it was practical, urgent, and theologically significant. The determination to proselytize was sometimes the source of a great deal of anger and even hatred toward Islam, especially since Muslim nations often forbid such proselytization. In theory, of course, there was an important distinction between proselytizing to Muslims and denigrating Islam, and the literature of mission organizations often highlighted their loving, respectful approaches to Muslims. Still, a proselytizing movement is by definition not an ecumenical movement; and loving individual Muslims (even as a goal) is not the same as respecting 'Islam' as a religion. The AD 2000 and Beyond movement founder Luis Bush had argued that Islam was dangerous precisely because Muslims were also gaining converts in various parts of the world. Islam was 'reaching out energetically to all parts of the globe; in a similar strategy, we must penetrate (its) heart with the liberating truth of the gospel.'[53]

It was not uncommon for well-known evangelicals to present Islam in a more complicated way – combining calls to love Muslims and a commitment to 'dialogue' with a deep conviction that Islam is a nightmare religion.

The Dutch-born evangelist Brother Andrew, who has written more than 11 books on evangelism and Islam, is enormously admired among evangelicals around the world.[54] Brother Andrew is also well known for his regular trips to the West Bank and Gaza, and for his insistence that evangelicals need to start acknowledging the terrible social conditions faced by Palestinians under Israeli occupation. He speaks passionately about the need for Christians to stop hating Muslims, and instead to start listening to them – and sympathizing with them. But Brother Andrew also writes frequently and passionately about the dangers of the 'rise of Islam.' And his 'sympathy' for Muslims is exactly that. Describing a lecture he gave at Hamas University (and, of course, his giving a Christian lecture to Hamas was no small coup), he told an interviewer:

> I stand there and I open the New Testament and I read about the cross, about forgiveness, and this concept of God's love. [For them] forgiveness is unknown.... They know nothing about the assurance of salvation. They're such uncertain people. Why are we not crying out with compassion and pity on a billion people like that?... They are human people that have the same fear and pain and anxiety and love that I have.[55]

Muslims need human compassion and pity. They also need to hear the promise of Christianity, since their religion leaves them 'uncertain people' who do not really understand God. But if they refuse to embrace the peace of Christ, they are doomed to be part of the 'Islamic insurgence' that is threatening Christianity.

It was within this context – the combination of hostility and sometimes problematic love – that many people in Iraq and in the Middle East more generally were quite suspicious of the motives of evangelical missionary and humanitarian organizations. Abbulaziz Sachedina, a scholar of Islam at the University of Virginia, argued that he believes that Iraqis appreciate aid from US organizations, but that they also feel a lot of suspicion about the agendas of humanitarian organizations:

> On the one hand, they [Iraqis] want [aid organizations] to come in; at the same time ... America does ... stand out as a Christian nation, as a Christian nation that is anti-Islamic at the moment. Therefore there's a lot of suspicion of what exactly the missions are trying to accomplish.[56]

In the first two years of the Iraq war, those suspicions had real consequences, and it became clear that the military-evangelism complex had failed in its mission. In fact, the arrival of American evangelicals did not help Christians or evangelism in Iraq. As liberal evangelical author and radio show host Tony Campolo wrote:

Sadly, one of the consequences of our support of our nation's foreign policies is that the doors for missionary work are being shut. ... In Iraq, Christians, who even during the evil days of the Hussein regime had the privilege of boldly worshipping and evangelizing, are now being threatened.[57]

Indeed, over the course of the five years between 2003 and March 2008, at least a dozen US and other foreign missionaries were attacked in Iraq. In the spring of 2004 alone, eight American missionaries were killed in drive-by shootings and six South Koreans were abducted.[58] Uncountable numbers of Iraqi Christians faced increased dangers, including a series of attacks on churches that led to a dramatic exodus among the already small Christian population. By 2005, every major Christian foreign aid organization, and most other humanitarian organizations, had pulled out of Iraq.[59]

Missionary work in Iraq was one 'sub-field' within the larger field of evangelical faith-politics. As US organizations and individuals took positions – made statements, sent medical supplies, or worked with Christians in the Middle East to try to start churches in Iraq – they also positioned themselves in relationship to each other, and as part of the larger American conversation about Islam. For proselytizing evangelicals like Franklin Graham, the opportunities opened up by the war were immediate and unproblematic, part of a global struggle for souls – and social power. Others saw the war as both opportunity and danger – whether or not they had supported the war, they might provide services in Iraq as part of incarnating their faith by serving those in need. But they could not separate themselves out by the nature of their intentions: the Iraq war was what Bourdieu would call the 'structuring structure' of the entire enterprise, and the 'clash' between Islam and Christianity was *made* real by the fact that some people (Muslim and Christian) enacted it on the ground.

IV Doubt: sin at Abu Ghraib

When the atrocities at Abu Ghraib were revealed in May 2004, the revelations were shocking, and polarizing, for the US public in general. Commentators from across the political spectrum tried to make sense of the images – the violence done to detainees, and the bodies naked and in pain, the smiling young people who were dragging prisoners on dog leashes.[60] But for evangelicals, especially those who had supported the war, the revelations at Abu Ghraib raised very particular moral and theological questions. This was not just a political issue, or a nationalist question about how Americans could behave so terribly. It was a question of sin.

When the photos from Abu Ghraib were published, the Vatican and mainline Protestant churches immediately spoke eloquently and angrily about what they had seen. One group of religious leaders developed an ad to run on two Middle East satellite stations, al-Jazeera and al-Arabiyya, that apologized for what happened at Abu Ghraib. Read by four different representatives – Jewish, Catholic, Protestant, and Muslim – the ad said in part: 'As Americans of faith, we express our deep sorrow at abuses committed in Iraqi prisons.... We condemn the sinful and systemic abuses committed in our name, and pledge to work to right these wrongs.'[61] Some evangelical groups also spoke out: the left-wing *Sojourners* called for Defense Secretary Donald Rumsfeld's resignation, arguing that he had known for months about the treatment of prisoners at Abu Ghraib. 'Such inaction and tolerance of human rights abuses is inexcusable,' *Sojourners* wrote in an email message to supporters: 'If these abuses were systemic, we cannot trust that same system – including military police and intelligence officials, the CIA, and independent military contractors – to correct them.'[62]

But in the first two or three weeks after the revelations, even months later, there was, as *Christianity Today* noted, a remarkable silence among most evangelicals. A largely conservative community, still strongly supportive of the war and the president, was slow to respond publicly. After an original quietude, however, evangelicals soon produced a broad range of commentary on the scandal. This commentary was much like its secular counterpart in some ways, musing on the horror of what the guards at Abu Ghraib had done, noting the sexual lewdness, commenting on the specifically anti-Muslim tenor of much of the torture.

Evangelicals had two concerns that differed from those of the secular press, however. The first was several of the perpetrators publicly identified as (Protestant) Christians. Spec. Charles Graner Jr., the ringleader of the group, had apparently evoked his faith in a disturbing way, when he described the sexual and physical abuse he and his colleagues were carrying out. 'The Christian in me says it's wrong,' he told Spec. James Darby, 'but the corrections officer in me says, "I love to make a grown man piss himself." '[63] Graner claimed to be a believer, then, but one who apparently did not find in his faith many resources for moral rectitude. Now, on display for the world, the image of American Christians as persecutors, as torturers – violators of fundamental human rights who also relished, and photographed, their abuses.

By 2004, human rights had been a topic in the evangelical public sphere for more than 20 years. Intellectuals and activists had written about human rights in journals like *Christianity Today*, in hundreds of books, and on activist/fundraising web sites. This reporting and activism had focused primarily on the oppression of Christians – often by Muslims. American evangelicals viewed images and heard stories of the suffering of Christians in the global south – people imprisoned, tortured, or driven from their homes; and they read, often, about the particular threat of Islam, since Muslims were presented as intolerant persecutors, the greatest threat to Christians since the fall of communism.[64] The 'persecuted Christians' movement had real political consequences; it led, in part, to the passage of the International Religious Freedom Act of 1998.[65] Its greatest significance, however, lay in the kinds of images it produced for American Christians *of themselves*. The suffering of Christians in the global south was the suffering of *their* people, and in identifying with that persecution, they created a sense of themselves too as under attack. It was a comfortable position, one that allowed a kind of solidarity with global Christians but which also fed into the more mundane sense of marginalization in US culture. Then, with the revelations at Abu Ghraib, American evangelicals had a very different vision – they had to grapple with the image of themselves as persecutors.

The second, related issue for evangelicals was theological, and it focused on the problem of sin. That is, there was a ready agreement among evangelicals (as well as among other Christians) that, whatever else it was, the situation at Abu Ghraib was a demonstration of the inherent sinfulness of human beings. Across the theological and political spectrum of American evangelicalism, believers highlighted the essentially 'fallen' nature of human beings. Southern Baptist Theological Seminary president Albert Mohler articulated a common sentiment, saying that 'moral romanticists' might be befuddled by what had happened, but 'Christians, on the other hand, are informed by the biblical teaching that human evil is written into the very warp and woof of humanity.'[66] Or, as Glen Stassen, professor of Christian ethics at the evangelical Fuller Theological Seminary would later put it: torture 'is the sin of usurping authority and making yourself the replacement for God, the sin of dominating the powerless, the sin of violating God's creation.'[67]

Evangelicals differed widely, however, on the implications of that understanding of sin as central to human nature. Gary Bauer of Focus on the Family, for example, insisted, as many secular conservatives did, that the events at Abu Ghraib were 'the perverse acts of a few,' caused by 'man's sinfulness multiplied by wartime pressures.'[68] In his view, Abu Ghraib said nothing about the situation in Iraq overall: our nature as sinners shows up in many situations, and while war often causes evil to manifest itself, neither the US leadership nor the war itself could be blamed. Individuals are responsible for their sin, not political leaders. Bauer's was a perfect example of a larger trend in thinking about Abu Ghraib – what Barthes calls the act of 'turning history into nature.' Using the doctrine of sin, he was able to efface the specifics of what happened at Abu Ghraib: the conditions in the prison and the powerful role of military intelligence there, the failures of command, the general anti-Muslim contexts of US culture in general and the military in particular. Instead of accounting for the history that made possible the abuses at Abu Ghraib, Bauer focused on universals – sinfulness and 'the stresses of war' – that can be treated as if they were 'just there,' without historical human cause.

That was one approach, but it was not the only one, even among conservatives. Some did see the sins of Abu Ghraib as firmly rooted in human causes – but those causes did not necessarily include the conduct of the Iraq war. Instead, domestic culture was the problem. The Abu Ghraib photos were clearly pornographic, and so, some conservatives rushed to conclude, it was pornography that caused the problem. Americans had allowed pornography to flourish, and without a steady diet of those images, the soldiers at Abu Ghraib would never have been able to *imagine* the things they did. (In that, we later learned that some of those treatments were actually suggested by senior officers in military intelligence). 'A good question for the public debate at the moment,' Chuck Colson commented, 'is whether we have brought all of this on ourselves by our addiction to or toleration for pornography.'[69]

And so, major evangelical conservatives responded to Abu Ghraib by positioning themselves as both horrified (in political or social terms) and worldly wise (they understood the fact of universal sin). Whatever their specific position – whether they focused on the social context of pornography as the problem or insisted that there was no problem beyond a crime committed by a few – most evangelical conservatives managed to deftly extract the sins of Abu Ghraib from the Iraq war itself, which was, on this model, neither context nor cause.

Moderate and left-liberal evangelicals responded with anger, not only at the images, but at the responses of the religious right. Samuel Rodriguez, head of the National Hispanic Leadership Conference, referred back to the seamless web argument: 'As a member of the steering committee of Evangelicals for Human Rights,' he wrote, 'I am troubled by evangelicals who embrace a Pro-Life platform yet refuse to address life issues outside the womb such as torture and cruel punishment.'[70]

Writing in *Christianity Today*, evangelical author and journalist Stephen Gertz roundly criticized Christian conservative leaders who had tried to push the scandal under the rug by blaming it on only a few 'bad apples.' Invoking the apostle Paul, Gertz argued that the soldiers' actions were indeed a symptom of sin, 'a disease we are all infected with.' Gertz's doctrine of sin as both original and individual was a view he shared with most Protestants. It required him to balance two precepts: after the expulsion from Eden, all people are sinful, by nature and inevitability; but we are also individually responsible for our sins, and will be held accountable. 'Let's rightly react with revulsion when we see these pictures, and call for an accounting for the crimes committed,' Gertz wrote.

> But let's also recognize the evil nature in ourselves, and out of this recognition ... [seek] to counter the evil done by Christians who have failed to live up to their calling. May God have mercy on us and the guards and prisoners of Abu Ghraib.[71]

Gertz had few specific recommendations for how other Christians should 'counter the evil' of Abu Ghraib, but his overall vision was clear: Christians constitute a community who somehow must atone for the failures of any part of that community.

If so, there were other histories, other sins, to speak to. Most of the white evangelical leaders, conservative and liberal, had seen Abu Ghraib in terms of sin, and perhaps saw that sin as located in the context of the larger war, but few commented on the particular history of race that the soldiers' photos evoked. The nationally renowned African American pastor and author TD Jakes, however, saw at Abu Ghraib the legacy of American racism. Jakes, who usually positioned himself as apolitical (with a conservative bent), told an interviewer that he was not surprised at the photos; he had seen similar things before, in the lynching photos from the Jim Crow south. Like some secular commentators, including Susan Sontag, Jakes saw echoes of America's racist past.[72]

> We grew up with stories of lynchings and beatings, and I've seen even as late as the 60s people beaten and left in cornfields in Mississippi.
>
> So it's very believable that somebody with too much power and privacy would pervert that power, and abuse someone who had no control. Or strip them down and tar and feather them as they did our forefathers, or rape our women. This has always been amidst the singing of hymns on Sunday morning. It was very believable to me.[73]

If Christians were the persecutors at Abu Ghraib, Jakes suggested another reminder to white evangelicals: it was not the first time.[74]

If what happened at Abu Ghraib had at first seemed singular in its grotesque horror, it soon became clear that this was just the first in a series of revelations of broad, systematic mistreatment of prisoners in US custody. Over the following year, the media reported accusations of torture at Guantanamo (soon borne out) and revealed the practice of 'extraordinary rendition' – sending prisoners to be interrogated by nations that were known to practice torture.[75] Again, there were many major religious right organizations who defended the Bush administration, or who remained strategically silent. Unlike Abu Ghraib, the torture issue could not be dismissed as a matter of individual choices made by soldiers. It was fundamentally linked to US policy in the 'war on terror.' As we have seen, many evangelicals were deeply invested in supporting the Iraq war; not a few also had a history of hostility to Islam. They were not inclined to be 'soft on terrorists' or to criticize the president; for these conservatives, human rights enforcement seemed to end at the White House door. In this, of course, they were joined by secular conservatives as well.

Other evangelicals, however, countenanced no such limitations to what they believed was the fundamental Christian conviction that each human life was sacred. This focus on the sacredness of life was linked, in part, to the religious-political idea of a 'seamless garment' or 'consistent ethic of life.' Associated originally with Catholic thinking, the idea linked opposition to abortion, the death penalty, and euthanasia with stances against poverty and oppression.[76]

A few months after the revelation of the 'torture memos,' *Christianity Today* ran a cover story: '5 Reasons Why Torture is Always Wrong; And Why There

Should Be No Exceptions.' Written by the widely recognized evangelical author and ethicist David Gushee, the story opens with descriptions of three people being tortured: one electrocuted, one asphyxiated, a third man humiliated in a bra and thong. '[W]e do not want to call torture what it is,' Gushee wrote. 'We deny that we are torturing ... We give every evidence of the kind of self-deception that is characteristic of a descent into sin.'[77]

In 2006, liberal evangelical author Randall Balmer published his account of the systemic denial among religious conservatives. In *Thy Kingdom Come: How the Religious Right Distorts the Faith and Threatens America*, Balmer describes how in 2005 he sent a query to eight religious right organizations asking for their statements on torture. Only two responded, and both defended the Bush administration, even as they claimed to oppose torture in principle. Balmer was disgusted: 'surely no one who calls himself a child of God or who professes to hear "fetal screams" could possibly countenance the use of torture' in any circumstances.[78]

In 2005, a group of evangelical intellectuals and activists began the two-year process of drafting 'An Evangelical Declaration against Torture,' issued in March 2007. David Gushee was the primary author; other drafters of the declaration included evangelical liberals Brian McLaren and Ronald Sider. Still others, however, were moderate conservatives like David Neff, editor of *Christianity Today*, Rebecca Hestenes, the minister at large for World Vision, and professors at several evangelical theological seminaries. 'We write this declaration to affirm our support for detainee human rights and our opposition to any resort to torture,' the group asserted. Basing its argument against torture on a human rights ethic and a commitment to the 'sanctity of life,' the declaration insisted that 'human rights places a shield around people, even when (especially when) our hearts cry out for vengeance.'[79]

The drafters insisted that the declaration was not an attack on the Christian right, or on 'the Republican president of the United States,' and it repeatedly praised the US military for its stances against torture and rules about interrogation. Still, the document was clearly intended as a space-clearing gesture, making room for an expansive interpretation of evangelical moral principles. The declaration made links to Catholic theology, the mainline Protestantism of Reinhold Niebuhr, and the global, secular human rights movement. It cited the Geneva Conventions in detail, implicitly honing to a strict view of what defined torture. The declaration also gestured repeatedly toward traditional evangelical moral concerns. It argued that human rights commitments were based on the Christian view of the 'sanctity of life,' mobilizing the hallmark language of the anti-abortion movement, and linking its anti-torture position to the key tropes of conservative evangelical activism.

The overall thrust of the document opened up the critique among evangelicals that had begun with Abu Ghraib. The issue was no longer just human sin, but also human responsibility to protect the dignity of others. For most evangelicals, that moral vision would not and could not be separated from opposition to abortion, but it was now commonplace to insist that life concerns extended beyond the womb. Human rights were not just about protecting the unborn, or other 'persecuted' Christians. 'We know we really care about human rights,' Gushee wrote, 'when we care about the rights of our enemies and those we fear, not just ourselves or our friends.'[80]

Shortly after it was issued, the declaration was endorsed by the generally conservative National Association of Evangelicals. As of 2007, it had been signed by 286 individuals.[81] Although the conservative reaction against the declaration came from a relatively small number of people, it was also fierce. Daniel Heimbach, who had been so important in crafting 'just war' theory to support the Iraq war, called the declaration a 'moral travesty' that was trying to divide evangelicals. A more serious and sustained critique by Keith Pavlischek argued, correctly, that the declaration had failed to define 'torture' with any precision. Nor did it discuss when or if it might be permissible to treat 'non lawful combatants' differently than POWs, or what, exactly, are the parameters of permitted government action. As Pavischek pointed out, the declaration achieved broad agreement by remaining vague on the most serious areas of contention among evangelical liberals and moderates.[82] But in some sense that was precisely the point; the declaration was an act of position-taking, one designed to mark evangelicals (at least those who signed the statement) as expansive in their moral vision, global in their orientation, yet pragmatic and diplomatic in their political approaches. It was the calling card of post-Moral Majority evangelical moderation, with all the possibilities and limits that such a position entailed.

V Endgame: changing views of the war

By mid-2006, white evangelicals' support for the war had fallen sharply – down to 58 percent from 77 percent in 2003 – and approval of President Bush had declined even more sharply, especially among young white evangelicals. Latino support was also dropping; in late 2006, Latino evangelicals were more likely than Latinos as a whole to say the Iraq war was the right choice, but the support had still dropped significantly, down to 49 percent.[83] On both counts, evangelical support was still higher than in the population as a whole, which by large margins wanted the United States out of Iraq, and increasingly saw the launching of the war itself as a mistake. By all accounts, those evangelicals in the pews who turned against the war did so for the same reasons the rest of the population did: higher numbers of US casualties (more than 3000 dead by mid-2006), and increasing sectarian violence in Iraq, with little in the way of real political solutions in sight. By and large, evangelicals did not raise specifically theological concerns about issues like Sunni–Shiite power-sharing, troop levels, timelines for pull out. (The exception here, as always, was the hyper-charged subset of prophecy-watching evangelicals; but, even there, the web discussants strained to make specific links to Iraq.)

While the rising evangelical criticism of the war after 2006 did not emerge for specifically evangelical reasons, the new position-takings did have a significant political effect within the evangelical community. Those evangelicals who had questioned the war from the beginning became increasingly self-confident and assertive. No longer content to argue reactively about the nature of just war or to defensively insist on their own patriotism, some members of the evangelical left called evangelical conservatives to repent of their previous views.

Writing in the *New York Times* in early 2006, Charles Marsh, a professor of religion at the University of Virginia and a self-described evangelical, excoriated his fellow believers for falling into line behind the Bush administration on the Iraq war. Marsh said he had recently re-read some of the sermons and statements delivered by influential American evangelicals between the fall of 2002 and March of 2003 when many of the most respected evangelical leaders had 'blessed the president's war plans, even when doing so required them to recast Christian doctrine.' Marsh commented that the sermons he reviewed may have quoted scripture or invoked the doctrine of just war, but they did both as a thin disguise for their determination to go to war:

> The single common theme among the war sermons appeared to be this: our president is a real brother in Christ, and because he has discerned that God's will is for our nation to be at war against Iraq, we shall gloriously comply.

In their near uniform support for the war, American evangelicals had been guilty of 'mistaken loyalty,' Marsh argued, putting nationalism and love of power before the Christian call to be peacemakers. 'The Hebrew prophets might call us to repentance,' he concluded, 'but repentance is a tough demand for a people utterly convinced of their righteousness.'[84]

The theme of 'repentance' is of course not the exclusive province of evangelicals; it has a long and rich history in both Christian and Jewish theology. The call to repent, however, have particular resonance when speaking to conservative evangelicals in the twenty-first century, who for 30 years had been insisting that the nation should repent of its 'sins' of sexual immorality, cultural relativism, and liberalism. Now, evangelical liberals were speaking broadly of the need for conservative evangelicals to repent – of support for the war, certainly, but also of a more general American arrogance. Jim Wallis, always a standard-bearer for anti-war evangelicals, titled the January 2008 cover story in *Sojourners* 'A Call to Repentance.' It was well past time for American Christians to examine their own instinctive nationalism, he wrote:

> Support for U.S. wars and foreign policy is still the area where American Christians are most 'conformed to the world' (Romans 12:2). This is our Achilles' heel, our biggest blind spot, our least questioned allegiance, the worst compromise of our Christian identity, and the greatest failing of our Christian obedience.[85]

To fully claim its membership in the transnational Christian community, Americans would need to join that community in its opposition to the war.

Similarly, author Randall Balmer, never one to mince words, wrote in *Thy Kingdom Come* that it was about time for the religious right to face what they had done in supporting the war. 'My Bible,' he wrote, 'teaches that those who refuse to act with justice or who neglect the plight of those less fortunate have some explaining to do.' But with repentance, even the religious right might be able to come into the fold. 'My evangelical theology assures me that no one, not even Karl Rove or James Dobson, lies beyond the reach of redemption, and that even a people led astray can find their way home.'[86] By August 2007, even the conservative American Baptist Press news wondered aloud: 'Did evangelicals' support for Iraq invasion damage credibility?'[87]

The scorn that some evangelicals heaped on the logic of support for the war was striking, and although it certainly did not represent the majority view, it did indicate the changing contours of evangelical opinion. In 2003, evangelical opponents of the war had not argued with quite the same kind of righteous anger. It had been the case that, from the beginning, the most outspoken anti-war contingent had been inclined to argue that their criticism of the war was indicative of a richer understanding of biblical justice in general – in other words, that they understood better than conservatives did 'what Jesus would do' about issues that went well beyond Iraq. By 2007, however, this group was beginning to make an even stronger claim: that the 'mistakes' of the pro-war camp were the sins of an evangelical conservatism that was now on the wane. And so Jim Wallis, who had something of a reputation for always being certain that change was just around the corner, nonetheless spoke for a larger community when he insisted on the emergence of a 'post-religious right America.'[88]

Of course, most evangelical conservatives did not consider *themselves* in danger of imminent demise, and they did not back down from their support of the war. Richard Land of the Southern Baptist convention continued to insist that the invasion of Iraq had been an act of liberation, although he was 'extremely disappointed in many aspects of the prosecution of the war.'[89] And Rick Scarborough, head of Vision America and a major standard bearer of the religious right, organized a conference in October 2007 in which he, Gary Bauer, and a number of others defended the Iraq war as a necessary front in the larger battle against terrorism. Not about to brook any territory to the moderates who were talking about torture as a 'sanctity of life' issue, Scarborough announced that this global battle was 'the ultimate life issue. If radical Islam succeeds in its ultimate goals, Christianity ceases to exist.'[90]

By 2007, however, the right-wing of evangelicals no longer had the easy ascendancy they once enjoyed. They were not about to go away, by any means, but they were now in a genuine competition with moderates, moderate conservatives, and liberals over the 'common sense' of the community. Among evangelicals, the term 'prophetic' is often used in a very specific way to mean a type of speech or action that speaks the truth in the face of a disbelieving world, regardless of the consequences. In that sense, the early opposition to the Iraq war by liberals and the evangelical left was not only marginal, but prophetic precisely *because* it was marginal; the evangelical left had been willing to speak truth to power. By 2007, that opposition to the Iraq war had positioned evangelical liberals as 'prophetic' in the more prosaic sense: they had correctly predicted that the war was not the path to peace. In the field of evangelicalism in America, the liberals were now stronger than they had been in 30 years. If that was not a particularly impressive statement, given the lock hold of the right on evangelicalism in the late twentieth century, it was nonetheless a remarkable development. The field was in flux, and the future was at hand.

Notes

1 NCC, 'NCC-Led Religious Leaders Mission to Iraq Concludes,' *National Council of Churches*, January 3, 2002, www.ncccusa.org/news/02news104.html; Associated Press, 'Bishop in President George W. Bush's church appears in new antiwar ad,' *Associated Press Worldstream*, January 31, 2003; Bill Broadway, 'TV Debate Delineates Christian Divide on War; Mainline Churches Against; Evangelicals For,' *Washington Post*, March 15, 2003.
2 'Panel of Christians Speaks Out on War with Iraq – transcript,' CNN Larry King Live, March 11, 2003, http://transcripts.cnn.com/TRANSCRIPTS/0303/11/lkl.00.html.
3 Most famously proclaimed by E.J. Dionne, *Souled Out: Reclaiming Faith and Politics after the Religious Right* (Princeton University Press, 2008). I discuss this topic with David Rutledge of Australian Broadcasting Corporation on 'Religion and the US Presidential Race,' March 21, 2008, at www.abc.net.au/rn/breakfast/stories/2008/2195254.htm.
4 Pierre Bourdieu, *The Field of Cultural Production: Essays on Art and Literature* (New York: Columbia University Press, 1993). Elsewhere, Bourdieu makes more use of the term 'habitus,' which he uses to describe the combination of social structure, individual calculation, and personal disposition that constitutes the site, limits, and possibilities for individual agency.
5 That is, even in religious traditions that are doctrine-oriented, as with evangelical Christianity, the connection adherents have to their faith is as much experiential as doctrinal. On this approach, see Talal Asad, *Genealogies of Religion: Discipline and reasons of power in Christianity and Islam* (Baltimore: The Johns Hopkins University Press, 1993); David D. Hall, *Lived Religion in America* (Princeton, NJ: Princeton University Press, 1997).
6 Laurie F. Maffly-Kipp, Leigh E. Schmidt, and Mark Valeri, 'Introduction,' in *Practicing Protestants: Histories of Christian Life in America, 1630–1965* (Baltimore: The Johns Hopkins University Press, 2006), 6.
7 Mark A. Noll, *American Evangelical Christianity: An Introduction* (Oxford: Blackwell Publishers, 2001).
8 The research on religious identification in the United States is myriad, contradictory, and deeply divided in how it deals with race in particular. The Pew Center for Religion and Public Life's 2008 survey counts 26 percent of Americans as evangelical Protestant, and just under 7 percent as members of historically black churches, for a total of 33 percent. See http://religions.pewforum.org/affiliations.
9 Alan Wolfe makes a similar point about the tendencies of researchers to exclude black and Latino evangelicals in his review of Michael Lindsay's *Faith in the*

Halls of Power; Alan Wolfe, 'Evangelicals Everywhere: Review of Faith in the Halls of Power,' *The New York Times*, November 25, 2007.

10 Luis Lugo, 'Pew Forum: Here Come "Los Evangélicos"!' *Pew Forum on Religion & Public Life, Event Transcript*, June 6, 2007, http://pewforum.org/docs/? DocID=220; Pew Forum on Religion and Public Life and Pew Hispanic Center, *Changing Faiths: Latinos and the Transformation of American Religion* (Washington, DC, April 2007), http://pewforum.org/surveys/hispanic.

11 See Michael O. Emerson and Christian Smith, *Divided by Faith: Evangelical Religion and the Problem of Race in America* (New York: Oxford University Press, 2000).

12 Specific numbers are hard to come by, but since 2000, both the Coalition of African American Pastors (CAPP) and the High Impact Leadership Coalition were formed by African American church leaders to support conservative causes, particularly opposition to same-sex marriage and abortion. See also Andrea Elliott, 'For New York Evangelicals, a Political Conversion,' *New York Times*, November 14, 2004; David D. Kirkpatrick, 'Black Pastors Backing Bush Are Rare, but Not Alone,' *New York Times*, October 5, 2004; Krissah Williams, 'Politics of Race and Religion; Moral Issues Leave Black Evangelicals Torn Between Parties,' *Washington Post*, November 26, 2007. On Latinos, see Paul Hughes, 'Continental Divide,' *Christianity Today*, February 2008, www.christianitytoday.com/ct/2008/february/13.14.html; Associated Press, 'Fewer Hispanics Identifying Themselves as Democrats,' Fox News, August 9, 2007, www.foxnews.com/story/0,2933,292653,00.html.

13 Phillips, 'The Religious Left's Moment,' and Beliefnet, 'Your Religion's Stance on Iraq,' *Beliefnet*, nd, www.beliefnet.com/story/121/story_12190_1.html.

14 'Mideast churches warn against Iraq invasion,' *Christian Century* 119, no. 18 (September 28, 2002), 15.

15 Staff writers, 'American, Canadian, British Church Leaders Call on U.S. to "Stop the Rush to War",' *National Council of Churches*, August 29, 2002, www.ncccusa.org/news/02news82.html; Religious Leaders for Sensible Priorities, 'President Bush, Let Jesus Change Your Mind,' *New York Times*, December 4, 2002, www.ccmep.org/2002_articles/Iraq/120402_president_bush.htm.

16 Pew Center for the People and the Press, *Different Faiths, Different Messages*, March 19, 2003, http://people-press.org/reports/display.php3?ReportID=176; Marshall Shelley, 'War Isn't Being Waged From the Pulpit,' *Christianity Today – web only*, March 2003, www.christianitytoday.com/ct/2003/marchweb-only/3–24–12.0.html; Peter Steinfels, 'Beliefs: In a Poll, Few Say that Religion Shaped their Views on Iraq. The Truth May be More Complex,' *New York Times*, March 22, 2003.

17 Jonathan Tilove, 'Blacks' Opposition to Iraq War Rooted in History,' *Newhouse News Service*, February 13, 2003. According to Zogby poll in March 2003, only 23 percent of African Americans supported the war. Liz Marlantes, 'From Alabama Pews, a Wary Look at War,' *Christian Science Monitor*, March 10, 2003.

18 Kevin Anderson, 'Hispanics Divided over Iraq War,' BBC News, April 12, 2003, http://news.bbc.co.uk/2/hi/americas/2941523.stm.

19 'Silent Evangelical Support of Bush's Proposed War Against Iraq,' NPR, February 26, 2003, www.npr.org/programs/morning/transcripts/2003/feb/030226. hagerty.html; Art Toalston and Dwayne Hastings, 'Land: Military Action Against Iraq Meets Ethical Standards for War,' *Baptist Press News*, September 9, 2002, www.bpnews.org/bpnews.asp?ID=14198.

20 Bill Broadway, 'Religious Leaders' Voices Rise on Iraq; Most Question U.S. Moves Toward War, but Evangelicals Embrace Bush Policy as Assault on Evil,' *Washington Post*, September 28, 2002; Editors, 'Bully Culprit,' *Christianity*

Today – web only, September 1, 2002, www.christianitytoday.com/ct/2002/septemberweb-only/9–30–11.0.html; Todd Hertz, 'Opinion Roundup: Is Attacking Iraq Moral?' *Christianity Today – web only*, September 1, 2002, www.christianitytoday.com/ct/articleid=7063.

21 For example, in September 2002, the National Council of Churches organized a call by religious leaders asking President Bush to reconsider war against Iraq. The statement was signed by Ronald Sider, head of Evangelicals for Social Action. Statement at www.ncccusa.org/news/02news83.html.

22 Marvin Olasky, 'Make Love, Not War: But What if Making War is the More Compassionate Response?' *World Magazine*, March 17, 2007, www.worldmag.com/articles/12778.

23 George Lopez, 'Just? Unjust? The Bush doctrine of Pre-emptive War has Opened up a New Front in the Debates over "Just War" Theory,' *Sojourners*, May 2004, www.sojo.net/index.cfm?action=magazine.article&issue=soj0405&article= 040520.

24 Heimbach describes the genesis in 'The Bush Just War Doctrine: Genesis and Application of the President's Moral Leadership in the Persian Gulf War,' in *From Cold War to New World Order: The Foreign Policy of George Bush*, Meena Bose and Rosanna Perotti, eds. (Westport, CT: Greenwood Press, 2002), 441–464. On Heimbach and the 2003 war, see Jason Hall, 'Panel: War is Justified according to Biblical Standard,' Baptist Press News, February 27, 2003, www.bpnews.net/bpnews.asp?id=15326.

25 Charles W. Colson, 'Just War in Iraq: Sometimes Going to War is the Charitable Thing to do,' *Christianity Today* 46, no. 13 (December 9, 2002), 72.

26 Jimmy Carter, 'Just war – or a Just War?' *New York Times*, March 9, 2003.

27 The signers included both leaders of mainline churches and core spokespeople for the evangelical left (Wallis, Ron Sider of Evangelicals for Social Action, pastor and radio commentator Tony Campolo, and David Beckman of Bread for the World). It was signed by several African American ministers as well, including Cheryl Sanders, a Church of God pastor in Washington DC and faculty at Howard Divinity School. See 'Disarm Iraq Without War: A Statement from Religious Leaders in the United States and United Kingdom,' November 2002, posted at Sojo.net, www.sojo.net/index.cfm?action=action.US-UK_statement. Jim Wallis discusses the statement, just war theory, and his work against the war in Jim Wallis, *God's Politics: Why the Right Gets It Wrong and the Left Doesn't Get It*, 1st edn (San Francisco: HarperSanFrancisco, 2005), 108–136.

28 Quoted by R. Drew Smith, 'Black Denominational Responses to US-Middle East Policy since 9/11,' *The Review of Faith and International Affairs* 6, no. 1 (Spring 2008), 5–18.

29 B. Keith English, 'War in Iraq Fails in Two Christian Traditions – re-posting from Commercial Appeal (Memphis),' *Sojo.net*, October 23, 2005, www.sojo.net/index.cfm?action=news.display_article&mode=s&NewsID=5001.

30 Bob Hyatt, 'Profoundly Disturbed on the Fourth of July: God, the Flag and the End of America,' *Open Source Theology*, June 25, 2004, www.opensourcetheology.net/node/391.

31 Tony Evans, *War with Iraq: A Biblical Perspective (Revelation 18: 1–11)*, Sermon series, available at TonyEvans.org.

32 The discussion sites on the Left Behind boards were abuzz with these topics; by 2004, they were available only to subscribers. Under the rubric of, for example, the thread 'President Bush/Anti-Christ????' was a mix of prophecy talk, hard-nosed political analysis, and personal revelation. There, posters criticized Bush's willingness to speak kindly about Islam, although most agreed the President was probably not the Antichrist. Thread at www.leftbehindcommunity.com/n/mb/message.asp?webtag=lb-prophecyclub&mag=1100.10.

33 Mark Bailey, 'The End Is Not Yet,' *Christianity Today* — *web only*, March 1, 2003, www.christianitytoday.com/ct/2003/marchweb-only/3–24–44.0.html; Todd Strandberg, 'The Iraq War Has Little Effect on the Rapture Index,' *Christianity Today* – *web only*, March 1, 2003, www.christianitytoday.com/ct/2003/marchweb-only/ 3–24–43.0.html.
34 Philip Jenkins, *The Next Christendom: the Coming of Global Christianity* (New York: Oxford University Press, 2002).
35 The changing nature of missionary work is a key theme in my forthcoming book, tentatively titled *Our God in the World: The Global Visions of American Evangelicals.*
36 Although this particular way of framing the different types of missions is my own, it echoes the formal and informal evaluations of those involved in aid programs. See, for example, the comments of the Jaisankar Sarma, on the staff of World Vision in India, in the question and answer session of a panel with Lamin Sanneh, 'Evangelicals, Islam, and Humanitarian Aid' (presented at the Ethics and Public Policy Center, Washington, DC, May 29, 2003), www.eppc.org/ conferences/pubID.1579,eventID.60/transcript.asp.
37 Alexandra Alter, 'Groups Weigh Risks, Morality of Evangelizing in Postwar Iraq,' *Religion News Service, reposted at Pew Forum on Religion and Public Life*, June 5, 2003, http://pewforum.org/news/display.php?NewsID=282.
38 At a 2007 conference on the global dimensions of faith-based organizations, Steven Weir of Habitat for Humanity International put it simply: 'Most [of us] would argue that the objective is not proselytization, but simply to demonstrate through our work the love of Jesus.' Habitat is an ecumenical rather than evangelical organization, but it includes a strong evangelical component. Steven Weir, 'A Discussion with Steven Weir,' in *Global Dimensions of Faith-Based Organizations* (Washington, DC: Berkley Center for Religion, Peace, and World Affairs, 2007), 14.
39 Deborah Dortzbach, 'A Discussion with Deborah Dortzbach,' in *Global Dimensions of Faith-Based Organizations* (Washington, DC: Berkley Center for Religion, Peace, and World Affairs, 2007), 49.
40 World Vision is now the largest privately funded charity in the world as well as the second largest recipient of US government funding for faith-based international organizations. For a more detailed discussion of the church-state issues involved in US government funding of international faith-based organizations, see R. Marie Griffith and Melani McAlister, 'Introduction: Is the Public Square Still Naked?,' *American Quarterly* 59, no. 3 (September 2007), 527.
    Several dissertations have examined World Vision's work in detail: Susan Mary McDonic, 'Witnessing, Work and Worship: World Vision and the Negotiation of Faith, Development and Culture' (Duke University, 2004); Stephen Kamau Githumbi, 'Formation of Missiological and Developmental Values in World Vision's projects Among the Poor in Nairobi' (Fuller Theological Seminary, School of World Mission, 1996).
41 Todd Hertz, 'Comments on Islam Endanger Missionaries, Letter Says,' *Christianity Today*, January 1, 2003, www.ctlibrary.com/ct/2003/januaryweb-only/ 1–13–53.0.html.
42 Cizik is quoted in 'Silent Evangelical Support Of Bush's Proposed War Against Iraq' (NPR, February 26, 2003), www.npr.org/programs/morning/transcripts/2003/feb/030226.hagerty.html; Bill Broadway, 'Evangelicals' Voices Speak Softly About Iraq,' *Washington Post*, January 25, 2003.
43 Among the many discussions of the allure of missions in Iraq, see Deborah Caldwell, 'Why Iraq Beckons,' *Beliefnet*, www.beliefnet.com/story/124/story_12448_1.html; 'Most Evangelical Leaders Favor "Evangelizing Muslims Abroad",'

Ethics and Public Policy Center, April 7, 2003, www.eppc.org/news/newsID.8/ news_detail.asp.

44 Luis Bush, 'Reaching the Core of the Core,' *Renewal Journal* 10, www. pastornet.net.au/ renewal/journal10/g-bush.html.

45 Staff, 'The Southern Baptists Restructure to Reach the Unreached Peoples: An Interview with Jerry Rankin, IMB President and Avery Willis, Senior Vice President for Overseas Operations,' *Mission Frontiers: The Bulletin of the US Center for World Mission* (October 1997), www.missionfrontiers.org/1997/0710/ jo976.htm.

46 Arian Eujung Cha, 'Christian Missionaries Battle For Hearts and Minds in Iraq,' *The Washington Post*, May 16, 2004; Alexandra Alter, 'News: Groups Weigh Risks, Morality of Evangelizing in Postwar Iraq,' *Religion News Service*, June 5, 2003, http://pewforum.org/news/display.php?NewsID=2282.

47 Broward Liston, 'Interview: Missionary Work in Iraq,' *Time Magazine*, April 15, 2003, www.time.com/time/world/article/0,8599,443800,00.html; Samuel Hugh Moffett, 'Why We Go,' *Christianity Today*, November 14, 1994, http:// ctlibrary.com/14532.

48 Sami Dagher, 'Personal interview,' Beirut, January 10, 2008.

49 Marvin Olasky, 'Refining Cruelty: An Army of Compassion Finds that War is Hell,' *World Magazine*, March 10, 2007, www.worldmag.com/articles/12756.

50 Teresa Watanabe, 'Seminary Is Reaching Out to Muslims; An Evangelical School Launches an Interfaith Effort to Allay Tensions Deriving from 9/11,' *Los Angeles Times*, December 6, 2003.

51 'Why We Should Listen to Muslim Voices' (presented at the IGE Global Leadership Forum, Washington, DC, September 22, 2007), www.globalen-gage.org/media/article.aspx?id=8306.

52 John Green, Ethics and Public Policy Center, and Beliefnet, 'Evangelical Views of Islam,' *Beliefnet*, April 7, 2003, www.beliefnet.com/story/124/story_12447.html; Deborah Caldwell, 'How Islam-Bashing Got Cool,' Beliefnet, www.beliefnet.com/story/110/story_11074_1.html.

53 Ibid.

54 His best-known book is Brother Andrew, *God's Smuggler* (New York: New American Library, 1967); see also Brother Andrew, *Secret Believers: What Happens When Muslims Turn to Christ?* (London: Hodder Christian, 2007).

55 Wendy Murray Zoba, 'Smuggling Jesus into Muslim Hearts,' *Christianity Today*, October 5, 1998, www.ctlibrary.com/1818.

56 Michael Lawrence *et al.*, 'Ministering to Those in Need: The Rights and Wrongs of Missions and Humanitarian Assistance in Iraq' (Washington, DC, June 4, 2003), http://pewforum.org/events/?EventID=46.

57 Tony Campolo, 'Is Christianity a Casualty of War?' *Huffington Post*, January 5, 2006, www.huffingtonpost.com/tony-campolo/is-christianity-a-casualt_b_13329.html.

58 Four American pastors were shot and killed in February 2004; four Southern Baptists killed in a car bomb in March 2004, several South Korean missionaries were abducted and later released. Doug Bandow, 'Christians in the Crossfire,' *American Conservative*, October 23, 2006, www.amconmag.com/2006/2006_10_23/article.html; Edward Wong and James Glanz, 'South Korean Is Killed in Iraq By His Captors,' *The New York Times*, June 23, 2004.

59 Mindy Belz, 'Kidnapped: Iraq: The terrorists' stock in trade – abduction – sows chaos and fear among churches,' *The World*, May 19, 2007, www.worldmag.com/articles/12951; Bill Broadway, 'For Iraqi Christians, A Shadow of Insecurity; War Has Brought "Very Real Freedom" – and Dangers, Archbishop Says,' *The Washington Post*, July 17, 2004.

60 Pew Center for the People and the Press, 'Iraq Prison Scandal Hits Home,' May 12, 2004, http://people-press.org/reports/pdf/213.pdf. I discuss the general

responses to Abu Ghraib in the final chapter of *Epic Encounters: Culture, Media, and U.S. Interests in the Middle East Since 1945*, Updated edn (Berkeley: University of California Press, 2005).

61 Mark Glassman, 'The Reach of War: Broadcast; U.S. Religious Figures Offer Abuse Apology on Arab TV,' *New York Times*, June 11, 2004; Don Lattin, 'TV ad by religious leaders apologizes to Arab world for abuses at Abu Ghraib,' *San Francisco Chronicle*, June 16, 2004.

62 Ted Olsen, 'Weblog: Rounding Up the Few Christian Voices on the Iraq Prison Scandal,' *Christianity Today – web only*, May 1, 2004, www.ctlibrary.com/ct/2004/mayweb-only/5-10-22.0.html.

63 Ted Olsen, 'Weblog: The Religious Side of the Abu Ghraib Scandal,' *Christianity Today – web only*, May 1, 2004, www.christianitytoday.com/ct/2004/mayweb-only/ 5-24-12.0.html.

64 Among many other examples of literature of this type, see Nina Shea, *In the Lion's Den: A Shocking Account of Persecuted and Martyrdom of Christians Today and How We Should Respond* (Broadman & Holman Publishers, 1997); Paul A. Marshall, *Their Blood Cries Out: The Untold Story of Persecution Against Christians in the Modern World* (Dallas: World Publishing, 1997).

65 Allen Hertzke, *Freeing God's Children: The Unlikely Alliance for Global Human Rights* (Lanham, MD: Rowman & Littlefield, 2004).

66 Albert Mohler, 'First Person: The prison abuse scandal & the human heart,' *Baptist Press News*, May 24, 2004, www.bpnews.net/bpnews.asp?id=18342.

67 Benedicta Cipolla, 'Taking on Torture,' *PBS Religion & Ethics NewsWeekly*, Web Exclusive, January 20, 2006, www.pbs.org/wnet/religionandethics/week921/exclusive.html.

68 Gary Bauer, 'Gary Bauer on the Iraq prisoner abuse scandal,' *Beliefnet*, May 10, 2004, www.beliefnet.com/story/145/story_14576_1.html.

69 Chuck Colson, 'Problems Abroad, Problems at Home,' *Prison Fellowship*, May 18, 2004, www.breakpoint.org/listingarticle.asp?ID=2219; Jane LaRue, 'News & Commentary: Abu Ghraib and Pornography,' *Concerned Women for America*, May 11, 2004, www.cwfa.org/articles/5653/LEGAL/pornography/index.htm.

70 Samuel Rodriguez, 'Torture, Hypocrisy, and Faith,' November 11, 2007, On Faith Blog, at http://newsweek.washingtonpost.com/onfaith/samuel_rodriguez.

71 Steven Gertz, 'I Was in Prison and You Abused Me,' *Christianity Today – web only*, May 1, 2004, www.ctlibrary.com/ct/2004/mayweb-only/5-24-53.0.html.

72 Susan Sontag, 'Regarding the Torture of Others,' *New York Times*, May 23, 2004.

73 Deborah Caldwell, 'T.D. Jakes talks about Mega fest, his role as a Christian, Osama bin Laden, and the war in Iraq,' *Beliefnet*, 2004, www.beliefnet.com/story/147/story_14791.html.

74 One interesting thing about Jakes' approach to the issue is that he, almost alone among evangelical commentators, did not discuss 'sin.' Jakes in fact has been criticized by other evangelicals for his theology on precisely this issue, since Oneness Pentecostals, who Jakes was associated with, have tended to de-emphasize sin and focus more on God's goodness. Jakes is also, in some fashion, an adherent of the prosperity gospel, which suggests that faithfulness to God leads to wealth and health in this life – another doctrine that leads to a decrease in attention to the issue of sin.

75 Mark Danner, *Torture and Truth: America, Abu Ghraib, and the War on Terror* (New York: New York Review Books, 2004); Karen J. Greenberg, Joshua L. Dratel, and Anthony Lewis, eds, *The Torture Papers: The Road to Abu Ghraib* (New York: Cambridge University Press, 2005).

76 Cardinal Joseph Bernardin articulated this idea in a famous 1983 speech, which he later expanded into a book, *Consistent Ethic of Life* (Kansas City, Mo, 1988).

'Seamless garment' is a biblical reference to John 19:23, a reference to Jesus's 'seamless' clothes taken from him at the cross. How much this ethic is enacted by the church is discussed in Timothy A. Byrnes, 'How "seamless" a garment? The Catholic bishops and the politics of abortion,' *Journal of Church & State* 33, no. 1 (Winter 1991), 17. Evangelicals have debated the idea often, including Randall L. Frame, 'Weaving a seamless garment out of peace, freedom, and security: the National Association of Evangelicals,' *Christianity Today* 31, no. 8 (May 15, 1987), 42–44; Charles Colson, 'Seamless garment or straitjacket?' *Christianity Today* 32, no. 16 (November 4, 1988), 72.

77 David Gushee, '5 Reasons Torture Is Always Wrong,' *Christianity Today*, February 2006, www.ctlibrary.com/38136. Tony Campalo, generally associated with the evangelical left, made a similar point on a blog posting. Talking to a group of evangelicals about the issue of torture, he found that most of them supported it in some cases.

> I came away from that discussion with a sense that many of us Evangelicals have given up our moral compasses and wandered into an ethical wasteland where we are not only losing our souls, but also losing our testimonies as good people. Checking around, I found very little condemnation of America's use of torture from those pundits of Christian Fundamentalism who usually can be counted on to speak out with righteous indignation whenever our government provides even the appearance of evil.
>
> (Tony Campolo, 'Is Christianity a Casualty of War?'
> *Huffington Post*, January 5, 2006)

78 Randall Balmer, *Thy Kingdom Come: How the Religious Right Distorts the Faith and Threatens America: An Evangelical's Lament* (New York: Basic Books, 2006).

79 Evangelicals for Human Rights, 'An Evangelical Declaration Against Torture: Protecting Human Rights in an Age of Terror,' *Review of Faith and International Affairs* 5, no. 2 (Summer 2007), 46.

80 David Gushee, 'How to Read "An Evangelical Declaration Against Torture",' *Review of Faith and International Affairs* 5, no. 2 (Summer 2007), 62.

81 Sarah Pulliam, 'NAE Endorses Statement Against Torture,' *Christianity Today – web only*, March 16, 2007, www.christianitytoday.com/ct/2007/marchweb-only/111–54.0.html; Peter Steinfels, 'An Evangelical Call on Torture and the U.S.,' *New York Times*, July 21, 2007.

82 Erin Roach, 'Ethicist: NAE torture declaration "irrational",' *Baptist Press News*, March 15, 2007, www.sbcbaptistpress.org/BPnews.asp?ID=25190; Keith Pavlischek, 'Human Rights and Justice in an Age of Terror,' *Human Rights and Justice in an Age of Terror*, October 2007, www.christianitytoday.com/books/web/2007/sept24a.html.

83 Dan Cox, 'Pew Forum: Young White Evangelicals: Less Republican, Still Conservative,' *Pew Forum on Religion & Public Life*, September 28, 2007, http://pewforum.org/docs/?DocID=250; Luis Lugo, 'Pew Forum: Here Come "Los Evangélicos"!' *Pew Forum on Religion & Public Life, Event Transcript*, June 6, 2007, http://pewforum.org/docs/?DocID=220.

84 Charles Marsh, 'Wayward Christian Soldiers,' *New York Times*, January 20, 2006.

85 Jim Wallis, 'A Call to Repentance,' *Sojourners*, January 2008, www.sojo.net/index.cfm?action=magazine.article&issue=soj0801&article=080110.

86 Randall Balmer, *Thy Kingdom Come: How the Religious Right Distorts the Faith and Threatens America: An Evangelical's Lament* (New York: Basic Books, 2006), 191.

87 Robert Marus, 'War and peace: Did Evangelicals' Support for Iraq Invasion Damage Credibility?' *ABPNews.com*, August 6, 2007, www.abpnews.com/2690.article. A Pew Forum survey in September 2007 that showed younger evangelicals' support for President Bush had dropped from 87 percent approval in 2002 to 45 percent in 2007: Dan Cox, 'Pew Forum: Young White Evangelicals: Less Republican, Still Conservative,' *Pew Forum on Religion & Public Life*, September 28, 2007, http://pewforum.org/docs/?DocID=250.

88 Jim Wallis, *The Great Awakening: Reviving Faith & Politics in a Post-Religious Right America* (New York: HarperOne, 2008). And Charles Marsh, writing now in the Boston Globe, argued that America was at the end of an era, and that evangelicalism had lost its relevance and their credibility: 'Conservative evangelical elites, in exchange for political access and power, have ransacked the faith and trivialized its convictions.' Charles Marsh, 'God and Country,' *Boston Globe*, July 8, 2007, www.boston.com/news/globe/ideas/articles/2007/07/08/god_and_country/. See also the Pew survey showing increased willingness of evangelicals to vote Democratic in 2008: John Green, 'Pew Forum: Religion and the Presidential Vote: A Tale of Two Gaps,' *Pew Forum on Religion & Public Life*, August 21, 2007, http://pewforum.org/docs/?DocID=240.

89 Randall Balmer and Richard Land, 'Evangelicalism: Richard Land and Randall Balmer discuss the politics of the religious right,' *On Faith*, Spring 2007, http://newsweek.washingtonpost.com/onfaith/evangelicalism.html.

90 Eric Gorski, '"Radical Islam" should Jolt Voters, Evangelicals Say,' *USA Today*, November 2007, www.usatoday.com/news/religion/2007-11-10-evangelicals N.htm.

8   Against everyone and no-one

The failure of the unipolar in Iraq and beyond

Scott Lucas* and Maria Ryan

On 30 January 2001, ten days after the inauguration of President George W. Bush, his closest advisors sat down for the first meeting of the National Security Council. The opening item on the agenda was 'Regime Change in Iraq.' Ensuing discussion took up specific measures from the pursuit of 'smart sanctions' to aerial assaults in the no-fly zones over northern and southern Iraq to the prospect of a coup that might topple Saddam Hussein, but there were also grand thoughts on the strategic and ideological potential of a new Iraq.

Offering perhaps the grandest thought, the new Secretary of Defense, Donald Rumsfeld, expounded, 'Imagine what the region would look like without Saddam and with a regime that is aligned with US interests. It would change everything in the region and beyond. It would demonstrate what US policy is all about.'[1] Rumsfeld's speculation both illuminates and complicates characterizations of the Bush Administration's approach to foreign policy. Iraq was clearly a demonstration case, but for what?

An initial starting point is the evaluation of Rumsfeld's statement as an exemplar of the American 'unipolar.' First set out for the public in 1990 by the columnist Charles Krauthammer, this was the assertion of a world in which 'the center of world power [was] the unchallenged superpower, the United States, attended by its Western allies.' Even more significantly, Krauthammer explained that 'the single pole of world power' would have the capability to be a 'decisive player *in any conflict in whatever part of the world it chooses.*'[2] Developed by officials in the George H. W. Bush Administration, notably Assistant Secretary of Defense Paul Wolfowitz and his staff member Zalmay Khalilzad, the unipolar moved from the identification of a unipolar moment into a quest for a unipolar era, translated into a Government strategy in which:

> our first objective [would be] to prevent the re-emergence of a new rival. This is a dominant consideration underlying the new regional defense strategy and requires that we endeavor to prevent any hostile power from dominating a region whose resources would, under consolidated control, be sufficient to generate global power. These regions include

Western Europe, East Asia, the territory of the former Soviet Union, and Southwest Asia.[3]

While it is unclear if Wolfowitz and Khalilzad were already envisaging one of the countries of Southwest Asia, Iraq, as a specific target of American action, the possibility was clearly present nine years later. With its degraded capabilities, Iraq was unlikely to put up great resistance to an overt display of American power, and with its oil reserves and its geographic and political significance for the Middle East, including the American relationship with Israel, it was of significance for American interests.

This begs the question, however, of why this grand demonstration was not embraced by the rest of the Administration in February 2001. The easy explanation – that the events of 11 September 2001 reconfigured international relations and US national security – takes us no further in ascertaining whether those events were cause or pretext. It is our contention that, for a meaningful analysis, the pursuit of the unipolar has to be considered in conjunction with the battle for influence within the bureaucracy of the Bush Administration. Put bluntly, the mobilization of US foreign policy to pursue regime change in Iraq as the demonstration of a revived American preponderance of power was the product of a small group of policy activists being in the right place at the right time. The tragedy of September 11 was the necessary catalyst to convert the abstracted notion of power versus 'everyone and no-one' into an applied blueprint linking capability-based and threat-based approaches.

This is not to deny that some of these key activists rested their ideas on the 1990s neo-conservative construction of security and American power, nor does this rule out ideological projection to rationalize preponderance: 'the balance of power that favors freedom.'[4] However, this hypothesis points to the imperative of a network which could not only set out the notion of a preponderant American power but could aggressively promote a particular bureaucratic and political strategy to convert the American exceptional into the global, not only as an idea but as a long-term political and military predominance. Some of the high-level members of the Bush Administration were active in this network in the 1990s – for example, Rumsfeld and Vice President Dick Cheney were both involved with the Project for a New American Century[5] – but most of the ideas that made up the pursuit of the unipolar came from activists who would serve in mid-level positions or would even be based outside the Administration. In that sense, a Rumsfeld, a Cheney, even a President Bush was vital not as originators of the grand unipolar strategy but as the officials who could ensure its adoption in American foreign policy.

The dynamics of this network point not only to the distinction of the Bush Administration's strategy but also to the significance of its eventual failure. For the pursuit of the 'unipolar' did not emanate from a consideration of local and regional political, economic, and cultural interactions but from an attempt to transcend them. While setting out the overriding importance of American power, these activists did not embed that power in a reconstruction of structures and systems (so-called 'nation-building') but situated it in an abstracted notion of indigenous recovery tenuously linked to specific 'locals,' usually exiles, who had been part of the network. Intelligence, analysis, and planning inside the US Government that did not suit this abstracted notion (or accept these networked 'locals') would be disregarded and, in key instances, quashed.

The pursuit of the unipolar would thus become a pursuit against everyone and no-one. It was against everyone because as Soviet power disappeared as both a symbolic and real opponent, it was replaced with a range of possible rivals over whom the US must be dominant. At the same time, it was against no-one because political cultures in these rival states were often abstracted or emptied of substance and significance beyond the invocation of tyrants, terrorists, and weapons of mass destruction.

But, of course, 'America' was not filling an emptied political space; rather, the US was entering countries and regions where there were numerous groups with their particular concerns, structures, and conceptions of power. Even for those 'liberated' by the exercise of American capabilities, those conceptions might not coincide with or even support American preponderance.[6] When this conflict between the specifics of the 'local' and the abstract of US power emerged, the unipolar – by its very nature – could offer no resolution through the reconstruction of indigenous institutions, at least those that were not closely and assuredly linked to American networks. All the unipolar offered, in the face of a raging Iraqi insurgency that seemed to prove the contrary, was the stale claim that America was 'the single pole of power,' able to exercise 'decisive' influence in any conflict it chose.

In these circumstances, the US Government had to rely upon the promotion of rationales that might obscure or transcend the tensions. The post-9/11 rationale of anti-terrorism, for the sake of intervention in Iraq, had given way to the rationale of security against rogue states and tyrants; now, amidst continuing and increasing insecurity, 'security' had to be replaced by the rationale of democracy, albeit an abstracted democracy that was synonymous with US power rather than the promotion of democratic practices and systems. This, however, would be a far from stable endpoint, given that peoples – inside Iraq and beyond – might use their democratic rights to support parties opposed to American interests.

Capabilities and power: searching for a strategy in the 2000 campaign

Part of the difficulty in interpreting the genesis of the Bush foreign policy lay in the rather general, emergent notion of the 'unipolar' in his 2000 Presidential campaign. Indeed, the candidate's initial focus was on military capabilities rather than an endpoint for the projection of American power. Addressing cadets at the University of the Citadel, Bush – after a rhetorical jab at Bill Clinton and Al Gore with his promise to 'renew the bond of trust between the American president and the American military' – set out the aims to 'defend the American people against missiles and terror' and to 'begin creating the military of the next century.' The only hint of a wider global mission came in a vague ambition

> to take advantage of a tremendous opportunity – given few nations in history – to extend the current peace into the far realm of the future, a chance to project America's peaceful influence, not just across the world, but across the years.[7]

The rather narrow focus, which substantively ended in support for Donald Rumsfeld's vision of transforming the military services, was all the more surprising given that the speech was shaped by a group of advisors led by Condoleezza Rice. The 'Vulcans,'[8] who included Paul Wolfowitz, Stephen Hadley, and Richard Armitage, had been meeting throughout the summer, but there was little in Bush's rhetoric pointing to any defined policy agenda.[9] So-called neo-conservative activists saw potential in the speech but they also worried over the lack of definition in the assertion of American power. Robert Kagan thought Bush sounded 'a great deal more like a classic realist, a great deal of emphasis being in areas where there are vital national interests at stake,'[10] a back-handed compliment at best given neo-conservative scepticism on 'realism.'

Responding in part to this critique, Bush offered the broadest of global visions for the projection of 'peaceful influence' six weeks later. This time, the symbolic setting was the Ronald Reagan Presidential Library, where the candidate linked his call for a strong defence to an invocation of ideological leadership. Establishing the 'negative' rationale for the unipolar – 'the vacuum left by [our] retreat would invite challenges to our power' – Bush added the 'positive' of complementary interests:

> America, by decision and destiny, promotes political freedom – and gains the most when democracy advances. America believes in free markets and free trade – and benefits most when markets are opened. America is a peaceful power – and gains the greatest dividend from democratic stability.

This attempted convergence of ideals and political and economic interests would later be enshrined in the 2002 National Security Strategy, with its endpoint of a 'balance of power that favors freedom' and the trinity of 'freedom, democracy, and free markets.'[11]

Conceptually, Bush was not breaking from the Clinton Administration's advocacy of an 'assertive multilateralism.'[12] Far from declaring a unilateral American project to remake the world, Bush used the foundation of American alliances to safeguard his venture into the global, concluding, 'We have partners, not satellites. Our goal is a fellowship of strong, not weak, nations. And this requires both more American consultation and more American leadership.' Even the United Nations, along with other international organizations, could 'serve the cause of peace.' At the same time, Bush was setting out a difference of degree from his predecessor, setting out the primacy of US direction. Europe could – and should – 'invest more in defense capabilities; and, when necessary, in military conflict'; the UN could 'help in weapons inspections, peacekeeping and humanitarian efforts.' In the end, however, the 'fellowship of strong, not weak, nations' rested upon 'both more American consultation and more American leadership.'[13] The US would act with alliances if possible but would act alone if necessary.

Bush's own assertiveness raised an immediate question. Was it necessary, in the emergent strategy of the unipolar, to define 'for' or 'against' whom America was pursuing its mission? Geographically, the candidate walked through a checklist of 'strong democratic allies in Europe and Asia' and 'a fully democratic Western Hemisphere, bound together by free trade.' He cited 'America's interests in the Persian Gulf' to arrive at his only specific commitment – beyond the implied perpetual of missile defence to 'check the contagious spread of weapons of mass destruction' – linking the 'advance [of] peace in the Middle East' to 'a secure Israel.' On China, Bush wandered between a competitive but sometimes co-operative coexistence with 'a free and prosperous' Beijing and containment of a rival. Similarly, the possibility of a working relationship with Moscow was hedged by calls for a halt to proliferation and a 'democratic and free Russia.'

The political answer to the question, staking out a distinctive approach while projecting the unipolar against everyone and no one, was to emphasize the commitment to capability through National Missile Defense (NMD). Bush's campaign advisor Robert Zoellick framed the challenge as 'a repeat of 1990–91 where this time Iraq has nuclear weapons and missiles to deliver them.'[14] After a May 2000 special press conference, in which Bush outlined his plans for missile defence and was supported by George Shultz, Henry Kissinger and Colin Powell, Robert Kagan praised the boldness of an approach that would transform the international environment 'in terms of our own power and our ability to maintain primacy.'[15]

For proponents of the unipolar, the Reagan Library speech was more than adequate reassurance. The details of specific objectives beyond NMD might be vague, but the potential that American power might be extended under the ideological umbrella of 'freedom' offered hope. As Kagan noted with approval, '[Bush] sounded a lot more like Ronald Reagan and spoke a great deal more about American primacy, American principles being at the forefront of his foreign policy.'[16] He and William Kristol believed that this was 'the strongest and clearest articulation of a policy of American global leadership since the end of the Cold War.'[17]

Bush's future Secretary of State was ready to go even further. In an article in *Foreign Affairs* at the start of 2000, Rice put power at the heart of a new post-Cold War pursuit of 'strategic opportunities' for the 'national interest,' combining an American exceptionalism of the 'remarkable position' of political and economic superiority and the transcendent virtue of being on 'the right side of history.' Assured of both might and right, she could be unapologetic about the unipolar against those who were so 'uncomfortable with the notions of power politics, great powers, and power balances' that they embraced 'a reflexive appeal ... to notions of international law and norms, and the belief that the support of many states − or even better, of institutions like the United Nations − is essential to the legitimate exercise of power.' Rather than 'multilateral agreements and institutions ... [as] ends in themselves,' Rice argued for unilateral capability to 'ensure that America's military can deter war, project power, and fight in defense of its interests if deterrence fails' and 'to deal decisively with the threat of rogue regimes and hostile powers, which is increasingly taking the forms of the potential for terrorism and the development of weapons of mass destruction.'

As with Bush, the question of the geopolitical framework for the exercise of that power remained. At first glance, Rice's 'post-Cold War' outlook had a distinctively Cold War resonance with the 'focus [of] US energies on comprehensive relationships with the big powers, particularly Russia and China, that can and will mold the character of the international political system.'[18] Yet, in line with both her candidate and the key advisors to the campaign, Rice's broader vision was of the unlimited projection of capabilities. Invoking the language of the 1992 Defense Planning Guidance, she claimed, 'The American military must be able to meet decisively the emergence of any hostile military power in the Asia-Pacific region, the Middle East, the Persian Gulf, and Europe.'[19]

Rice had answered the question left by Bush's speeches − 'Was it necessary, in the emergent strategy of the unipolar, to define "for" or "against" whom America was pursuing its mission?' − with a clear No. When they were not in office, Bush's 'Vulcans,' as they dubbed themselves, enjoyed the luxury of being able to advocate a theory of hegemonic stability that did not necessarily require a specific adversary: 'unipolarism' was a good in its own right; a way to *prevent* threats emerging or, if they did emerge, deal with them decisively.

Finding an example for the unipolar

The potential problem for the campaign was how to project the unipolar to the general public.[20] More prominent were its 'negative' aspects, that is, the need to detach or distance the United States from commitments such as the Anti-Ballistic Missile Treaty, the Oslo peace process between Israel and Palestine, and peacekeeping in areas such as the Balkans. In contrast, when the unipolar was asserted 'positively' in the name of the national interest, at least with respect to specific cases, it was done so hesitantly. Military projection, as in Kosovo, was to be encouraged for the sake of American leadership but political and economic projection, particularly in post-conflict areas, was to be considered with caution. As Rice argued, '[The US military] is not a civilian police force. It is not a political referee. And it is most certainly not designed to build a civilian society.'[21]

This caution extended even to potentially key cases such as the American handling of 'rogue states.' Far from placing such enemies at the centre of an American strategy, Bush made almost no reference to them, apart from his general insistence at the first debate amongst Republican candidates, 'I wouldn't ease the sanctions, and I wouldn't try to negotiate with [Saddam Hussein] ... I'd be helping the opposition groups. And if I found in any way, shape, or form that he was developing weapons of mass destruction, I'd take 'em out.'[22] Rice offered only general references to the Iraqi and North Korean menace of weapons of mass destruction and Iran's support of terrorism and threat to Israel. Instead, when other advisors such as Rumsfeld paid attention to the 'rogue states' of Iran and North Korea, they did so primarily to justify the pursuit of Ballistic Missile Defence.[23]

Up to and beyond the Presidential election in November 2000, the often abstract call for the display of military capability, as well as the open disavowal of nation-building and peacekeeping, gave the impression that the Bush Administration would retreat from overseas commitments rather than embrace intervention. Dick Cheney, condemning the Clinton Administration for 'overused' military forces, called for a selective approach in the demonstration of power: 'It is important that we make sometimes difficult choices about when we're going to actually use military force, that we need to avoid situations where we commit troops because we can't think of anything else to do.' Beyond the rejection of the US occupation of Haiti in 1994 and a call for ground troops to be removed from Kosovo, the prospective Vice President 'did not spell out a specific doctrine that he and Gov. George W. Bush ... would follow if they won the election.'[24] In his debates with Democratic nominee Al Gore in October, Bush stated repeatedly that the purpose of the military was 'to fight and win war and therefore prevent war from happening in the first place' but preceded this with the pointed rejection of a protracted post-war commitment, 'I don't think we can be all things to all people in the world.... I would be very careful about using our troops as nation builders.'[25]

Iraq's immediate significance was as a possible way out of this conundrum, providing a 'positive' assertion of American power linked both to security against Iraqi weapons of mass destruction and to the freeing of an oppressed people. The Republican platform supported the Iraq Liberation Act of 1998 as 'a starting point in a comprehensive plan for the removal of Saddam Hussein.' How to proceed from aspiration to achievement in this demonstration of the unipolar was a different matter however. Robert Kagan asked pointedly, 'It's easy and fine for George Bush to say he would support the Iraq Liberation Act, but it seems to me the responsible question is, what do you do next if Saddam starts slaughtering the opposition?'[26]

Nascent planning focused instead on the pursuit of specific interests and, significantly, came from 'private' channels beyond the neo-conservative network and Bush advisors. In November 2000 the Baker Institute – named after James W. Baker III, long-time advisor to Bush father and son – issued a warning about 'the potential leverage of an otherwise lesser producer [of oil] such as Iraq' with Saddam Hussein a 'destabilizing influence to the flow of oil to international markets from the Middle East.' Officials from the Institute met members of the Council on Foreign Relations, who then reported on the economic and geopolitical problem of Iraq as a 'swing producer' of oil.[27]

By mid-December the Vice President-elect was making clear, in security briefings for the transition of administrations, that he wanted to focus on Iraq. Meeting Bill Clinton for the first (and only) time, Bush confirmed that his chief concerns were missile defence and Iraq; when Clinton raised issues from al Qaeda to Middle Eastern diplomacy to North Korea and nuclear weapons in South Asia, Bush offered no response.[28] Still, on the eve of the Inauguration, it was not certain that Iraq was destined to be the top issue for the Administration. The appointment of the Secretary of Defense, for example, did not point towards an immediate drive on Baghdad. Instead at the press conference unveiling Rumsfeld, both the President and his nominee focused on military transformation and missile defence.[29] The National Intelligence Estimate released in December carried the headline, 'Iraq: Steadily Pursuing WMD Capabilities,' but the text was more cautious, 'stating that Iraq did not appear to have taken significant steps toward the reconstitution of the [nuclear] program.'[30]

Instead, the establishment of Iraq as a demonstration case for the American unipolar came from deeper within the Bush bureaucracy, notably at the Pentagon. Rumsfeld quickly established a 'Kitchen Cabinet' of assistants like Steve Cambone, Martin Hoffman, M. Staser Holcomb, and Steve Herbits.[31] Cambone had served in Cheney's Department of Defense from 1990 to 1993 and had been staff director for the Rumsfeld Commission on Ballistic Missile Defense. Hoffman, Holcomb, and Herbits had an even longer association with the Secretary of Defense, working with him since the late 1960s and 1970s.[32]

Even more importantly, Richard Perle, who had lost his chance at a high-level post because of an ill-timed intervention on the Israeli–Palestinian issue during the campaign,[33] shrewdly re-established his influence. He turned down the offer of Undersecretary of Defense for Policy, the number-three post in the Pentagon; instead he recommended a protégé, Douglas Feith, for the job while taking up the chairmanship of the advisory Defense Policy Board.[34] Perle's position, formally working 'outside' the formal bureaucracy while having a significant de facto presence within it, was further buttressed with the appointments of Dov Zakheim and Peter Rodman to influential positions in the Department. Harold Rhode, officially assigned to the Pentagon's Office of Net Assessment, worked with Feith to set out the Pentagon line that there would be no more 'bartering in the bazaar,' purging permanent staff who did not agree.[35] This nexus of officials, working in combination with others such as David Wurmser in Cheney's office and Elliot Abrams at the National Security Council, put Iraq at the top of the Bush agenda, even before the formal confirmation of Feith and Paul Wolfowitz as Undersecretary of Defense.[36]

For these officials, the liberation of Baghdad would be one piece of a long-envisaged re-arrangement of the region. In 1996 Perle, Feith, and Wurmser, writing for the Israeli Prime Minister Benjamin Netanyahu, set out the proposal 'A Clean Break: A Strategy for Securing the Realm.' The paper focused on Israel's immediate neighbours to suggest military assaults against Lebanon and Syria, but this 'prelude to a redrawing of the map of the Middle East which would threaten Syria's territorial integrity' was linked to co-operation with Jordan and Turkey to overthrow Saddam and restore the Hashemite dynasty to the Iraqi throne.[37] Perle saw a leadership role for the Iraqi National Congress (INC) and its head, Ahmad Chalabi, whom he considered 'a modern liberal leader.' Two years later, as Wurmser was seeking Israeli support for US Congressional funding of the INC, Perle emphasized the need for Tel Aviv to focus on Saddam as well as the ayatollahs of Iran: 'One can only speculate what it might accomplish if it decided to focus its attention on Saddam Hussein.'[38]

As soon as he took up his post with Vice President Cheney, Wurmser set out the 'Clean Break' approach. Emphasizing that 'America's and Israel's responses must be regional, not local,' he proposed that Washington and Tel Aviv should 'strike fully, not merely disarm, the centers of radicalism in the region – the regimes of Damascus, Baghdad, Tripoli, Tehran, and Gaza.'[39] Perle complemented this with a public call for 'democratization':

> I think there is a potential civic culture in Arab countries that can lead to democratic institutions and I think Iraq is probably the best place to put that proposition to the test because it's a sophisticated educated population that has suffered under totalitarian rule.[40]

By 30 January and the first meeting of the National Security Council, this group – through their connections in the 1990s with officials like Rumsfeld and Cheney, their roles in the Presidential campaign, and their places in the emerging Bush Administration bureaucracy – had ensured their aspirations were voiced at the top of the Executive Branch. The President set out, 'We're going to correct the imbalances of the previous administration on the Mideast conflict. We're going to tilt it back to Israel.' When Secretary of State Colin Powell, taken by surprise, objected that ending efforts for an Israeli–Palestinian settlement might unleash the Israeli army, Bush responded, 'Sometimes a show of strength by one side can really clarify things.'[41] Then, making the link that Perle and his associates desired, Bush asked Condoleezza Rice, the new National Security Advisor, to outline 'How

Iraq is Destabilizing the Region.' Rice in turn was supported by the Director of Central Intelligence, George Tenet, with a briefing including a photograph of 'a plant that produces either chemical or biological materials for weapons manufacture.'[42]

Thus, Rumsfeld's appeal two days later to 'imagine what the region would look like' was not just the vision of the unipolar but the framing for a specific strategic approach to link the demonstration of American strength with the establishment of long-term predominance. It did not, however, mark the success of that approach. Although his intervention had checked Colin Powell's opening proposal of 'targeted sanctions' and assurances that Saddam had 'not developed any significant capability' in WMDs,[43] it did not end in an approved course of action. In part, this was because Rumsfeld, either because he was not inclined to do so or had not been asked to do so by his assistants, did not push the option of the overthrow of Saddam: while the enforcement of no-fly zones in northern and southern Iraq might help opposition groups, he added, 'I'm after the weapons of mass destruction. Regime change isn't my prime concern.'[44] In part, this was because the President was reluctant to set out a defined course of action; as a White House official later reflected, 'Faced with a dilemma, he has this favorite phrase he uses all the time: Protect my flexibility.'[45] For this flexibility, the NSC authorized three working groups: one to consider covert pressure to topple Saddam, one to study intensified American action over the no-fly zones, and one to evaluate targeted sanctions.

The Iraq resolution also awaited the initial steps towards the unipolar, signalled during the campaign, through the development of capabilities and detachment from international agreements and bilateral negotiations. Rumsfeld's pursuit of military transformation, almost to the point of obsession,[46] was twinned with the ever-present of Missile Defense through Bush's emphasis on new systems and reform in the Pentagon.[47] The Administration turned its back on its predecessor's talks to suspend the North Korean nuclear programme and signalled that it would abrogate the 1972 Anti-Ballistic Missile Treaty as well as reject agreements on the environment, the International Criminal Court, and chemical and biological weapons.[48] Key officials thus hedged their bets on intervention in Iraq. At his confirmation hearings, Paul Wolfowitz professed his desire for the overthrow of Saddam Hussein but, when asked if there was a feasible plan to achieve this, admitted, 'I haven't seen it yet.'[49] Cheney said inspections of Iraqi facilities 'may not be as crucial if you've got other measures in place.'[50]

At lower levels, however, the activists ensured that their plans were further developed, to the point that they constituted a de facto policy. Within hours of the initial NSC meetings, information leaked to the press that 'the Bush administration has given Iraqi opposition groups permission to resume their activities inside Iraq with American funding,' finally releasing the first tranche of $4 million from the 1998 Iraq Liberation Act.[51] United Press International reported,

What distinguishes this training from previous courses for the INC ...
such as emergency medical care, public relations and war-crimes investi-
gations ... is that the rebels attending the five-day seminar would also
learn how to use pistols, Kalishnikov rifles, 12-gauge shotguns and a
variety of other firearms.[52]

Bush announced on 6 February that the US would resume the funding of
opposition efforts inside Iraq for the first time since 1996.[53] Ten days later,
the moves for covert operations were complemented by the most extensive
bombing of Iraqi positions – approved by members of the NSC, including
Powell, and recommended to the President – since December 1998.[54] Perle
in particular maintained the pretext of Saddam Hussein's imminent threat
to the United States, telling Congress:

Does Saddam now have weapons of mass destruction? Sure he does.
How far he's gone on the nuclear-weapon side I don't think we really
know. My guess is it's further than we think. It's always further than we
think, because we limit ourselves, as we think about this, to what we're
able to prove and demonstrate.[55]

Equally important, these plans and operations always had the potential to
become part of the larger conception of the American unipolar in the Middle
East, especially if they found a high-level supporter who could bring Government and the private sector together in discussion. Cheney soon filled this
role as he sought a re-definition of foreign policy linked to control of energy
resources, taking in hand the warning of the Baker Institute's report that 'the
US remains a prisoner of its energy dilemma.'[56] A National Security Council
directive of February 3 commanded NSC staff to co-operate with the Energy
Task Force, led by the Vice President, as it pursued the 'melding' of 'the
review of operational policies towards rogue states' with 'actions regarding
the capture of new and existing oil and gas fields.'[57] Industry executives and
Cheney's staff pored over a map of Iraq, void of all features except the location
of its main oil deposits, divided into nine exploration blocks.[58]

By mid-March, some in the State Department and the CIA were so
worried about the increasing support for the INC that they fed a press
campaign questioning the group's efficacy. According to officials,

despite millions of dollars in U.S. aid, the leading Iraqi opposition
group has proved ... hapless in making use of the money, accounting
for it, finding recruits for Pentagon training and preventing its own
fragmentation.... The Iraqi National Congress also now is so out of
favor in the Arab world and Turkey that all but one of the states border-
ing Iraq have made clear to Secretary of State Colin Powell and other
U.S. officials that they won't allow the group to operate out of their
territory.[59]

The backing of the INC appears to have cut across another initiative for regime change, led by the National Security Council, in early 2001. Falah Aljibury, an Iraqi-born oil executive and Ronald Reagan's back channel to Saddam Hussein in the 1980s, hosted a discussion group led by Pamela Quanrud, an NSC economics expert. Plans were developed for the replacement of Saddam Hussein by a former Ba'athist general; one of those approached was General Nizar Khazrahi, who was in Denmark awaiting trial on war crimes charges.[60]

Amidst this bureaucratic manoeuvring and conflict, covert action remained at the forefront of planning, even if it was never accepted as the central American approach. Richard Haass, the director of policy planning at the State Department and the head of the interagency group overseeing the three options for Iraq, recommended 'an uprising by a popular rebel group, while simultaneously recruiting and supporting high-ranking Iraqi military officers willing to oust Saddam's regime.' The strategy was considered from late April to the end of July in 'deputies' meetings' of high-ranking CIA officials, Deputy Secretary of State Richard Armitage, Paul Wolfowitz and Cheney's national security adviser, I. Lewis Libby, and in the Principals Committee of Rice, Cheney, Tenet, and Powell.[61] Wolfowitz, pressing the activist agenda, proposed the bombing of dams to 'recreate' the marshlands in Iraq and, with his assistant Zalmay Khalilzad, drafted further proposals for the arming and training of insurgents.

Further space for covert moves came with the failure of the 'smart sanctions' strategy, buried by Russian opposition at the UN Security Council. A 'top Bush aide' declared, 'People are now going to say, "Is it time to take another look at regime change?"'[62] Rumsfeld, however, continued to prefer the overt challenge through the bolstering of the no-fly zones.[63] Thus while 'A Liberation Strategy' was put forth on 1 August with reliance on Iraqi opposition groups and consideration of circumstances for overt military action, no specific recommendations were put to the President.[64]

Beyond this internal manoeuvring, the major challenge to the Iraqi demonstration case was coming from events beyond Baghdad. The most significant of these came in April with the downing of an American reconnaissance plane in the South China Sea. The subsequent mini-crisis, with 24 US crewmen held by the Chinese for 11 days, dominated headlines and tested Rice's approach to Beijing as 'strategic competitor' rather than strategic partner.[65] The Pentagon and many in Congress demanded a firm response, but diplomatic considerations and economic interests as well as the risks of military confrontation checked any US intervention. A 'senior official' admitted, 'There aren't a lot of good options.'[66] When the US offered a qualified apology to obtain the release of the crewmen and the return of the plane (dismantled and in boxes), the unipolar appeared to have been circumscribed.[67] Kagan and Kristol wrote of 'A National Humiliation' in which the American expression of regret was 'a partial capitulation, with real-world consequences.'[68]

With the Administration also occupied or constrained by the escalation of violence in Israel and Palestine, 'terrorism' (including consideration of action to undermine or topple the Taliban and break up al Qaeda),[69] and hostility to American policy in Europe and beyond, the focus had to remain on capabilities and the clearing of political and military space for unilateral action. The orchestrated denunciation of the Anti-Ballistic Treaty coupled with warnings of Pearl Harbor and surprise attacks, rejection of the International Criminal Court, sustained opposition to the Kyoto agreement, and a 'policy review' on North Korea all pointed towards development of the potential for selective, American-defined action.

Bush, often away from Washington, seemed detached from day-to-day discussions, let alone policymaking.[70] Instead, it was Rumsfeld and Cheney who persisted with the broadest conception of the use of American power. In an interview with the *New Yorker*, the Vice President spoke of 'an organizing principle for US foreign policy that could be compared to the Cold War':

> There are still regions of the world that are strategically vital to the U.S.... And anything that would threaten their independence or their relationships with the United States would be a threat to us. Also, you've got to worry about North Korea. You've got to worry about the Iraqis, what ultimately develops in Iran ... I think we have to be more concerned than we ever have about so-called homeland defense, the vulnerability of our system to different kinds of attacks. Some of it homegrown, like Oklahoma City. Some inspired by terrorists external to the United States.... The threat of terrorist attack against the U.S., eventually, potentially, with weapons of mass destruction – bugs or gas or biological or chemical agents, potentially even someday nuclear weapons.[71]

This was far from enough for those who had pressed for the American unipolar. Kagan and William Kristol complained that Bush 'may go down in history as the man who let American military power atrophy and America's post-Cold War pre-eminence slip away.'[72] In Kristol's *Weekly Standard*, Reuel Marc Gerecht asked if the US was serious about toppling Saddam and claimed 'the Bush Administration has continued and actually surpassed its predecessor's display of timidity in the Middle East.'[73]

The criticism was premature and possibly misguided, in part because of the immediate focus upon cases such as China and Iraq. By September, Rumsfeld's capabilities-based approach was ready to be linked to Cheney's attention to 'regions of the world.' The Secretary of Defense was basing an expansion of military power on a new doctrine of pre-emption: 'If we are to extend this period of peace and prosperity, we need to prepare now for the new and different threats we will face in the decades ahead – not wait until they fully emerge.' Possible targets of American action were Iraq and North Korea, as Rumsfeld pondered, 'What checks and balances are there on

Saddam Hussein or Kim Jong Il?... We cannot rely on them being deterred.'[74]

The catalyst of 9/11: capitalizing on opportunity

Then, on 11 September 2001, aircraft commandeered by al Qaeda hijackers struck the World Trade Center and the Pentagon. Condoleezza Rice asked her staff, 'How do you capitalize on these opportunities?' a sentiment repeated by President Bush to his closest advisors, 'This is a great opportunity. We have to think of this as an opportunity.'[75] The Quadrennial Defense Review, drafted in the summer but revised after al Qaeda's attacks, stated:

> [T]hese attacks confirm the strategic direction and planning principles that resulted from this review, particularly its emphasis on homeland defense, on surprise, on preparing for asymmetric threats, on the need to develop new concepts of deterrence, on the need for a capabilities-based strategy, and on the need to balance deliberately the different dimensions of risk. However, the attack on the United States on September 11, 2001 will require us to move forward more rapidly in these directions, even while we are engaged in the war against terrorism.[76]

Specifically this new, unified approach could now take up the demonstration case of Iraq. On 10 September Rumsfeld was telling his staff that the major American adversary was not 'one of the last decrepit dictators of the world' but 'the Pentagon bureaucracy.'[77] Less than 48 hours later, he was commanding, 'best info fast. Judge whether good enough hit S.H.' – meaning Saddam Hussein – 'at same time. Not only UBL [Osama bin Laden].... Go massive, sweep it all up. Things related and not.'[78] (Once again, Bush was in step with his advisors, allegedly telling the counter-terrorism co-ordinator Richard Clarke, 'I want you to find whether Iraq did this'[79]). Where planning before September 11 had only gone as far as 'a propaganda campaign against the Saddam Hussein regime ... [with] a satellite television station ... beaming programmes into Iraq from London and Washington,'[80] Perle could now lobby for an accelerated campaign for regime change, allegedly telling officials, 'Iraq has to pay a price for what happened yesterday. They bear responsibility.'[81]

By 13 September Rumsfeld had asked for scenarios for an assault upon Iraq and for a specific contingency plan to seize and hold the southern Iraqi oilfields, complementing and moving beyond a plan for an attack by 10 000 insurgents supported by US airpower; however, after extensive debate, the NSC rejected the proposal, tabled by Wolfowitz, to hit Iraq immediately.[82] For the President, however, it was quite clear that operations to remove the Taliban from power were a stepping stone to regime change in Baghdad, who he believed 'was involved' in the strikes on the World Trade Center and the Pentagon.[83] As he told British Prime Minister Tony Blair on 20 September

'We must deal with this first. But when we have dealt with Afghanistan, we must come back to Iraq.'[84]

Having put the idea of Iraq as demonstration case on the agenda in January, the activists at working levels could now set up the pretext for overt as well as covert operations. On 18–19 September, Perle's Defense Planning Board met to discuss the topic of Saddam Hussein and regime change. Their featured guest was Ahmad Chalabi, who assured the gathering that Iraq was both an incubator for terrorists and a possessor of weapons of mass destruction.[85] In October, Douglas Feith set up the 'Policy Counter-Terrorism Evaluation Group' (PCEG) to convert such assertions into the 'intelligence' that would be presented as the casus belli against Iraq.[86] (Francis Brooke, Chalabi's Washington aide, summarized the process, 'I sent out an all-points bulletin to our network, saying, "Look, guys, get me a terrorist, or someone who works with terrorists. And, if you can get stuff on W.M.D., send it!"'[87]) A few months later, the PCEG was supplemented by the 'Office of Special Plans,' a war-planning unit under Wolfowitz and Feith's direction.[88] Bush gave the ad hoc units political cover; as he told a group of Senators meeting with Rice, 'Fuck Saddam. We're taking him out.'[89]

The collapse of the unipolar

The subsequent narrative of American intervention in Iraq is now generally known. On 21 November 2001, before the 'liberation' of Afghanistan was completed, Bush asked Rumsfeld to draw up plans for the invasion of Iraq.[90] In early March 2002, as US forces were failing to capture Osama bin Laden in the Tora Bora Mountains, Cheney was travelling to the United Kingdom and Arab countries to announce the shift in attention from the Afghan theatre to Baghdad.[91] When this initial attempt was checked by the scepticism of Arab leaders, the escalating crisis between Israel and a lack of 'intelligence' that could be presented as pretext for military operations,[92] the Bush Administration adjusted its timetable and rolled out the campaign for action in August, beginning with Cheney's speech at the Veterans of Foreign Wars National Convention warning of an imminent Iraqi nuclear weapons capability.[93]

Similarly, the devolution of 'Mission Accomplished' into a protracted occupation of Iraq, with chaos rather than stability and a very untidy 'freedom,' is now being well-documented. From the killing of at least 17 Iraqi demonstrators in Fallujah by US forces at the end of April, the cycle of American and insurgent violence was soon established. By August 2003, when the UN headquarters in Baghdad was bombed, killing 17 including the special envoy Sérgio Vieira de Mello, 'liberation' had turned into a muddled campaign of 'coalition' forces versus 'foreign fighters,' 'Ba'athists,' and 'dead enders,' a presentation that obscured rather than clarified the sources of dispute. Even the capture of Saddam Hussein in December 2003 was little more than a short-term public relations reprieve from the worsening situation.

This ongoing story of Iraq still does not get to the heart of the Bush Administration's strategy and, thus, the reasons for the failure of the 'unipolar.' The problem was that the invasion of Iraq was never pursued with attention to the specific conditions of the country but as the demonstration of a US preponderance of power, beyond Baghdad, 'against everyone and against no-one.' The military assault could demonstrate American capabilities. It could see the extension of American capabilities through with the acquisition and development of US influence over the Iraqi economy and resources. It could even be heralded as the catalyst for a regional transformation that would both demonstrate 'freedom' and establish an order supporting the long-term maintenance of those American capabilities and interests.

The unipolar was being projected, however, in an arena emptied of 'local' political, economic, and cultural meaning. Indeed, by definition, the unipolar could not recognize the possibility of alternative loci of power. Actors in Iraq, apart from Saddam and his henchmen, were reduced to the passive recipients of Bush's invocation in the 2000 campaign, 'If we're a humble nation, but strong, they'll welcome us.'[94] The 'new' Iraqi political system would be brought in from outside through the exiles, such as Ahmad Chalabi and the Iraqi National Congress, supported by the civilian leadership in the Pentagon. This in part explained how the general aversion to 'nation building' expressed in the 2000 Presidential campaign became a specific avoidance of planning for post-war Iraq (and, before that, post-war Afghanistan).[95] Before the invasion, the State Department's 'Future of Iraq' project – based on detailed studies of the country's political and economic structures and involving more than 300 Iraqi participants – was thrown out by Rumsfeld; after 'liberation' the struggles of Jay Garner, the first American representative in Baghdad, for a coherent (or even a rudimentary) approach to reconstruction were dismissed in favour of the sweeping edicts of his successor, Paul Bremer.

When that failure to address local structures and dynamics, including the rejection of elections throughout 2003, fed growing Iraqi dissatisfaction and then resistance, the Bush Administration's rationale for the unipolar was turned against itself. Expressed in the President's West Point speech in June 2002, the American premise was that the display of military capability would prompt others – inside Iraq, throughout the Middle East, and throughout the world – to follow US political and economic agendas.[96] But when those general agendas were exposed with social breakdown in Iraq, then the American 'demonstration' of capabilities came under scrutiny. Instead of post-Saddam Iraq serving as a model for other countries that the US wanted to transform, it provided the rationale for others in those countries who wished to challenge an American preponderance. Ironically, the architects of the 1996 'Clean Break' had been proven correct in their vision of a regional transformation; however, instead of enhancing US power, the 'domino effect' was a regional (and global) increase in anti-Washington sentiment and an exacerbation of existing conflicts.

For a brief period at the start of 2005, there was a false dawn for the unipolar with the first Iraqi national elections and a wave of demonstrations and uprisings from the Ukraine to Georgia to Lebanon. Shifting from a security-based rationale ('we fight them over there so we don't have to fight them here') to one based on ideological projection, the Bush Administration proclaimed a 'freedom agenda' that would uphold the benevolent, transforming potential of American power. The President proclaimed in his 2005 State of the Union address, 'We are all part of a great venture: To extend the promise of freedom in our country, to renew the values that sustain our liberty, and to spread the peace that freedom brings.'[97]

The problem was that this American proclamation of 'freedom' was just as abstracted, and just as detached from local political, economic, and cultural conditions, as the US military intervention that had preceded it. Elections in Iraq would not lead to stability. The demonstrations in Lebanon, as well as American pressure, might have accelerated a withdrawal of Syrian forces but they did not produce either the welcoming of US influence or a lasting political accommodation. Even the less problematic cases such as Ukraine and Georgia would be complicated by internal political turmoil that fractured 'pro-Western' governments, suspended Parliaments, and led to the imposition of emergency rule.

And, inevitably, the American unipolar faced the tensions and even contradictions between its threat-based and ideology-based rationales. The June 2005 call of Condoleezza Rice, now Secretary of State, in Cairo to stand with those 'demanding freedom for themselves and democracy for their countries'[98] was soon overtaken by the Egyptian Government's crackdown on dissent and political and religious opposition. Democracy in Palestine led to the popular election of Hamas in Gaza, a result that cut against the Bush Administration's strategy for 'security' and against 'terrorism' in the area. And, somewhat ironically, the US Government retreated from any call for liberation in North Korea because this would complicate efforts to deal with Pyongyang's possible capability in nuclear weapons. By 2006 the Administration had effectively abandoned the 'freedom agenda,' apart from the set pieces of Bush's meetings with dissidents and a short-lived initiative at the G8 summit in Prague in June 2007.

Conclusion: an empire of capabilities?

Months before the Bush Administration came into office, Paul Wolfowitz wrote, 'Even if the chances of another assault on world peace are remote, what is at stake is too great to permit complacency or neglect of America's responsibility as the world's dominant power.'[99]

Wolfowitz's candid profession of the endpoint of American foreign policy did not outline the complexities of this pursuit of the unipolar. The quest for power was bound up with other considerations and rationalizations that distinguished the positions of activists. Brent Scowcroft, the National Security Advisor to the first President Bush, captured the tensions of ideology and geopolitics in a cogent assessment of the second President Bush's Administration:

> If you talk about the two real neocons, there's Richard Perle and Paul Wolfowitz, and they're very different. Paul Wolfowitz is an idealist, but he's prepared to impose democracy by the sword. Perle's not about that. I don't think Perle gives a shit about democracy. Fundamentally, it's all a means to an end.[100]

Within weeks of the 'liberation' of Iraq, Wolfowitz outlined the tangle of considerations that lay behind the American invasion:

> There have always been three fundamental concerns. One is weapons of mass destruction, the second is support for terrorism, the third is the criminal treatment of the Iraqi people. Actually I guess you could say there's a fourth overriding one which is the connection between the first two.... The third one by itself, as I think I said earlier, is a reason to help the Iraqis but it's not a reason to put American kids' lives at risk, certainly not on the scale we did it. That second issue about links to terrorism is the one about which there's the most disagreement within the bureaucracy.[101]

Perle was even blunter in framing the 'spread of democracy' as a rationalization for other objectives: 'It is not always in our power to do anything about [undemocratic governments], nor is it always in our interest, but when it is in our power and our interest, we should toss dictators aside.'[102]

   Yet these divergences were not fundamental, provided the unipolar was always held up as the unifying end. What was needed was not a resolution of the 'spread of democracy' or of a specific position vis-à-vis a rival, be that the post-Cold War China or Russia or one of the numerous rogue states, but a platform for a demonstration of American capabilities. As Perle told George Packer, when 'the world began on 9/11,' people were already in place to give President Bush a strategy and a world-view.[103] That world-view, which propelled the plans of the Pentagon in particular, was set out by Robert Kagan and William Kristol in 1996:

> The most difficult thing to preserve is that which does not appear to need preserving.... The ubiquitous post-Cold War question – where is the threat? – is thus misconceived. In a world in which peace and American security depend on American power and the will to use it, the main threat the United States faces now and in the future is its own weakness. American hegemony is the only reliable defense against a breakdown of peace and international order.[104]

But as the Project for a New American Century, which included Kagan, Kristol, Perle, and Wolfowitz as members, admitted in 2000, to implement this policy and ensure its acceptance by the public, what was needed was 'a catastrophic and catalyzing event – like a new Pearl Harbor.'[105]

Yet, in all this consideration of the conditions in and beyond the United States that both mandated and permitted the quest for the unipolar, those who would either accept American preponderance or be on the receiving end of American capabilities were little more than an abstracted Other. US power might remove a Saddam Hussein but offered little consideration of the political, economic, or cultural circumstances that followed regime change. In such a context, failure lay not – as 'neo-conservatives' claimed – in the negligence or dismissal of 'American hegemony' but within the concept itself.

Recognition of this inherent flaw complicates many explanations not only of the Bush Administration ('neo-conservative,' 'neo-Wilsonian,' 'assertive nationalist,' etc.) but of the place of hegemony in present and future US foreign policy. Bruce Berkowitz's concern with predominance does not extend beyond the 'sustainability' of capabilities.[106] Robert Kagan persists in an assertion of American power which ignores any substantive consideration of the 'recipients' of that power:

> American predominance in the main categories of power persists as a key feature of the international system. The enormous and productive American economy remains at the center of the international economic system. American democratic principles are shared by over a hundred nations. The American military is not only the largest but the only one capable of projecting force into distant theaters.[107]

Unable or unwilling to evaluate America in relation to the 'other,' Kagan can only fall back on the assertion that the issue is simply one of the United States overcoming its 'crisis of legitimacy.' Meanwhile Joseph Nye, even as he criticizes the manner and approach of the Bush Administration, does not question the notion of American hegemony; he merely searches for a kinder, gentler way of achieving it: 'Soft power is the ability to get what you want by attracting and persuading others to adopt your goals.'[108]

Others put forth simplistic representations of American power as an 'empire' to be embraced. John Gaddis comfortably asserts,

> Empire is as American as apple pie.... It seems to me on balance American imperial power in the 20th century has been a remarkable force for good, for democracy, for prosperity. What is striking is that great opposition has not arisen to the American empire.[109]

When this empire is not welcomed, then the explanation must lie in an equally sweeping representation of opposition. Francis Fukuyama, having broken with former allies of a preponderance of power, sees a world 'characterized by American hegemony and a global anti-Americanism backlash.'[110]

However perhaps the most provocative, and ultimately counterproductive, simplification is the equation of American power with the spread of freedom. With an added emphasis and, some would say, validity because it is offered by those who were not supporters of the Bush Administration, this 'liberal intervention' sets up liberation as the end of foreign policy. As Michael Ignatieff defined the approach just before the Iraq war,

> The choice is one between two evils, between containing and leaving a tyrant in place and the targeted use of force, which will kill people but free a nation from the tyrant's grip.... This is finally what makes an invasion of Iraq an imperial act: for it to succeed, it will have to build freedom.[111]

Unfortunately, the pursuit of the unipolar is not the pursuit of freedom, and its framing of 'people' goes no further than as a passive entity to be freed from tyrants or defended from terrorists, a vacuous signifier for the legitimate basis of American power. The 'imperialism' in the actions of the Bush Administration lay not in the purported outcomes set out by Ignatieff; instead it resided in the exercise of the actions in and of themselves and in the assurance, through capabilities and the control of resources supporting them, that this exercise could continue in perpetuity.

Notes

* The authors thank the Leverhulme for support for research for this chapter.
1 Ron Suskind, *The Price of Loyalty: George W. Bush, the White House, and the Education of Paul O'Neill* (New York: Simon and Schuster, 2004), 85.
2 Charles Krauthammer, 'The Unipolar Moment,' *Foreign Affairs*: America and the World 1990/01, www.foreignaffairs.org/19910201faessay6067/charles-krauthammer/ the-unipolar-moment.html. This notion of the unipolar should be distinguished from previous constructions of American 'preponderance,' such as that set out by State Department official George Kennan in the Truman Administration. See, for example, the analysis in Melvyn Leffler, *A Preponderance of Power: National Security, the Truman Administration, and the Cold War* (Stanford, CA: Stanford University Press, 1992).
3 See 'Excerpts From the Pentagon's Plan: "Prevent the Re-emergence of a New Rival",' *New York Times*, 8 March 1992.
4 National Security Strategy of the United States of America (henceforth 2002 NSS), September 2002: Introduction, www.whitehouse.gov/nsc/nss/2002/nssintro.html.
5 See for example, the Project for the New American Century's Statement of Principles, 3 June 1997, signed by both Rumsfeld and Cheney, www.new americancentury.org/statementofprinciples.htm, 1 February 2008.
6 In the aftermath of the fall of the Ba'athist regime, on the base of the demolished statue of Saddam in Fardus Square that a US tank had famously helped to pull down, an Iraqi had graffitied the words 'All done, go home.' See 'The Iraqi Media Three Months after the War: A New But Fragile Freedom,' *Reporters Without Borders*, 22 July 2003, www.rsf.org/article.php3?id_article=7583.
7 Speech by Governor George W. Bush, 'A Period of Consequences,' The Citadel, South Carolina, 23 September 1999, www.citadel.edu/pao/addresses/pres_bush.html.

8   The group adopted this nickname in reference to the hometown of Rice (and of one of the authors of this chapter), Birmingham, Alabama, which features a giant statue of the Roman god of fire and metalworking on a mountaintop over-looking the city.

9   'Black Max,' *This Far and No Further: A Timeline of Events Surrounding the Radical Right's Attempts to Subvert American Democracy*, 1999, www.iraqtimeline.com/1 999.html, 13 February 2008.

10 'How Would George W. Bush Govern in Foreign Policy?,' American Enterprise Institute, Transitions to Governing Project, 22 June 2000, debate transcript, www.aei.org/events/filter.,eventID.276/transcript.asp.

11 Speech by George W. Bush, 'A Distinctly American Internationalism,' Ronald Reagan Presidential Library, Simi Valley, California, 19 November 1999, www.mtholyoke.edu/acad/intrel/bush/wspeech.htm. See also 2002 NSS Introduction.

12 See the analysis in Stephen Erlanger, 'The U.S. and the U.N.: Now, Who Needs Whom More?' *New York Times*, 7 July 1996.

13 Bush, 'A Distinctly American Internationalism.'

14 AEI Transitions to Governing Project debate, 22 June 2000.

15 Kagan quoted in AEI Transitions to Governing Project debate, 22 June 2000. For the press conference with Shultz, Kissinger, and Powell, 23 May 2000, see www.washingtonpost.com/wp-srv/onpolitics/elections/bushtext052300.htm, 13 January 2008.

16 AEI Transitions to Governing Project Debate, 22 June 2000.

17 William Kristol and Robert Kagan for the Editors, 'A Distinctly American Internationalism,' *Weekly Standard*, 29 November 1999: 7. In 2003 Kristol told PBS:

> Bush gave speeches that we could have written, and the fact that we did help write, or friends of ours did help write, a very strong speech on distinctly American internationalism – it goes into Reagan Library in late 1999 – but he gave other speeches in which he said, "We have to be humble. We're over-extended. We don't need to spend much more on the military."
>
> (Interview with William Kristol, PBS Television, *Frontline*,
> 'The War Behind Closed Doors,' transcript,
> www.pbs.org/wgbh/pages/frontline/shows/iraq/interviews/kristol.html,
> 5 December 2007)

18 This outlook was also put forward by Wolfowitz, who considered China the 'single most important foreign policy challenge of the coming decades.' [Ambassador Paul Wolfowitz to the Heritage Foundation, 'Asian Democracy and American Interests,' 29 September 2000, www.heritage.org/Research/AsiaandthePacific/upload/12268_1.pdf].

19 Condoleezza Rice, 'Promoting the National Interest,' *Foreign Affairs*, January/February 2000, www.foreignaffairs.org/20000101faessay5/condoleezza-rice/campaign-2000-promoting-the-national-interest.html.

20 Indeed, in its widest projection, Bush's consideration of foreign policy verged on self-promoted caricature, as in his statement of his credentials at the first debate of Republican candidates: 'I have had foreign policy as the governor of Texas, and that is with Mexico, and I've handled it well.' See 'Text from New Hampshire Debate Involving G.O.P. Presidential Candidates,' *New York Times*, 3 December 1999, www.nytimes.com/library/politics/camp/120399wh-gop-debate-text.html.

21 Rice, 'Promoting the National Interest.'

22 Text from New Hampshire Debate, *New York Times*.
23 Zoellick was asked by a journalist whether Bush would be

> willing to resort to a pre-emptive strike [against Iraqi WMDs], which
> seems to me to be eminently sensible, why does he want to build a missile
> defense, which would be far more costly and wait for them to maybe
> launch something?

He replied,

> Well, I think that question is too clever by half. I mean obviously, we don't
> always know when people have … For the same reason that Israel feels it's
> important to have a missile defense system and that we are not necessarily
> aware of what North Korea had when [sic.] and what Iraq has now.
> (AEI Transitions to Governing Project Debate, 22 June 2000)

24 Michael Cooper, 'Cheney Urges Rethinking Use of U.S. Ground Forces in
   Bosnia and Kosovo,' *New York Times*, 1 September 2000.
25 This was repeated twice in the first Bush–Gore Presidential debate, 3 October
   2000, www.debates.org/pages/trans2000a.html. It was repeated three times in the
   second Bush–Gore Presidential debate, 11 October 2000, www.debates.org/pages/
   trans2000b.html. See also excerpts from Bush's speech to the American Legion
   Convention in Milwaukee, 6 September 2000, www.pbs.org/newshour/bb/
   politics/july-dec00/stump.html.
26 AEI Transitions to Governing Debate, 22 June 2000. When pressed on this
   point by Kagan, Perle refused to comment on exactly what further measures a
   Bush Administration might take, countering that it was an inappropriate level
   of detail at that stage and that although Bush was committed to supporting the
   opposition, it would be 'impossible to describe second and third and fourth
   moves' if their offensive were to fail.
27 Greg Palast, *Armed Madhouse: Undercover Dispatches From a Dying Regime*
   (London: Penguin, 2007), 120–121.
28 Michael Gordon and Bernard Trainor, *Cobra II: The Inside Story of the Invasion and
   Occupation of Iraq* (London: Atlantic, 2006), 13–14.
29 'Comments by Bush and Rumsfeld on Selection of the Secretary of Defense,'
   New York Times, 29 December 2000.
30 Gordon and Trainor, *Cobra II*, 125–126; James Risen, 'Spy Notes on Iraqi Aims
   Were Shelved, Suit Says,' *New York Times*, 1 August 2005.
31 Bob Woodward, *State of Denial* (New York: Simon and Schuster, 2006).
32 For Cambone's involvement in the Rumsfeld Commission, see the Executive
   Summary of the Report of the Commission to Assess the Ballistic Missile Threat
   to the United States, 15 July 1998, www.fas.org/irp/threat/bm-threat.htm. For
   Hoffman's position, see Bill Gertz and Rowan Scarborough, 'Inside the Ring,'
   Washington Times, 23 March 2001. On Rumsfeld's relationship with Holcomb,
   see 'Rumsfeld on High Wire of Defense Reform,' *Washington Post*, 20 May 2001.
   For a profile of Steve Herbits, see Chris Bull, 'The Quiet Crusader,' *The Advocate*,
   23 July 2002, http://findarticles.com/p/articles/mi_m1589/is_2002_July_23/
   ai_89871724/print.
33 Stefan Halper and Jonathan Clarke, *America Alone: The Neoconservatives and the
   Global Order* (Cambridge: Cambridge University Press, 2004), 116–117.
34 Halper and Clarke, *America Alone*, 119–120.
35 Robert Dreyfuss and Jason Vest, 'The Lie Factory,' *Mother Jones*, January/
   February 2004, www.motherjones.com/news/feature/2004/01/12_405.html.

36 Halper and Clarke, *America Alone*, 120–121.

37 *A Clean Break: A New Strategy for Securing the Realm*, Institute for Advanced Strategic and Political Studies, June 1996, www.iasps.org/strat1.htm. The Hashemite regime, which included King Hussein of Jordan, had ended in Iraq in 1958 with the revolution that toppled King Feisal.

38 James Bamford, *A Pretext for War: 9/11, Iraq and the Abuse of America's Intelligence Agencies* (New York: Doubleday, 2004), 293–294. Perle's emphasis on Iraq was shared by others. In January 1998, the Project for the New American Century issued a public letter to President Clinton calling for 'the removal of Saddam Hussein's regime from power.' There were 18 prominent signatories, including Perle, Elliott Abrams, John Bolton, Zalmay Khalilzad, Donald Rumsfeld and Paul Wolfowitz. See 'Letter to President Clinton on Iraq,' 26 January 1998, www.newamericancentury.org/iraqclintonletter.htm.

39 David Wurmser, 'Middle East "War": How Did It Comes to This?,' *AEI On the Issues*, 1 January 2001, www.aei.org/publications/pubID.12266/pub_detail.asp.

40 Cited in Halper and Clarke, *America Alone*, 148.

41 Bamford, *Pretext for War*, 265; Suskind, *The Price of Loyalty*, 72.

42 Suskind, *The Price of Loyalty*, 70–73.

43 See Bamford, *Pretext for War*, 268; Ivo Daalder and James Lindsay, *America Unbound* (Washington DC: Brookings Institution), 129; Ray McGovern, 'Why Plame Matters,' 18 July 2005, www.tompaine.com/articles/2005/07/18/why_plame_matters.php.

44 Suskind, *The Price of Loyalty*, 85.

45 David Rose *et al.*, 'The Path to War,' *Vanity Fair*, May 2004, 106.

46 In February 2001 Rumsfeld tried to avoid attendance at a meeting of NATO defence chiefs in Munich, claiming he needed to remain in Washington to oversee the Pentagon. He eventually went to Germany, only to give a speech holding forth on missile defence and belittling European military approaches (Gordon and Trainor, *Cobra II*, 6).

47 Daalder and Lindsay, *America Unbound*, 63. Bush, in his first State of the Union address in February 2001, stated, 'Our military was shaped to confront the challenges of the past. So I've asked the Secretary of Defense to review America's Armed Forces and prepare to transform them to meet emerging threats.' (George W. Bush, Address Before a Joint Session of Congress, 27 February 2001, www.presidency.ucsb.edu/ws/index.php?pid=29643).

48 On North Korea, see James Mann, *Rise of the Vulcans: A History of Bush's War Cabinet* (New York: Viking, 2004), 277–280; Daalder and Lindsay, *America Unbound*, 66–67, 74, and 176–177. On Kyoto, see Halper and Clarke, *America Alone*, 124 and Daalder and Lindsay, *America Unbound*, 65.

49 Halper and Clarke, *America Alone*, 148; Andrew Bacevich, *American Empire: The Realities and Consequences of American Diplomacy* (Cambridge: Harvard University Press, 2002), 207. Wolfowitz's statement appears to have been a tactical evasion rather than an expression of the truth, given his open support for the Iraqi National Council's plan of an invasion of exiles supported by US airpower. He endorsed this in a November 1997 article co-authored with Zalmay Khalilzad in *The Weekly Standard* and also in testimony to two Congressional hearings in 1998. In April 1999, Wolfowitz and Stephen Solarz wrote a letter to *Foreign Affairs* in which they again endorsed the INC plan but with the corollary that the use of US ground troops should not be ruled out. (Paul Wolfowitz and Zalmay Khalilzad, 'Overthrow Him!' *Weekly Standard*, 1 December 1997, 14–15; Wolfowitz prepared testimony to the House International Relations Committee, 25 February 1998, *Iraq Watch*, www.iraqwatch.org/government/US/HearingsPreparedstatements/ wolfowitz-hirc-2–25–98.htm; Wolfowitz testimony of 16 September

1998, reproduced by the Project for a New American Century, www.ncwameri-cancentury.org/iraqsep1898.htm; Stephen J. Solarz and Paul Wolfowitz, 'Letter to the Editor,' *Foreign Affairs*, March/April 1999, 160–161).

50 Quoted in John Prados, *Hoodwinked: The Documents that Reveal How Bush Sold Us a War* (New York: New Press, 2004), 4.

51 Nicholas Arons, 'US Supported Iraqi Opposition,' *Foreign Policy In Focus*, April 2001, www.fpif.org/briefs/vol6/v6n10iraq.html.

52 Eli J. Lake, 'US to Give Iraq Rebels Weapons, Security Training,' *United Press International*, 13 February 2001.

53 Arons, 'US Supported Iraqi Opposition.'

54 Bacevich, *American Empire*, 207–208; 'Is There a Strategy?,' *Inter Press Service*, 20 February 2001, www.highbeam.com/doc/1P1–42047216.html; Alan Sipress and Dan Balz, 'Bush Signals Escalation in Response to Hussein,' *Washington Post*, 17 February 2001; Woodward, *State of Denial*, 22.

55 Harold Meyerson, 'Intelligence Designed: How the Pentagon Mimicked Enron,' *The American Prospect*, 23 May 2004, www.prospect.org/cs/articles?article= intelligence_designed.

56 Michael Meacher, 'This War on Terrorism is Bogus,' *Guardian* (London), 6 September 2003.

57 Jane Mayer, 'Contract Sport: What Did the Vice-president Do for Halliburton?' *The New Yorker*, 16 February 2004, www.newyorker.com/archive/2004/02/16/040216fa_fact?printable=true.

58 Mark Levine, 'Waist Deep in Big Oil,' *The Nation* (New York), 12 December 2005, www.thenation.com/docprem.mhtml?i=20051212&s=levine. It is likely that Cheney would have been sympathetic to this argument because he had called for end to Iraqi sanctions in 1990s. 'We seem to be sanction-happy as a government,' Cheney said at an energy conference in April 1996, which was reported in the oil industry publication Petroleum Finance Week. 'The problem is that the good Lord didn't see fit to always put oil and gas resources where there are democratic governments.' The Clinton Administration blocked one of Halliburton's attempted deals with Iraq, although Cheney later claimed that he 'had a firm policy that we wouldn't do anything in Iraq, even arrange-ments that were supposedly legal.' (Jason Leopold, 'Cheney's Lies About Halliburton and Iraq,' *Counterpunch*, 19 March 2003, www.counterpunch.org/leopold03202003.html).

59 'Hapless Hussein Opposition Has U.S. Looking Elsewhere,' *Los Angeles Times*, 19 March 2001. In April 2001, the *Washington Post* reported, 'Otherwise unidentified State Department officials have followed up an energetic trashing of the existing sanctions regime in the press with a campaign of character assas-sination aimed at Saddam's opponents, who are largely guilty of being friends of the diplomats' enemies at the Pentagon.' (Jim Hoagland, 'Policy Wars Over Iraq,' *Washington Post*, 8 April 2001). See also James Risen, *State of War: The Secret History of the Bush Administration and the CIA* (New York: Free Press, 2006), 75.

60 Palast, *Armed Madhouse*, 52–54; Greg Palast, 'Secret US Plans for Iraq's Oil,' *BBC Newsnight*, 17 March 2005, http://news.bbc.co.uk/1/hi/programmes/newsnight/4354269.stm; 'Secret US Plans for Iraq's Oil Spark Political Fights Between Neocons and Big Oil,' *Democracy Now!*, 21 March 2005, www.democracynow.org/2005/3/21/u_s_broadcast_exclusive_secret_u.

61 'US Considers Iraqi Coup,' *NewsMax.Com Wires*, 28 April 2001, http://archive.newsmax.com/archives/articles/2001/4/27/211326.shtml; Lewis D. Solomon, *Paul Wolfowitz: Visionary Intellectual, Policymaker, Strategist* (Westport: Praeger Security International, 2007), 89.

62 'Iraqi Sanction Reform Stymied; US Urged to Seek "Regime Change,"' *Knight Ridder/Tribune News Service*, 4 July 2001.

63 Gordon and Trainor, *Cobra II*, 14–15.

64 Solomon, *Paul Wolfowitz*, 89.

65 According to James Mann, the National Security Advisor – anticipating conflict with Beijing – was seeking a showdown sooner rather than later and well in advance of the Chinese Communist Party's Congress in autumn 2002. (Mann, *Rise of the Vulcans*, 281).

66 David Sanger, 'Powell Sees No Need for Apology; Bush Again Urges Return of Crew,' *New York Times*, 4 April 2001.

67 Mann, *Rise of the Vulcans*, 281–285; Daalder and Lindsay, *America Unbound*, 67–70.

68 Halper and Clarke, *America Alone*, 130–131.

69 Solomon, *Paul Wolfowitz*, 71–73; Mann, *Rise of the Vulcans*, 298–299; Meacher, 'This War on Terrorism is Bogus'; Woodward, *Bush at War*, 35.

70 Bush controversially took a month-long vacation in August 2001, going home to his ranch in Texas. See Katharine Seelye, 'President Is on Vacation, Mostly Not Taking It Easy,' *New York Times*, 7 August 2001.

71 Cited in Nicholas Lemann, 'The Quiet Man,' *The New Yorker*, 7 May 2001, http://web.archive.org/web/20040918102730/www.newyorker.com/archive/content/?040906fr_archive06.

72 Robert Kagan and William Kristol, 'No Defense,' *Weekly Standard*, 23 July 2001, 13.

73 Reuel Marc Gerecht, 'Liberate Iraq,' *Weekly Standard*, 14 May 2001, 23.

74 Rumsfeld testimony to Senate Armed Services Committee, 21 June 2001, http://armed-services.senate.gov/statemnt/2001/010621rumsfeld.pdf.

75 Rice cited in Nicholas Lemann, 'The Next World Order,' *The New Yorker*, 1 April 2002, www.newyorker.com/archive/2002/04/01/020401fa_FACT1?currentPage=2; Woodward, *Bush at War*, 26–32.

76 Quadrennial Defense Review Report, 30 September 2001, www.comw.org/qdr/qdr2001.pdf.

77 Jeremy Scahill, 'A Very Private War,' *Guardian* (London), 1 August 2007.

78 'Plans for Iraq Attack Began on 9/11,' *CBS News*, 4 September 2002, www.cbsnews.com/stories/2002/09/04/september11/main520830.shtml. Rumsfeld also clashed with Powell over hitting Iraq first rather than al Qaeda. (Halper and Clarke, *America Alone*, 149).

79 Rose *et al.*, 'Path to War,' 108.

80 Andrew Buncombe and Kim Sengupta, 'Bush Backs Air Waves Assault on Saddam,' *The Independent* (London), 29 August 2001.

81 Richard Perle, 'How the CIA Failed America,' *Washington Post*, 11 May 2007; George Tenet, *At the Center of the Storm: My Years at the CIA* (New York: Harper Collins, 2007).

82 Solomon, *Paul Wolfowitz*, 80; Daalder and Lindsay, *America Unbound*, 105; James Fallows, 'Blind into Baghdad,' *The Atlantic*, January/February 2004, www.theatlantic.com/doc/200401/fallows; Gordon and Trainor, *Cobra II*, 15–17 and 19–20; Woodward, *Bush at War*, 97–99.

83 George Packer, *The Assassin's Gate: America In Iraq* (London: Faber and Faber, 2005), 41. Bush reiterated to the National Security Council on September 28 that Saddam 'was probably behind this in the end.' (Solomon, *Paul Wolfowitz*, 81).

84 Rose *et al.*, 'Path to War,' 110. On 17 September Bush signed a two-and-a-half page order that laid out his plan for the invasion of Afghanistan and also directed the Pentagon to begin planning military operations for an invasion of Iraq. As he told reporters in the White House Rose Garden, 'Afghanistan is

just the beginning.' (Bamford, *Pretext for War*, 287; Solomon, *Paul D. Wolfowitz*, 82–83).

85   Bamford, *Pretext for War*, 287; Rose *et al.*, 'Path to War,' 108.
86   Bamford, *Pretext for War*, 289–291.
87   Jane Mayer, 'The Manipulator,' *The New Yorker*, 7 June 2004, www.new yorker.com/archive/2004/06/07/040607fa_fact1.
88   Dreyfuss and Vest, 'The Lie Factory.'
89   Daniel Eisenberg, 'We're Taking Him Out,' *Time*, 13 May 2002.
90   Woodward, *State of Denial*, 81–82.
91   Gordon and Trainor, *Cobra* II, 40–43; Steve Richards and Rupert Cornwell, 'United They Stand. But Will Tony Follow George All the Way to Baghdad?' *The Independent* (London), 10 March 2002; Toby Harnden, 'Cheney Begins Mission to Win Arab Minds,' *Daily Telegraph*, 13 March 2002.
92   As David Manning, the chief foreign policy advisor to British Prime Minister Tony Blair, wrote after meetings with Rice, 'Bush has yet to find the answers to the big questions' such as 'how to persuade international opinion that military action against Iraq is necessary and justified' and 'what happens on the morning after?' Blair, after meeting Bush in Crawford, Texas, in April, promised British support for the war if 'efforts had been made to construct a coalition/shape public opinion, the Israel–Palestine Crisis was quiescent, and the options for action to eliminate Iraq's WMD through the UN weapons inspectors had been exhausted.' (Walter Pincus, 'Memo: US Lacked Full Post-War Iraq Plan,' *Washington Post*, 12 June 2005).
93   Vice President Speaks at VFW 103rd National Convention, 26 August 2002, www.whitehouse.gov/news/releases/2002/08/20020826.html. When Richard Haass asked Rice if it made sense to put Iraq at the centre of American planning in the midst of a global war on terror, she responded, in Haass' words, 'That decision's been made; don't waste your breath.' Foreign Secretary, Jack Straw, informed the British Cabinet, 'It seemed clear that Bush had made up his mind to take military action.' (Nicholas Lemann, 'How It Came to War,' *The New Yorker*, 25 March 2003, www.newyorker.com/archive/2003/03/31/030331fa_ fact; Pincus, 'From Memos, Insight Into Ally's Doubts on War,' *Washington Post*, 28 June 2005).
94   Bush–Gore Presidential Debate, 11 October 2000, www.debates.org/pages/trans2000b.html.
95   On Afghanistan, see Daalder and Lindsay, *America Unbound*, 112 and 115.
96   'President Bush Delivers Graduation Speech at West Point,' 1 June 2002, www.whitehouse.gov/news/releases/2002/06/20020601-3.html.
97   Bush State of the Union address, 2 February 2005, www.whitehouse.gov/news/releases/2005/02/20050202-11.html.
98   Rice remarks at the American University in Cairo (accessed 11 February 2008), www.state.gov/secretary/rm/2005/48328.htm.
99   Solomon, *Paul Wolfowitz*, 53.
100 Alan Weisman, *Prince of Darkness: Richard Perle – The Kingdom, The Power & The End of Empire in America* (New York: Union Square Press, 2007). Joseph Nye observed, 'There really isn't a coherent Bush ideology but three strands of opinion competing with each other. That's why the administration has been so divided.' On Iraq, 'first there was WMD – which appeals to traditional security people. Then the connection with 9/11 – which appeals to assertive nationalists. And finally democratising the Middle East – which appeals to the Wilsonians.' (Quoted in Mark Leonard, 'The Burning of Bush,' *Financial Times* [London], 25 June 2004).
101 William Kristol, 'What Wolfowitz Really Said,' *Weekly Standard*, 9 June 2003.

102 Richard Perle and David Frum, *An End to Evil: How to Win the War on Terror* (New York: Random House, 2003), 113–114 (italics added).

103 Packer, *Assassin's Gate*, 41.

104 William Kristol and Robert Kagan, 'Toward a Neo-Reaganite Foreign Policy,' July/August 1996, 22–23.

105 Project for the New American Century, *Rebuilding America's Defenses: Strategy, Forces and Resources for a New Century*, September 2000, 51, www.newamerican-century.org/RebuildingAmericasDefenses.pdf.

106 Bruce Berkowitz, 'Strategy for a Long Struggle,' *Policy Review*, February/March 2007, www.hoover.org/publications/policyreview/5516406.html.

107 Robert Kagan, 'End of Dreams, Return of History,' *Policy Review*, August & September 2007, www.hoover.org/publications/policyreview/8552512.html.

108 Joseph S. Nye, Jr., 'Soft Power: Propaganda Isn't the Way,' *International Herald Tribune* (Paris), 10 January 2003, www.iht.com/articles/2003/01/10/ednye_ ed3_.php; Joseph S. Nye, Jr., *Soft Power: The Means to Success in World Politics* (New York: Public Affairs, 2004).

109 John Gaddis and Paul Kennedy, 'Kill the Empire! (Or Not),' *New York Times*, 25 July 2004.

110 Francis Fukuyama, *America at the Crossroads* (New Haven: Yale University Press, 2006). An alternative version of this binary is an outcome of either freedom or oppression as in Michael Kelly's claim,

> The argument concerns whether the employment of this almost unfath-omable power will be largely for good, leading to the liberation of a tyran-nized people and the spread of freedom, or largely for bad, leading to imperialism and colonialism, with a consequent corruption of America's own values and freedoms. This question is real enough and more: probably the next hundred years hinges on the answer.
>
> (Michael Kelly, 'What Now?,' *The Atlantic*, May 2003)

111 Michael Ignatieff, 'The Burden,' *New York Times Magazine*, 5 January 2003. On the drift in mainstream liberal thinking towards a more militant foreign policy on humanitarian grounds, see Tony Smith, *A Pact with the Devil: Washington's Bid for World Supremacy and the Betrayal of the American Promise* (New York: Routledge, 2007).

9 George W. Bush, American exceptionalism and the Iraq War

Trevor B. McCrisken

'We have no ambition in Iraq, except to remove a threat and restore control of that country to its own people.'[1] With these words, on the evening of 19 March 2003, US President George W. Bush announced to the American people that war with Iraq had begun. Like so many presidents before him, Bush was couching military action against another state in terms consistent with a benign meta-narrative of US foreign policy. This meta-narrative holds that the United States does not go to war in order to pursue pure self-interest or to conquer or control foreign lands, but rather that it does so to advance higher principles and to bring greater freedom, democracy and modernity to the peoples of the world. This benign meta-narrative is rooted in the belief in American exceptionalism – a belief that the United States is unique among nations and that it has a particular destiny to improve the human condition. Bush's adherence to exceptionalist ideas about the role of the US in the world has had significant consequences for his foreign policy and particularly for the war in Iraq. This chapter explores Bush's exceptionalist thinking and its impact on his foreign policy agenda both before and after 11 September 2001. The main focus is on Bush's war in Iraq and how his exceptionalist beliefs not only helped shape the arguments for war but also how they contributed to his determination to see the war through even as it became increasingly complex and unpopular.

American exceptionalism and US foreign policy

The belief in American exceptionalism forms a core element of American national identity and is a major part of the foundational myth of the United States. It is a belief rooted in the earliest colonial times and has developed and gained strength in the decades and centuries since.[2] Exceptionalism is an idea that takes many forms and is open to wide and varied interpretation but its fundamental basis is shared broadly among Americans and accepted almost as common sense, forming the framework within which elite and popular thinking takes place about the role of the US in the world and its foreign policy.[3] The belief in American exceptionalism is reinforced by symbolism and ritual on a daily basis across the United States from the reciting of the Pledge of Allegiance in public schools to the singing of the 'Star Spangled Banner' at even minor sporting events. It has also had a significant presence in most presidential rhetoric, especially in relation to US foreign affairs.

The basic assumptions of the belief in American exceptionalism can be summarised as follows:

1   That the United States is a special nation chosen by Providence to play a special role in human history.
2   That the unique blend of values and principles on which US society and American national identity are built have universal appeal and application, are desired by the rest of the world, and should be adopted globally for the betterment of all human kind.
3   That although it is not without its faults, US society is at the forefront of human progress and provides an invaluable example or model for the rest of the world to follow. Mistakes will be made, but the US will always overcome them and revert to first principles in order to move ever forward toward making a more perfect union and a more perfect world.
4   That because US objectives globally are rooted in values and principles that have universal applicability, US foreign policy should not be regarded as anything other than benign.
5   That, ultimately, the United States is a 'force for good in the world'.

Although these assumptions, or variations on them, form the foundation of most if not all exceptionalist thinking, their meaning, significance and consequences have been interpreted in different ways by different Americans at different times in their history. This variety of interpretations can be aggregated into two main strands of exceptionalist thought: the exemplary strand and the missionary strand.[4] The exemplary strand was the first form of exceptionalism to have a major influence upon foreign policy decision making in the United States. This strand holds that because the United States is an exceptional nation it should provide an example to the rest of the world but that wherever possible it should remain aloof from the problems and conflicts besetting other states and focus on perfecting its own society rather than interfering with others. This strand dominated thinking during the early years of the republic and can be seen clearly in the calls for 'non-entanglement' in foreign affairs advocated by Presidents George Washington and Thomas Jefferson.[5] It is a sentiment that has seen expression across the American political spectrum, from the anti-imperialists at the end of the nineteenth century, to the 'isolationists' of the 1920s and 1930s, to the 'America First' advocates of the late twentieth century. Throughout US history, however, there has been tension between this exemplary strand and the missionary strand; a tension that has usually played out in debates over the appropriate direction for US foreign policy.[6]

Advocates of the missionary strand of American exceptionalism argue that being an example to the world is not enough, that the United States has a right and a duty to take an active role in world affairs in order to promote its agenda and objectives. While they tend to admit that this engagement promotes the self-interest of the United States, they also insist that US intentions are benign and designed to promote certain values and principles that will further human development and improve the lot of all humankind. As US power and influence globally became stronger across the nineteenth and particularly the twentieth century, the missionary strand began to dominate US foreign policy making, though again in differing forms that straddle the political spectrum: 'Manifest Destiny' and westward expansion in the nineteenth century; 'imperialism' at the turn of the twentieth century; 'Wilsonianism' before and during World War I; 'internationalism' during the interwar years and into World War II; and 'free world leadership' during the Cold War. While there may be disagreement over what exceptionalism amounts to and what its consequences for foreign policy making should be, a belief in the fundamentals of American exceptionalism has framed the discourse and debate over US foreign relations through most of its history.[7]

This belief in American exceptionalism has also faced significant challenges to its continued existence at various points in US history: the Civil War, the imperialism debate, World War I, the Great Depression, World War II, the Korean War, and the Vietnam War have all caused critics and analysts to signal the 'end of American exceptionalism'.[8] Yet the belief has been remarkably resilient and despite decay over time it has been prone to replicate, refresh and reassert itself. Rather than finally writing exceptionalism's obituary, for example, US presidents from Gerald Ford onward responded to the defeat in Vietnam and the attendant doubts over the power and morality of the US by reasserting the belief in American exceptionalism and calling for a return to the values and principles that lie at its core.[9]

George W. Bush and exceptionalism

While his father had problems with what he rather disparagingly referred to as 'the vision thing',[10] George W. Bush has had no such concerns. Even before he became president, Bush had expressed clearly his adherence to many of the core assumptions of American exceptionalism. At an early campaign speech in November 1999 at the Ronald Reagan Presidential Library, for example, then Governor Bush admitted that, in the defence of the nation, every president 'must be a clear-eyed realist', but he also made clear that 'realism must make a place for the human spirit'. He called for 'an American foreign policy that reflects American character' and contended that

> Some have tried to pose a choice between American ideals and American interests – between who we are and how we act. But the choice is false. America, by decision and destiny, promotes political freedom – and gains the most when democracy advances.

In keeping with the benign meta-narrative of US foreign relations, Bush insisted that 'America is a peaceful power' that has 'no territorial objectives' but gains 'the greatest dividend from democratic stability'.[11]

George W. Bush carried these beliefs about the US role in the world into his presidency. He set the tone in his First Inaugural Address on 20 January 2001, in which he expressed a clear affinity with the core ideals of American exceptionalism. Although he admitted that Americans were 'flawed and fallible', Bush nonetheless asserted that they were 'united across the generations by grand and enduring ideals'. The adherence to these ideals meant, according to Bush, that in foreign policy toward allies, rivals and enemies alike: 'we will speak for the values that gave our nation birth'. He reaffirmed the idea that the US is a chosen nation by stating that 'we are guided by a power larger than ourselves who creates us equal in His image'. He also made clear that he viewed US intentions toward the world as benign, echoing the words of many of his predecessors by stating categorically that the US is 'a power that went into the world to protect but not possess, to defend but not to conquer'.[12] Bush developed these exceptionalist themes further in his first address to a Joint Session of Congress on 27 February 2001. Reiterating his campaign message, he argued that the US under his leadership would pursue 'a distinctly American internationalism'. The US would, in conjunction with its allies, operate as 'a force for good and a champion of freedom' in the world promoting 'values' and 'peace'.[13] This perception of the US as being a force for good in the world would become a major theme of the Bush administration and a claim that the president would frequently repeat in the months and years to come. It is a claim firmly within the tradition of the benign meta-narrative of US foreign relations. Bush's adherence to exceptionalism is more than simply a rhetorical tool, however. As Stanley Renshon argues, Bush is a 'traditional patriot' who 'truly loves and admires his country'. His belief in American exceptionalism is deeply held and provides much of the framework for his thinking about the US and its role internationally. According to Renshon, Bush is 'unabashedly proud of the United States, clearly feels that its virtues easily outweigh its failures, respects its traditions and institutions, and takes seriously and personally his oath to protect and preserve'.[14]

The fullest expression of Bush's exceptionalist claims came in his Second Inaugural Address, four years into his presidency with the 'war on terror' far advanced and the conflict in Iraq stagnating. Bush attempted to draw together the pragmatic and ideological aspects of his foreign policy to set an agenda for the rest of his presidency. He argued that 'America's vital interests and our deepest beliefs are now one', suggesting that the only way to secure the United States and its interests and also the 'best hope for peace in our world' was 'the expansion of freedom in all the world'. He claimed, therefore: 'It is the policy of the United States to seek and support the growth of democratic movements and institutions in every nation and culture, with the ultimate goal of ending tyranny in our world.' Bush insisted that there was nothing belligerent about adopting such a policy: 'America will not impose our own style of government on the unwilling. Our goal instead is to help others find their own voice, attain their own freedom, and make their own way.'[15] The speech, and more generally Bush's assertive promotion of US democratic principles globally, met with a good deal of criticism, particularly outside the United States. A State Department assessment of foreign media coverage of the Second Inaugural found serious doubts abroad about the benign intentions of the US since the administration had spent its first term promoting democracy via a combination of 'intimidation' and 'the use of force'.[16]

Although much was made of the Bush administration's often aggressive promotion of democracy, there was nothing particularly novel about a US president advocating global democracy promotion or utilising force to achieve it. In fact, the emphasis on democracy and freedom drew upon a long tradition. For all the limitations on democracy within the United States itself, from its earliest days the US had promoted the idea that democracy and freedom were the cornerstones of its political culture. This emphasis on democracy and its promotion gained strength and impact as US global power increased. By the time of World War I, President Wilson could claim the US was entering the conflict to 'make the world safe for democracy'; Franklin D. Roosevelt sought to protect and promote the 'Four Freedoms' in World War II; at the dawning of the Cold War, President Truman's eponymous doctrine was predicated on the idea that the US would protect the rights of free, democratic peoples the world over; John F. Kennedy would famously 'pay any price, bear any burden, meet any hardship, support any friend, oppose any foe to assure the survival and success of liberty'; during his presidency, Ronald Reagan promised the US would 'again be the exemplar of freedom and a beacon of hope for those who do not now have freedom'; and George W. Bush's predecessor Bill Clinton, who like Bush gave much credence to 'democratic peace theory', believed his administration must give emphasis to enlarging the number of liberal democracies in the world and was not shy of threatening or using force to achieve those aims, as in Haiti and Kosovo. For all the talk of the radical departures taken by the Bush administration in foreign affairs, there is much in its tone and emphasis, particularly on the importance of spreading freedom and democracy, that demonstrates significant continuity with many of its predecessors and indeed that it is continuing the emphasis on the exceptional dedication to what are perceived as benign, universally applicable values.

Much of the democracy and freedom focused exceptionalist rhetoric adopted by Bush and his advisers is widely attributed to the influence of so-called neoconservatives both within and connected to his administration. Neoconservatives hold that US interests are best served by the aggressive promotion and spread of democracy throughout the globe. Both their ideas and their advocacy of active promotion place the views of neoconservatives firmly within the missionary strand of American exceptionalism. The US is regarded by neoconservatives very much as the pinnacle of human development and there is an unflinching acceptance of the idea that to spread the American way of life will not only be of benefit to the United States in terms of increasing the number of friendly states in the world but will also be of great benefit to the peoples in those countries that are democratised as they will be able to turn away from 'regressive' behaviours and fully embrace an American version of modernity. The dominance of their influence on the Bush administration, however, is often overstated. None of the principle foreign policy advisers to the president were true neoconservatives. For example, although at times their agendas did fit very neatly with neoconservative thinking, Secretary of Defense Donald Rumsfeld, National Security Adviser Condoleezza Rice, and Vice President Dick Cheney are better categorised as conservative nationalists rather than neoconservatives.[17] Indeed, for each of them the neoconservative focus on values, principles and nation-building did not sit well with their strong sense of pragmatism and their understanding of international power relations. It was at the second tier of foreign policy making that true neoconservatives held positions of influence – Deputy Secretary of Defense Paul Wolfowitz and Undersecretary of Defense for Policy Douglas Feith for example. This is not to say that the neoconservative influence did not exist but it is worth remembering that while important it was not wholly dominant and neoconservatives did not get everything their way. Significantly, it is clear that Bush's adherence to exceptionalist ideas runs much deeper than the influence of Wolfowitz, Feith and others. As Daalder and Lindsay argue, the belief that 'the United States is a unique great power and others see it as such' was one of the central tenets of what they call the 'hegemonist faith' that best describes the form of realist thinking that underpinned foreign policy making in the Bush administration.[18] American exceptionalism is not a neoconservative idea but has far deeper and older roots. For example, even Henry Kissinger, that thoroughbred realist, has admitted that 'Moral purpose was a key element of motivation behind every American policy and every war in the twentieth century.'[19]

In the initial months of his presidency, the most obvious consequence of Bush's emphasis on a 'distinctly American internationalism' was the apparent resurgence of what was widely criticised as unilateralism in world affairs. The administration saw American primacy as all important and identified key interests that required the US to pull back from some of the multilateral arrangements that President Clinton and several of his predecessors had expended energy on building up. The details are well known: the Bush administration withdrew US support from the Kyoto Agreement on climate change that had stalled in the Senate anyway, opposed the foundation of the International Criminal Court, rejected the Comprehensive Test Ban Treaty, and withdrew from the Anti-Ballistic Missile (ABM) Treaty in order to revitalise the Missile Defense programme. Placing US interests first, being reticent about if not hostile toward participation in international organisations, and listening to allies but only following their advice if it affirmed Bush's positions – these were the main characteristics of the first eight months of the Bush presidency. They reflected a more self-interested version of exceptionalist thinking about the US role in the world than had been adopted by the Clinton administration. In its first eight months, the Bush administration remained determinedly internationalist but very much on its own terms, essentially reasserting the idea of non-entanglement in international agreements which had been a core characteristic of US foreign policy following the republic's founding. Yet the United States was firmly entangled in global affairs at the beginning of the twenty-first century and no president could prevent the world from intruding on his foreign policy agenda. On a crisp September morning, events proved once more that much that happened in the world was outside the control of 'the exceptional nation'.

'9/11', exceptionalism and the 'war on terror'

The meaning given to the events of 11 September 2001 and the subsequent policy decisions were the result of a process of social construction rather than being some 'normal' or 'commonsense' response.[20] This 'framing' of '9/11' was rooted in assumptions about the exceptional nature of the United States. Indeed, on September 11 itself, President Bush argued that America's exceptionalism was the very reason it had been attacked by terrorists. In his Address to the Nation that evening he stated: 'America was targeted for the attack because we're the brightest beacon for freedom and opportunity in the world.'[21] Bush constructed the meaning of that day and the subsequent 'war on terror' in terms that drew on the deepest elements of American national identity to help the US public comprehend what had happened to them, how it would affect their place in the world, what the nature of the threat was that they faced, and how the nation should best respond. The terrorist attacks were perceived by the Bush administration as being an attempt to bring down the whole fabric of American society – international terrorism was portrayed as an existential threat to the United States that must be met with all the resources the US has at its disposal. As Secretary of State Colin Powell told the House International Relations Committee, the September 11 terrorists had launched 'an attack against who we are, our value systems, our belief in the dignity of the individual, our belief in democracy, our belief in the free enterprise system – that is what it is an attack against'.[22]

The language used particularly by Bush but also by other members of his administration, including Powell, as they constructed the central narrative elements of the 'war on terror' was steeped in exceptionalist claims. The president in particular made a number of highly simplified, black-and-white, Manichaean statements that clearly privileged the United States above all other states in terms of morality and legitimacy, and demanded that other states either sided with the US or they could be expected to be treated as enemies. The day after the attacks, following a National Security Council meeting, Bush told the White House press corps that these had been 'more than acts of terror. They were acts of war.' Bush characterised the conflict with terrorist groups as 'a monumental struggle of good versus evil' in which he confidently expected good to prevail.[23] In an Address to a Joint Session of Congress on 20 September 2001, Bush appealed to other nations to join the US in its fight to rid the world of terrorism. It was not, he assured them, 'just America's fight'. It was 'the fight of all who believe in progress and pluralism, tolerance and freedom' across the globe. The administration, therefore, was asking 'every nation to join us'. Bush, however, allowed no rhetorical space for doubt, ambivalence or prevarication on the part of other states in the ensuing battle with al Qaeda. He warned in stark Manichaean terms that: 'Either you are with us, or you are with the terrorists.'[24]

Bush's preference in the 'war on terror', its opening salvo in Afghanistan, and then the war in Iraq, was to work with coalition partners, provided they agreed with US objectives and were willing to accept US leadership. Those that would not, France being the most public example, were ostracised and portrayed as being out of step with the priorities of the free world. The break with past administrations in this emphasis on unilateralist decision making was again not as great as is often supposed. Exceptionalism, whether in its exemplary or missionary forms, presupposes the primacy of American views, priorities, interests and objectives above those of others. The emphasis on seeing the US as the world's leading nation makes it easy if not natural for presidents to set policy and expect others to follow. Some administrations may have been willing to take on advice from their foreign allies and even adjust policy to some extent, but the usual approach has been to decide upon US priorities and objectives then to build coalitions around that policy whenever possible. President Clinton is often remembered as a committed multilateralist, yet he frequently referred to the US as 'the world's only indispensable nation', emphasised that 'there is no substitute for American leadership', and intervened militarily only when, where and how it suited his administration's priorities rather than being drawn unwillingly into conflicts by the demands of allies or international organisations. The broad coalition building of George H.W. Bush is often contrasted with his son's apparent unilateralism, yet is clear that he too would have gone it alone to remove Iraq from Kuwait in 1991. Bush admits in his memoirs that he was always 'prepared to deal with this crisis unilaterally if necessary'. Bush's National Security Adviser, Brent Scowcroft, confirms the White House held no concern that a UN mandate was necessary for it to act to reverse the Iraqi invasion. Indeed, Scowcroft argues that the UN 'provided an added cloak of political cover. Never did we think that without its blessing we could not or would not intervene'.[25] George W. Bush similarly went the UN route to gather legitimacy for his preferred policy toward Iraq in 2002–2003, and did also garner support (even if it was mostly very limited) from a number of allies, not least Britain. There is little doubt that he would have acted entirely alone if necessary and that the degree to which the Iraq invasion was a legitimate, multilateral affair is highly contestable and has met with considerable opposition, even contempt, among the administration's critics and detractors. Nonetheless, Bush's approach was in keeping with that taken by predecessors on matters concerning the use of force and very much within the bounds of the missionary strand of American exceptionalism. As Daalder and Lindsay put it: 'If the townspeople did not want to ride out to meet the bad guys, Washington would happily take on the role of Gary Cooper in *High Noon* and face the bad guys alone.'[26]

Iraq, exceptionalism and the coming of war

The Bush administration constructed an argument for war with Iraq based mostly on what turned out to be spurious claims that Iraq was hiding weapons of mass destruction from UN inspectors, and dubious accusations that linked Saddam Hussein's regime to al Qaeda and the terrorist attacks of 11 September 2001. Bush's belief in American exceptionalism can go some way toward explaining why and how the administration continued to cling to these arguments even as the weapons failed to materialise and the terrorist linkages proved elusive. George W. Bush has placed Ronald Reagan in pole position on his list of political heroes and has often evoked Reagan's memory and his apparent achievements in speeches, press conferences and other public and private pronouncements. The degree to which this personal affinity has translated into similarities between the two presidencies has become a matter of much critical scrutiny.[27] There is at least one way in which the two presidents are alike, however, and that is their shared faith in the main tenets of American exceptionalism. Reagan was a true believer in the exceptional nature of the United States. Chief among the characteristics that disposed him towards exceptionalism were his profound optimism and self-confidence. George W. Bush is also a supremely confident individual and a man of 'strong convictions'.[28] As he told a press conference following the 2002 congressional elections: 'I don't take cues from anybody, I just do what I think is right.'[29] Despite widespread criticism that he gives too much influence to close advisers, Bush has been consistently forthright about knowing his own mind, acting on his convictions, and leaving little if no room for doubts. As he told the journalist Bob Woodward:

> a president has got to be the calcium in the backbone. If I weaken, the whole team weakens. If I'm doubtful, I can assure you there will be a lot of doubt. If my confidence level in our ability declines, it will send ripples throughout the whole organization. I mean, it's essential that we be confident and determined and united.... I don't need people around me who are not steady.... And if there's a hand-wringing attitude going on when times are tough, I don't like it.[30]

At the core of Ronald Reagan's convictions was the notion that the United States was the greatest nation on earth that was capable of overcoming any problem, no matter how big, if its people believed enough in themselves and their abilities. Reagan held an undying faith that being optimistic about things, as he was and he believed the American people always should be, would eventually enable any person or even a nation state to transcend any problem. Reagan believed in overcoming problems through motivation and was convinced that if something could be said repeatedly enough it would eventually come true. The resolution to each problem and issue the country faced was to Reagan what Garry Wills termed 'a truth waiting to happen' that could actually be willed into existence.[31] George W. Bush appears to share much of this same optimism and faith in 'truths waiting to happen'. Nowhere is this more apparent than in the arguments Bush and his advisers made to justify going to war with Iraq.

The first 'truth waiting to happen' regarding Iraq was that Saddam Hussein's regime had stockpiles of chemical and biological weapons together with an active programme to develop nuclear weapons, all of which it was successfully hiding from the UN inspection teams led by Hans Blix. There was at least some basis to such claims. Iraq had used chemical and biological weapons before, both in its war with Iran and against its own citizens. There was also sufficient evidence to suggest that Iraq was seeking a nuclear capability and developing further chemical and biological weapons for the UN Security Council to authorise inspections to take place and to insist that Baghdad cooperate fully or face grave consequences. Bush declared tirelessly, for well over a year before the US led invasion, that Iraq was developing weapons of mass destruction which it continued to 'hide from the civilized world' and that as a result it posed a 'a grave and growing danger' to the United States and the wider world.[32] Bush repeated time and again with the utmost confidence that

> The Iraqi regime possesses biological and chemical weapons. The Iraqi regime is building the facilities necessary to make more biological and chemical weapons.... The regime is seeking a nuclear bomb, and with fissile material, could build one within a year.[33]

The full weight of the administration's diplomatic, military and intelligence services, including a powerful submission to the UN by sceptical Secretary of State Colin Powell, was thrown behind the campaign to convince the US Congress, the American public, and indeed global opinion that Saddam Hussein's regime did have weapons of mass destruction and that it was seeking to develop ever more powerful weapons to threaten its neighbours and even states further afield. Bush's closest ally Britain played its part, the Blair government adding the claim that Iraq could launch a chemical or biological weapon within 45 minutes of the order being given. Saddam Hussein's regime itself did little to counter the claims being made in Washington and London, indeed its 'elaborate deceptions, denials and evasions' about its weapons programmes and the extent of its remaining arsenal simply added strength to the arguments of those insisting that the WMD threat from Iraq was both 'credible' and 'immediate'.[34] Yet when the invasion came and the rule of Saddam Hussein was brought to a swift and decisive end, the fiction of the Iraqi WMD programme was revealed as US and coalition forces failed to find any trace of significant stockpiles or weapons development programmes. On the eve of invasion, Bob Woodward had drafted a report for the *Washington Post* that he and his colleagues decided was too strong and contrary to the established wisdom to publish in which he cited various officials and sources who admitted 'confidentially that the intelligence on WMD was not as conclusive as the CIA and the administration had suggested', indeed that the evidence was 'pretty thin'.[35] The Bush administration had succeeded in pushing so hard the 'truth that was waiting to happen' about Iraqi weapons of mass destruction that much of the argument had become unassailable. This happened not least because the argument fit so well, at least within the United States, with the benign meta-narrative of US foreign policy. In accordance with this narrative, the US was going to war with Iraq to rid the world of an evil dictator and the threat that he posed not only to peace and stability in the region but also to the very existence of his many and varied enemies.

The second 'truth waiting to happen' about Iraq was that its regime was connected to al Qaeda and that, in fact, Saddam Hussein was directly responsible for the attacks on the World Trade Center and the Pentagon. Such a claim might be dismissed as just another internet fantasy about '9/11' were it not for the lengths taken by the Bush administration, in particular Dick Cheney, Paul Wolfowitz and the president himself, to build a case with which to convince the American public that the linkage was true. On 12 September 2001, Bush asked his National Coordinator for Security, Infrastructure and Counterterrorism, Richard Clarke, to 'See if Saddam did this. See if he's linked in any way.' Clarke admits he was 'taken aback, incredulous', since all the intelligence pointed to al Qaeda as being responsible and, as he reminded the president, 'we have looked several times for state sponsorship of al Qaeda and not found any real linkages to Iraq'.[36] The threat of terrorism had not been made an immediate priority by the Bush administration when it took office, in fact it was downgraded from the high level of concern it had been given by the Clinton White House. It was not discussed in a major committee meeting until April 2001, and then only at the Deputies Committee level, not among the principals from the NSC, State, Defense and the other key national security departments and agencies. Clarke's efforts at this meeting to emphasise the threat posed by al Qaeda were undercut by Wolfowitz's insistence that the real problem was state-sponsored terrorism, and specifically that sponsored by Iraq. Clarke and the deputies from the CIA and the FBI agreed that there was 'no evidence of any active Iraqi terrorist threat against the US', but Wolfowitz was having none of it. He insisted that al Qaeda could not perpetrate attacks like that on the World Trade Center in 1993 'without a state sponsor' and was convinced that Iraq was to blame: 'Just because FBI and CIA have failed to find the linkages does not mean they don't exist.'[37] The Iraq–al Qaeda link was simply a 'truth waiting to happen'.

Following the September 11 attacks there was a relatively heated discussion at Camp David concerning whether to strike Iraq first in the newly declared 'war on terror' but the measure was rejected, at least at that point, by all the principle advisers and Bush agreed that it should not be pursued. The only strong advocate in favour of striking Iraq first was Paul Wolfowitz who again claimed there was a link between Iraq and al Qaeda, in fact declaring that there was a '10 to 50 per cent chance Saddam was involved in the 9/11 attacks' even though there was no real evidence to support his view.[38] By January 2002, however, Bush had become convinced that there must be a link between al Qaeda and Iraq, a conclusion fuelled by the fear verging on paranoia in Washington generated by the anthrax attacks of October to December 2001 and the shred of evidence linking the leading hijacker of the '9/11' attacks, Mohammed Atta, to an Iraqi intelligence officer he had allegedly met in Prague that spring.[39] In his 2002 State of the Union Address, Bush declared starkly that 'Iraq continues to flaunt its hostility toward America and to support terror', implying none too subtly that like Iran and North Korea, Iraq was developing weapons of mass destruction in order to give them to 'terrorists'.[40] As the march toward war with Iraq gathered pace, Bush honed his argument and together with Cheney, Rumsfeld, Wolfowitz and others repeatedly claimed that the Iraqi regime was in league with al Qaeda and implied that Saddam Hussein was responsible for or at least connected to the '9/11' attacks. By September 2002, Bush was confidently telling congressional leaders that 'The [Iraqi] regime has long-standing and continuing ties to terrorist organizations. And there are al Qaeda terrorists inside Iraq.'[41] Richard Clarke and other intelligence officers continued to deny that any substantive connection existed, concluding in his memoirs that 'Any Iraqi "link" to al Qaeda is a minor footnote when compared to the links with other regimes', including most significantly the close US ally of Saudi Arabia, and that 'none of the possible "links" between Iraq and al Qaeda rise to the level of noteworthy assistance and support'.[42] The '9/11 Commission' also concluded in June 2004 that there had been no 'collaborative relationship' between Iraq and al Qaeda.[43] Yet despite all the evidence to the contrary, the *Washington Post* found in September 2003 that 69 per cent of Americans 'thought it at least likely that Hussein was involved in the attacks on the World Trade Center and the Pentagon'.[44] By consistently repeating the claim that al Qaeda and Iraq were linked and by implying that Saddam Hussein was an accomplice in the '9/11' attacks, the Bush administration had willed fiction into 'truth' for a sizeable majority of the US public. Soon after this poll was published, Bush finally went on record to say that 'We've had no evidence that Saddam Hussein was involved with the September 11th' but even then he continued to insist: 'There's no question that Saddam Hussein had al Qaeda ties.'[45] The irony is, of course, that the US occupation of Iraq has done exactly what Bush's critics feared would happen – it has created an al Qaeda–Iraq link as al Qaeda operatives now regard Iraq as the obvious place to take the 'war on terror' to the Americans by attacking its forces.

Bush's personal confidence, his exceptionalist beliefs, and his conviction that the attacks upon the US on '9/11' must be avenged combined with an assertive nationalism among his top advisers, the neoconservative priorities of their deputies, and the hubris generated by the apparently swift and decisive victory in Afghanistan to enable policy making that centred its targets on the decade long problem of Iraq. Much of the argument for war reflected supreme confidence in the righteousness of that cause, even if that meant accepting evidence that was little more than truths waiting to happen.

The Iraq War, Bush and exceptionalism

A major facet of exceptionalist thought in the US has been the view that all the people of the world want to be like Americans, a point affirmed by the constant influx of immigrants from across the globe. Although a distinctly American mix of values and principles – what Samuel Huntington referred to as the 'American Creed' – lies at the core of the belief in American exceptionalism, these values and principles are held to be universal in their appeal and application. Loren Baritz has shown how this kind of 'solipsistic thinking' about Vietnam and the Vietnamese led US policy makers to assume that their intervention in that country would be welcomed and supported. Solipsism means that 'someone believes that he is the world'. When combined with the characteristically high degree of self-belief and optimism inherent in exceptionalism, Baritz argues, this solipsistic thinking can create an 'enabling ignorance' about other peoples, their customs, beliefs and practices, that causes the US to intervene abroad without due attention to local circumstances and with an unshakeable belief that its actions will be understood and accepted, even desired, by the local population. Forty years ago, this combination of solipsism and optimism 'made the detailed particularities of Vietnam's otherness beside the point'. Similar conclusions can be reached concerning the Bush administration's approach to Iraq. Indeed, Baritz's argument still holds if Vietnam is replaced with Iraq:

> The myth of the city on a hill combined with solipsism in the assumptions about [Iraq] made by the American war planners. In other words, we assumed that we had a superior moral claim to be in [Iraq], and because, despite their quite queer way of doing things, the [Iraqis] shared our values, they would applaud our intentions and embrace our physical presence.[46]

As they contemplated war with Saddam Hussein's Iraq in 2002 and early 2003, Bush and his foreign policy advisers had been buoyed by the seemingly decisive and swift defeat of the Taliban in Afghanistan. Their solipsism convinced them that the US would be welcomed with opened arms by the Iraqi population who would be grateful that Saddam Hussein's regime was no more. Paul Wolfowitz, for example, was confident that: 'The

Iraqi people understand what this crisis is about. Like the people of France in the 1940s, they view us as their hoped-for liberator.'[47] General Tommy Franks, CENTCOM Commander and architect of the Iraq war plan, assumed the Iraqi people would turn against Saddam Hussein's regime if the US demonstrated sufficient resolve and commitment as it invaded. As Bob Woodward points out, however, this argument was 'based less on solid intelligence from inside Iraq than assumptions about how people *should* feel toward a ruthless dictator'.[48]

This combination of optimism and solipsism contributed to the slipshod planning for what the US should do with Iraq once Saddam Hussein's government had been removed, and even caused some clear advice about the potential difficulties to be ignored or downgraded as the war planning developed. George Tenet, the CIA Director, warned the president that Iraq would not be like Afghanistan, where the US had successfully utilised relationships with opposition groups and leaders in its campaign to overthrow the Taliban. The CIA's relationships with Kurdish and Shi'ite groups in Iraq were in tatters since the US had 'abandoned' them so many times. Tenet concluded that 'the people in Iraq were sceptical' about US intervention.[49] The State Department proposed plans for a new Iraqi civil administration that would focus on the crucial needs of electricity, water and communications but this was rejected by the Pentagon's Undersecretary for Policy, Douglas Feith.[50] The majority of the principle planning for the war was focused on defeating the Republican Guard and removing Saddam Hussein's government from power rather than being concerned with the aftermath. As Bush made clear in an NSC meeting nine days into the conflict, 'only one thing matters: winning. There's a lot of second-guessing regarding the post-Saddam world.... Don't worry about the carping and the second-guessing. Rise above it, be confident ... It's not a matter of timetable, it's a matter of victory.'[51]

Although Bush declared 'victory' in Iraq with his 1 May 2003 speech on the USS *Abraham Lincoln*, the violence continued. An insurgency of disparate groups grew and became more organised and effective in its attacks on US and other coalition forces as the complex divisions within Iraqi society became increasingly apparent the more that stabilisation and reconstruction efforts faltered. The solipsism that had accompanied planning prior to the war continued to impact on thinking about the insurgency and how best to deal with it. US policy makers in Washington and in Iraq itself seemed somewhat shocked by the strength of opposition to their occupation as the insurgency unfolded. Their perspective was so firmly set around the enabling ignorance that had coloured their view of how Iraqis would react to the invasion that it also hampered their ability to understand the complexity of the situation they had entered into. The White House gave great emphasis to the significance of 'foreign Islamist fighters' and members of al Qaeda who were allegedly stirring up or even orchestrating the insurgency.[52] As early as September 2003, Bush declared that Iraq was now 'the central front' in the war on terror that would 'take time and require sacrifice' to pacify. He vowed that 'we will do what is necessary, we will spend what is necessary, to achieve this essential victory in the war on terror'.[53] Yet there was substantial evidence to suggest that Bush and his advisers were misjudging the nature of the insurgency. Far from being an insurgency directed by outside forces, the number of 'foreigners' among the Iraqi insurgents was very small. US experts and Iraqi officials admitted in November 2005, for example, that at least 90 per cent of the insurgents were Iraqi and that this percentage could be as high as 96 per cent. Official sources also showed that only 3.8 per cent of the 13 300 detainees within Iraq by October 2005 were foreign.[54] Although the impact of foreign fighters and the ability of al Qaeda to recruit in Iraq have had serious consequences, it is nonetheless the case that, as Toby Dodge has concluded, they are not 'the main or most important forces sustaining the insurgency' which is very much 'a home-grown phenomenon'.[55] Just as his predecessors had misjudged and misunderstood the nature and strength of the enemy in Vietnam, so George W. Bush, aided by his unbridled faith in the righteousness of the American position, has misunderstood the potential for civil breakdown in Iraq leading to serious miscalculations of how best to deal with the post-Saddam situation.

Yet despite all the setbacks and problems in Iraq, the President's determination that the US will 'win' in Iraq has barely faltered with speech after speech reiterating how crucial to his foreign policy and the war on terror success in Iraq remains and how undeniable it is that the goal will be achieved: 'To retreat before victory would be an act of recklessness and dishonor, and I will not allow it.'[56] Even five years after the invasion began, with the death toll of US forces about to reach 4 000, Bush insisted that 'Removing Saddam Hussein from power was the right decision – and this is a fight America can and must win.'[57] The message from Bush is clear: We are Americans, therefore we are right, and therefore we will win.

Iraq, the war on terror and the end of exceptionalism (again)

When Daniel Bell and other critics in the 1970s argued that any remaining sense of American exceptionalism had come to an end as a result of the US experience in Vietnam, a major part of their argument focused upon the ways in which the war had been fought and the morality of the strategy, tactics and individual acts that had been carried out in the name of the United States. The same charges can be levelled against the Bush administration in its conduct of the 'war on terror' and the war in Iraq. The administration and its defendants have argued that the post-9/11 period is an exceptional time that calls for exceptional measures to be adopted in order to combat the existential threat posed by international terrorism and its supporters.[58] These 'exceptional measures' include the adoption of highly questionable interrogation techniques that opponents have condemned as torture; the forced removal or 'rendition' of individuals suspected of being terrorists or sympathising with their cause; the physical and mental abuse of prisoners at Guantanamo Bay in Cuba and at the Abu Ghraib prison in Iraq; and the high levels of civilian casualties in both Afghanistan and Iraq. Yet far from accepting the arguments of administration officials that the threats to the US are so great that the 'war on terror' must be prosecuted by any means necessary, critics have countered that in fact these 'exceptional measures' are undermining if not destroying any remaining sense of American exceptionalism. During the build-up to war, for example, House Republican Majority Leader Dick Armey objected to the potential invasion of Iraq on exceptionalist grounds arguing that the US could not 'make an unprovoked attack on another nation' because 'It would not be consistent with what we have been as a nation or what we should be as a nation.'[59] The *New York Times* ran an editorial in October 2007 in which it condemned the Bush administration for adopting positions on the use of torture that 'mock American values':

> Once upon a time, it was the United States that urged all nations to obey the letter and the spirit of international treaties and protect human rights and liberties. American leaders denounced secret prisons where people were held without charges, tortured and killed. And the people in much of the world, if not their governments, respected the United States for its values.

The Bush administration has dishonoured that history and squandered that respect.[60]

Bush and his advisers have remained adamant throughout the war on terror that they do not condone or allow torture to be carried out by the United States, insisting that 'America stands against and will not tolerate torture' because 'freedom from torture is an inalienable right'.[61] Following the revelations of abuse at Abu Ghraib prison, Bush claimed to 'view those practices as abhorrent'. He too invoked the belief in American exceptionalism to show how out of character such actions were for Americans: 'what took place in that prison does not represent America that I know. The America I know is a compassionate country that believes in freedom.'[62]

The long term commitment of US troops to suppress an insurgency following an invasion of questionable origin, the indefinite holding of prisoners without charge at what can be regarded effectively as a concentration camp, and the use of interrogation methods such as waterboarding to coerce captives, led one Harvard academic to conclude that such events 'sounded the close of the America exceptionally blessed among the nations'.[63] Yet the events to which this particular academic, Charles Eliot Norton, referred were not those associated with Iraq and the 'war on terror', but with the Spanish American War of 1898 and the suppression of the 'Philippine Insurrection' that followed it. The anti-imperialists declared the end of American exceptionalism over 100 years ago for many of the same reasons that critics of the Bush administration are making the argument today. Yet the belief in

American exceptionalism, as the last century has demonstrated, is incredibly resilient and there is every indication that it will again survive this latest challenge to its existence and continue to be a major influence upon US foreign policy making beyond Bush and beyond his legacy in Iraq.

Notes

1 George W. Bush, 'President Addresses the Nation', White House Office of the Press Secretary, Press Release, at www.whitehouse.gov/news/releases/2003/03/20030319-17.html, 19 March 2003.

2 See Jack P. Greene, *The Intellectual Construction of America: Exceptionalism and Identity from 1492 to 1800* (Chapel Hill, NC: University of North Carolina Press, 1993).

3 See Trevor B. McCrisken, *American Exceptionalism and the Legacy of Vietnam: US Foreign Policy Since 1974* (Basingstoke, UK/New York: Palgrave Macmillan, 2003); H.W. Brands, *What America Owes The World: The Struggle for the Soul of Foreign Policy* (Cambridge: Cambridge University Press, 1998).

4 McCrisken, *American Exceptionalism*, 8–14; H.W. Brands uses the terms 'exemplarist' and 'vindicationist' to describe these two main strands of exceptionalist belief, see Brands, *What America Owes*; similarly, Michael Hunt identifies two persistent 'visions' of what he calls American national greatness: 'the dominant vision equating the cause of liberty with the active pursuit of national greatness in world affairs and the dissenting one favoring a foreign policy of restraint as essential to perfecting liberty at home'. See Michael H. Hunt, *Ideology and US Foreign Policy* (New Haven, CT: Yale University Press, 1987), 43.

5 See George Washington, 'Farewell Address, United States, 17 September 1796', *A Compilation of the Messages and Papers of the Presidents, 1789–1902*, ed. James D. Richardson (Washington, DC: Bureau of National Literature and Art, 1907), vol. I, 222–223; Thomas Jefferson, 'First Inaugural Address at Washington, DC, 4 March 1801', *Inaugural Addresses of the Presidents of the United States from George Washington 1789 to George Bush 1989* (Washington, DC: United States Government Printing Office, 1989), 15.

6 McCrisken, *American Exceptionalism*, 11–17.

7 McCrisken, *American Exceptionalism*, 11–17; see also Trevor B. McCrisken, 'Exceptionalism' in Alexander DeConde, Richard Dean Burns, and Fredrik Logevall, eds, *Encyclopedia of American Foreign Policy*, Second Edition (New York: Charles Scribner's Sons, 2002), vol. 2, 63–80.

8 See, for example, Daniel Bell, 'The End of American Exceptionalism', *The Public Interest* (Fall 1975), reprinted in Daniel Bell, *The Winding Passage: Essays and Journeys 1960–1980* (New York: Basic Books, 1980).

9 McCrisken, *American Exceptionalism*, Chs. 3–7.

10 See, for example, David Mervin, *George Bush and the Guardianship Presidency* (Basingstoke: Macmillan, 1996) esp. 28–37, 210–214; also McCrisken, *American Exceptionalism*, 131–134.

11 Governor George W. Bush, 'A Distinctly American Internationalism', Ronald Reagan Presidential Library, Simi Valley, California, 19 November 1999, at www.mtholyoke.edu/acad/intrel/bush/wspeech.htm.

12 Bush, 'President George W. Bush's Inaugural Address', White House Office of the Press Secretary, Press Release, www.whitehouse.gov/news/inaugural-address.html, 20 January 2001.

13 Bush, 'Address of the President to the Joint Session of Congress', www.whitehouse.gov/news/releases/2001/02/20010228.html, 27 February 2001.

14 Stanley A. Renshon, *In His Father's Shadow: The Transformations of George W. Bush* (New York/Basingstoke, UK: Palgrave Macmillan, 2004), 141–142.

15 Bush, 'President Sworn-In to Second Term', www.whitehouse.gov/news/releases/2005/01/20050120–1.html, 20 January 2005.

16 US Department of State, 'Foreign Media Reaction to Bush Inauguration: Second Term Vision v. First Term Legacy', www.globalsecurity.org/military/library/news/2005/01/wwwh50121.htm, 21 January 2005.

17 Stefan Halper and Jonathan Clarke, *America Alone: The Neo-Conservatives and the Global Order* (Cambridge: Cambridge University Press, 2004), 14.

18 Ivo H. Daalder and James M. Lindsay, *America Unbound: The Bush Revolution in Foreign Policy* (Washington, DC: Brookings Institution Press, 2003), 40–47.

19 Quoted in Halper and Clarke, *America Alone*, 23.

20 Stuart Croft, *Culture, Crisis and America's War on Terror* (Cambridge: Cambridge University Press, 2006), 40.

21 Bush, 'Statement by the President in His Address to the Nation', www.whitehouse.gov/news/releases/2001/09/20010911–16.html, 11 September 2001.

22 Colin Powell, 'Campaign Against Terrorism, Secretary Colin L. Powell, House International Relations Committee, Washington, DC, US Department of State website, at www.state.gov/secretary/former/powell/remarks/2001/5572.htm, 24 October 2001.

23 Bush, 'Remarks by the President in Photo Opportunity with the National Security Team', www.whitehouse.gov/news/releases/2001/09/20010911–16.html, 12 September 2001.

24 Bush, 'Address to a Joint Session of Congress and the American People', www.whitehouse.gov/news/releases/2001/09/20010920–8.html, 20 September 2001.

25 George Bush and Brent Scowcroft, *A World Transformed* (New York: Alfred A. Knopf, 1998), 303–304, 313, 416.

26 Daalder and Lindsay, *America Unbound*, 44.

27 See Lou Cannon and Carl M. Cannon, *Reagan's Disciple: George W. Bush's Troubled Quest for a Presidential Legacy* (New York: Public Affairs, 2008).

28 Renshon, *In His Father's Shadow*, 84–96.

29 Bush, 'President Outlines Priorities', White House Office of the Press Secretary, Press Release, www.whitehouse.gov/news/releases/2002/11/20021107–2.html, 7 November 2002.

30 Quoted in Bob Woodward, *Bush at War* (New York: Simon & Schuster, 2002), 259.

31 Garry Wills, *Reagan's America* (New York: Penguin, 1988), 383–384; McCrisken, *American Exceptionalism*, 86–87.

32 Bush, 'The President's State of the Union Address', White House Office of the Press Secretary, Press Release, www.whitehouse.gov/news/releases/2002/01/20020129–11.html, 29 January 2002.

33 Bush, 'President Bush Discusses Iraq with Congressional Leaders', White House Office of the Press Secretary, Press Release, www.whitehouse.gov/news/releases/2002/09/20020926–7.html, 26 September 2002.

34 Michael Clarke, 'The Diplomacy that Led to War in Iraq', in Paul Cornish, ed., *The Conflict in Iraq, 2003* (Basingstoke: Palgrave Macmillan, 2004), 32.

35 Bob Woodward, *Plan of Attack* (New York: Simon & Schuster, 2004), 354–356.

36 Richard A. Clarke, *Against All Enemies: Inside America's War on Terror* (New York: Free Press, 2004), 32.

37 Clark, *Against All Enemies*, 231–232.

38 Woodward, *Plan of Attack*, 25–26.

39 David Frum, *The Right Man: An Inside Account of the Surprise Presidency of George W. Bush* (London: Weidenfeld & Nicolson, 2003), 176–181, 235–239.

40 Bush, 'State of the Union 2002'.

41 Bush, 'Congressional Leaders'.

42 Clarke, *Against All Enemies*, 270.

43 Walter Pincus and Dana Milbank, 'Al Qaeda–Hussein Link is Dismissed', *Washington Post*, 14 June 2004, A1, www.washingtonpost.com/wp-dyn/articles/A47812–2004Jun16.html.

44 Dana Milbank and Claudia Deane, 'Hussein Link to 9/11 Lingers in Many Minds', *Washington Post*, 6 September 2003, A1, www.washingtonpost.com/ac2/wp-dyn/A32862–2003Sep5.

45 Bush, 'Remarks by the President After Meeting with Members of the Congressional Conference Committee on Energy Legislation', White House Office of the Press Secretary, Press Release, 17 September 2003.

46 Loren Baritz, *Backfire: A History of How American Culture Led Us into Vietnam and Made Us Fight the Way We Did* (New York: Ballantine Books, 1985), 15–18.

47 Paul Wolfowitz, 'Remarks as Delivered to Veterans of Foreign Wars, Omni Shoreham Hotel, Washington, DC', United States Department of Defense, Press Release, www.dod.mil/speeches/2003/sp20030311-depsecdef0082.html, 11 March 2003.

48 Woodward, *Plan of Attack*, 81.

49 Ibid., 64.

50 Halper and Clarke, *America Alone*, 322.

51 Quoted in Woodward, *Plan of Attack*, 406–407.

52 See George W. Bush, 'President Outlines Strategy for Victory in Iraq, 30 November 2005', White House Press Release, www.whitehouse.gov/news/releases/2005/11/20051130–2.html; *National Strategy for Victory in Iraq*, Washington, DC: National Security Council, November 2005.

53 George W. Bush, 'President Addresses the Nation', White House Office of the Press Secretary, Press Release, www.whitehouse.gov/news/releases/2003/09/20030907–1.html, 7 September 2003.

54 Anthony H. Cordesman, *Iraq and Foreign Volunteers*, Washington, DC: Center for Strategic and International Studies, 2005, 2–3.

55 Toby Dodge, *Iraq's Future: The Aftermath of Regime Change*, Adelphi Paper 372 (Abingdon, UK/New York: Routledge, 2005), 12, 18–19.

56 Bush, 'President's Address to the Nation', White House Office of the Press Secretary, Press Release, www.whitehouse.gov/news/releases/2005/12/20051218–2.html, 18 December 2005.

57 Bush, 'President Bush Discusses Global War on Terror', White House Office of the Press Secretary, Press Release, www.whitehouse.gov/news/releases/2008/03/20080319–2.html, 19 March 2008.

58 Croft, *America's War on Terror*, 52–53.

59 Quoted in Daalder & Lindsay, *America Unbound*, 136–139.

60 'On Torture and American Values', *New York Times*, 7 October 2007, www.nytimes.com/2007/10/07sun1.html.

61 Seymour M. Hersh, *Chain of Command: The Road from 9/11 to Abu Ghraib* (London: Allen Lane, 2004), 367.

62 Bush, 'President Bush Meets with Alhurra Television on Wednesday', White House Office of the Press Secretary, Press Release, www.whitehouse.gov/news/releases/2004/05/20040505–5.html, 5 May 2004.

63 Quoted in Robert L. Beisner, *Twelve Against Empire: The Anti-Imperialists, 1898–1900* (Chicago: University of Chicago Press, 1985), 81.

10 The Middle East and the Persian Gulf as the gateway to imperial crisis
The Bush administration in Iraq

Cary Fraser

What we're seeing here, in a sense, is the growing – the birth pangs of a new Middle East and whatever we do we have to be certain that we're pushing forward to the new Middle East not going back to the old one.

Condoleezza Rice, July 21, 2006

The people of England have been led in Mesopotamia into a trap from which it will be hard to escape with dignity and honour. They have been tricked into it by a steady withholding of information. The Baghdad communiqués are belated, insincere, incomplete. Things have been far worse than we have been told, our administration more bloody and inefficient than the public knows. It is a disgrace to our imperial record, and may soon be too inflamed for any ordinary cure. We are to-day not far from a disaster.

A Report on Mesopotamia by T. E. Lawrence,
The Sunday Times, 22 August 1920

The search for a new Middle East posited by the American Secretary of State in 2006 was a central objective of the Bush administration from the inception of its term in 2001. Following the inauguration of the new President in January 2001, on February 6, 2001, elections in Israel resulted in the establishment of a new government headed by Ariel Sharon, the long-time champion of aggressive Israeli military posture in the region and of territorial expansion in the Occupied Territories adjoining Israel. One indication of the significance of the strategic shift that resulted from the restoration of Sharon was the Bush administration's decision to abandon the Clinton administration's efforts to forge a peace agreement between Israel and the Palestinian Authority that would result in the creation of a Palestinian homeland. According to the *New York Times*, 'The Bush administration formally abandoned the Middle East peace proposals of President Clinton today, saying they belonged to the former president and did not apply now that Ariel Sharon has been elected prime minister of Israel.'[1] In a subsequent editorial, the *New York Times* expressed the view that: '...it makes sense for Mr. Bush to step back from his predecessor's intense personal involvement in peace talks. But the new administration would do well to avoid any return to the petulant chilliness that sometimes characterized the administration of the elder George Bush, as when his secretary of state, James Baker, haughtily instructed Israel's leaders, "when you are ready for peace, call us," and read aloud the White House telephone number.'[2]

It was this emergence of a strategic axis between the Bush administration and the Sharon government that would shape the American search for a new Middle East in which an Anglo-American-Israeli entente, led by the Bush administration, would redefine the Middle East and the Persian Gulf. By abandoning its predecessor's approach to the Israeli-Palestinian conflict, the Bush administration signalled that it was committed to the marginalization of both the Arab states and Iran within the new dispensation that it sought to establish in the region. It was a strategy that may have been framed by the belief that the American military garrisons in Saudi Arabia, its aircraft carrier deployments in the region, increased intelligence coordination among the three nuclear partners, and the fact that both the United States and the United Kingdom were permanent members of the UN Security Council, would provide the basis for long-term American domination of the Middle East and the Persian Gulf – at the expense of other major powers, including China which had begun to establish a significant presence in the region. The Anglo-American control over much of Iraqi airspace which had been authorized by the UN Security Council in the wake of the 1991 Gulf War had led to the expansion of American force projection capabilities in the region, and that process may have whetted the Anglo-American-Israeli appetite for a new strategic dispensation that would allow the three powers to consolidate their military control over the region. Key to the Bush administration's strategy for the region was a focus on the containment and weakening of Iraq as a way to ensure that American strategic power would continue to shape the strategic environment of the Middle East and the Persian Gulf.[3]

The strategic vision pursued by the Bush administration was heavily influenced by the views articulated by The Project for the New American Century (PNAC), a non-profit, educational organization committed to the maintenance of America as the dominant global power. In a report, 'Rebuilding America's Defenses,' the organization acknowledged that:

we saw the project as building upon the defense strategy outlined by the Cheney Defense Department in the waning days of the Bush administration. The Defense Policy Guidance (DPG) drafted in the early months of 1992 provided a blueprint for maintaining U.S. preeminence, precluding the rise of a great power rival, and shaping the international security order in line with American principles and interests. Leaked before it had been formally approved, the document was criticized as an effort by 'cold warriors' to keep defense spending high and cuts in forces small despite the collapse of the Soviet Union; not surprisingly, it was subsequently buried by the new administration.

Although the experience of the past eight years has modified our understanding of particular military requirements for carrying out such a strategy, the basic tenets of the DPG, in our judgment, remain sound. And what Secretary Cheney said at the time in response to the DPG's critics remains true today: 'We can either sustain the [armed] forces we require and remain in a position to help shape things for the better, or we can throw that advantage away. [But] that would only hasten the day when we face greater threats, at higher costs and further risk to American lives.'[4]

Given Vice President's Cheney extraordinarily influential role in the George W. Bush administration, and his previous service as the Secretary of Defense in the George Herbert Walker Bush administration (1989–1993), it was evident that the new administration was committed to accomplishing the goals that had been identified in 1992. With one of his key allies and mentors, Donald Rumsfeld, returning to the post of Secretary of Defense in the new administration, Cheney was well-placed to pursue the 'restoration' of American military power as the key instrument in projecting American influence across the entire international system in line with his own thinking and that of The Project for the New American Century.

It was this emphasis on military power that led to the Bush administration's early embrace of Ariel Sharon's approach to the Middle East which emphasized discounting the Palestinian Question and focusing upon the 'rogue states with missiles [which] are the region's biggest geo-political challenge.'[5]

The administration's rush to embrace Sharon, given his long record of systematic and gratuitous violence against Palestinians, and his role during the 1982 Israeli invasion of Lebanon which led to the massacre of Palestinian refugees in the Sabra and Shatilla, boded ill for American policy in the Middle East under the new administration.[6]

The Bush administration had clearly embarked upon a strategy that signalled its willingness to dismiss both the Palestinian cause in the struggle against Israeli Occupation, and sentiment in the Arab and wider Islamic world which had seen the Clinton administration pursue a solution to the conflict. The Bush administration's *volte-face* was a slap at the hopes of the Arab states that America would continue to pursue a solution that would be acceptable to both Israelis and Palestinians. The new administration's shift also represented an abandonment of the traditional American effort to maintain some 'equidistance' between Israel and Arab states. The US had supported the creation of Israel under the Truman administration and had established itself after 1948 as a guarantor of Israel's survival in the region. However, given the importance of the Middle East as an energy supplier for Europe and Japan, and the role of American oil majors in the region, the US had also ensured that its support for Israel did not jeopardize its access or influence with the major oil producing Arab states. These considerations remained central to American policies from the 1950s until the Bush administration began to signal its new policy in 2001.

The new policy that promoted a strategic alliance between Israel and the United States, and increased military coordination with Britain in preventing the re-emergence of Iraq as a major player in the region, marked a return to the Western imperial endeavors that had emerged during World War I as Britain, France, and Czarist Russia sought to dismember the Ottoman Empire. The European search for strategies of control over the carcass of the Ottoman Empire had led to the expansion of Russian/Soviet influence in the successor states that emerged in the Southern and Eastern European areas of the Ottoman regions while Britain and France had concentrated their efforts to secure their influence in the Middle East among the Arab populations. It was the Balfour Declaration (1917) – promising a Jewish homeland in Palestine – issued by the British wartime government during the European efforts to divide the Ottoman Empire that would ultimately lay the seeds for the conflict that remains at the heart of the Arab–Israeli relations today.[7]

From World War I to the present, European efforts to exercise suzerainty in the Arab world has implied a commitment to Israel at the expense of Arab interests. The British-French-Israeli military attempt to seize control of the Suez Canal in 1956 crystallized that sentiment in the Arab world and it led to the unravelling of the British and French imperial projects in the Middle East and North Africa. The Eisenhower administration's decision to oppose the military intervention of its allies and Israel opened the way for an expanded American influence in the Middle East among Arab states at the expense of its European allies. The Soviet Union's backing of Egypt against France, Britain, and Israel also brought the Cold War into the region and accelerated the decline of British and French influence. Israel recognized the transformation of the region that ensued and began to assiduously court the United States in search of an American commitment to its long-term survival. For the United States, its new role required American efforts to mediate Israeli–Arab disputes, the challenge of Arab nationalism to the European presence in the region, and the challenge from the Soviet Union as it sought to use Arab nationalism and radical politics to secure its own influence in the region.[8]

If the strategic competition with the Soviet Union helped to keep the US focused upon maintaining a balanced relationship between Israel and America's Arab allies in the Middle East, the late 1970s transformed the region and the role of the United States therein. First, the Soviet intervention in Afghanistan led to the enunciation of the Carter Doctrine which indicated that the United States would deploy its military forces to ensure the security of energy resources in the region. As a consequence, the major Arab oil producers were provided with a military umbrella from the United States and there was an expectation of a greater American military role in maintaining the security environment.

Second, the overthrow of the Shah of Iran occasioned by the Iranian Revolution led to the American loss of a major pillar of influence in the region since Iran had served as a counterweight to the Arab states who posed a threat to both Israel and the United States. Iran under the Shah had been seen as a key ally of the US, and the emergence of a radical Islamist regime disrupted American visions of a secular Iranian regime that would continue the Shah's policy of accommodating American concerns. Further, as the level of hostility between the revolutionary regime and the United States escalated, it became clear that Iran was prepared to extend the range of its challenge to American influence across the entire region.

Third, the Camp David Accords that led to a negotiated peace between Egypt and Israel placed the American government under increased pressure to deliver a wider peace agreement between Israel and its Arab neighbors. Iran's support for the Palestinian Liberation Organization (PLO), and Syria – both of which expected that the land-for-peace principle established by the Camp David Accords – complicated the American problem since Iran had now emerged as a new source of pressure in the Arab–Israeli dispute. When the Israeli invasion of Lebanon of 1982, tacitly supported by the US, failed to destroy the PLO, it created an even larger problem – the rise of Hezbollah as a military and political force representative of the Shia community in Lebanon. With Iranian and Syrian support, Hezbollah emerged as a militant nationalist group that ultimately forced the departure of the Israelis from Lebanon. Iran's revolutionary regime had transformed the region by becoming a sponsor of a Shia resurgence in the Islamic world and its influence began to emerge in the intra-Arab disputes among Sunni and Shia Muslims. Iran also played an increasingly important role in the Israeli–Arab conflicts by lending support to Syria and for the Palestinian struggle against Israel.

Finally, the major Arab states, in collaboration with the United States, backed a war by Iraq against Iran in a search for ways to cripple the new revolutionary regime. The Iraqi war on Iran was an indication of the increasing dependence of the major Arab oil-producing states upon the United States to secure themselves from the strategic challenge posed by the Iranian Revolution. The rise of radical Islam had begun to reshape the Middle East and Persian Gulf, and the Arab states sensed their vulnerability in this new context. In effect, the American military had become the de facto security guarantor of these states as the Iran–Iraq war consumed resources and people for much of the decade of the 1980s – ending in military stalemate and military exhaustion for both sides.

The exhaustion of Iraq and Iran through the war ultimately strengthened American influence and opened the way for the United States to expand its military presence as a way of becoming the military arbiter of the Middle East and the Persian Gulf. The retreat of the Soviet Union from Afghanistan after its defeat by radical Islamic insurgents supported by Iran, the United States and Arab regimes in the Middle East, presaged a larger disengagement from the Middle East and the Persian Gulf. The collapse of the Cold War offered the US an unprecedented opportunity to become the dominant power in the region with all of the trappings of an 'informal empire.' This opportunity was consolidated when the US-led war to reverse the Iraqi invasion and attempted annexation of Kuwait ended in the defeat and destruction of much of Iraq's military capability. The Gulf War of 1991 destroyed Iraq as an independent military power and reinforced the role of the United States when it created huge military bases in Saudi Arabia that could be used to enforce a Pax Americana in the Persian Gulf. With Iraqi military power effectively crippled and the country under sanctions authorized by the United Nations, including ceding control over large sections of its airspace, and with Iran focused upon its post-war reconstruction, the US had secured a level of control over the region that the British had sought earlier in the twentieth century but which it had not been quite able to achieve.

In this context, the United States launched the effort to negotiate an end to the Israeli–Palestinian dispute by backing the creation of a Palestinian Authority run largely by the PLO. It was a strategy premised upon the belief that the United States could effectively use its leverage over Israel and the Arab states to push them to set the terms of a settlement that all parties would accept given the military ascendancy that the US had acquired over the region. The military, strategic, and economic weakness of Iraq, and the focus of Iran upon its post-war reconstruction, had created a context in which American ambitions to dominate the region could be systematically pursued. In effect, conditions seemed ripe for the creation of a Pax Americana in the region. This process was set in train by the Bush administration in the wake of the American-led victory against Iraq in 1991 and was adopted by its successor, the Clinton administration. The search for a negotiated peace between Israel and the Palestinian Authority continued up until the arrival of the George W. Bush administration and the elevation of Ariel Sharon to the office of Prime Minister of Israel in January 2001, at which point, the new Bush administration changed tack and moved to implement its new strategic alliance with Israel at the expense of the Palestinians, the other Arab states, and Iran.

It was an audacious reorientation of American foreign policy in the Middle East and was undoubtedly motivated by the strategic vision of the PNAC and its proponents within the ranks of the new administration. However, Richard Falk has suggested that this new approach to the Middle East was shaped by a larger global strategy embedded within the PANC document, namely:

(2) the shared conviction that Europe was no longer the main arena of geopolitics, but rather that the defining issues in world politics in the near future would involve a struggle for control over the Middle East and, secondarily, a decision as to how to manage the containment (or alternatively to provoke a confrontation) with China; . . .

(4) that sufficient military capabilities accompanied by an interventionary diplomacy and the correct strategic goals would alone make it possible for the United States to act forcibly and effectively to reshape

the political landscape of the Middle East, and maybe additionally, to confront China in a manner that intimidated Beijing, even at the risk of provoking a war with China, hoping to blunt any Chinese regional challenge before China became too strong to defeat at an acceptable cost.[9]

Falk's assessment speaks to a broader vision of the Bush administration's strategy for the reorientation in American foreign policy from 2001 onwards. However, it is also important to recognize that the question of China in the Middle East had agitated American policy in the decade prior to the arrival of the Bush administration. By the mid-1980s, China had emerged as a secret supplier of medium range missiles to Saudi Arabia, thus offering an alternative source of weaponry for the Saudi kingdom and lessening its dependency upon the United States.[10] Those missiles had the range to strike both Teheran and Tel Aviv, thus allowing the Saudis to maintain a credible threat to both Iran as a military and ideological threat, and Israel as a military threat. It was a remarkable statement that even as it grew increasingly dependent upon the growth of American influence in the region, the Saudis were quite prepared to seek room for maneuver in the complex game of mutual interdependence in its relationship with the US. Thus, China's emergence as an advanced weapons supplier to Saudi Arabia, and a potential supplier to others, had breached the American pretensions to an exclusive zone of influence in the region.[11] Worse from the American perspective was the discovery that the Chinese were installing 'a nationwide fiber optic communications network for Saddam's regime: the key nodes of this system were destroyed by U.S. airstrikes in January 2001.'[12] The ubiquitous presence of the Chinese in the development of the military capabilities of the Arab states and Iran had effectively compromised American regional influence.

In effect, by 2001 China had emerged as an alternative strategic partner for regional states. For the Bush administration, this development was a source of serious concern as it posed a threat to the American efforts to assert exclusive influence over the region. China had emerged as a strategic competitor for the United States at both the global level and in the Middle East. China had also begun to emerge as a major purchaser of energy resources and a source of investment which opened avenues for an even greater role in the region as an economic partner to the Arab states and Iran. In addition, Israeli arms sales to China promised to dilute American influence even further. The Bush administration's decision to pursue a new regional strategy was, in the final analysis, directed at stimulating 'the birth pangs of a new Middle East' in which America, with the support of its Israeli surrogate, would hold uncontested sway over the region and Chinese influence would be diminished. This image of American influence in the region, ironically, represented a return to the idea that the eastern provinces of the Ottoman Empire could be ruled from an imperial center. Implicitly and explicitly, the Middle East had become, in the eyes of the Bush administration, the place to revitalize the American *imperium* in both material and psychological terms.[13]

However, the regional states were not necessarily persuaded by the American shift in strategy. One of the early signs of the displeasure among Arab states was their rejection of American efforts to organize a new sanctions regime against Iraq and the organization of a pan-Arab 'Intifada Fund' administered from Saudi Arabia. Kuwait indicated that it would support the reintegration of Iraq into the trade among the states of the region and also provided a donation $150 million to the fund for the Palestinians. It was an indication of the shift in opinion among the Arab states that even Kuwait, which had been the victim of Iraqi aggression and occupation, and the most ardent advocate of sanctions against Iraq was willing to move toward the position adopted by other members of the Arab League in dealing with Iraq.[14] Other American allies, like France and Turkey, were also critical of the American effort to impose new sanctions.[15] The American effort to organize the sanctions regime was running into opposition that was fed by both the growing evidence of serious humanitarian consequences for ordinary Iraqis and a widespread willingness of Iraq's neighbors and other major powers to violate the sanctions regime. As a consequence, the Bush administration's abandonment of the Clinton administration's pro-active policy of helping to negotiate the terms of a durable Israeli–Palestinian peace accord, and the resumption of violence in the Occupied Territories in late 2000 and early 2001, had changed the political climate within the region.[16]

For the Bush administration, it was becoming evident that it was losing ground in the struggle to redefine the future of the region. The Bush administration was moving in a direction that had opened a serious rift with the Arab world and other players in the region. In effect, the Palestinian Question and the future of Iraq would become the terrain within which the issues of American influence and policies would be contested. The level of Arab disaffection with the Bush administration's shift in policy was apparently severe enough for the President's father and former President, George H.W. Bush, to place calls to Crown Prince Abdullah of Saudi Arabia in order to reassure the Saudis that his son would 'do the right thing.' The calls from the former President on his son's behalf were apparently in response to the Crown Prince's 'unusually blunt' criticism of the Bush administration's warm embrace of Ariel Sharon and its failure to be even-handed in handling of the Israeli–Palestinian issue. Abdullah's level of displeasure was also signalled in his evasive responses to the administration's invitations to visit the United States. The situation was further complicated when Brent Scowcroft, the National Security Advisor to the former President Bush, expressed the view that the new administration had 'let down its friends during the current Israeli–Palestinian conflict....'[17] The Saudi concerns about the Bush administration's strategy continued to be communicated to Washington even after the former President's calls to Crown Prince Abdullah. According to Eric Rouleau:

A month before September 11 [2001], the crown prince had already warned Bush about the rising danger, asking him to intervene in the

Middle East to bring about a 'balanced' settlement of the Israeli–Palestinian conflict. According to his close aides, however, Abdullah's early oral and written messages were treated with skepticism in Washington, leading the prince, in an unprecedented gesture, to refuse an invitation to visit the White House.[18]

The fraying of the Saudi–American relationship in the period prior to 11 September 2001 was symptomatic of the growing divergences between the Bush administration's desire to establish a dominant strategic position in the region and the increasing Saudi concern about the American tilt toward Israel.[19] As a consequence, the embrace of Ariel Sharon's government in Israel, and the abandonment of a pro-active stance on Israeli–Palestinian peace negotiations, had created a climate of hostility which was worsened by the destruction of New York's World Trade Center on 11 September 2001 by a group of 19 al Qaeda operatives, 15 of whom were of Saudi origin. With this attack, al Qaeda, as a challenger to American policy in the Arab world, had dealt a severe blow to the Saudi–American relationship and forced both countries to reappraise their relationship and their respective roles in the Middle East and the Persian Gulf.

For the United States, it was evident that its reliance on Saudi Arabia as a strategic partner in the region had helped to fuel the radicalization of anti-American sentiment across the Arab world. The earlier bombing of the Khobar Towers complex in Saudi Arabia in 1996 paled into insignificance with the destruction of the World Trade Center, but it had been an early signal of the growing problem that the American military presence in Saudi Arabia posed for the Saudi–American relationship.[20] In effect, the American military presence in Saudi Arabia had done little to provide an anchor for the American security umbrella in the region. Al Qaeda was thus responsible for forcing the United States to begin seeking an alternative site and strategic partner for housing American military forces.

For Saudi Arabia, al Qaeda's activities demonstrated that the kingdom's strategic alliance with the United States, and the American bases in the country, had helped to crystallize opposition to the expansion of American influence and its presence in Saudi Arabia. Al Qaeda's activity had also helped to expose the vulnerabilities of the Saudi royal family since the Saudi Kingdom's religious authority was based in large part on its 'guardianship' of Mecca and Medina, the two holiest sites of Islam. The presence of American bases in the kingdom raised the profoundly disturbing issue of whether the royal family had lost its own sense of legitimacy through its increasing dependence upon the American military.[21] In the wake of the destruction of the World Trade Center, Crown Prince Abdullah moved very quickly to put distance between the Saudi Kingdom and the United States by way of a peace initiative backed by the Arab League in March 2002 'promising full normalization of relations between Israel and the entire Arab world in exchange for the implementation of the UN's resolutions on Palestine. The pcace deal – extended directly 'to the government and the people of Israel' – was clearer and more precise than any that had been formulated since the creation of the Jewish state.'[22] By seizing the initiative in focusing international attention upon the need to resolve the Israeli–Palestinian conflict, Abdullah upstaged the Bush administration's strategy of deference to Israel and demonstrated its leadership of the Arab world in confronting the US agenda.[23] In the final analysis, the Saudi proposal had effectively crippled American efforts to establish terms of settlement for the Israeli–Palestinian dispute which would be to the advantage of Israel. The Saudi proposal also had the virtue of being directed at Israel, and it was a clear message that the Arab states were prepared to engage Israel directly without the United States as an intermediary.

The shift in the Saudi position on its relationship with the United States that began before the September 11, 2001 attack continued after the attack even as the two sides sought ways to ensure that neither side was rushed into adopting positions that could undermine the basis of their long-standing relationship: oil. In January 2002, the then White House Chief of Staff, Andrew Card admitted that the United States was seeking to reduce the American 'footprint' [military presence] in Saudi Arabia and 'I think it's been a long-term interest of both countries.'[24] In May 2003, Deputy Secretary of Defense, Paul Wolfowitz, confirmed the importance of American troops being removed from Saudi Arabia in an interview in *Vanity Fair*:

> There are a lot of things that are different now, and one that has gone by almost unnoticed – but it's huge – is that by complete mutual agreement between the U.S. and the Saudi government we can now remove almost all of our forces from Saudi Arabia. Their presence there over the last 12 years has been a source of enormous difficulty for a friendly government. It's been a huge recruiting device for al Qaeda. In fact if you look at bin Laden, one of his principle grievances was the presence of so-called crusader forces on the holy land, Mecca and Medina. I think just lifting that burden from the Saudis is itself going to open the door to other positive things.[25]

Thus, the al Qaeda attacks on the World Trade Center had served as a catalyst for the redefinition of the Saudi–American relationship with significant consequences for the entire Middle East. The emergence of a Saudi Kingdom increasingly willing to distance itself from the United States implied that the US would have to redefine its strategy for asserting its influence in the region.

The recognition of the growing distance between the United States and Saudi Arabia over Iraq, over the Israeli–Palestinian dispute, and over the presence of US troops in Saudi Arabia, seems to have led the Bush administration toward the decision to pursue the overthrow of Saddam Hussein. While considerable attention has been paid to the issues of weapons of mass destruction, the control over Iraqi oil reserves, the establishment of a democratic Iraq, overthrowing a dictator who had little support in the region and whose departure would be little mourned by many of his former foes – Iran, Kuwait, Israel – the importance of Iraq as a site for permanent military bases to maintain American influence and readiness to intervene has not received the attention that the issue deserves. It would appear that the Bush administration may have been seeking to replace the bases in Saudi Arabia with bases in Iraq. Given the Bush administration's commitment to the projection of its military power as part of the effort to dominate the international system, the importance of a permanent large-scale American military presence in Iraq should not be underestimated. According to Kenneth Pollack, the former Director for Persian Gulf Affairs in the National Security Council during the Clinton administration, the United States 'has an interest in maintaining military access to the Persian Gulf because of the region's geostrategically critical location, near the Middle East, Central Asia, eastern Africa, and South Asia.'[26] Like their British imperial predecessors who had used its Suez base as its platform for the projection of power into Asia, the region has assumed a similar importance in American global strategy.

Again, like the British in the 1950s, the Bush administration has been attempting to hold on to military bases in the region at a time that the region's political climate is marked by a deep hostility to Western imperial projects. Thus, imperial hubris has again reared its head in the relationship among the Western powers and the states of the Middle East and the Persian Gulf. A very blunt assessment of this American hubris was given by the former President Jimmy Carter in 2006. In a live interview with Larry King on CNN, Carter expressed the view that:

> There are people in Washington now, some of our top leaders, who never intend to withdraw military forces from Iraq ... because that was the reason we went into Iraq was to establish a permanent military base in the Gulf region and I have never heard any of our leaders say that they would commit themselves to the Iraqi people that ten years from now there will be no military bases of the United States in Iraq.
>
> I would like to hear that. But that's one of the things that concerns Iraqi people. And when I meet with Arab leaders around the world they all have noticed this. They're the ones that have brought it to my attention and I think it's an accurate statement.[27]

Carter's observation captures the ambiguities that surrounded the purposes of the American invasion of Iraq. Earlier speculation about his issue in the popular press had emerged as journalists began to examine American military operation in the aftermath of the American invasion of Iraq. As early as April 20, 2003 the *New York Times* was reporting that the Bush administration is planning a long-term military relationship with the emerging government of Iraq, one that would grant the Pentagon access to military bases and project American influence into the heart of the unsettled region, senior Bush administration officials say.... Whether that can be arranged depends on relations between Washington and whoever takes control in Baghdad. If the ties are close enough, the military relationship could become one of the most striking developments in a strategic revolution now playing out across the Middle East and Southwest Asia, from the Mediterranean to the Indian Ocean. A military foothold in Iraq would be felt across the border in Syria, and, in combination with the continuing United States presence in Afghanistan, it would virtually surround Iran with a new web of American influence.[28]

On March 23, 2004, the *Chicago Tribune* published an article in which it quoted senior American military officers in Iraq:

'Is this a swap for the Saudi bases?' asked Army Brig. Gen. Robert Pollman, chief engineer for base construction in Iraq. 'I don't know.... When we talk about enduring bases here, we're talking about the present operation, not in terms of America's global strategic base. But this makes sense. It makes a lot of logical sense.'

Bri. Gen. Mark Kimmitt, deputy chief of operations for the coalition in Iraq, said the military engineers are trying to prepare for any eventuality. 'This is a blueprint for how we could operate in the Middle East,' Kimmitt said. '[But] the engineering vision is well ahead of the policy vision. What the engineers are saying now is: Let's not be behind the policy decision. Let's make this place ready so we can address policy options.'[29]

Later in 2004, the *Christian Science Monitor* returned to this issue. It reported that:

So far, the Bush administration has not publicly indicated that it will seek permanent bases in Iraq to replace those recently given up in Saudi Arabia, a possibility mentioned by Deputy Defense Secretary Paul Wolfowitz before US forces moved into Iraq. The US already has bases in Kuwait and Qatar. At an April 2003 press conference, Defense Secretary Donald Rumsfeld said any suggestion that the US is planning a permanent military presence in Iraq is 'inaccurate and unfortunate.' With the presidential election weeks away, he is unlikely to alter that pronouncement on such a politically touchy matter. Such a move would almost certainly attract fire from Democratic candidate John Kerry. Nonetheless, several military experts in Washington assume that Iraq's new government will need the support of American troops – and thus 'permanent' bases – for years, perhaps decades to come.[30]

The American effort to use the invasion of Iraq to consolidate a long-term military presence in the Middle East and Persian Gulf in order to dominate the region, even at the expense of alienating its close ally, Saudi Arabia, over the Israeli–Palestinian dispute, was a sign of the growing gulf between the US and the regional states. In many ways, the Bush administration's occupation of Iraq followed the precedent set by Israel's occupation of the Palestinian territories and, like Israel's occupation, American actions in Iraq have created a crisis of credibility and a crisis of legitimacy for the United States in the region. In early 2007, King Abdullah of Saudi Arabia, at a summit meeting of Arab leaders, spoke of the American occupation of Iraq as an 'illegitimate foreign occupation.' The blunt assessment from the Saudi King came at the same time that former Secretary of State Henry Kissinger observed in a speech in Tokyo that: 'A military victory in the sense of total control over the whole territory, imposed on the entire population, is not possible' in Iraq.[31]

These statements by the Saudi monarch and Kissinger pointed to the growing sense of failure that informed assessments of the Bush administration's efforts to consolidate its influence over the Middle East and Persian Gulf. However, the assessments were also informed by the failure of the Israeli invasion of Lebanon in 2006 in response to the kidnapping of Israeli soldiers by Hezbollah militants. The Israelis unleashed an extraordinary aerial bombardment of Beirut and the civilian infrastructure of the country, and then sent Israeli forces into ground combat against Hezbollah units in Southern Lebanon. Hezbollah's ability to counter the Israeli ground forces using anti-tank weapons, and its use of a sustained barrage of mobile short range rockets against Northern Israel, eventually led to the intervention of the United Nations Security Council to pass a resolution leading to an end to the military conflict.

The Israeli military which had hitherto been seen as unchallengeable in conventional war in the region, given American support, found itself out-maneuvered on the ground in Southern Lebanon, and frustrated by Hezbollah's use of short-range rockets to provoke the flight of the Israeli population of Northern Israel into safer areas in the south of the country. For the Israeli military to be humbled by an Arab military force was a major shift in the strategic environment of the region. It was clear that Israeli armoured units could be halted on the ground in Lebanon, and that Israel was vulnerable to missile attacks. For the states with larger conventional forces, it was clear that Hezbollah had exposed the vulnerabilities of Israeli conventional forces and those lessons were not lost on other states in the region. Just as important, the limits of Israeli military strategy in the region replicated the failures of American military strategy in Iraq in the face of the growing insurgency that had crippled the American effort to impose its control over the entire country. The disproportionate military advantages enjoyed by both Israel and the United States in their respective excursions into war against irregular forces in Lebanon and Iraq had failed to change the political reality on the ground; neither Lebanon nor Iraq had ceased to be a threat to American and Israeli strategy in the region.[32]

It was against the background of the Israeli failure in Lebanon and the intractability of the Iraqi insurgency that a bipartisan critique of the Bush administration emerged. The Iraq Study Group, co-chaired by the Former Republican Secretary of State, James Baker, and the former Democratic Congressman, Lee Hamilton, issued a report in December 2006 that called for a reorientation of American policy toward the Middle East and Persian Gulf and the removal of American forces from Iraq. The report indicated that:

> Our most important recommendations call for new and enhanced diplomatic and political efforts in Iraq and the region, and a change in the primary mission of U.S. forces in Iraq that will enable the United States to begin to move its combat forces out of Iraq responsibly. We believe that these two recommendations are equally important and reinforce one another.
>
> [and]
>
> The United States cannot achieve its goals in the Middle East unless it deals directly with the Arab-Israeli conflict and regional instability. There must be a renewed and sustained commitment to by the United States to a comprehensive Arab-Israeli peace on all fronts: Lebanon, Syria, and President Bush's June 2002 commitment to a two-state solution for Israel and Palestine.[33]

In effect, the recommendations were a clear statement – from the American political establishment across the two major parties, Democrat and Republican – that the Bush administration had erred. It was a repudiation of the Bush administration's strategy for an Anglo-American-Israeli military condominium that would dominate the region.[34]

This bipartisan repudiation of the Bush administration's strategy in the Middle East marked the growing realization that the insurgency in Iraq had become a quagmire for the American military. More important, it was an unambiguous call for the Bush administration to rethink its focus upon military force as the default strategy for dealing with the region. The report's emphasis upon the need for an active American diplomacy to bring Iraq's neighbors into the search for a strategy to reconstitute a sovereign Iraqi state formed part of the emphasis upon American military disengagement from Iraq. This emphasis upon diplomacy was designed to refocus the Bush administration's energies toward working in a multilateral framework with both regional states, and other interested parties including the United Nations Security Council, in creating a new regional framework within which a reconstituted Iraqi state could be integrated.

The Iraq Study Group Report signalled that the Bush administration's strategy of using Iraq to establish its military dominance within the region, in partnership with the United Kingdom and Israel, had failed. More important, like the Suez Crisis of 1956, the American invasion of Iraq failed to stem the tide of anti-Western sentiment in the region and has accelerated the search by regional states and external powers including Russia, India, China, France, and Germany for a new security framework for the region. The American imperial project has foundered upon the resurgence of both nationalism and Islam in the Middle East and the Persian Gulf. In a fitting footnote to this misadventure, on December 12, 2007, Al-Jazeera reported that Iraq's National Security Advisor, Mowaffaq al-Rubaie, had indicated that the US would not be allowed to establish permanent military bases in the country since it 'cannot be accepted by any nationalist Iraqi.'[35]

The American experience in Iraq has also served as a reminder of Hannah Arendt's acute observation:

> The amount of violence at the disposal of a given country may no longer be a reliable indication of that country's strength or a reliable guarantee against destruction by a substantially smaller and weaker power. This again bears an ominous similarity to one of the oldest insights of political science, namely that power cannot be measured by wealth, that an abundance of wealth may erode power, that riches are particularly dangerous for the power and well-being of republics.[36]

The Middle East has once again proven to be a graveyard for Western imperial projects, as it did in the twentieth century.

Notes

1 Jane Perlez, 'Bush Officials Pronounce Clinton Mideast Plan Dead,' *New York Times*, February 9, 2001.
2 Editorial, *New York Times*, February 10, 2001.
3 Anthony Cordesman, 'No Choice But to Strike,' *New York Times*, February 17, 2001.
4 'Rebuilding America's Defenses: Strategy, Forces and Resources For a New Century,' A Report of The Project for the New American Century, September 2000, ii. www.newamericancentury.org.
5 William A. Orme, Jr., 'Disillusionment With a Friend,' *New York Times*, March 25, 2001.
6 For an account of the Israeli invasion of Lebanon, see Ze'ev Schiff and Ehud Ya'ari, *Israel's Lebanon War* (London: Unwin Paperbacks, 1984).
7 For an excellent overview of Western efforts to dominate the Middle East as the Ottoman Empire foundered, see D. K. Fieldhouse, *Western Imperialism in the Middle East* (New York: Oxford University Press, 2006).
8 For accounts of the Suez Crisis, see Peter L. Hahn, *The United States, Great Britain, and Egypt, 1945–1956* (Chapel Hill, NC: UNC Press, 1991); Keith Kyle, *Suez* (New York: St. Martin's Press, 1991); and Diane B. Kunz, *The Economic Diplomacy of the Suez Crisis* (Chapel Hill, NC: UNC Press, 1991).
9 Richard A. Falk, *The Costs of War: International Law, the UN, and World Order After Iraq* (New York: Routledge, 2008), 54.
10 Elaine Sciolino, 'Chinese Missiles Sold in Mideast Worrying Shultz,' *New York Times*, July 16, 1988.
11 After 2001, the US concerns about Chinese influence in the region were complicated by the tensions that arose over Israeli arms sales to China, leading to

American pressure on Israel over the issue. See 'US "Anger" at Israel Weapons Sale,' British Broadcasting Corporation News, December 16, 2004. The Clinton administration had earlier expressed similar concerns about Israeli arms exports to China and China's sale of weapons to both Iran and Saudi Arabia. See Steven Lee Myers, 'U.S. seeks to Curb Israeli Arms Sale to China Air Force,' *New York Times*, 11 November 1999.

12 Kenneth M. Pollack, 'Next Stop Baghdad?' *Foreign Affairs*, vol. 81, no. 2, 2002.
13 George W. Bush, in a speech to the American Enterprise Institute on February 26, 2003, invoked the American responsibility to the 'civilized world' as the final arrangements for the invasion of Iraq were being implemented. According to Bush: 'In Iraq, a dictator is building and hiding weapons that could enable him to dominate the Middle East and intimidate the civilized world – and we will not allow it.' The full text of Bush's speech was published in the *Guardian* (London), February 27, 2003. This invocation of American military intervention in defense of civilization was central to President Theodore Roosevelt's Corollary to the Monroe Doctrine which justified American military intervention and occupation of Caribbean countries at the beginning of the twentieth century.
14 Orme, 'Disillusionment With a Friend.'
15 John F. Burns, '10 Years Later, Hussein is Firmly in Control,' *New York Times*, February 26, 2001.
16 John F. Burns, 'Why Saddam Hussein is Back Onstage,' *New York Times*, March 4, 2001.
17 Jane Perlez, 'Bush Senior, on His Son's Behalf, Reassures Saudi Leader,' *New York Times*, July 15, 2001.
18 Eric Rouleau, 'Trouble in the Kingdom,' *Foreign Affairs*, vol. 81 no. 4, 2002.
19 The *Washington Post* reported that George W. Bush's response to a question about the Israeli–Palestinian conflict at a press conference on August 24, 2001 triggered an adverse reaction from the Saudi Crown Prince Abdullah. Abdullah reportedly telephoned the Saudi Ambassador, Prince Bandar bin Sultan, and instructed him to deliver a message to the Bush administration. The message was delivered to both Secretary of State Colin Powell, and National Security Advisor Condoleezza Rice. According to the *Washington Post*, a summary from a Senior Saudi official indicated that the message was: 'We believe there has been a strategic decision by the United States that its national interest in the Middle East is 100 percent based on [Israeli Prime Minister Ariel] Sharon.' This was America's right, the message continued, but Saudi Arabia could not accept the decision.... 'From now on, we will protect our national interests, regardless of where America's interests lie in the region.' Bandar was instructed to cut off further discussion between the two countries. The time had come to 'get busy rearranging our lives in the Middle East.' Robert G. Kaiser and David B. Ottaway, 'Saudi Leader's Anger Revealed Shaky Ties,' *Washington Post*, February 10, 2002.
20 Philip Shenon, '23 U.S. Troops Die in Truck Bombing in Saudi Base,' *New York Times*, June 26, 1996.
21 Rouleau, 'Trouble in the Kingdom.'
22 Rouleau, 'Trouble in the Kingdom.'
23 Saudi Arabia's views about the importance of settling the Israeli–Palestinian conflict was shared by other Arab Gulf States. See Eric Rouleau, 'Gulf States: Ambivalent Allies,' *Le Monde Diplomatique* (Paris), December 2001.
24 CNN Wolf Blitzer Reports, Interview with Saudi Prince Turki al Faisal, Aired February 1, 2002 – 19:00 ET.
25 Deputy Secretary Wolfowitz Interview with Sam Tannenhaus, Vanity Fair, May 9, 2003, www.defenselink.mil/transcripts/transcript.aspx?transcriptid=2594.

26 Kenneth Pollack, 'Securing the Gulf,' *Foreign Affairs*, vol. 82 no. 3, 2003.

27 CNN.com – Transcripts, CNN Larry King Live, Interview with Jimmy Carter, Aired February 1, 2006 – 21:00 ET.

28 Thom Shanker and Eric Schmitt, 'A Nation At War: Strategic Shift; Pentagon Expects Long-Term Access to Key Iraq Bases,' *New York Times*, April 20, 2003.

29 Christine Spolar, '14 "Enduring Bases" Set in Iraq: Long-term Military Presence Planned,' *Chicago Tribune*, March 23, 2004.

30 David R. Francis, 'US bases in Iraq: Sticky Politics, Hard Math,' *Christian Science Monitor*, September 30, 2004.

31 Hans Greimel, 'Iraq Military Victory No Longer Possible, says Henry Kissinger,' Associated Press, April 1, 2007.

32 For assessments of the war, see Alastair Crooke and Mark Perry, 'How Hezbollah Defeated Israel,' *Asia Times Online*, October 12–14, 2006; Congressional Research Service Report for Congress (online), Lebanon: The Israel-Hezbollah Conflict, August 14, 2006; Gary C. Gambill, Implications of the Israel-Hezbollah War, Mideast Monitor vol. 1 no. 3, 2006, www.mideastmonitor.org/issues/0609/0609_2.htm; Center for Strategic and International Studies, Press Briefing, 'A Visit to the Israel-Lebanon Front: Lessons of the War and Prospects for Peace and Future Fighting,' Anthony H. Cordesman, August 17, 2006, Transcript by Federal News Service, Washington, DC.

33 James A. Baker III, and Lee H. Hamilton (co-Chairs), *The Iraq Study Group Report* (New York: Vintage Books, 2006), xiii–xv.

34 The fact that the report was co-authored by none other than James Baker who was the architect of the strategy that had brought George W. Bush to office in the wake of the disputed 2000 Presidential election, and who had served as the former Secretary of State in the administration of George H.W. Bush, the father of the current President. Doubly humiliating was the fact that Sandra Day O'Connor, one of the five Supreme Court Justices who was a signatory to the Court's decision in the case that decided the election of 2000 in favor of George W. Bush, was also a member of the Iraq Study Group. See Cary Fraser, 'End of Illusion and End of Era,' *Trinidad and Tobago Review*, January 1, 2007.

35 Al-Jazeera.net, 'Iraq Rejects Permanent US Bases,' December 12, 2007.

36 Hannah Arendt, 'Reflections on Violence,' *New York Review of Books*, February 27, 1969.

11 The Imperial Presidency Redux
Presidential power and the war in Iraq

Jon Roper

When Arthur Schlesinger Jr. published *The Imperial Presidency* in 1973, its title reflected the mood of the moment. The President was too powerful. Congressional prerogatives had been usurped. Constitutional proprieties had been set aside. The nation had been led into an unwinnable war. The White House had condoned criminal activities. The core argument was straightforward enough. Schlesinger described how America's rise to a position of international pre-eminence had helped the President, the most important actor in deciding and conducting the nation's foreign policy, to assume a position of unrivalled authority within the American political system. Furthermore, the Commander-in-Chief's arrogation of the war-making initiative eroded Congress's constitutional power to declare war. It gave Presidents the vital capacity to back diplomatic language with the threat or use of military force. At the same time war had fuelled the Executive's insurgent assault on the framework of American constitutionalism. If World War II saw the Presidency 'resurgent', during the Korean War it was 'ascendant' and by the Vietnam War it was 'rampant'. As it reached its apogee, therefore, the Imperial Presidency, 'essentially the creation of foreign policy', had 'overwhelmed the traditional separation of powers in foreign affairs' and had started 'to aspire toward an equivalent centralization of power in the domestic polity'.[1]

The constitutional crisis which ended with Richard Nixon's resignation from office in August 1974 led to the pendulum of power oscillating from the Executive towards the Legislature, as Congress became more assertive in checking and balancing Presidential authority. This chapter traces the reaction of those who clung to the wreckage of the 'Imperial Presidency' and who developed a constitutional theory that legitimised the rehabilitation of presidential power: the 'Unitary Executive'. It argues that after its adherents moved into positions of influence in George W. Bush's administration, their aggressive attempt to expand the sphere of presidential authority, particularly in the aftermath of the events of 11 September 2001, foundered as a result of the war in Iraq. Schlesinger's analysis, which is based on Max Weber's typology for the legitimisation of political power, is discussed in relation to the fate of this 'Imperial Presidency Redux'. The chapter concludes that the erosion of George W. Bush's charismatic authority as his political credibility evaporated is the latest example of the dangers of leading the nation into dubious battle: misuse of the war power is the most effective restraint on Executive aggrandisement.

The Imperial Presidents

The political context which informed Schlesinger's argument – the deepening ideological divisions caused by the Vietnam War and the revelations of the Watergate scandal – was not the inevitable outcome of the structural trends that he saw as encouraging presidential pre-eminence. He recognised that the Presidency is an institution moulded not only by historical developments and political circumstances but also by the personalities and character of those who occupy the White House. Despite the increasing potential for the assumption of unconstitutional power, not all Presidents were tempted to act imperiously. Roosevelt 'delighted in power' but used it effectively and responsibly. Although Truman committed American forces to fight in Korea without a congressional declaration of war, for Schlesinger, he remained: 'far too spontaneous an American democrat to fit comfortably into the imperial Presidency.' Similarly, Eisenhower and then Kennedy, whose 'ironic and sceptical intelligence customarily kept the Presidency in healthy perspective', managed to avoid the excesses of what Senator William Fulbright famously referred to in a separate but related context as the 'arrogance of power'.[2]

The Imperial Presidency might be instead better entitled *The Imperial Presidents.* In coining his catch-phrase Schlesinger focused on two Presidents whose conduct in office had, he argued, broken through the barriers of constitutional restraint. His political antipathy towards Lyndon Johnson and Richard Nixon, both of whom he regarded as illegitimate occupants of the office, fuelled his argument. The memory of the Kennedys, both Jack and Robert, whose assassinations had deprived the United States of the prospect of charismatic leadership, is the shadow from which *The Imperial Presidency* emerged. Indeed, the book might have been left unwritten had the brothers survived. Schlesinger's conclusions about the development of presidential power ultimately derive from his characterisation of Johnson and Nixon as a usurper and an interloper in what might have been, but for the tragedies in Dallas and Los Angeles, a very different decade in the history of the Presidency. For Schlesinger, Johnson thus 'poured an insatiable personality, a greed for consensus and an obsession with secrecy into the institution. The office now began to swell to imperial proportions.' Then,

> with Nixon there came, whether by weird historical accident or by unconscious national response to historical pressure and possibility, a singular confluence of the job with the man. The Presidency, as enlarged by international delusions and domestic propulsions, found a President

whose inner mix of vulnerability and ambition impelled him to push
the historical logic to its extremity.[3]

The Imperial Presidency portrays a Chief Executive who has strayed from the
reservation of American constitutionalism, unaccountable except during
re-election campaigns, claiming popular legitimacy by virtue of having
won a mandate to govern in the only national contest for office and remov-
able only through the politically controversial process of impeachment.
Although the original 'genius' of this ultimate sanction 'lay in the fact that
it could punish the man without punishing the office', Schlesinger nevertheless recognised that it might in fact do both. Instead 'the trick was
to preserve presidential power but to deter Presidents from abusing that
power' because 'the nation required both a strong Presidency for leadership
and the separation of powers for liberty'.[4] In other words, using the typology
for the legitimisation of political power first advanced by Max Weber,
Schlesinger's ideal was to preserve a combination of charismatic and legal
rule. In fact the blunt instrument of impeachment proved unnecessary. Its
threat was sufficient. Nixon took pre-emptive action and resigned before
Congress could determine his political fate. However, the problem of recon-
ciling strong presidential leadership and the separation of powers remained.

If the Imperial Presidency crashed in the maelstrom of opposition to
the Vietnam War and burned in the all-consuming inferno of Watergate,
Johnson and Nixon were not its only casualties. The ideological consensus
that Schlesinger had championed during Truman's presidency as *The Vital
Center* was eviscerated.[5] In its place, polarised attitudes now informed
political perspectives on the proper parameters of constitutional authority.
Conservatives emerged as the advocates of a strong Executive, particularly
when Republicans occupy the White House. Through re-interpreting the
Constitution in such a way as to legitimise the President's re-colonisation of
a sphere of pre-eminence, they helped to design a new model of presidential
power. It was this creation, the 'Unitary Executive' which became, for liberals, 'The Imperial Presidency Redux': its potential abuses of power thrown
into sharp relief by another war: Iraq.

Presidential wars

The defining characteristic of the 'Imperial Presidency' was the Commander-
in-Chief's capacity to order American forces into battle without a congressional declaration of war. Truman, whose doctrine defined the terms of Cold
War American foreign policy, is the *eminence grise* behind the contemporary
Executive's assumption of this power. His decision to commit forces to
combat in Korea, as Schlesinger pointed out,

> beguiled the American government first into an unprecedented claim
> for inherent presidential power to go to war and then into ill-advised

resentment against those who dared to bring up the constitutional issue ... by insisting that the presidential prerogative alone sufficed to meet the requirements of the Constitution, Truman ... dramatically and dangerously enlarged the power of future Presidents to take the nation into major war.[6]

Congress became a bystander as Truman took 'police action' in Korea. When, after the outbreak of hostilities, he finally addressed a joint session of the legislature on 19 July 1950 it was to explain his decision to go to war and to report a *fait accompli*. He had earlier dismissed the possibility of requesting a congressional resolution endorsing his action because he was concerned that his successors, in similar situations, might have to follow his precedent without the guarantee of the congressional support that he took for granted. As Averell Harriman, one of Truman's advisers recalled:

> among other things I recommended to the president was that he get a Joint Resolution from Congress.... Mr. Truman said he had considered such a move; if he got a Joint Resolution it would tie the hands of a successor. He was always thinking about his responsibility to the presidency.... I thought it was a mistake and so did many others at that time. But the President's inclination to protect the office – not to allow anything or anybody to weaken the authority of the president of the United States – that was something to which President Truman paid a great deal of attention.[7]

Truman's unilateral action in Korea mortgaged his political future to the outcome of the war. As the conflict became a stalemate of attrition, public opinion turned against the President. In March 1951, Senator Robert Taft argued that the war was the result of 'an absolute usurpation of authority by the President'.[8] His critics, including Arthur Schlesinger, dismissed 'Mr. Republican' as an advocate of the 'New Isolationism', but Taft's comment reflected the growing sense of unease at the President's unilateral commitment of forces overseas.

Despite his desire not to establish a precedent which could restrict the freedom of manoeuvre of his successors, Truman's experience over Korea ironically encouraged them to seek congressional resolutions to endorse potential or intended military actions.[9] Lyndon Johnson's sense that Truman had made a mistake in not involving the legislature in his decision to go to war informed his action in persuading it to pass the Tonkin Gulf Resolution: the 'blank cheque' which he subsequently cashed in escalating America's involvement in the Vietnam War.

The Tonkin Gulf Resolution gave legal force to the power that Truman had assumed. Congress ceded its right to declare war to the President. In granting Johnson authority 'to take all necessary measures to repel any armed attack against the forces of the United States and to prevent further aggression' in Southeast Asia, the legislature gave the executive an expansive discretion to take military action.[10] As Truman found out over Korea, however, once presidential wars become unpopular, Congress ducks for cover. It was Johnson who was held responsible for his failure to extricate America from the quagmire he had created, leaving his successor a dubious political inheritance.

Bob Haldeman, Nixon's White House Chief of Staff, was convinced that 'without the Vietnam war there would have been no Watergate'.[11] The scandal which engulfed the Nixon administration became a shorthand expression for Presidential corruption. It was also the product of the undermining of Executive credibility that the Vietnam War had precipitated the gap between the President's claim that the conflict was both necessary and winnable, and the widespread perception that it was neither of those things. Nixon's behaviour while in office became another example of the flawed morality that many believed had underscored America's involvement in Southeast Asia. It flowed naturally into a growing cynicism. The President's protestation that he was not a crook did nothing to convince a sceptical public.

As Theodore White put it:

> of all the political myths out of which the republic was born ... none was more powerful than the crowning myth of the Presidency – that the people, in their shared wisdom, would be able to choose the best man to lead them. From this came the derivative myth – that the Presidency, the supreme office, would make noble any man who held its responsibility.[12]

If the first of Schlesinger's Imperial Presidents, Lyndon Johnson, inherited an office that imbued its holders with charismatic authority, that legacy was squandered once he involved the nation in the Vietnam War. Richard Nixon then drained the Presidency of any remaining deference that had been its due. As White observes, Nixon's 'lawlessness exploded the legends'.[13] In Weberian terms, executive power is legitimated if it remains within the parameters of legal rule and if the President retains charismatic authority. What Truman's and Johnson's experiences demonstrate is that unpopular presidential wars undermine the credibility on which charismatic leadership is based. With Watergate, the 'Imperial Presidency' imploded. In the aftermath of Nixon's resignation, however, conservatives developed a constitutional theory which attempted to rehabilitate an expansive view of presidential power, hoping thereby to re-establish public faith in the office and the authority of its predominantly Republican incumbents.

The 'Unitary Executive'

Even before Nixon left office, Congress had begun to re-assert itself through legislation that aimed to limit the scope of presidential autonomy. In

November 1973, the same month that *The Imperial Presidency* was published, it overturned the President's veto of the War Powers Resolution. Six months later, in July 1974, and weeks before he resigned, Nixon reluctantly signed the Congressional Budget and Impoundment Control Act which prevented the Executive ignoring the Legislature's wishes by refusing to spend appropriations agreed for specific purposes. The reverberations from the Watergate era continued to inform Congress's efforts to oversee the Executive's actions. In 1978 it passed the Foreign Intelligence Surveillance Act, establishing procedures for the gathering of information from other than domestic sources and also the Ethics in Government Act, which established the office of the special prosecutor to investigate alleged Executive misdemeanours. These legislative constraints defined the political terrain that those who advocated strong presidential leadership battled to recover.

It was a conservative cause. As the Democrats controlled Congress, Republicans looked to the White House as their principal source of power. However, in the immediate aftermath of Watergate, President Gerald Ford had little room for political manoeuvre, particularly after he used his power of pardon to spare his predecessor the ignominy of appearing in court. In April 1975, he failed to persuade Congress to agree to his request for $300 million to aid South Vietnam, which was crumbling in the face of invasion from the North. On 30 April the South Vietnamese surrendered. Just over two weeks later, on 15 May Ford had the unique distinction of becoming the only President thus far to comply with section 4(a) of the War Powers Resolution, informing Congress that he had authorised military action to rescue the crew of the *Mayaguez* which had been seized by Cambodian patrol boats. In his report he cited his executive power under the Constitution and his authority as Commander-in-Chief as justification for ordering the operation. Elsewhere the President made it clear that he would have taken action irrespective of any objections from the Legislature.

Ford left the White House convinced that the War Powers Resolution was unconstitutional and chafing at such congressional efforts to curb presidential prerogatives. In an interview with *Time* magazine in 1980, he argued:

> Some people used to complain about what they called an 'imperial presidency', but now the pendulum has swung too far in the opposite direction. We have not an imperial presidency but an imperiled presidency. Under today's rules, which include some misguided 'reforms', the presidency does not operate effectively. That is a very serious development, and it is harmful to our overall national interests.[14]

Ford's comments appeared six days after Ronald Reagan had been elected President. Coincidentally, James Baker, then chief-of-staff designate, talked with Dick Cheney, who had occupied the same position in Ford's White House. As Jeffery Rosen has observed: Cheney had been one of a number of 'young conservatives' working in that administration who felt besieged by the post-Watergate laws that Congress had passed to restrain the president, in particular the War Powers Resolution ... When Congress voted to cut off funding in South Vietnam in 1975, they felt it had undermined Ford's foreign policy and usurped power from the executive branch.[15]

According to a profile of Cheney published in the *Washington Post* in 2007, in the course of their conversation, Baker had noted some advice: 'Restore power & auth to Exec Branch – Need strong ldr'ship. Get rid of War Powers Act – restore independent rights.... Central theme we ought to push.'[16] As the Republicans re-gained the White House after the Carter inter-regnum, at the end of which the President's weakness had been symbolised by the lengthy Iranian hostage crisis and the failure of his mission to rescue them, conservatives retained an ambition to repair what they saw as the damage done to the Presidency in the aftermath of Vietnam and Watergate.

During the Reagan years their project took shape. The territory that would be occupied by the 'Unitary Executive' began to be staked out. Within the Justice Department, it was the Office of Legal Counsel (OLC), charged with providing advice to the President as to the boundaries of the Executive's constitutional authority, which, as Rosen points out 'became known as a center of conservative intellectual thought, and as such attracted lots of bright, young, true believers'. They took their cue from Alexander Hamilton's argument in *Federalist 70* that: 'a feeble Executive implies a feeble execution of the government. A feeble execution is but another phrase for a bad execution; and a government ill executed, whatever it may be in theory, must be, in practice, a bad government.' Hamilton's first 'ingredient' for 'energy in the executive' was 'unity'.[17] The 'Unitary Executive' thus described the vigorous assertion of presidential power that conservative legal theorists argued was part of the Founders' original intent.

Samuel Alito, who George W. Bush would appoint to the Supreme Court, worked in the OLC during the Reagan administration and was among those who became, in his words, 'strong proponents of the theory of the unitary executive, that all federal executive power is vested by the Constitution in the President'. For Alito, moreover, 'this theory best captures the meaning of the Constitution's text and structure'.[18] In a memorandum written in February 1986, he outlined a way of putting the idea into practice through the exploitation of what was then seen as an innocuous device: the presidential signing statement. Alito discussed 'the novelty of the proposal', for which Stephen Calabresi, then working in the Justice Department as a special assistant to Attorney-General Ed Meese took credit, that 'Presidential signing statements be used to address questions of interpretation' of the law. Although Presidents had historically issued statements when signing acts of Congress as a comment on the legislation, 'they have seldom explained in any depth or detail how they have interpreted the bills they have signed. Presidential approval is usually accompanied by a statement that is often little more than a press release.'

Alito argued that issuing interpretative signing statements would have 'two chief advantages'. Not only would it 'increase the power of the Executive to shape the law' but also 'by forcing some rethinking by courts, scholars and litigants, it may help to curb some of the prevalent abuses of legislative history'. While outlining some of the possible objections to this strategy, among them that 'it seems likely that our new type of signing statement will not be warmly welcomed by Congress', he recommended that:

> the Department should continue and intensify its internal consideration of the theoretical problems posed by the proposed expanded role for Presidential signing statements. Once a few of (sic) signing statements of this new type have been issued, discussion in legal journals may be stimulated and should be encouraged.[19]

In the same month that Alito composed his memorandum, Ed Meese announced in an address at the National Press Club in Washington that:

> to make sure that the President's own understanding of what's in a bill is the same ... or is given consideration at the time of statutory construction later on by a court, we have now arranged with the West Publishing Company that the presidential statement on the signing of a bill will accompany the legislative history from Congress so that all can be available to the court for future construction of what that statute really means.[20]

The publication he referred to, the *US Code Congressional and Administrative News* is the authoritative collection of legislative history and as such an important source for the subsequent interpretation of the law.

While the promotion of interpretative signing statements represented one attempt to reconfigure presidential power, Congress's refusal to fund Reagan's 'freedom fighters' in Nicaragua and provide American support for the contra opposition to the Sandinista government there, showed that the President's autonomy was still constrained. The Iran-Contra scandal then further demonstrated the continuing propensity for the Executive to stray beyond the boundaries of constitutional conduct in pursuit of its overseas ambitions. Lieutenant Colonel Oliver North may have believed that using the proceeds of illegal arms sales to Iran to fund an insurgency in Nicaragua was a 'neat idea', but it amounted to the privatisation of American foreign policy. The Iran-Contra scandal demonstrated that Presidents could still act imperiously and face the consequences of being caught out. Reagan survived the political firestorm which in different circumstances might have led to his impeachment.

When the majority report of the Congressional Committees that investigated the administration's actions was published in November 1987 it concluded that

> the Iran-Contra affair was characterized by pervasive dishonesty and inordinate secrecy.... Secrecy became an obsession. Congress was never informed of the Iran or the contra covert actions, notwithstanding the requirement in the law that Congress be notified of all covert actions in a 'timely fashion'.

It was clear who should be held to account: 'The Constitution requires the President to "take care that the laws be faithfully executed". This charge encompasses a responsibility to leave the members of his Administration in no doubt that the rule of law governs.' In a sideswipe at those who believed in the 'Unitary Executive', the report observed that

> in a constitutional democracy, it is not true, as one official maintained, that 'When you take the king's shilling, you do the king's bidding.' The idea of monarchy was rejected here 200 years ago and since then, the law – not any official or ideology – has been paramount. For not instilling this precept in his staff, for failing to take care that the law reigned supreme, the President bears the responsibility.[21]

Not all members of the Congressional Investigating Committees agreed. A Minority Report was issued in which it was argued that:

> judgments about the Iran-Contra Affair ultimately must rest upon one's views about the proper roles of Congress and the President in foreign policy.... Much of what President Reagan did in his actions toward Nicaragua and Iran were constitutionally protected exercises of inherent Presidential powers.[22]

It was evident that the perspective on Presidential power of one of its signatories, the Republican representative from Wyoming, had not changed when he had moved from the Executive to the Legislature. Dick Cheney's robust defence of Reagan's actions was consistent with the views he had adopted while working in the White House.

As Reagan's presidency came to an end, the idea of the 'Unitary Executive' had been advanced but it had gained limited traction beyond conservative political and legal circles. In 1989, the Supreme Court disagreed with the argument that the post-Watergate law which allowed independent investigation of possible abuses of Executive power was an infringement upon presidential prerogatives. In *Morrison v. Olson*, it decided that the provisions in the Ethics in Government Act relating to the special prosecutor (by then re-named independent counsel) did not contradict the principle of the separation of powers and intrude on the President's sphere of constitutional authority. The sole dissenter from the decision was Antonin Scalia. Before Reagan had appointed him to the Court in 1986, Scalia had formerly worked in the OLC during the Nixon and Ford administrations and had argued the case for Nixon's legal ownership of the tapes and documents that were the incriminating evidence of the President's involvement in Watergate. His opinion in that matter had been dismissed by the Court.

For Scalia, however, the issue remained the same. The problem was 'Power. The allocation of power among Congress, the President, and the courts in such fashion as to preserve the equilibrium the Constitution sought to establish.' In his view: 'The purpose of the separation and equilibration of powers in general, and of the unitary Executive in particular, was not merely to assure effective government but to preserve individual freedom.' A politically motivated independent counsel could investigate the President's actions: 'in an area where so little is law and so much is discretion'. This potentially inhibited Executive autonomy in ways that ran counter to the intent and spirit of the Constitution. Scalia saw circumstances in which:

> 'what would normally be regarded as a technical violation', could assume a significance out of all proportion for the independent counsel. It 'may in his or her small world assume the proportions of an indictable offense. What would normally be regarded as an investigation that has reached the level of pursuing such picayune matters that it should be concluded, may to him or her be an investigation that ought to go on for another year.'

The President was faced with the 'frightening' prospect of agreeing to the appointment of an independent counsel and staff 'with nothing else to do but to investigate you until investigation is no longer worthwhile' and then

> to have that counsel and staff decide, with no basis for comparison, whether what you have done is bad enough, wilful enough, and provable enough, to warrant an indictment. How admirable the constitutional system that provides the means to avoid such a distortion. And how unfortunate the judicial decision that has permitted it.[23]

Republicans were used to controlling the White House, which they occupied for 20 of the 24 years between 1968 and 1992. They were also accustomed to being a minority in the House of Representatives and more often than not in the Senate as well. When Bill Clinton became President that changed. Scalia's analysis ironically and neatly encapsulated the battles that emerged between Clinton and Kenneth Starr, the independent counsel appointed to pursue the Whitewater investigation into alleged improprieties in real estate dealings while the President was Governor of Arkansas. With the Republicans now ascendant in Congress, a Democrat President became the lightening rod for a conservative campaign that culminated in his impeachment after a scandal in which the investigation of the independent counsel played a pivotal role. Clinton was acquitted in February 1999. By then, his was not the only reputation that had been tarnished. Starr was widely vilified for the way in which he had made the President's private morality grounds for potential political humiliation. In June, Congress, in a move supported by the then Attorney-General Janet Reno and by Starr himself, allowed the independent counsel law to expire.

During the Clinton administration and into George W. Bush's presidency conservatives continued to advance the theoretical case in favour of the 'Unitary Executive'. In 1997, Stephen Calabresi published the first in a series of articles with Christopher Yoo, then a law professor at Vanderbilt University, that underpinned the concept within the context of an expansive interpretation of presidential power. Their aim, according to the third of their surveys published in 2004 was to provide 'a comprehensive chronicle that places the battles between the President and Congress over control of the administration of federal law in historical perspective'. For Calabresi and Yoo, 'all three branches of the federal government have the power and the duty to interpret the Constitution'. Moreover, 'the meaning of the Constitution is determined through the dynamic interaction of all three branches'. In tracing the ways in which Presidents had historically claimed a position of primacy within the system of separated institutions sharing powers, they also saw nothing wrong with the politically charged term that Schlesinger had first used to describe a constitutionally unhinged Executive. On the contrary, they concluded that:

> strong presidents like the two Roosevelts and Wilson ... helped remake the institution of the presidency into the primary institution for mobilizing and implementing political will. Their administrations set the stage for the imperial presidency that would dominate modern times.[24]

From 'Unitary Executive' to 'Imperial Presidency Redux'

By the end of the twentieth century, the script had been written. It remained for the actors to take centre stage. 'After George W. Bush took office in 2001', as Jeffery Rosen observes, 'the various threads of pro-executive power conservatism – the Watergate-scarred Ford veterans, the Reagan OLC team – united with younger members of the Bush OLC to embrace aggressively the idea of the unitary executive.'[25] Dick Cheney had a major part to play in this development. In his interview with *Time* in 1980, Gerald Ford had argued that to overcome many of the difficulties afflicting the 'imperilled presidency' the Vice-President should become:

> a real Chief of Staff, both to control the administrative bureaucracy and to see that Administration relations with the Congress really

mesh.... This would be comparable to what happens in a well-organized business, where you have a chief executive officer and a chief operating officer. The President is the chief executive officer.... But you then have the Vice President as the chief operating officer ... the Vice President should be in the job of making the Administration work.[26]

In 2001, the first President with a Harvard MBA entered the White House with Ford's former Chief of Staff as Vice-President cast in just such a role.

The defining moments of Bush's presidency – the events of 11 September 2001 and his unilateral declaration of a 'war on terror' – confirmed the conservatives' assumption that authority and power should be concentrated in the Executive. After the retributive use of force to topple the Taliban regime in Afghanistan, however, it was the action that was taken in support of the 'Bush Doctrine' of pre-emptive war, the invasion of Iraq and its aftermath that raised the spectre that the 'Unitary Executive' was simply the 'Imperial Presidency Redux'.

On 14 September in a replay of its action in passing the Tonkin Gulf Resolution, Congress gave the President sweeping authorization

to use all necessary and appropriate force against those nations, organizations, or persons he determines planned, authorized, committed, or aided the terrorist attacks that occurred on September 11, 2001, or harbored such organizations or persons, in order to prevent any future acts of international terrorism against the United States by such nations, organizations or persons.[27]

The OLC used this as one element in its subsequent legal justifications for the President's expansive use of his powers as Commander-in-Chief, based on its ideological mantra: the 'Unitary Executive' as the focal point of constitutional authority. The President's unfettered capacity to use military force in the 'war on terror' was outlined in a memorandum from the OLC drafted by John Yoo (Christopher Yoo's brother) less than two weeks after Congress had passed the resolution. It asserted that 'the President has the constitutional power not only to retaliate against any person, organization, or State suspected of involvement in terrorist attacks on the United States, but also against foreign States suspected of harboring or supporting such organizations'. In addition: 'The President may deploy military force pre-emptively against terrorist organizations or the States that harbor or support them, whether or not they can be linked to the specific terrorist incidents of September 11.'

In language by now familiar, the memorandum argued that the Constitution:

secures all federal executive power in the President to ensure a unity in purpose and energy in action.... The centralization of authority in the

President alone is particularly crucial in matters of national defense, war, and foreign policy, where a unitary executive can evaluate threats, consider policy choices, and mobilize national resources with a speed and energy that is far superior to any other branch.

Alexander Hamilton, this time writing in *Federalist 74*, was quoted with approval: 'Of all the cares or concerns of government, the direction of war most peculiarly demands those qualities which distinguish the exercise of power by a single hand.'[28] Before the end of the year, the Taliban regime in Afghanistan which had provided a base for Osama Bin Laden and al Qaeda terrorist training camps had been overthrown by an American led military coalition operating with United Nations approval.

On 13 November 2001, President Bush issued a military order concerning the 'Detention, Treatment, and Trial of Certain Non-Citizens in the War Against Terrorism'. It authorised the detention 'at an appropriate location designated by the Secretary of Defense outside or within the United States' of those who were not citizens of the United States and who were believed to be either members of al Qaeda or suspected of having 'engaged in, aided or abetted, or conspired to commit' acts of terrorism. Such detainees could be tried by Military Commissions.[29] The way in which this order was formulated and approved revealed much about the way the President construed his powers as Commander-in-Chief in the aftermath of September 11. The legal arguments in support of the action were prepared by the OLC. David Addington, the Vice-President's long-time legal adviser, was also influential in shaping the proposal. According to the *Washington Post*, on the day the order was issued, Cheney had shown it to Bush at their weekly lunch. Afterwards,

> in less than an hour, the document traversed a West Wing circuit that gave its words the power of command. It changed hands four times, according to witnesses, with emphatic instructions to bypass staff review. When it returned to the Oval Office, in a blue portfolio embossed with the presidential seal, Bush pulled a felt-tip pen from his pocket and signed without sitting down. Almost no one else had seen the text.[30]

At that time, congressional reaction was muted. The President enjoyed widespread popular support for his aggressive stand against terrorism. It was only after the establishment of the detention centre at Guantanamo Bay graphically illustrated the consequences of Bush's action that it became, for his critics in the Legislature and in the country, an enduring example of the imperious use of presidential power.

As had been the case in Vietnam, political opposition to such controversial actions began to be voiced in the context of the Executive's persistence in pursuing an increasingly unpopular military campaign. Following the initial response to 9/11, and as his administration's next target for military action became clear, the broad political and popular support for the President fractured. From the end of 2001 onwards, the continuing and inconclusive conflict in Afghanistan was relegated to a side-show as attention was focused on the nation that some of Bush's most senior advisers, including the then Defense Secretary Donald Rumsfeld, felt should have been its first target after the September 11 attacks: Iraq.

In January 2002, in the President's State of the Union Address, it became a charter member of the 'Axis of Evil'. Five months later, in his speech at West Point, the President revealed publicly that the ground was being prepared. In formulating the 'Bush Doctrine', he warned that:

> The gravest danger to freedom lies at the perilous crossroads of radicalism and technology. When the spread of chemical and biological and nuclear weapons, along with ballistic missile technology – when that occurs, even weak states and small groups could attain a catastrophic power to strike great nations. Our enemies ... have been caught seeking these terrible weapons ... unbalanced dictators with weapons of mass destruction can deliver those weapons on missiles or secretly provide them to terrorist allies.

The United States needed 'to be ready for preemptive action when necessary to defend our liberty and to defend our lives'.[31] There was no doubt which 'unbalanced dictator' he had in mind.

Saddam Hussein was toppled soon after the war began in March 2003 but despite the President's confident assertion that it had been 'Mission Accomplished', the conflict continued. American troops remained in Iraq. Casualties mounted. At the end of April 2004, the United States surrendered most of its remaining moral high ground in the court of world opinion when images of prisoner abuse at Abu Ghraib were released. Nevertheless the Bush administration remained obdurate. In approving the Defense Appropriations Act of 2006, which incorporated Senator John McCain's amendment prohibiting the inhumane treatment of military prisoners, including those still held in Guantanamo Bay, the President issued an interpretative signing statement that reserved the right to: 'construe Title X [of the Detainee Treatment Act] relating to detainees, in a manner consistent with the constitutional authority of the President to supervise the unitary executive branch...' As Jim Pfiffner points out: there was 'a distinct similarity' with President Nixon's use of the impoundment of funds to circumvent legislation to which he objected. 'In both cases the presidents were asserting the constitutional authority to ignore the law and accomplish, in effect, a line-item or absolute veto.' The President had lobbied Congress not to pass the McCain Amendment. Now, he had effectively 'announced that he would accomplish administratively what he had failed to do through the constitutional legislative process'.[32]

The signing statement that accompanied the Defense Appropriations Act highlighted the administration's reliance on the powers inherent in its concept of the 'Unitary Executive'. As President Bush's second term unraveled and the war in Iraq became a focal point of opposition, the use of such devices was the subject of increasing criticism. At the same time, the revelation in the *New York Times* in December 2005 that, armed with a legal justification from the OLC, the President had authorised the National Security Agency (NSA) to conduct electronic surveillance of American citizens without obtaining warrants from the courts and effectively by-passing the provisions of the 1978 Foreign Intelligence Surveillance Act provoked a similar firestorm of controversy. The image of a President who continued to fight an unpopular war, ignored congressional legislation as it suited his purpose, condoned actions which flouted the law, had an obsession with secrecy which he justified on the grounds of national security, and who threatened civil liberties and the constitutional separation of powers had a particular resonance.

The prototypical 'Imperial Presidents', Johnson and Nixon, had abused their Executive power in pursuing the Vietnam War and constructing the 'plebiscitary presidency'. Similarly, the war in Iraq and the view of presidential power inherent in the 'Unitary Executive' allowed George W. Bush's critics to characterise his administration as the 'Imperial Presidency Redux'. Once again, the continuing imbroglio of American forces overseas led to the collapse of a President's credibility. In the toxic political atmosphere surrounding the continuing conflict in Iraq, the charge that George W. Bush's administration has systematically flouted the constitutional framework of the rule of law was more easily made and became more widely believed.

Charisma, 'caesarism' and credibility

Gerhard Casper, the former President of Stanford University, has argued in Weberian terms that the contemporary justification of presidential 'caesarism' has relied upon:

> collecting, summarizing, and expanding diverse, limited, and sometimes petty constitutional authorities into undifferentiated executive powers. [It] has, for many decades now, been the technique for denying the constitutional primacy of Congress and limiting the role of the courts. Would-be caesars rule with the aid of such abstractions as *the* executive power, *the* 'inherent' powers of the commander-in-chief, *the* war power, *the* foreign affairs power, *the* emergency power. Sweeping congressional resolutions such as the Authorization for Use of Military Force are also invoked, but only as a back-up for the fainthearted, since the alleged constitutional powers are generally considered as sufficient authority.

It has been a trend 'pushed by elevating discrete executive authorities to ever higher constitutional levels, *seeking cover behind the legitimacy of the constitution*'.[33]

As Casper also suggests, quoting Suetonius on Caesar: 'Conciliato populi favore....' ('Having won the favor of the masses...'), is an apt Weberian motto for the leader whose charismatic authority is legitimated through the democratic electoral process.[34] Schlesinger's 'plebiscitary presidency' or, as Casper styles it, 'plebiscitary caesarism' thus by-passes constitutional conventions and rests directly on a popular mandate: both Johnson in 1964 and Nixon in 1972 won landslide electoral victories and in 2004, as Dick Cheney pointed out, Bush won 'the greatest number of popular votes of any presidential candidate in history'.[35] The Executive, relying upon the support of the people (Nixon's 'Silent Majority'), is potentially able to dominate the political process irrespective of constitutional constraints.

It was Weber, however, who also issued advice relevant to those tempted to exploit their electoral mandate in order to extend the sphere of their political power: 'One take care – as to any attempt, on the part of the president, to infringe the laws or to govern autocratically – that "the gallows and the rope" be always before his eyes.'[36] In the United States, the threat of impeachment, the possibility of repudiation at the polls and ultimately the fact that nowadays a President has a maximum of eight years in office remain potential countervailing pressures to discourage the excesses of 'caesarism'. As Casper observes: 'To use Weber's colorful metaphor, "the gallows and the rope" remained before Nixon's eyes.' Moreover, 'if the Nixon case illustrates "situational gallows", then Lyndon Johnson's 1968 decision not to run for reelection represents a kind of "imagined gallows" and the constitutional term limit for presidents constitute "mandatory gallows".'[37] To evade the political noose, a President needs to retain a reservoir of charismatic authority. If that evaporates, loss of credibility is a sign that the court of public opinion has given its verdict.

Following his re-election in 2004, George W. Bush faced the 'mandatory' rather than 'situational' or 'imagined' scaffold, but it was built upon a similar foundation to those erected for Johnson and Nixon. The common thread that unites the 'Imperial Presidency' and the 'Imperial Presidency Redux' is the Executive's persistence in fighting wars while faced with a growing popular perception that America is on the losing side.

A self-evident truth in the history of Presidential politics is that when the nation confronts an existential threat, the Commander-in-Chief who leads America to victory in war emerges with an enhanced reputation. Such is the case even if the national emergency has required them to press the powers of the office to their constitutional limit and to behave as potential 'Imperial Presidents': witness Abraham Lincoln in the Civil War and Franklin Roosevelt during World War II. It is equally apparent that within the context of long-running existential conflicts, the Cold War and now the 'war on terror', Presidents who invest substantial political capital in committing military forces overseas take a gamble. If their actions mire the country in situations where there are no easy exit strategies and the prospects of victory seem progressively to diminish, public confidence in their leadership rapidly ebbs away: witness Truman in Korea, Johnson and Nixon in Vietnam, and now George W. Bush in Iraq. Without such public trust, they have no credibility.

For Weber, therefore, 'by its very nature, the existence of charismatic authority is specifically unstable'. Moreover: 'it is recognition on the part of those subject to authority which is decisive for the validity of charisma' but its legitimacy 'lasts only so long as the belief in its charismatic inspiration remains'.[38] As Eric Posner and Adrian Vermeule have observed:

> For Presidents, credibility is power. With credibility, the formal rules of the separation of powers system can be bargained around or even defied, as Lincoln and FDR demonstrated. Without credibility, a nominally powerful president is a helpless giant. Even if legal and institutional restraints are loose and give the president broad powers, those powers cannot effectively be exercised if the public believes that the president lies or has nefarious motives.[39]

In 1952, with his public approval ratings at a low ebb because of the Korean War, Harry Truman faced the 'imagined gallows' following his defeat by Estes Kefauver in the New Hampshire primary. Like Lyndon Johnson in 1968, Truman withdrew from the political fray rather than risk further humiliation at the polls.[40] Throughout his second term, the increasing criticism of his competence – the reaction to Hurricane Katrina – and a lack of faith in his insistence that progress was being made in Iraq effectively eroded George W. Bush's political authority in the same way that Korea, Vietnam (and the Watergate scandal which flowed from it) moulded attitudes towards Truman, Johnson and Nixon.

Conclusion

Once the perceived failure of America's military intervention in Iraq began to undermine President Bush's political credibility, the administration's justification for the expansive use of presidential power – the 'Unitary Executive' – was held up to public scrutiny, with its legal and constitutional basis becoming a matter of political debate. Even some conservatives in the OLC began to retreat from the outposts of executive authority whose occupation their colleagues had advocated in the immediate aftermath of September 11. Jack Goldsmith, who took charge of the OLC in 2003, rescinded several of the Department's opinions including those which had supported the coercive interrogation of terrorist suspects. He resigned in July 2004, after repeated confrontations with other administration officials, principally David Addington, as he tried to place 'deeply flawed' opinions which were 'sloppily reasoned, overbroad, and incautious in asserting extraordinary constitutional authorities on behalf of the President' on a firmer legal footing.[41] Such revelations helped to frame the liberal critique of George W. Bush's abuse of power: those who put forward his case for an expansive interpretation of Executive autonomy had stitched together the Imperial President Redux's new clothes, which now became invisible except to those ideologues within the administration for whom political ends outweighed constitutional concerns.

The Constitution constrains Executive authority. Modern democratic politics nevertheless creates the potential for the emergence of the Imperial President: an American 'Caesar'. In an essay written in 1917, Weber suggested that:

> Every kind of direct popular election of the supreme ruler and, beyond that, every kind of political power that rests on the confidence of the masses and not of parliament ... lies on the road to these 'pure' forms of caesarist acclamation. In particular, this is true of the position of the President of the United States, whose superiority over parliament derives from his (formally) democratic nomination and election.[42]

During the Cold War, in the face of a perceived existential threat from nations whose dictators cultivated a cult of personality, there was a desire for strong presidential leadership. Respect for the institution of the Presidency imbued the office and by implication its incumbents with an inherent charismatic authority. Furthermore, as Casper points out:

> In ordinary political language, 'charisma' often refers to no more than the capacity to inspire enthusiasm. However, if we widen the focus to those aspects of the Weberian concept that describe the caesarist-charismatic leader as somebody who is firmly committed to a cause, who wants to set his own limits, who does not consider himself confined by technical jurisdiction, a fair number of presidents qualify as charismatic.[43]

It is a characterisation that Casper applies to George W. Bush, but it is also a definition that could include Truman, Johnson and Nixon.

What these Presidents also share is their association with increasingly unpopular wars: Korea, Vietnam and Iraq. Their experiences show that the tipping point that turns charismatic leadership into the 'Imperial Presidency' or alters the 'Unitary Executive' into the 'Imperial Presidency Redux' occurs when the Commander-in-Chief's credibility evaporates. All that is then left to them is the sight of the scaffold. George W. Bush is the latest American 'Caesar' to become a casualty of a failed war that lost him the public confidence necessary to the exercise of effective presidential power. 'Caveat imperator', emperor beware.

Notes

1 Arthur Schlesinger Jr., *The Imperial Presidency* (Boston: Houghton Mifflin Company, 1989 edition), chs 5–7 and p. 208.

2 Schlesinger, *Imperial Presidency*, 213–214. See also J. William Fulbright, *The Arrogance of Power* (New York: Random House, 1967).

3 Schlesinger, *Imperial Presidency*, 214, 216.

4 Schlesinger, *Imperial Presidency*, 415, 417.

5 Arthur Schlesinger Jr., *The Vital Center* (Boston: Houghton Mifflin Company, 1949).

6 Schlesinger, *The Imperial Presidency*, 135.

7 Harriman's comment was made at a Truman Library Institute Conference in 1975, 'The Korean War – establishing a position: July 2–5 1950', Truman Presidential Library, www.trumanlibrary.org/whistlestop/study_collections/korea/large/kwarj2thru5.htm#ah1.

8 See Schlesinger, 'The New Isolationism', *The Atlantic*, May 1952. He described Taft as 'a man in transition, an Old Isolationist trying hard to come to terms with the modern world'. Taft's quote is from J. Moser, 'Principles Without Program: Robert A. Taft and American Foreign Policy', Ashbrook Center for Public Affairs, www.ashbrook.org/publicat/dialogue/moser.html.

9 For a discussion of the presidential use of congressional resolutions, see Jon Roper, 'Europe's Vietnam Syndrome: America and the Quagmire of Iraq', in John Dumbrell and David Ryan, eds. *Vietnam in Iraq: Tactics, Lessons, Legacies and Ghosts* (London: Routledge, 2007), 139–158.

10 See H.J. Res 1145, Joint Resolution of Congress, 7 August 1964.

11 H.R. Haldeman, *The Ends of Power* (London: Sedgwick & Jackson, 1978), 79.

12 Theodore White, *Breach of Faith: The Fall of Richard Nixon* (New York: Atheneum Publishers, 1975), 322.

13 White, *Breach of Faith*, 323–324.

14 'Two Ex-Presidents Assess the Job', *Time*, 10 November 1980. The other ex-President was Richard Nixon.

15 Jeffrey Rosen, 'Bush's Leviathan State', *New Republic*, 24 July 2006.

16 Barton Gellmann and Jo Becker, 'Cheney on Presidential Power' in 'Angler: The Cheney Vice Presidency', *Washington Post*, 24–27 June 2007.

17 Rosen, 'Bush's Leviathan State'.

18 Alito's remarks, made in a speech given in November 2000 to the Federalist Society were raised as an issue during his confirmation hearings. See, for example, 'Schumer Questions Nominee's Theory on Executive Role', *Boston Globe*, 10 January 2006, which quotes these views. The Federalist Society was formed in 1982 as a 'group of conservatives and libertarians dedicated to reforming the current legal order', The Federalist Society for Law and Public Policy Studies, www.fed-soc.org/aboutus/id.28/default.asp.

19 Memorandum to the Litigation Strategy Working Group, 5 February 1986, Samuel L. Alito Jr. 'Using Presidential Signing Statement (sic) to Make Fuller Use of the President's Constitutionally Assigned Role in the Process of Enacting Law', US Department of Justice Office of Legal Counsel, www.archives.gov/news/samuel-alito/accession-060-89-269/Acc060-89-269-box6-SG-LSWG-Alito toLSWG-Feb1986.pdf.

20 Quoted by Walter Dellinger, 'The Legal Significance of Presidential Signing Statements', Memorandum Prepared for Bernard N. Nussbaum, Counsel to the President, 3 November 1993, www.usdoj.gov/olc/signing.htm.

21 Daniel K. Inouye, Senate Select Committee, and Lee H. Hamilton, House Select Committee, Report of the Congressional Committees Investigating Iran–Contra

Affair with Supplemental, Minority and Additional Views (Washington, DC: GPO, 1987).

22 Richard Cheney, 'Cheney In His Own Words', November 1987, *PBS Frontline*, www.pbs.org/wgbh/pages/frontline/darkside/themes/ownwords.html, citing Daniel K. Inouye, Senate Select Committee, and Lee H. Hamilton, House Select Committee, Report of the Congressional Committees Investigating Iran-Contra Affair with Supplemental, Minority and Additional Views (Washington, DC: GPO, 1987).

23 U.S. Supreme Court, Morrison v. Olson 487 U.S. 654 (1988).

24 Christopher Yoo and Stephen Calbresi, 'The Unitary Executive During the Third Half Century, 1889–1945', *Public Law and Legal Theory Working Paper No. 04–11* (Vanderbilt University Law School), abstract, 4 and 124. The article was also published, with Laurence Nee cited as a co-author, in the *Notre Dame Law Review*, vol. 80, no. 1, November 2004.

25 Rosen, 'Bush's Leviathan State'.

26 'Two Ex-Presidents Assess the Job', *Time.*

27 The Joint Resolution of Congress, S.J.Res 23, was signed into law by President Bush on 18 September 2001.

28 John C. Yoo, 'The President's Constitutional Authority to Conduct Military Operations against Terrorists and Nations Supporting Them', Memorandum Opinion for the Deputy Counsel to The President, *Office of Legal Counsel*, www.usdoj.gov/olc/warpowers925.htm, 25 September 2001.

29 The White House, 'President Issues Military Order: Detention, Treatment, and Trial of Certain Non-Citizens in the War Against Terrorism', *Office of the Press Secretary*, www.whitehouse.gov/news/releases/2001/11/20011113–27.html, 13 November 2001.

30 Gellmann and Becker, 'Angler: The Cheney Vice Presidency', *Washington Post*, 24–27 June 2007.

31 The White House, 'President Bush Delivers Graduation Speech at West Point United States Military Academy West Point, New York', *Office of the Press Secretary*, www.whitehouse.gov/news/releases/2002/06/20020601–3.html, 1 June 2002.

32 I am grateful to Jim Pfiffner for letting me see the manuscript of chapter seven, 'The Power to Ignore the Law: Signing Statements' in his *Power Play: The Bush Presidency and the Constitution* (Washington, DC: The Brookings Institution Press, 2008).

33 Gerhard Casper, 'Caesarism in Democratic Politics: Reflections on Max Weber', Robert G. Wesson Lecture in International Relations Theory and Practice (Stanford: The Freeman Spogli Institute for International Studies, 2007), 19.

34 Casper, 'Caesarism', 2.

35 Cheney's remarks were made on 3 November 2004. See transcript, 'President Bush Gives Victory Speech; How Bush Won; Interview With Presidential Historian Robert Dallek', CNN.com transcripts aired 3 November 2004, http://transcripts.cnn.com/TRANSCRIPTS/0411/03/bn.07.html.

36 Quoted in Casper, 'Caesarism', 12.

37 Quoted in Casper, 'Caesarism', 17.

38 Shmuel Eisenstadt, *Max Weber on Charisma and Institution Building* (Chicago: University of Chicago Press, 1968), 22, 49, 52.

39 Eric Posner and Adrian Vermeule, 'The Credible Executive', *Olin Working Paper no. 309* (Chicago: University of Chicago Law School, 2006), 36.

40 In his memoirs, Truman claimed that it was never his intention to run for re-election in 1952, begging the question of why he initially allowed his name to go forward in the primaries. See Harry S. Truman, *Memoirs by*

Harry S. Truman (New York: Doubleday & Co., Inc., 1956), vol. 2, 488 489. He makes no mention of the New Hampshire result.

41 Jack Goldsmith, *The Terror Presidency* (New York: W. W. Norton, 2007), 10.
42 Quoted in Casper, 'Caesarism', 9.
43 Quoted in Casper, 'Caesarism', 18.

12 Securing the state

The US and post-war Iraqi border security dynamics

James Denselow

Iraq's borders have been suffering a crisis of identity since the US invasion of 2003. The six neighbouring states have been forced to reconfigure their political and functional relationships with the emerging and deeply fragmented Iraqi body-politic, as well as with the extra-regional US custodian and its allies. This chapter utilises a localised approach to the understanding of present day border security issues. It argues that action above and below the level of the state results in blurred scales of boundary operation as state to state polices are by no means in synchronisation with local relations in and around the border. Such blurred levels of operation across the Middle East are by no means unique to post-2003 Iraq, in fact they stem from the initial importation of the state system into the region following World War I. Since that time, political frontiers, in the European sense of the word, have struggled to manifest themselves.

Changes in border function can be said to mirror changes in political relationships. We cannot therefore hope to understand these borders in a political vacuum. This chapter examines the reasons for the Iraqi border's current identity crisis; reasons that have been triggered by the fallout from the 2003 invasion of the country and the subsequent disintegration and partial rebuilding of the Iraqi state. Despite General Petraeus' policy shift in 2007 with 'the surge' that moved US strategy from a 'top down' to 'bottom up' approach, border security dynamics remain important indices of the identity and capabilities of the emerging 'new Iraq'.

This chapter gives an insight into the present situation on the ground by connecting its historical origins with the more recent past. It provides a critical analysis of the impact that the war has had on Iraq's relations with its neighbours with particular focus on the Iraqi–Syrian border. It also examines the evolution of the border management techniques employed by the neighbouring states and by the US and Iraqi governments. It ends by providing a policy audit, assessing the successes, failures and recommendations for any future strategy to secure Iraq's borders.

Right from the start the complexity of international borders can be seen in the particular characteristics and functionality of each of Iraq's six international borders. To the east, the border with Iran is described as 'one of the great ethnic and cultural divides on the earth's surface'.[1]

Thousands of Iranian pilgrims have crossed the border to visit the holy Shi'a cities of Najaf and Karbala following the war. The Iranian government meanwhile has also been linked to the training and arming of groups across Iraq, including provision of 'explosive formed projectiles' (EFPs), advanced improvised explosive devices (IEDs) that are responsible for the majority of Multinational Force (MNF) deaths.

To the north is the rugged, mountainous border with Turkey. Huge numbers of Turkish troops have been present in the area fighting a low-level Kurdish insurgency. Turkey has intervened into northern Iraq and threatens to escalate such action if the Kurdish Regional Governorate (KRG) are not able to suppress the Kurdistan Workers Party (PKK), which may mean that what has in the past been the safest area of Iraq may slide into chaos.

To the south and west the Saudi and Kuwaiti borders are characterised by high-tech border fences that boast the ability to hermetically seal a border line through remote sensing weapons and state-of-the-art detection gear. Likewise, the Jordanian border is complete with sensors that can alert to the transit of WMD material.

The Syrian connection

This chapter's main focus however, is on the western Syrian–Iraqi border, the source of the brunt of jihadi transit, the *New York Times* once called it 'Iraq's Ho Chi Minh Trail',[2] and one of the driving factors shaping US–Syrian relations to the present day. It is based on research carried out in Syria over the past four years on the evolution of the geopolitics of this borderland as well as political relations between Damascus, Baghdad and Washington.

This story has proved an ever-changing narrative. It tells of Washington's ideological-strategic conundrum in dealing with Syria in respect to its Iraq policy. The US project in Iraq, which Thomas Ricks has described as a 'fiasco', has blunted the Bush Doctrine of pre-emptive regime change. The shifts in Iraq policy from the 2006 mid-term elections, the Baker–Hamilton Iraq Study Group report and the Petraeus 'surge' has led to a variety of engagements with Syria and Iran. Yet the nature of such engagement is somewhat disputed, made up of low-level regional conferences and Washington giving the 'green light' towards improved and more public bilateral ties being made by the respective states.[3]

So where does the narrative begin? Arguably the most obvious trigger was the much debated Coalition Provisional Authority's (CPA) decision to disband the Iraqi Security forces including the dissolution of a 35 000-strong Iraqi border guard that had been responsible for guarding six international borders covering a distance of over 3 000km.[4] The impact of dismissing the last bastions of the guardians of Iraq's frontiers was exacerbated by the geopolitical fallout from the invasion itself, not only in Iraq but throughout the region as the battle lines were drawn into three groups.

First the US and its 'moderate' allies: Turkey, Israel, Jordan, Egypt, Saudi Arabia and the Gulf States, the 'radical' states that opposed the US-led agenda: Iran, Syria and sections of Lebanon, and finally the non-state actors that flourished in the vacuums of sovereignty that followed state collapse in Afghanistan, Iraq and Lebanon: al Qaeda, Hizbullah and Fatah al-Islam, for instance.

Egyptian president Hosni Mubarrak warned that the invasion had created a hundred Bin Ladens[5] and US President George W. Bush famously urged them to 'bring it on'. And on they came; although it is widely accepted that the foreign fighters who travelled into Iraq have never comprised more than 10 per cent[6] amongst a largely Sunni-Iraqi insurgency estimated at points in 2005 and 2006 to stand at 30 000 to 60 000 strong.

In February 2006 the then Director of US National Intelligence, John Negroponte, delivered the annual threat assessment to the Senate Select Committee on Intelligence. His appraisal of the role of Syria is illuminating. He described it as that of a 'pivotal – but generally unhelpful – player in a troubled region'. Historian Philip Hitti, however, writing in 1951, described Syria as 'perhaps the largest small country on the map, microscopic in size but cosmic in influence'.[7] Visiting London in September 2006, Syrian Information Minister Dr. Mohsen Bilal responded to a question on why the US should engage Syria by stressing that Syria had influence 'beyond its borders'.[8] Jubin Goodarzi, speaking at Chatham House, London, the following month, stressed that Syria's inability to steer the region contrasts with its ability to 'thwart the ambitions of others'.[9]

Synthesising these views with the aim of defining a policy approach to the country suggests one that must balance Syria's pivotal role with its role as a spoiler. Such pragmatic and sensitive balancing of realities and ideas has not fit easily into the foreign policy machine of President George W. Bush however. Rather, his preference for black/white, evil/good solutions[10] has previously driven the now somewhat stalled 'Global War on Terror'.

Indeed, this is a key building block of this chapter's argument; that the US foreign policy machine has in the period 2001–2007 tended to churn out policy based on an often ideologically charged sense of how things should be done, rather than taking stock of realities on the ground and how things actually can be done. This changed considerably following the change of strategy in Iraq in 2007. In Washington Rumsfeld was replaced by the softly-spoken Robert Gates, who was a member of the Baker–Hamilton commission. In Iraq the rhetoric of General Casey was replaced by the pragmatism of General David Petraeus and throughout Baghdad officials in the Green Zone[11] tell of the replacement of personnel, from fresh-faced Republican ideologues in 2003–2004 to hard-bitten Arabist realists from 2006 onwards.

Thus the reasons behind the identity crisis of Iraq's borders can be seen both in the fallout from the invasion and in the post-9/11 paradigm shift from the ideas of a borderless world, to borders as barriers against the threat of terrorism. All of this comes up against the varying dynamics of six international borders whose histories and functionalities were and are far from modern Western norms.

Such a security-first paradigm would provide the context for the story of the Syrian management of its shared border with Iraq, that of a developing country being asked to seal, unilaterally and hermetically, a porous and largely desert line without US or international technical aid and in the face of an ever-volatile security situation on the Iraqi side. It is also the story of the way in which a seemingly functional issue such as border management can be caught up in the maelstrom of international relations and in particular highlights the inherent contradictions in the US government's overall policy approach to the regime in Damascus. Simply put – US animosity towards Syria post-9/11 led to the scenario in which Washington refused to help Syria help Iraq, and Damascus in turn looked to do its minimal best.

This chapter will now elaborate the dynamics introduced above by outlining the origins of the present day situation. It will briefly touch upon historical antecedents and outline borderland geography before attempting a critical appraisal of Syria's attempts at managing its border with Iraq following the 2003 invasion of the country by the US-led coalition.

Again, the significant point and crux of the argument is that a functional issue such as border securitisation has been transformed into a political football that has been kicked back and forth between the Syrian regime and the US administration with little input from either the nascent Iraqi government or its fledgling border guard.

Historical origins

In Ottoman times, desert regions such as the Iraqi–Syrian borderland tended to favour tribal autonomy. Mobile, nomadic communities, by their very nature, are more inclined and able to resist or evade central government. The Ottoman Empire never had more than nominal control over its Arabian subjects and was never able to collect taxes from any desert nomads.

Following World War I, the present borderland area was a 'no mans land'. The Arab Syrian government was only able to maintain a thin veneer of authority outside Damascus, despite the Sykes–Picot agreement of 1916 having placed the border at Raqqah, thereby including Mosul Vilayet in Syria. Because Iraqi officers were fighting in the Arab army the line was significantly shifted to Abu Kamal on the Euphrates, although British discovery of oil around Mosul meant that it was packaged into Iraq. This pre-state land swap prompted by colonial energy concerns rather than local characteristics is described by Tauber as a 'historical absurdity' that led to the creation of the border.[12]

After the post-war Paris peace conference and the imposition of French and British mandates onto the region, the Iraq–Syria boundary, which was agreed in the 'Franco-British convention' of 1920, was further defined in accordance with points connected to the mandates for Syria and Mesopotamia. As the implications of the finer details of such agreements evolved over time it became clear that officials on both the French and the British sides realised the futility of attempting to create lines of absolute sovereignty in an area characterised by historical freedoms from such control. In respect of the administration of the borderland between French mandated Syria and Mesopotamia, Gertrude Bell and A. T. Wilson presented the reality of what was likely to occur at the periphery of both administrations' control: 'It is clear that no Government will exercise effective control over Syrian desert. Governments are concerned only with the administration of settled districts and the relations of tribes to borders of cultivated land.'[13] Yet despite little hope for 'effective control', the 1920 convention went far in setting up policies to lead to such an end. Article 2 of the convention promised a more precise territorial definition than ever before, establishing a commission to 'trace on the spot the boundary line'. Article 3 of the convention promised to be a harbinger of future functional border issues; it outlined the need to come to an agreement over irrigation plans and the use of Tigris and Euphrates water, to avoid the French 'diminishing' Mesopotamian supplies. Functional agreements were also outlined in respect to railway networks with the British securing 'the right to transport troops'[14] across French mandated territory. The 1920 convention went so far as to grant railway lines their own 'extra-territoriality' status, such was their importance to British strategic thinking. Final delimitation details were settled in the League of Nations' report of the commission entrusted by the council with the study of the frontier between Syria and Iraq in 1932.

Syrian officials describe their border with Iraq as a difficult and harsh environment, a reflection both of its geography and the political history that has occurred in creating and developing it.[15] It is 376 miles in length. Beginning at the Turkish tri-point, at the confluence of the Tigris and the Lehabur rivers, the boundary follows the thalweg[16] of the Tigris downstream about 3.2 miles where it leaves the river. The boundary then trends in straight-line segments first south-westward about 68 miles and then southward about 153 miles to the Euphrates River. The boundary then continues in a straight line south-westward for a distance of about 152 miles to the Jordanian tri-point.

In terms of population and socio-economics it is worth emphasising the poverty of the borderland area, as well as recognising the tripartite division in terms of regional dynamics:[17]

1   From the Jordanian tri-point to the Euphrates River the border runs through full desert. It is a sparsely populated and a challenging environment, home to small Bedouin settlements, nomadic farming and little else.
2   North of the Euphrates is a more built-up area with villages on and along the border line. Villages such as Al Baguz are examples of settlements whose houses virtually cross the international border line itself.

Unsurprisingly perhaps this section of the border witnesses the highest incidence of illegal trade and border crossings.

3   The north-east corner of Syria, known as the 'Jazira' is characterised both by a history of more organised border control measures on either side as well as by the worst incidence of national poverty. The greater security both at and behind the border itself is linked to internal Syrian concerns with the indigenous Kurdish population and its connections with other Kurdish groups across the borders with Turkey and Iraq. In the Jazira ethnic-identity politics is exacerbated by the poverty; a UNDP report[18] identified that 58.1 per cent of the poor in Syria live in the north-east region[19] with 21 per cent of the rural population living on less than \$2 a day. Such poverty is visible in terms of poor quality housing, service provision, high unemployment and poor quality water sanitation supply systems.

Beyond a socio-economic description of the borderland itself it is important to understand the local people's attitude towards the border and what it actually means to them. The post-World War I carve up of historical 'greater Syria' into Palestine, Lebanon, Jordan and northern Iraq created a fundamental absence of legitimacy with regard to both Syria and Iraq's territorial parameters. Their shared boundary was perhaps the most overtly artificial colonial imposition of all, drawn up at a peripheral geo-strategic location vis-à-vis Damascus and Baghdad, the two centres of state power.

The implications were considerable. Both states devolved power to tribal proxies in order to maintain a nominal level of control at the borderland. The emergence of Ba'athist Arab nationalists from the ashes of colonial rule did not hugely alter this form of relationship. Border areas proved relatively infertile ground for the Ba'athist ideology. Tribal Sheikhs continued to play real leadership roles in the community providing their co-option to the state in exchange for increased levels of autonomy.

Tauber has argued that no two Arab states have endured as poor relations as Syria and Iraq.[20] This seemingly paradoxical conflict between two pan-Arab states lasted from 1968 to the mid-1990s. It witnessed cyclical periods of consolidation and conflict for regional influence and resources. Both sides supported proxies in the other's territory. Syria backed the Kurdish Democratic Party (KDP) and Patriotic Union of Kurdistan (PUK), while Iraq supported the Muslim Brotherhood in Syria and backed General Michel Aoun and the Maronites in Lebanon. Throughout the 1980s the states used posturing at the border to reflect general tensions between Damascus and Baghdad; they argued over Euphrates water resources, transit costs of Iraqi oil and at times moved large troop numbers to their respective frontiers.

Nevertheless, neither state fundamentally altered the peripheral autonomy in terms of society, economics and movement which existed at the borderland between them. Syrian officials wryly pointed out that in the 1980s they were unable to stop Saddam's truck bombs entering from Iraq and that if they could not protect themselves, what made Washington think that they could protect Iraq?[21]

In addition, both states historically have had larger priorities in terms of border security; Israel occupies the Syrian Golan Heights and, until 2005, Syria maintained a quasi-legitimate presence in Lebanon. Meanwhile, Iraq has experienced cyclical border disputes and actual conflict with Iran and Kuwait.

The invasion

Following this review of the Iraqi–Syrian border, it is necessary to analyse how the border issue became politicised to such a degree. Syria, through its own belligerence as well as its enemies' aggressive posturing, found itself at the epicentre of the 'Iraqi blame game'.

In the run up to the actual 2003 invasion, in line with both Syria's public opinion and geo-strategic interests at the time, President Assad was the region's most vocal critic of the US invasion. Marwan Qabalan of the Syrian National College of Defence argued that, 'Syria should have played the [Iraqi] game in a better way'.[22] Meanwhile, US officials in Damascus admit that the lack of support for the US invasion 'allowed Syria to enter the gun sights of people who hate Syria'.[23] Ammar Abdul Hamid of the Brookings Institute criticised a small number of people within the regime who benefited from the huge sums of illegal oil revenue crossing the Iraqi border prior to the war, a trade with an estimated annual value of $2 billion.[24]

In December 2004 as the security situation in Iraq continued to slide, President Bush urged Syria to 'stop the flow' of jihadis across the border. Concerns over the forward frontiers of US security meant that suddenly the functionality of Iraq's borders became an issue of concern in Washington. US attitudes towards border security had undergone a paradigm shift following the events of 9/11; there is now an overwhelming refocusing on 'preventing the entry of terrorists and weapons of mass destruction'[25] into the US. The 9/11 Commission Report stated clearly that 'countering terrorism has become, beyond any doubt, the top national security priority for the United States'.[26] John Donaldson, an International Boundary Research Unit (IBRU) research associate, is clear that 'we have witnessed the death of the concept of a borderless world'.[27] Indeed, Fukuyama's ideas of an 'end of history', characterised by the triumph of capitalist free markets that cross increasingly virtual borders, has been usurped by the re-branded US 'Long War' on global terror. This in turn has sparked massive debate in the US on border security and immigration issues. That President Bush promised to deploy an extra 6000 National Guard troops as part of a $1.9 billion refit to the security of the 2000 mile-long border with Mexico in May of 2006 was symptomatic of this shift in policy towards border management.

This institutional change, and in particular the 2002 Homeland Security Act that created the Department of Homeland Security, has significant implications for the future not only of US border management but also in the trickle-down effect that such changes will bring in terms of the standards and functions expected of other countries' control of their boundaries around the world.

In January 2005, the then Interim Iraqi Government Security official, Kasim Daoud, accused Iran and Syria of being 'two naughty boys'[28] for having been directly involved in assisting fighters transiting into Iraq. Reliable sources told the story of busloads of would-be fighters leaving from outside the Iraqi embassy in Damascus prior to the outbreak of war.[29] However there is no evidence that Syria *directly* facilitated even medium scale fighter transit following the outbreak of hostilities and the fall of the Iraqi regime. Instead, Syria's immediate reaction was to do its minimum best with regard to border security.

Border security starts with a good, solid strategy along the border itself, reinforced by policing and intelligence gathering behind the border. Along the actual frontier Syria claims that since 2005 it has made significant progress towards tightened security. The conclusion taken from the combination of these actions is that Syria is by no means an easy place from which to enter Iraq. However, there are also some glaring negative characteristics of the Syrian border security arrangements (explained below) which allow the issue of foreign fighters crossing from Syria to Iraq to remain a live issue of contention.

Yet it is worth noting that the Iraqi insurgency that emerged post-war constituted a largely indigenous force, with foreign elements playing regular deadly cameo appearances as 'force multipliers': those carrying out comparatively rare but highly destructive suicide attacks. The 'Iraqi' nature of the insurgency was reinforced as extremist foreign fighters such as Abu Musab al-Zarqawi were marginalised within the Mujahaddine Shura council, an umbrella organisation of Sunni Islamist groups, and the co-option of many fighters into groups of 'concerned citizens' following the shift in 2007 to the 'surge' strategy.

Syria has justified all changes to its border security along two lines. First, that once Iraq retains its security it can lead to the provision of a timetable for the withdrawal of coalition troops from their eastern neighbour, and second to prevent the 'bleed-back' of terrorists entering Syria from Iraq. In doing this the regime has taken a number of steps towards changing border function from what was a porous and nominally administrative line prior to the war to a security filter to personnel and materials crossing in either direction.

The development and improvement of this filter has been part of the Iraqi–Syrian reconciliation that followed the two countries re-establishing relations in 2006. In terms of the principle that border security starts with a good, solid strategy along the border itself, one can note that Syria has undertaken the following:

- The construction of 557 border posts situated along the border. Each spaced between 1 km and 3 km apart as imposed by the topographical nature of the terrain. Each post is manned by between 5 and 8 soldiers equipped with personal weapons and one fixed heavy weapon.

- The construction of an earth fence at a height of between 2 to 4 m.
- The upgrading of the three official crossing points. Although depending on security concerns 1 out of 3 of the crossings has been closed since 2004. Al Yaroubiyeh, in the north-east of the country, and Al-Tanf, close to the Jordanian tri-point have seen steadily increasing flows of both people and goods in both directions. The need for building materials and other goods in the relatively stable Kurdish Regional Government (KRG) controlled north, has seen a boom in traffic at the Al Yaroubiyeh crossing. This is characterised by queues of over 30 km of lorries backed-up on the Syrian side. There is also a rail service that travels across this border with two trains a day mainly carrying freight cargo.
- The overall size of the Syrian border security force numbers has oscillated around 10 000, troops having been redeployed to the east following the 2005 withdrawal from Lebanon. To put this reinforcement in context, prior to the war the guard on the Iraq border numbered only 700.

Furthermore, Western defence attachés in Syria have admitted that the Syrians have deployed over time and that a 'satisfactory' system of border coverage is in place.[30]

The Syrian Ministry of Interior has also introduced a new integrated computer system for all border entry points. This helps compensate for the fact that those from Arab countries have not required visas to enter. However, in October 2005 the Ministry of Interior issued a circular informing immigration and security officers that non-permanent resident males between the ages of 18–30 could be denied entry under a number of conditions, including travelling alone, student or recent graduate status, residence in a country other than their own, or suspicious travel abroad. Efforts were clearly being made to meet US concerns over the border.

By 2006, according to security officials,[31] Syrian efforts to control the border had resulted in the detention of over 1 300 extremists of different nationalities who were handed over to their country of origin through embassies and security channels. Syria then had 70 non-Syrian nationals in detention and at that time over 4 000 Syrians attempting to travel to Iraq illegally had been interrogated. Unsurprisingly there has been little work confirming these statistics. What work has been done looking at the numbers and backgrounds of would-be fighters has pointed to Saudi Arabia as the largest country of origin.[32] This said the weaknesses of Syrian efforts to control its border with Iraq have to be placed in the context of shifts in expectations of control informed by the paradigm shift in security dynamics.

A problem that has consistently impacted on all regional stakeholders has been the absence of communication. At a tactical level there is a complete absence of communication between the Syrian and US–Iraqi border patrols.[33] Syrians bemoan this fact that was born of the poverty of state to state relations. President Assad has used the absence of international support to defend Syrian actions; in 2004 he asked: 'Who to cooperate with? If you go to the border there are only Syrian guards on our side. But if you look at the Iraqi side there is nobody.'[34] Certainly the Iraqi border guards remain years from achieving both total border guard deployment and the actual ability to control the borders, following Paul Bremmer's ill-fated decision to disband the Iraqi armed forces, including a 35 000 strong border guard.

A simple incident highlights the absence of communication. When US forces closed the al-Qaim crossing in 2005 after taking fire from both sides of the border, they communicated the border's closure by using a catapult to send the message to the Syrian side of the border. Furthermore, a decision was taken banning local level communication from the Syrian border guard until state-to-state relations were improved. Such an absence of communication has inevitably led to failures of joint-intelligence. The Syrians claimed in 2006[35] that over 100 incidents have been recorded of US/Iraqi border guards targeting Syrian forces by accident. In such incidents the Syrians report six killed and 17 injured.

Non-state actors have looked to take advantage of the glaring weaknesses of the states within which they operate. In the case of foreign fighters crossing from Syria many take advantage of the inability of the Syrian military to patrol effectively at night. This is due to a combination of poor training and equipment. Syrian efforts to secure such equipment came close to fruition in 2005 when the British were involved as providers. However the 14 February 2005 assassination of former Lebanese Prime Minister Rafik Hariri put a halt to such a deal.

Two-man Syrian patrols, regardless of reinforcement numbers, have been unable or unwilling to challenge well-equipped and often large numbers of smugglers who are familiar with the terrain. What is more it is often the 'flight' stage of crossing the actual border line that is the most difficult to prevent. Pre-border interdiction remains a more effective means of control, especially considering the sparsely populated borderland area. However, preventative policing of 'would-be fighters' is proving a significant challenge to the Syrians. The profiling of those crossing; mainly Arabs, most with no criminal record and not carrying weapons, means that, in a country which welcomes significant numbers of Arab visitors each year, finding the guilty is not easy.

In addition the distance of the border from large cities such as Aleppo and Damascus means that the actual period of flight can occur within 24 hours. Poor airport screening[36] and high levels of corruption amongst Syrian officials, combine to make it easier for people to enter into Iraq. The border line itself is characterised by an ease of crossing as, unlike fenced or walled frontiers, the sand bearm border is easy to traverse on foot. Nor is it particularly difficult to move enough of it with a shovel to secure access for a four by four vehicle. The bearm has been in place for over four years and has suffered a large degree of natural weathering.

Future dynamics

It is recognised by Western officials in Damascus that the Syrians have done as much as they can to secure their border with Iraq.[37] Put simply, the reality is that Syria is doing well and that their Iraqi counterparts are a long way behind.[38]

In March 2005 General Abizaid, then head of CENTCOM, admitted that 'the Syrians had moved against the foreign fighters', yet the level of political sensitivity over isolating Syria and excusing the poor situation in Iraq saw President Bush in a speech in the same month blame al Qaeda fighters coming in from Syria as the enemy that US troops are presently engaged with.[39] One of the major reasons for the success of the 2007 'surge' strategy in reducing violence in Iraq was linked to the co-option of Iraqi Sunnis into 'concerned citizens' militias and using them to target foreign fighter al Qaeda elements.

On the other side of the border the Syrians have pushed border security high up their reform agenda. Their current approach can be characterised as a transition from the 'stone age to the space age' as old fashioned human-based approaches are replaced by state-of-the-art alternatives.

In 2006 a British security solution provider was contacted by the Syrian Ministry of Interior with the question 'what can we do to improve border security?'[40] The firm suggested the Syrians should acquire a full border perimeter security solution consisting of a 3 m high double-line security fence fitted with micro-strain fibre optic sensing equipment. This would be monitored by thermal imaging surveillance cameras which would transfer information to a network-able command and control centre. Yet implementation of such ideas remained on hold as the Syrians were looking for international finance for such schemes.[41]

In January 2008 reports suggested that behind the scenes deals had been made and that the State Department had provided the license for the sale of advanced computers for a Syrian border surveillance programme. US firm Cisco would supply $2.2 million in equipment for the 'Modernization of Syrian Customs Directorate' which was scheduled for completion sometime in 2008.[42]

Furthermore, customs control steadily emerged to the forefront of Syria's recent regional economic policy. In light of the security issues at the Iraqi and Lebanese borders, the government commissioned the UNDP in 2005 to improve custom measures at the 65 international entry points into Syria.[43]

The UNDP, in conjunction with the Customs Department, the EU and UNCTAD, by 2008 are scheduled to complete a three year process designed to implant automation at Syria's border posts. Although motivated primarily by security concerns in light of international concerns over WMD, weapons and terrorist transits, the program aimed to increase transparency, facilitation of trade and general customs services. Custom Project-Director Dr. Ihab Wattar gave the example of their forthcoming ability to trace vehicles trying to enter Syria within 24 hours of a 'security incident' from any neighbouring country such as Iraq, Jordan and Lebanon.[44]

Syria will be the only Arab country equipped with ASYCUDA World – a computerised customs management system which covers most foreign trade procedures. The system handles manifests and customs declarations, accounting procedures, and transit and suspense procedures. The ASYCUDA system allows vehicles and goods to be tracked in and out of separate entry and exit points. It also cuts out any cash transactions at customs posts, thereby significantly reducing the potential for corruption. The estimated cost of the project is \$8.5m, of which 5–10 per cent is paid for by the UNDP.[45]

Conclusions

US policy towards securing Iraq's borders has evolved steadily from the 2003 invasion from a policy premised on hope to one that recognises realities. The dismantling of Iraqi state structures and disbanding of all security forces combined an internal weakness with a US regional agenda that encouraged neighbouring enemies such as Syria and Iran to allow external factors to exacerbate the situation in the country.

Iranian policy, not the subject of this chapter, has arguably been the more pro-active whilst the Syrian–Iraqi border and its evolution from a line in the sand patrolled by a few hundred guards to a effective security filter buffered by thousands, is a reflection of how the post-9/11 paradigm shift has altered the perception of how forward borders should function.

The shift in strategy following the Baker–Hamilton report and the birth of the surge was combined with a regional security outreach alongside the co-option of elements of the insurgency to fight a wider war against al Qaeda. Securing the support of the people on both sides of the border in addition to kinetic security measures is a reflection of how the hearts and minds approach can be transferred to the complex social science phenomena that are international boundary lines.

Notes

1 Tahir-Kheli and Ayubi, *The Iran-Iraq war: New Weapons, Old Conflicts* (New York: Praeger, 1983), 5.
2 John Burns, 'Iraq's Ho Chi Minh Trail', *New York Times*, 5 June 2005, www.nytimes.com/2005/06/05/weekinreview/05burn.html.
3 Syria and Iraq restored diplomatic ties in November 2006 in what Iraqi Foreign Minister Zebari described as 'a new page in relations between the two countries'. *Al Jazeera*, http://english.aljazeera.net/NR/exeres/ECCAE12E-EDA5–473C-BBF2-B4BC8B839433.htm.
4 By way of comparison that is only slightly shorter than the US–Mexican border.
5 'Mubarak Says Iraq War Will Produce "100 bin Ladens"', Reuters, 31 March 2003, www.commondreams.org/headlines03/0331–01.htm.
6 Brian Whitaker, 'Report attacks "myth" of foreign fighters', *Guardian* (London), 23 September 2005, www.guardian.co.uk/world/2005/sep/23/iraq.ewenmacaskill.

7 Philip Hitti, *History of Syria, Including Lebanon and Palestine* (London: Macmillan, 1951), 3.
8 Anonymous interview, London, September 2006.
9 Jubin Goodarzi, 'Syria and Iran: An Enduring Alliance – 1979 to Present', speech by Middle East analyst and author of *Syria and Iran: Diplomatic Alliance and Power Politics in the Middle East* (London: I.B. Tauris, 2006); Chatham House Event, 2 October 2006.
10 David Ryan, *Frustrated Empire: US Foreign Policy from 9/11 to Iraq* (London: Pluto, 2007).
11 Anonymous interview, March 2007.
12 E. Tauber, *The Formation of Modern Syria and Iraq* (Ilford: Frank Cass, 1995), 43.
13 Note by India Office on Foreign Office Memorandum (November, 1918). British National Archives.
14 Franco-British Convention, Anglo-French Negotiations over the Boundaries of Palestine, 1919–1920, John J. McTague Jr., *Journal of Palestine Studies*, vol. 11, no. 2 (Winter, 1982), pp. 100–112.
15 Anonymous interview, July 2005.
16 Central flow of a river.
17 Note this information was obtained through participant observation and the author actually living and visiting all sections of the border at various times between 2005 and 2007.
18 'Poverty in Syria', UNDP Report, June 2005, www.undp.org.sy/publications/national/Poverty/Poverty_In_Syria_en.pdf.
19 Which in their survey included Idleb, Aleppo, Al Raqqa, Deir Ezzor and Hassakeh.
20 Tauber, *Formation of Modern Syria*, 56.
21 Anonymous interview, July 2005.
22 Anonymous interview, August 2006.
23 Anonymous interview, August 2006.
24 Anonymous interview, August 2006.
25 US Patrol, May 2005, www.globalsecurity.org/security/library/report/2005/050524-border-final-version.pdf.
26 T. Kean and L. Hamilton, *The 9/11 Commission Report* (New York: W. W. Norton, 2004).
27 Anonymous interview, June 2006.
28 Al Pessin, 'Iraqi Official says Syria and Iran Helping Insurgents', IWS, 27 January 2005, www.iwar.org.uk/news-archive/2005/01–27.htm.
29 Anonymous interview, August 2006.
30 Anonymous interviews, August 2006.
31 Anonymous interview, August 2006.
32 Ian Black, 'Saudis Make up 41 per cent of Foreign Fighters in Iraq', *Guardian* (London), 23 November 2007, www.guardian.co.uk/world/2007/nov/23/iraq.saudiarabia.
33 The US and Iraqi security forces are combined here as some form of integrated force structure has largely been in place – whether logistical or intelligence support, or embedded troops.
34 Speech of President Bashar al-Assad, Damascus University, June 2004, www.cggl.org/scripts/document.asp?id=46245.
35 Anonymous interview, June 2006.
36 Officials have described how 'eyeballing' potential criminals is as high-tech as it gets, Anonymous interviews, August–September 2006.
37 Anonymous interviews, August 2006.
38 Anonymous interviews, August 2006.

39 George Bush, President Discusses War on Terror, White House, 8 March 2005, www.whitehouse.gov/news/releases/2005/03/20050308-3.html.
40 Anonymous interview, March 2006.
41 Anonymous interview, August 2006.
42 'U.S. Sells Syria Dual-use Tech That Could be Used by Iran', *World Tribune*, 31 January 2008 www.worldtribune.com/worldtribune/WTARC/2008/ss_Syria_01_30.asp.
43 Modernization of the Customs Directorate Project, UNDP Report, 12 December 2007, www.undp.org.sy/pdf/customs.pdf?phpMyAdmin=OczIuASiMipdGobrTTvqOorif0d.
44 Anonymous interview, August 2006.
45 Background interview with UNDP official (anonymous), August 2006.

Bibliography

Aburish, Said, *A Brutal Friendship: The West and the Arab Elite*, New York: St. Martin's Press, 1998.

——. *Saddam Hussein: The Politics of Revenge*, New York and London: Bloomsbury Publishing, 2000.

——. *Nasser: The Last Arab*, New York: St. Martin's Press, 2004.

Amirahmadi, H. (ed.), *The United States and the Middle East: A Search for New Perspectives*, Albany: State University of New York, 1993.

Amnesty International, *Beyond Abu Ghraib: Detention and Torture in Iraq*, 2006.

Asad, Talal, *Genealogies of Religion: Discipline and reasons of power in Christianity and Islam*, Baltimore: Johns Hopkins University Press, 1993.

Bacevich, Andrew, *American Empire: The Realities and Consequences of American Diplomacy*, Cambridge: Harvard University Press, 2002.

Baker, James A. and Lee H. Hamilton, *The Iraq Study Group Report*, New York: Vintage Books, 2006.

Balmer, Randall, *Thy Kingdom Come: How the Religious Right Distorts the Faith and Threatens America: An Evangelical's Lament*, New York: Basic Books, 2006.

Bamford, James, *A Pretext for War: 9/11, Iraq and the Abuse of America's Intelligence Agencies*, New York: Doubleday, 2004.

Baritz, Loren, *Backfire: A History of How American Culture Led Us into Vietnam and Made Us Fight the Way We Did*, New York: Ballantine Books, 1985.

Batutu, Hanna, *The Old Social Classes and the Revolutionary Movements of Iraq*, Princeton: Princeton University Press, 1982.

Bell, Daniel, *The Winding Passage: Essays and Journeys 1960–1980*, New York: Basic Books, 1980.

Ben-Ami, Shlomo, *Scars of War, Wounds of Peace: The Arab–Israeli Tragedy*, London: Phoenix, 2006.

Bill, James, *The Eagle and the Lion: The Tragedy of American-Iranian Relations*, New Haven: Yale University Press, 1988.

Blackwell, Stephen, 'Pursuing Nasser: The Macmillan Government and the Management of British Policy Towards the Middle East Cold War, 1957–63', *Cold War History*, vol. 4, no. 3 (April 2004).

Blum, William, *Killing Hope: US Military and CIA Interventions Since World War II*, Monroe, Maine: Common Courage Press, 2004.

Bose, Meena and Rosanna Perotti (eds), *From Cold War to New World Order: The Foreign Policy of George Bush*, Westport, CT: Greenwood Press, 2002.

Bouillon, Markus, David Malone and Ben Rowsell (eds), *Preventing Another Generation of Conflict*, Boulder, CO: Lynne Rienner Publishers, 2007.

Bourdieu, Pierre, *The Field of Cultural Production: Essays on Art and Literature*, New York: Columbia University Press, 1993.

Bowen, Jeremy, *Six Days: How the 1967 War Shaped the Middle East*, London: Pocket, 2004.

Bradford, J. A., *Proconsuls and CINCs from the Roman Republic to the Republic of the United States of America: Lessons for the Pax Americana*, Fort Leavenworth, KS: School of Advanced Military Studies, 2001.

Brands, H. W., *What America Owes The World: The Struggle for the Soul of Foreign Policy*, Cambridge: Cambridge University Press, 1998.

Bremer, L. Paul., with Malcolm McConnell, *My Year in Iraq. The Struggle to Build a Future of Hope*, New York: Simon & Schuster, 2006.

Brzezinski, Z., *Power and Principle: Memoirs of the National Security Adviser, 1977–1981*, New York: Farrar, Straus, Giroux, 1983.

Bush, George and Brent Scowcroft, *A World Transformed*, New York: Alfred A. Knopf, 1998.

Cannon, Lou and Carl M. Cannon, *Reagan's Disciple: George W. Bush's Troubled Quest for a Presidential Legacy*, New York: Public Affairs, 2008.

Caton, Steven C., *Lawrence of Arabia: A Film's Anthropology*, Berkeley, CA: University of California Press, 1999.

Chesterman, Simon, *You, the People: The United Nations, Transitional Administrations, and State-building*, Oxford: Oxford University Press, 2004.

Chomsky, Noam, *World Orders, Old and New*, New York: Columbia University Press, 1994.

Clarke, Michael, 'The Diplomacy that Led to War in Iraq', in Paul Cornish, (ed.), *The Conflict in Iraq, 2003*, Basingstoke: Palgrave Macmillan, 2004.

Clarke, Richard A., *Against All Enemies: Inside America's War on Terror*, New York: Free Press, 2004.

Cordesman, Anthony H., *Iraq and Foreign Volunteers*, Washington, DC: Center for Strategic and International Studies, 2005.

Croft, Stuart, *Culture, Crisis and America's War on Terror*, Cambridge: Cambridge University Press, 2006.

Daalder, Ivo H. and James M. Lindsay, *America Unbound: The Bush Revolution in Foreign Policy*, Washington, DC: Brookings Institution Press, 2003.

Dallek, Robert, *Nixon and Kissinger: Partners in Power*, New York: Harper Collins, 2007.

Dann, Uriel, *Iraq Under Qassem: A Political History, 1958–1963*, New York: Praeger, 1969.

Danner, Mark, *Torture and Truth: America, Abu Ghraib, and the War on Terror*, New York: New York Review Books, 2004.

Darwish, Adel, *Unholy Babylon: The Secret History of Saddam's War*, New York: St. Martin's Press, 1991.

Diamond, Larry, *Squandered Victory: The American Occupation and the Bungled Effort to Bring Democracy to Iraq*, New York: Times Books, 2005.

Dionne, E. J., *Souled Out: Reclaiming Faith and Politics after the Religious Right*, Princeton University Press, 2008.

Dodge, Toby, *Inventing Iraq: The Failure of Nation-building and a History Denied*, New York: Columbia University Press, 2003.

——. 'The Invasion of Iraq and the Reordering the Post Colonial World', *Newsletter of the British International Studies Association* (no. 79, January 2004).

——. 'Iraqi Transitions: From Regime Change to State Collapse', *Third World Quarterly*, vol. 26, no. 4 (2005).

——. *Iraq's Future: The Aftermath of Regime Change*, Adelphi Paper 372, Abingdon: Routledge for the International Institute for Strategic Studies, 2005.

——. 'The Sardinian, the Texan and the Tikriti: Gramsci, the Comparative Autonomy of the Middle Eastern State and Regime Change in Iraq', *International Politics*, vol. 43, no. 4 (2006).

——. 'Review Essay. How Iraq was Lost', *Survival*, vol. 48. no. 4 (Winter 2006–07).

Dumbrell, John and David Ryan (eds), *Vietnam in Iraq: Tactics, Lessons, Legacies and Ghosts*, London: Routledge, 2007.

Eisenstadt, Shmuel, *Max Weber on Charisma and Institution Building*, Chicago: University of Chicago Press, 1968.

Emerson, Michael O. and Christian Smith, *Divided by Faith: Evangelical Religion and the Problem of Race in America*, New York: Oxford University Press, 2000.

Eppel, Michael, *Iraq from Monarchy to Tyranny: From the Hashemites to the Rise of Saddam*, Gainesville: University Press of Florida, 2004.

Fain, W. Taylor, 'John F. Kennedy and Harold Macmillan: Managing the "Special Relationship" in the Persian Gulf Region, 1961–63', *Middle Eastern Studies*, vol. 38, no. 4 (October 2002).

Falk, Richard A., *The Costs of War: International Law, the UN, and World Order After Iraq*, New York: Routledge, 2008.

Farouk-Sluglett, Marion and Peter Sluglett, 'The Historiography of Modern Iraq', *The American Historical Review*, December 1991.

——. *Iraq Since 1958: From Revolution to Dictatorship*, rev. edn, London: I. B. Tauris, 2001.

Fieldhouse, D. K., *Western Imperialism in the Middle East*, New York: Oxford University Press, 2006.

Fisk, Robert, *The Great War for Civilisation: The Conquest of the Middle East*, London: Fourth Estate, 2005.

Freedman, Lawrence and Efraim Karsh, *The Gulf Conflict: Diplomacy and War in the New World Order*, London: Faber, 1993.

Fromkin, David, *A Peace to End All Peace*, New York: Henry Holt, 1989.

Frum, David, *The Right Man: An Inside Account of the Surprise Presidency of George W. Bush*, London: Weidnfeld & Nicolson, 2003.

Fukuyama, Francis, *After the Neocons: America at the Crossroads*, London: Profile, 2006.

Fulbright, J. William, *The Arrogance of Power*, New York: Random House, 1967.

Fursenko, Aleksandr and Timothy Naftali, *Khrushchev's Cold War: The Inside Story of an American Adversary*, New York: W. W. Norton, 2006.

Gaddis, John Lewis, 'A Grand Strategy of Transformation', *Foreign Policy*, November/December 2002.

Galula, David, *Counterinsurgency Warfare: Theory and Practice*, PSI, 2006.

Garthoff, Raymond, *Détente and Confrontation: American-Soviet Relations from Nixon to Reagan*, Washington, DC: Brookings Institution, 1994.

Gasiorowski, Mark J., 'The 1953 Coup d'Etat in Iran', *International Journal of Middle East Studies*, vol. 19, no. 3 (August 1987).

Gender, Irene L., *Notes from the Minefield: United States Intervention in Lebanon and the Middle East, 1945–1958*, New York: Columbia University Press, 1997.

Gold, D., *America, the Gulf and Israel: CENTCOM (Central Command) and Emerging US Regional Security Policies in the Middle East*, Jerusalem: Jaffee Center for Strategic Studies, 2003.

Goldsmith, Jack, *The Terror Presidency*, New York: W. W. Norton, 2007.

Goodarzi, Jubin, *Syria and Iran: Diplomatic Alliance and Power Politics in the Middle East*, London: I. B. Tauris, 2006.

Gordon, Michael and Bernard Trainor, *Cobra II: The Inside Story of the Invasion and Occupation of Iraq*, London: Atlantic, 2006.

Greenberg, Karen J., Joshua L. Dratel, and Anthony Lewis (eds), *The Torture Papers: The Road to Abu Ghraib*, New York: Cambridge University Press, 2005.

Greene, Jack P., *The Intellectual Construction of America: Exceptionalism and Identity from 1492 to 1800*, Chapel Hill: University of North Carolina Press, 1993.

Gregory, D., *The Colonial Present: Afghanistan, Palestine, Iraq*, Oxford: Blackwell, 2004.

Griffith, R. Marie and Melani McAlister, 'Introduction: Is the Public Square Still Naked?', *American Quarterly*, vol. 59, no. 3 (September 2007).

Hahn, Peter L., *The United States, Great Britain, and Egypt, 1945–1956*, Chapel Hill: University of North Carolina Press, 1991.

Haldeman, H. R., *The Ends of Power*, London: Sedgwick & Jackson, 1978.

Hall, David D., *Lived Religion in America*, Princeton, NJ: Princeton University Press, 1997.

Halper, Stephan and Jonathan Clarke, *America Alone: The Neo-Conservatives and the Global Order*, Cambridge: Cambridge University Press, 2004.

Hanhimaki, Jussi, *Flawed Architect, Henry Kissinger and American Foreign Policy*, New York: Oxford University Press, 2004.

Harvey, D., *The New Imperialism*, Oxford: Oxford University Press, 2005.

Hendrickson, David C., *The Imperial Temptation: The New World Order and America's Purpose*, New York: Council on Foreign Relations, 1992.

Hersh, Seymour M., *Chain of Command: The Road from 9/11 to Abu Ghraib*, London: Allen Lane, 2004.

Hertzke, Allen, *Freeing God's Children: The Unlikely Alliance for Global Human Rights*, Lanham, MD: Rowman & Littlefield, 2004.

Hitti, Philip, *History of Syria, including Lebanon and Palestine*, London: Macmillan, 1951.

Hodson, Joel, *Lawrence of Arabia and American Culture*, Westport, Conn.: Greenwood Press, 1995.

Hunt, Michael H., *Ideology and US Foreign Policy*, New Haven: Yale University Press, 1987.

Ikenberry, G. J., 'America's Imperial Ambition', *Foreign Affairs*, September/October, 2002.

International Crisis Group, 'In their Own Words: Reading the Iraqi Insurgency', *Middle East Report*, no. 50, 15 February 2006.

Isaacson, Walter, *Kissinger: A Biography*, London: Faber and Faber, 1992.

Jabar, F. A., *The Shi'ite Movement in Iraq*, London: Saqi, 2003.

Jenkins, Philip, *The Next Christendom: The Coming of Global Christianity*, New York: Oxford University Press, 2002.

John Nagl, *Learning to Eat Soup with a Knife: Counterinsurgency Lessons from Malaya and Vietnam*, Chicago: University of Chicago Press, 2005.

Kean, T. and Lee Hamilton, *The 9/11 Commission Report*, New York: W. W. Norton, 2004.

Kinzer, Stephen, *All the Shah's Men: An American Coup and the Roots of Middle East Terror*, Hoboken, NJ: John Wiley & Sons, 2003.

——. *Overthrow: America's Century of Regime Change from Hawaii to Iraq*, New York: Times Books, 2004.

Kissinger, Henry, *White House Years*, Boston: Little Brown, 1979.

——. *Years of Renewal*, New York: Simon & Schuster, 1999.

Klare, Michael, *Resource Wars: The New Landscape of Global Conflict*, New York: Owl Books, 2002.

——. *Blood and Oil: The Dangers and Consequences of America's Growing Dependency on Imported Petroleum*, New York: Owl Books, 2004.

Klein, Naomi, *The Shock Doctrine: The Rise of Disaster Capitalism*, New York: Metropolitan Books, 2007.

Krauthammer, Charles, 'The Unipolar Moment', *Foreign Affairs*: America and the World 1990/1.

Krepinevich, Andrew, *The Army and Vietnam*, Baltimore: Hopkins Press, 1986.

Kuklick, Bruce, *Blind Oracles: Intellectuals and War from Kennan to Kissinger*, Princeton: Princeton University Press, 2006.

Kyle, Keith, *Suez*, New York: St. Martin's Press, 1991.

Leffler, Melvyn, *A Preponderance of Power: National Security, the Truman Administration, and the Cold War*, Stanford, CA: Stanford University Press, 1992.

Lesser, I. O., *Oil, the Persian Gulf, and Grand Strategy: Contemporary Issues in Historical Perspective*, Santa Monica, CA: RAND Corporation, 2001.

Levite, A. E., B. W. Jentleson, and L. Berman (eds), *Foreign Military Intervention: The Dynamics of Protracted Conflict*, New York: Columbia University Press, 1992.

Little, Douglas, 'His Finest Hour? Eisenhower, Lebanon, and the 1958 Crisis in the Middle East', *Diplomatic History*, vol. 20, no. 1 (Winter 1996).

——. *American Orientalism: The United States and the Middle East since 1945*, Chapel Hill: University of North Carolina Press, 2002.

——. 'Mission Impossible: The CIA and the Cult of Covert Action in the Middle East', *Diplomatic History*, vol. 28, no. 5 (November 2004).

McAlister, Melani, *Epic Encounters: Culture, Media, and U.S. Interests in the Middle East Since 1945*, updated edn, Berkeley: University of California Press, 2005.

McCrisken, Trevor B., 'Exceptionalism', in Alexander DeConde, Richard Dean Burns, and Fredrik Logevall, eds, *Encyclopedia of American Foreign Policy*, 2nd edn, New York: Charles Scribner's Sons, 2002.

——. *American Exceptionalism and the Legacy of Vietnam: US Foreign Policy Since 1974*, Basingstoke: Palgrave Macmillan, 2003.

McMahon, Robert J., 'Credibility and World Power: Exploring the Psychological Dimension in Postwar American Diplomacy', *Diplomatic History*, vol. 15, no. 4 (Fall 1991).

McNaugher, T.L., *Arms and Oil: U.S. Strategy and the Persian Gulf*, Washington, DC: Brookings Institution, 1985.

Mann, James, *Rise of the Vulcans: A History of Bush's War Cabinet*, New York: Viking, 2004.

Marshall, Paul A., *Their Blood Cries Out: The Untold Story of Persecution against Christians in the Modern World*, Dallas: World Publishing, 1997.

Martin, R., *An Empire of Indifference: American War and the Financial Logic of Risk Management*, Durham: Duke University Press, 2007.

Mervin, David, *George Bush and the Guardianship Presidency*, Basingstoke: Macmillan, 1996.

Mirsky, Jonathan, 'Reconsidering Vietnam', *The New York Review of Books*, vol. 28, no. 15 (10 October 1991).

Morris, L. Robert and Lawrence Raskin, *Lawrence of Arabia: The 30th Anniversary Pictorial History*, New York: Doubleday, 1992.

Morrissey, John, *Negotiating Colonialism*, London: HGRG, Royal Geographical Society, 2003

———. 'War, Geopolitics and Imaginative Geographies', in J. Morrissey, U. Strohmayer, Y. Whelan and B. Yeoh, *Key Concepts in Historical Geography*, London: Sage, forthcoming.

Noll, Mark A., *American Evangelical Christianity: An Introduction*, Oxford: Blackwell Publishers, 2001.

Nye Jr., Joseph S., *Soft Power: The Means To Success In World Politics*, New York: Public Affairs, 2004.

Oren, Michael, *Six Days of War: June 1967 and the Making of the Modern Middle East*, London: Penguin, 2003.

Osgood, Kenneth, *Total Cold War: Eisenhower's Secret Propaganda Battle at Home and Abroad*, Lawrence: University Press of Kansas, 2006.

Ovendale, Ritchie, 'Great Britain and the Anglo-American Invasion of Jordan and Lebanon in 1958', *International History Review*, vol. 16, no. 2 (May 1994).

Packer, George, *Assassins' Gate. America in Iraq*, New York: Farrar, Straus and Giroux, 2005.

Palast, Greg, *Armed Madhouse: Undercover Dispatches From a Dying Regime*, London: Penguin, 2007.

Perle, Richard and David Frum, *An End to Evil: How to Win the War on Terror*, New York: Random House, 2003.

Pfiffner, Jim, *Power Play: The Bush Presidency and the Constitution*, Washington DC: The Brookings Institution Press, 2008.

Phillips, David L., *Losing Iraq. Inside the Post-war Reconstruction Fiasco*, New York: Basic Books, 2005.

Podeh, Elie, '"Suez in Reverse": The Arab Response to the Iraqi Bid for Kuwait, 1961–63', *Diplomacy & Statecraft*, vol. 14, no. 1 (March 2003).

Pollack, Kenneth M., 'Next Stop Baghdad?' *Foreign Affairs*, vol. 81, no. 2 (2002).

———. *The Threatening Storm: The Case for Invading Iraq*, New York: Random House, 2002.

———. 'Securing the Gulf', *Foreign Affairs*, vol. 82 no. 3 (2003).

Powell, Colin, *A Soldier's Way: An Autobiography*, London: Hutchinson, 1995.

Prados, John, *Hoodwinked: The Documents that Reveal How Bush Sold Us a War*, New York: New Press, 2004.

Quandt, William, Fuad Jabber, Ann Mosley Lesch, *The Politics of Palestinian Nationalism*, Berkeley: University of California Press, 1973.

Quandt, William, *Peace Process: American Diplomacy and the Arab–Israeli Conflict Since 1967*, Washington: Brookings Institution, 2001.

Rabinovich, Abraham, *The Yom Kippur War: The Epic Encounter that Transformed the Middle East*, New York: Shocken Books, 2004.

Randall, Stephen, *United States Foreign Oil Policy Since World War I: For Profits and Security*, Toronto: McGill-Queens University Press, 2005.

Record, Jeffrey, *The Rapid Deployment Force and U.S. Military Intervention in the Persian Gulf*, Washington, DC: Institute for Foreign Policy Analysis, 1981.

——. *Making War, Thinking History: Munich, Vietnam, and Presidential Uses of Force from Korea to Kosovo*, Annapolis: Naval Institute Press, 2002.

Renshon, Stanley A., *In His Father's Shadow: The Transformations of George W. Bush*, New York: Palgrave Macmillan, 2004.

Reveron, D. S. (ed.), *America's Viceroys: The Military and U.S. Foreign Policy*, New York: Palgrave Macmillan, 2004.

Risen, James, *State of War: The Secret History of the Bush Administration and the CIA*, New York: Free Press, 2006.

Robinson, W. I., *Promoting Polyarchy, Globalization, US Intervention and Hegemony*, Cambridge: Cambridge University Press, 1996.

Roper, Jon, 'Europe's Vietnam Syndrome: America and the Quagmire of Iraq', in John Dumbrell and David Ryan, eds, *Vietnam in Iraq: Tactics, Lessons, Legacies and Ghosts*, London: Routledge, 2007.

Rouleau, Eric, 'Trouble in the Kingdom', *Foreign Affairs*, vol. 81 no. 4 (2002).

Ryan, David, *US Foreign Policy in World History*, London: Routledge, 2000.

——. *Frustrated Empire: US Foreign Policy, 9/11 to Iraq*, London: Pluto Press, 2007.

Said, Edward, *Covering Islam: How the Media and the Experts Determine How We See the Rest of the World*, London: Vintage, 1997.

Salinger, Pierre, with Eric Laurent, *Secret Dossier: The Hidden Agenda behind the Gulf War*, London: Penguin, 1991.

Schiff, Ze'ev and Ehud Ya'ari, *Israel's Lebanon War*, London: Unwin Paperbacks, 1984.

Schlesinger Jr., Arthur, *The Vital Center*, Boston: Houghton Mifflin Company, 1949.

——. *The Imperial Presidency*, Boston: Houghton Mifflin Company, 1989.

Schwarzkopf, Norman H., *It Doesn't Take a Hero*, New York: Bantam Books, 1992.

Shapiro, M. J., *Violent Cartographies: Mapping Cultures of War*, Minneapolis: University of Minnesota Press, 1997.

Shawcross, William, *The Shah's Last Ride: The Story of the Exile, Misadventures and Death of the Emperor*, London: Pan Books, 1989.

Shea, Nina, *In the Lion's Den: A Shocking Account of Persecuted and Martyrdom of Christians Today and How We Should Respond*, Nashville, TN: Broadman & Holman Publishers, 1997.

Shemesh, Haim, *Soviet–Iraqi Relations, 1968–1988: In the Shadow of the Iraq-Iran Conflict*, Boulder, CO: Lynne Rienner, 1992.

Shlaim, Avi, 'Israel, the Great Powers, and the Middle East Crisis of 1958', *Journal of Imperial and Commonwealth History*, vol. 12, no. 2 (May 1999).

——. *Lion of Jordan: The Life of King Hussein in War and Peace*, London: Allen Lane, 2007.

Sifry, Micah L. and Christopher Cerf (eds), *The Gulf War Reader: History, Documents, Opinions*, New York: Random House, 1991.

Smith, N., *The Endgame of Globalization*, New York: Routledge, 2005.

Smith, Tony, *A Pact with the Devil: Washington's Bid for World Supremacy and the Betrayal of the American Promise*, New York: Routledge, 2007.

Smolansky, Oles and Bettie Smolansky, *The USSR and Iraq: The Soviet Quest for Influence*, Durham, NC: Duke University Press, 1991.

Solomon, Lewis D., *Paul Wolfowitz: Visionary Intellectual, Policymaker, Strategist*, Westport: Praeger Security International, 2007.

Statler, Kathryn C. and Andrew L. Johns (eds), *The Eisenhower Administration, the Third World, and the Globalization of the Cold War*, Lanham, Md.: Rowman and Littlefield, 2006.

Suri, Jeremy, *Power and Protest: Global Revolution and the Rise of Détente*, Cambridge: Harvard University Press, 2003.

Suskind, Ron, *The Price of Loyalty: George W. Bush, the White House, and the Education of Paul O'Neill*, New York: Simon & Shuster, 2004.

Takeyh, Ray, *The Origins of the Eisenhower Doctrine: The US, Britain and Nasser's Egypt, 1953–57*, New York: St. Martin's Press, 2000.

Tal, Lawrence, 'Britain and the Jordan Crisis of 1958', *Middle East Studies*, vol. 31, no. 1 (January 1995).

Tauber, E., *The Formation of Modern Syria and Iraq*, Ilford: Frank Cass, 1995.

Telhami, S., *The Stakes: America and the Middle East*, Boulder, CO: Westview Press, 2002.

Tenet, George, *At the Center of the Storm: My Years at the CIA*, New York: Harper Collins, 2007.

Tripp, Charles, *A History of Iraq*, Cambridge, UK: Cambridge University Press, 2000.

Truman, Harry S., *Memoirs by Harry S. Truman*, New York: Doubleday & Co, Inc., 1956.

Wallis, Jim, *God's Politics: Why the Right Gets It Wrong and the Left Doesn't Get It*, San Francisco: HarperSanFrancisco, 2005.

——. *The Great Awakening: Reviving Faith & Politics in a Post-Religious Right America*, New York: HarperOne, 2008.

Weisman, Alan, *Prince of Darkness: Richard Perle – The Kingdom, The Power & The End of Empire in America*, New York: Union Square Press, 2007.

White, Theodore, *Breach of Faith: The Fall of Richard Nixon*, New York: Atheneum Publishers, 1975.

Williamson, Daniel C., 'Understandable Failure: The Eisenhower Administration's Strategic Goals in Iraq, 1953–1958', *Diplomacy & Statecraft*, vol. 17, no. 3 (September 2006).

Wills, Garry, *Reagan's America*, New York: Penguin, 1988.

Woodward, Bob, *The Commanders*, New York: Simon & Schuster, 1991.

——. *Bush at War*, New York: Simon & Schuster, 2002.

——. *Plan of Attack*, New York: Simon & Schuster, 2004.

——. *State of Denial*, New York: Simon & Schuster, 2006.

Yaqub, Salim, *Containing Arab Nationalism: The Eisenhower Doctrine and the Middle East*, Chapel Hill: University of North Carolina Press, 2004.

Yergin, Daniel, *The Prize: The Epic Quest for Oil, Money, and Power*, New York: Free Press, 1991.

Index